TEST <u>YOUR</u> MEMORY

1. Who is the heroine of *Gone With The Wind?*
2. Who was Harry Truman's second vice-president?
3. What kind of road starts with "Mac"?
4. What is the "tail" of a neuron called?
5. Why is Abbey Road famous?

How did you do? If your memory is a little hazy, check the answers below. Think you'll remember them?

---

1. Scarlett O'Hara. 2. Alben W. Barkley 3. macadam. 4. axon 5. It's the site of the Beatles' recording studio

---

In TOTAL RECALL, you'll find dozens of foolproof tips and techniques—and enjoy that excellent memory you've always wanted!

TOTAL RECALL

How To Boost
Your Memory Power

By Joan Minninger, Ph.D.

PUBLISHED BY POCKET BOOKS NEW YORK

To Bob and Mary Goulding

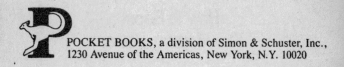

POCKET BOOKS, a division of Simon & Schuster, Inc.,
1230 Avenue of the Americas, New York, N.Y. 10020

Copyright © 1984 by Joan Minninger
Cover photo copyright © 1986 Comstock

Published by arrangement with Rodale Press
Library of Congress Catalog Card Number: 84-9958

All rights reserved, including the right to reproduce
this book or portions thereof in any form whatsoever.
For information address Rodale Press, 33 East Minor Street,
Emmaus, Pennsylvania 18049

ISBN: 0-671-60452-X

First Pocket Books printing May, 1986

10 9 8 7 6 5 4 3 2 1

POCKET and colophon are registered trademarks
of Simon & Schuster, Inc.

Printed in the U.S.A.

Contents

Part I
WHY WE FORGET

Part II
HOW WE REMEMBER

Part III
HOW TO

Acknowledgments

With special appreciation to Eleanor Knowles Dugan, whose humor, brilliance, and generosity are woven through the fabric of this book; to Mark Harrington, whose intelligence and tenacity make him the ideal researcher; to Robert L. Goulding, M.D., and Mary McClure Goulding, M.S.W., who taught me how to move my clients through memory blocks using Redecision Therapy; to all the conceptualizers and researchers from Aristotle to Alan Baddeley whose contributions to the understanding of memory have enriched this book; to Colgan Schlank, who foresaw the book; and to Charles Gerras, superlative editor, who said "Yes!"

Introduction: What Do You Want to Remember?

Students at a memory workshop were asked what they wanted to remember:

"Names and events."

"I want to connect names and faces."

"Remember what I read."

"Not to forget appointments."

"My mother-in-law's birthday."

"The key points and not get bogged down in detail."

"Where I put my shopping list."

Most people go around saying they have a terrible memory. They use their "bad memories" as a tool to protect, comfort, annoy, or sabotage themselves.

It may comfort you to think of your memory—what it is, how it works, what it retains, and what it loses—as something outside yourself that has nothing to do with what you do and who you are, but this just isn't so. Once you find out *why* you forget and *how* you remember, you can decide what you want to do about it.

The most important discovery you can make is to realize that *you* alone decide what you will remember. This discovery doesn't have to be threatening or involve drudgery either. It can be invigorating, liberating, and even pleasurable.

Remembering in new ways stretches the mind like a new exercise stretches the body. Imagine your mind togged out in a bright, new exercise suit, jogging in place, ready to try something new.

How do you want to remember differently when you finish this book? Make a statement.

"I want to _____
_____."

PART I

Why We Forget

1

How Much Can People Remember?

A typical adult's brain contains 15 billion to 100 billion neurons. If we accept the lower figure, this means that you can remember two-to-the-ten-billionth-power bits of information. Just to write out this number that represents the items your mind is capable of holding, you would have to write a zero a second for 90 years, says neurologist Richard M. Restak. Popular science writer Carl Sagan uses the higher figure, representing the equivalent of information in 10 billion encyclopedia pages. The brain, he says, is a very big place in a very small space.

The glory of the human mind centers in its ability to be bombarded with a million bits of diverse information every day and convert them to intelligent thought. It does this by evaluating, sorting, deciding and redeciding on sequences and relationships, discarding the irrelevant, filling in the blanks with bits of information from its files, and filing the new images for later use.

The key word here is *evaluating*. By placing a value on a bit of information we let it advance to the forefront or recede to form a part of a larger picture. We can do this temporarily or permanently, and we can convert the images later if we want to. No tape recorder, camera, or even computer can do all of this. Computers, in fact, are just very fast, efficient morons, with neither imagination nor common sense. It takes a computer four minutes to work out the right combination for a Rubik's Cube, considering every possible turn until all the correct ones have been made. An efficient teenager can do it in two minutes and the 16-year-old 1982 World Champion did it in 22.95 seconds!

Discarding information is essential for remembering. According to *Science Digest* (November, 1983), scientists estimate that we remember only 1 out of every 100 pieces we receive. If we remembered everything, they say, we would be "paralyzed by information overload." A good memory must be selective.

Imagine yourself strolling through a park. You hear the babble of children's voices, the twittering of birds, and the sound of traffic in a nearby street. The mother on the bench hears her own child's voice. The bird watcher hears the mating call of the yellow-breasted titmouse. The car enthusiast recognizes the familiar hum of his friend's souped-up T-bird. Each individual automatically tunes in the sounds that have value and blocks out the extraneous ones.

This blocking process is part of intelligence, but it can also lead to problems. What happens when our natural blocking process becomes a handicap? And what about blocks caused by illness, injury, fatigue, or misunderstanding? We are going to look at three kinds of memory blocks:

emotional, mechanical, physical.

We filter noise for information that interests us: a mother hears her child; a bird watcher hears the yellow-breasted titmouse's song; a teenage boy hears the hum of a friend's souped-up T-bird.

2

Emotional Blocks

People are upset when they forget what they want to or need to remember. The result of their memory "blocks" can be anything from a casual annoyance to a major inconvenience to a life-threatening disaster.

At the very least, memory blocks affect how we feel about ourselves. How do you feel when you forget? People at my memory workshops say:

"I go blank."
"I feel frustrated."
"Selfish."
"It embarrasses others and makes me look silly."
"Disappointed."
"Stupid."
"Guilty."
"It doesn't bother me at all."

How do you feel when someone forgets your name? "If one of my bosses forgets my name, I feel pretty worthless," said one of my students. "I assume others feel that way when I forget their names."

Memory blocks can even threaten how we live, our health, our personal relationships, and our income:

"I lose a lot of business contacts."
"My wife is furious with me."
"I waste so much time."
"I really mess things up at work. I may lose my job."
"My employees think I don't like them."
"My life is a wreck."

Protecting Ourselves with Blocks

Some memory blocks are curious, dramatic, and specific to the people who have them. These people are unconsciously protecting themselves in some way.

Gisela attended a workshop I did for the Civil Service Commission. She worked in a typing pool for 20 men, and her goal was to be able to walk down the hall at work and address her bosses by name: "Good morning, Mr. Thompson. Good morning, Mr. Harris." When her turn came to recount the names of those in the workshop, she remembered all the women's names but none of the men's.

My attempts to resolve this curious memory block ran up against a blank wall time after time. Finally, we recreated her office setting in the workshop and invited her to "walk down the hall," saying hello to the men as she passed them. She seemed embarrassed and didn't look them in the eye.

"What are you feeling when you look away?" I asked.

"Guilty," she replied.

"Why?" I asked.

"Well, I'm a married woman."

"Yes?"

"The Bible says that 'he who lusts after a woman in his own heart is guilty of adultery' and I think that applies to women, too. I get very excited when I see these men, and I don't want my mind and heart feeling that way about anyone but my husband."

In time I was able to convince Gisela that remembering the names of men she encounters socially or in business need not affect her morals. She had been confused. She really thought that having warm, happy feelings about a man and subconsciously acknowledging him by remembering his name was to betray her husband. She had no idea that much of the human race walks around having warm, happy feelings about much of the rest of the human race (both sexes!) without violating even the strictest moral code.

She decided to try looking men in the eye. When she risked it, she found she could remember the men's names as well as the women's.

Marty, a singer from San Diego, had trouble remembering song lyrics. "No matter what I do," he said, "I forget words to songs. I repeat them over and over in my head, but it doesn't help."

"What do you do when you're performing and you forget the words?" I asked.

His face lit up. "I tell jokes and stories."

"Does the audience like them?"

"Oh, yeah! People laugh and laugh." Marty had never really thought of laughter as the root of his problem. Now he understood. The positive response he got for burlesquing his forgetfulness was an incentive *not* to remember.

"If you cut out the jokes and stories, you'll be able to remember the lyrics," I said.

"Oh, I can't do that. That's the best part of the act."

Marty had developed this wonderful way to amuse, but part of him kept saying, "You *should* remember the lyrics to the songs." It was a happy block. He decided to stop arguing with himself and tell jokes.

Louise from Seattle could remember first names, but not last names. Several sessions in which we practiced techniques for remembering last names proved fruitless. "How do you feel about last names, Louise?" I asked one day.

She wasn't sure what I meant, thought a minute, then said flatly, "I hate them. Last names mean somebody owns you. First I had my father's last name. Then I had my first husband's last name. Then I had my second husband's last name. Then I had my third husband's last name. I'm so sick and tired of men's last names. Only my first name is really mine.

"When I was a little girl, I always had to call people 'Mr.' or 'Mrs.' so-and-so while they called each other by their first names and had a lot more fun."

She realized her inability to remember last names was entirely self-imposed. She had a choice: stay angry and refuse to learn last names or drop her anger and remember them.

Dan, a policeman, wanted help in remembering phone numbers. He was particularly annoyed at his inability to remember the number for police headquarters. For the past five years he had had to call headquarters every 90 minutes while on duty, and he had to look the number up each time.

This seemed incredible to me until I learned that Dan

was a 20-year veteran of the force. His feelings soon came out. "For 15 years, they trusted me; and now I've got all these procedures like I'm a little kid. I resent it! My mind refuses to learn that number!"

"Well, who has to look it up each time?" I asked. He raved and ranted about unfairness and bureaucracy, but he finally recognized the connection and realized he had a choice.

Wally was the driver of a cab I hailed at the Boston airport. On our way into the city, he learned that I was there to do a memory workshop. "Oh, boy, I could sure use that!" he cried.

At least twice a week Wally forgot his driver's license and had to make a long trip home to get it. "I get so mad. I pound my head against the wall!" he reported.

I don't usually do therapy on wheels, but this case intrigued me. When we couldn't find any hidden benefit to his frequent trips home, I asked: "Did anyone ever pound your head on the wall?"

"That's what my old man used to do when I ran away naked," he replied. When Wally had been four years old, his mother was very ill. His father had no time for Wally, so Wally devised a clever way to get his attention. He would take off all his clothes and run as far from home as he could get. When the police brought him home, his father would rage at him and pound his head against the wall, screaming "How can you do this when your mother is so sick?"

After Wally's mother died, Wally's father retreated into alcoholism, banging Wally's head any time he was frustrated with his son. Since that was the only attention Wally knew from his father, it became a valued form of recognition. Banging his head as an adult allowed him to feel in contact with his father and postpone his acknowledgment that his father was never going to give him what he needed and deserved from him.

Barbara wanted to remember addresses and telephone numbers. She could remember only three—those of her home, her office, and a close friend's. In one of their sessions Barbara's therapist wrote down his own phone number and asked her how she felt about it. She stared at it quietly for a long time.

Finally she said: "I haven't thought about this in years.

When I was 12 years old, I read in the newspaper about people having numbers tattooed on their arms. Then they were taken off to concentration camps. I think I decided then that I'd never associate a number with a person. I don't think I want to give that up." This was her way of seeing people as individuals, and it gave her a sense of power.

Blocks That Mean You Care

Forgetting doesn't always mean you don't want to remember. Here is some news. Write it down. Embroider it on a tea towel. Chisel it in stone.

Caring Can Cause Memory Blocks

Sometimes we try so hard to remember that we end up defeating ourselves. Forgetting doesn't necessarily mean that we don't care. Sometimes it means just the opposite.

Much of this became clear to me while I was working on my own memory problem through several sessions with Arthur Rissman, a specialist in helping people break through creative blocks.

"What's the problem?" Art asked.

"I need to know how to remember students' names," I told him. "I sometimes have over 150 students a year in my university courses. I've resorted to taking their pictures, writing the names underneath, and covering each name as I look at the picture. But when I try to recall them, I wind up with a bunch I consistently forget or confuse."

"Tell me how you feel about the people whose names are in the bunch you forget."

Startled, I heard myself saying, "Why, those are the people I like best!"

Part of Art's genius is his uncanny ability to ask the right questions. This time he followed-up with: "Can you now see the playmates you had as a child?"

"No," I answered, "we didn't live near other children."

"Can you see the person who took care of you the most?"

"During the day I was with housekeepers."

"Did you like them?"

"Oh, yes," I told him.

"What were their names?"

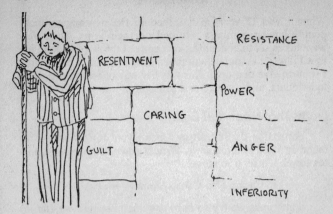

RESENTMENT

RESISTANCE

POWER

CARING

GUILT

ANGER

INFERIORITY

We can shut ourselves into a prison that denies us freedom to remember.

"I can't remember. We moved a lot."

"What do your former housekeepers and your students whose names you can't remember have in common?" he asked.

"They both came and went," I said.

"My hunch," said Art, "is that missing people was less painful for you if you forgot their names."

"Of course!" I shouted.

"You are still protecting yourself in this way. Do you need to?"

"Obviously not. I know and enjoy a lot of people and see them when I want to."

"Is it okay for you to remember the names of the students you like?"

"Sure," I said.

"Will you?"

"Sure."

My block had been useful because it *protected* me from *caring.* I no longer needed it and could discard it. However, I had one more conflict. Sometimes I confused names.

"There are two students I like in my class whose names are Bill and John. I keep calling Bill 'John' and John 'Bill,' and never remember which is which. Each has taken to writing his name in chalk on the sole of his shoe so he can hold it up when I call him by the other name."

"How are they alike?" Art asked.

"They both are warm and friendly."

"How are they different?"

"One talks more than the other."

"Got it?" he asked.

"Right," I agreed.

"Now, just notice which one talks more and you won't confuse them."

Blocks Because Nobody Cares

When my workshops meet, I usually canvas the room, asking the students what they hope to achieve in the class. An older woman in one group had a rather unusual request: "I want to remember my trip to China."

Several of the workshop members looked incredulous or stifled startled giggles. "You went to China and you don't remember it?" I asked.

"Very little. When I try to tell my friends about the highlights of the trip, my mind becomes a blank. They go to lots of exotic places. I want to impress them; but since I got back from China I can't remember much of what I saw."

I wondered if she had somehow failed to notice what was around her through preoccupation or some block. "Did you have experiences that delighted you?"

"Yes, of course."

"Then imagine you are where you usually talk to your friends. Start to tell them about your fascinating experiences and notice their responses."

Her face went blank and then looked sad. "My friends are very . . . animated. They have so many exciting things happening to them. They don't seem to want to listen when I talk unless I talk about them. Mostly they just want me to listen, and they sure don't want to hear about something they didn't do themselves."

I went to the blackboard and picked up a piece of chalk. "How many people here have ever been to China?" I asked. Several raised their hands and several more commented that they had read a lot about the country.

"Notice the attention you are getting here," I said. "Tell

us about the first city you visited." As she talked, I wrote down the highlights of each remembrance on the blackboard. Slowly, she began to glow as she summoned up rich images of seven different places she had visited. Sometimes she couldn't recall the name of the city, but when people in the class called out suggested names, she was able to recognize it.

Obviously she had enjoyed her trip and remembered it in great detail. However, she had blocked the information because it had not served its purpose—to make her important in the eyes of her friends.

What Causes Emotional Blocks?

All these blocks grew out of conflict. Each of these people used memory blocks as protection from something. If you want an inscription for your thinking cap, here it is:

> A memory block is a mental barrier that we use to protect ourselves from what we perceive as harm, error, or ridicule.

Our blocks exist to protect us. When we forget some things and not others, there may be an internal conflict about the material that makes us anxious and prevents remembering. We sense that remembering may be dangerous, inconvenient, or embarrassing.

Forgetting may be protective, but it can also be a dreadful nuisance. We can eliminate some of these blocks when we understand the cause. Others may be easier to live with than to change. Still others are desirable and should be maintained.

Resolving Emotional Blocks

You've seen how several people came to terms with their emotional memory blocks. If you suspect that you may also have an emotional block, you have several choices:

- Discard your block because you no longer need it.
- Develop new strategies for dealing with your block.
- Make friends with your block.

When to Keep Your Blocks

It is important not to discard a block until you are sure you can live without it. Your block may be protecting you in ways that you don't fully understand or appreciate.

For most of us the ultimate fear is death. This sounds melodramatic, but in one bizarre case, I encountered a woman who was certain that she would die if she remembered. The woman was the mother of my friend, Florence Mischel, and her strange story began in Europe at the end of the last century. Florence's mother, Rose, was born in Russia in 1889, the ninth of 11 children in a Jewish family. During the pogroms, the family fled to Romania.

To fully understand the implications of this story, you must appreciate the great reverence and thirst for education possessed by all Jews. "Even the poorest Jewish family," recalled Rose, "had a little tin box on the mantle where they would put coins to send boys to study the Torah."

All the children in Rose's family were remarkably bright; but as they reached their teens, they died one by one, in the order of their birth. They may have succumbed to some genetic disorder or to the hardships and diseases common at the time, but Rose's mother began to wonder if there was a curse on her family.

One of Rose's older sisters was a brilliant scholar, and her parents were preparing to send her to the university, something unheard of for a female. Then the girl died. Rose was just nine and remembered that the entire village closed their shops and went into mourning for this remarkable young woman.

Rose's mother was desolate and frantic at the relentless toll death was taking on her children. She consulted the village rabbi (literally "teacher") to try to understand why God was punishing her in this way.

Now, the rabbi may have been a stupid man; or he may have been the product of an era in which men genuinely believed that women should not be educated; or he may have been misunderstood by Rose's mother. In any case, Rose's mother returned home with the rabbi's judgment: "God is angry because you worship education more than you worship Him." Rose's mother resolved that none of her surviving children would ever attend school.

Times were hard and Rose's father set out on foot to find a better life for his family. He walked across Europe, reached Glasgow, and took passage to the United States. After working in New York City for a year or two, he sent for his family. Rose was now 14 and went directly to work, but her younger sister, Leah, was required to attend school. After a year of education, Leah died.

Despite Rose's inability to read and write, she was very clever. It was common for sweatshop owners to cheat their uneducated workers, but Rose could figure the wages owed her in a few seconds—"I did 6 wool dresses at $0.27 each plus $0.04 a dress bonus for black-on-black, 8 silk dresses at $0.31 each, and 17 shirtwaists at $0.12 each, you owe me $6.38." When the garment factories were unionized, she became a shop steward. Rose was beautiful and talented; but throughout her adult life, she maintained that she couldn't read a word. Despite the efforts of her children to teach her, she would cross her arms, press her lips together, and say, "I'm just a dummy."

Yet Rose was somewhat embarrassed by her illiteracy and made every effort to hide it from outsiders. Once, in her later years, she was going to travel cross-country on the luxury train, the Super Chief. It was customary for passengers to read the menu and write their meal orders on little cards, something Rose could not do. Florence discreetly contacted the waiters ahead of time. She told them her mother had very poor eyesight and was too vain to wear glasses. Florence would be so grateful if they would read her the menu and write her order for her. Well tipped, the waiters complied.

Still Rose disdained information from books. "What, you made it from a cookbook?" she would say to her daughters. "*I* never cook from books!" It was the ultimate dismissal.

When Rose was in her seventies and bored with inactivity, Florence hired a reading teacher to come three or four times a week. Still Rose would not learn to read. Florence began to speculate on what had happened. Rose had been nine and *must* have known how to read before her mother's fateful visit to the rabbi. After that, Florence suspected, Rose had been so terrified by the deaths of her beloved sisters that she blocked all memory of how to read. Her own life would be forfeit if she committed such a blasphemy. Remembering meant dying.

Florence tried a new approach. "Mother," she said, "you are very smart and have a fantastic memory. I know you're not a dummy and you have had to work very hard for many years *not* to learn to read. It must have been very difficult for you." To her surprise, her mother began to cry. "It's true," she admitted. For a long time they talked about Rose's dead sisters and whether God would really punish anyone for learning to read.

Then Florence said, "Mother, you are 75 years old. That's a good, long life. Suppose that God would strike you dead tomorrow if you learned to read? So what? Why not risk it?"

Somewhat reluctantly, Rose consented. Florence made flash cards for her with pictures and the English words. When Rose went to sound out a word like "cat" or "dog" she would say it backwards from right to left as Hebrew is written, showing that she really had learned Hebrew as a child!

Rose died at 95, still not fully literate, but almost convinced that God would not strike her dead for remembering how to read.

What Does It Mean When You Always Forget?

Much of this book will urge you not to harass yourself when you have good reasons of forgetting. But what happens when forgetting becomes a major disruption in your life?

Stop and ask yourself these questions:

- Do you frequently exceed an acceptable level for errors caused by forgetting? (This level will vary widely from person to person and situation to situation.)
- Are you forgetting more than you can emotionally and physically afford to forget? (This frequently depends on temperament, upbringing, and profession.)
- Has forgetting become physically or emotionally threatening? Is it even self-destructive?

If you answer yes to any or all of these questions, it may be time to get outside help. If you constantly forget, and if that forgetting is *constantly* distressing, destructive, or dangerous, then you need more help than this book can offer.

When the disasters of forgetting become the central issue in a person's life, when the stress of forgetting gets irreversibly bound up in the stress of social, financial, and personal failure, then it's time to look for fundamental causes. Extreme stress, in itself, can produce memory loss. Self-destructive urges can make us sabotage ourselves, and poor emotional health in general can create a climate in which "everything goes wrong."

If neither old nor new memory structures work, despite all our energies, and the everyday reasons for forgetting don't seem to be the cause, then it's time to seek professional help.

Being in Therapy

Many of us resist therapy as a resolution to our personal concerns, including memory blocks. Therapy has a broad range of techniques and approaches, each has a particular strength or effectiveness with individual persons and psychological problems.

In my own practice I have found Redecision Therapy to be of particular value to clients who berate themselves over their poor memory. This is a short-term results-oriented therapy developed by Robert L. Goulding, M.D., and Mary McClure Goulding, M.S.W., that asks the client to make a contract to change something in his life—not to "work on it" or describe it or justify it, but *change* it. The contract can be for something as seemingly trivial as not biting your nails during the next week or as urgent as not committing suicide during the next 24 hours.

Redecision Therapy has proven successful with people who realize they are at an impasse and are willing to look for a different way to solve an old problem. Because logic and "ought to" have already failed, Redecision Therapy gets the client to experience his *feelings* and then decide if he is willing to trade "safe" old feelings, however unpleasant, for positive new feelings. As Eric Berne explained in *Games People Play* (New York: Ballantine, 1978), there is usually a "con" that we give ourselves to keep playing the game, even though we "lose" all the time. Redecision Therapy differs from traditional analysis in its emphasis on resisting the "con" or bad feeling payoff and on focusing on "what you want to change today." *You* do it, not the therapist. You can't just "work on"; you must change. Your goal is to change *now*.

Leslie, a divorced mother of three, was a very successful real estate salesperson. To make more business contacts, she joined many civic and business associations and worked for the local Chamber of Commerce. Several times a week she made presentations to local businesses and to major corporations around the country to encourage them to move their plants to the area. She was a popular speaker and she self-published several travel guides which sold well to tourists. As her career expanded, she acquired a housekeeper, secretary, bookkeeper, accountant, and agent. Her busy life should have run very smoothly . . . but "should" doesn't always mean "did."

Leslie started her session by stating, "I want to find things more easily." When asked for an example, Leslie became a little tearful. "Last week, my daughter sent me a birthday present. It came four days before my birthday and on the wrapping it said, 'Do not open until Friday.' I was so excited, I wanted to open it right then, but I forced myself to put it away. Now I can't find it anywhere."

Going back to Leslie's original statement, I asked her, "What does 'find things' mean to you?"

"To be able to go right where I put it and enjoy it." She smiles ruefully. "I'm not losing things for fun. I really wanted that present. I know it's something she made herself. I wanted it so badly, I put it in a special place." I asked her what she would like her contract to be.

"I want to put things so I know where they will be when I want to get them back. There is so much stuff that comes in."

I quizzed her further and found out that she "loses everything, forgets everything." (This is a parental judgment and obviously not true.) The previous weekend Leslie had gone off to a much-anticipated vacation at the beach with her family and forgotten her suitcase. "There I was, trying to walk through the sand in panty hose, silk dress, and high heels."

I asked Leslie if she sometimes felt like a little girl when she lost things. A mischievous look came into her eye. I then asked her if she would be willing to think like the little girl who dropped things everywhere, and to talk to her adult self about how the little girl felt. "I'm going to ask you to switch places, to sit in that chair and be a little girl." Leslie agreed.

"Little girl Leslie, how do you feel about putting things away?"

Leslie the adult businesswoman and Leslie the child discussed the old "bad feelings" about being forced to remember to put things away. Leslie recalled that her father yelled at her and her mother threatened punishment when she lost or forgot things. In other words, she got lots of attention for forgetting. Her parents were preoccupied with their business. They were inclined not to give her attention unless she created a problem. Leslie learned to get negative attention rather than no attention. Now mom and dad are no longer around to punish little Leslie, so adult Leslie and little girl Leslie were able to strike a bargain: "I don't have to feel bad about forgetting where I put things."

Leslie can now *choose* to feel bad and continue to harass herself or she can solve the problems her forgetting sometimes creates and *choose* to feel all right about it.

"Imagine it's tomorrow, Leslie," I said. "You can't find your shoes and the phone number you need. How are you feeling?"

"Terrible . . . but I will stop it, stop feeling that way. I can make myself stop if I notice it."

"So when you start feeling terrible because you've lost something, you can make yourself feel better? You can stop harassing yourself?"

Leslie smiled. "Yes, I think so."

"So what is your decision?"

Leslie leaned back in her chair. "My decision . . . is that when I notice I am making myself feel bad because I've lost something . . . I will choose to feel good anyway. I will solve the problem, instead of harassing myself, and feel good about solving it."

This conclusion may not sound like a solution to all of Leslie's problems, and it isn't. But she frees herself of her guilt long enough to see the cycle of self-harassment and self-sabotage that she has set up. She sees that, as an adult, she has choices about how to feel, as well as about where she puts things.

Once she deliberately chooses her feelings, it is a short step to deliberately choosing her actions, to *noticing* where she puts things and remembering where they are. In the past, the more she forgot, the more she harassed herself, and the more she harassed herself, the more she forgot. By removing her bad feeling payoff, Leslie is removing her unconscious reason for forgetting. Eventually she will stop losing things because there is no payoff.

Try This . . .
for a Fresh Attitude Toward Forgetting

Here are some options that you have about memory:
- I can remember and feel good.
- I can remember and feel miserable.
- I can forget and feel miserable.
- I can forget and feel good.

In this chapter, I told you some ways that people in my workshops said they felt about forgetting: "I feel frustrated," "Selfish," "It embarrasses others and makes me look silly," "Stupid," "Guilty," "It doesn't bother me at all."

Make a note of some ways *you* react when you forget something: _____
_____.

Don't decide which is "right." Don't even decide which option you usually choose. You are experimenting with new ways to do things and new ways to feel about what you do. Don't lock yourself into an old pattern by labeling it as yours.

3

Mechanical Blocks

"Quick, name a West Coast sound."

"Ah, er, the Grateful Dead."

"No, Puget."

When we can't remember something, the cause isn't always an emotional or physical block. A misperception or an interruption, either from outside or of our own making, can block memory just as effectively. For convenience we'll clump these together and call them "mechanical" blocks.

These blocks can take three forms. Sometimes we misunderstand something we see or hear and so we misfile the information. Sometimes we're distracted before we can file the information. And sometimes we're distracted during the retrieval process. We start hunting thought a mental file drawer and find another captivating through that diverts us or the phone rings or our bus comes. In all three instances, the result is the same. We "forget."

Misfiled Information

This happens when incoming signals aren't recorded properly. Your chances of summoning up Puget Sound from your memory file would be close to zero if you were searching for the name of a California-based rock group. Focusing on the word *sound* in one context makes it just about impossible to find the answer in another. This is called "the specificity of encoding."

Misfiled information, information that isn't coded properly before we tuck it away, is a major source of "forgetting."

There are many homonyms and words of multiple meanings in English to add to our confusion. Jam—session or strawberry? Read/reed? Weak/week? Guilt/gilt?

What about English words that have opposite meanings?

- rent—pay for the use of and be paid for use
- fast—go fast or stick fast
- sanction—allow or prevent
- overlook—see or fail to see

And what does this sentence, taken from a newspaper article, actually mean? "He was shot at once."

When we don't give sufficient context—encoding—to a bit of information, we will forget it. This is one reason foreign languages can be so difficult to learn.

An example is the Frenchman who endeavored to remember the English phrase "Thank you" by rhyming it with "Saint Cloud" (pronounced "San Clue"), a suburb of Paris. When his American sweetheart next complimented him, he blushed and stammered, "Montmartre."

What Do You See?

Memory is complicated by how we perceive the sights, sounds, and sensations that surround us. The possibilities for variations in encoding are almost infinite. Some things that may affect how we evaluate information are our age, sex, intelligence, education, disposition, our nationality and social status, our political and religious beliefs, our physical appearance, income, the weather, the people around us, where we are, and the time of the day, month, and year.

Consider reading about a war in the history books of the opposing countries. Or the un-universality of music—how the sound of bagpipes, rock and roll, or Chinese opera can enchant or torment different listeners.

What do people remember when they look at you? No two people see exactly the same thing. Depending on who is doing the looking, they may see a parent, a child, a spouse, a lover, a friend or a foe, a menacing foreigner or a kindred spirit, someone too fat or too thin, too young or too old, too rich or too poor, useful, lovable, or dangerous. Yet each viewer is looking at the same collection of atoms.

No two people see exactly the same thing. It depends on who is doing the looking.

Creating Reality

"Reality is not so much recorded as constructed," says neurologist Richard M. Restak. If we are walking down a sunny hallway and a figure suddenly appears ahead of us, we assume that he has stepped through a doorway. If we are walking down a spooky, dark hallway and a figure suddenly appears ahead of us, we might assume that he has stepped through a wall and is a ghost.

We shape the recorded information to our expectations, to our template of reality at that moment. We discard information that doesn't fit (Mrs. Throgbottom appeared to walk through a wall, so there must be a door in that alcove) and adapt information that is out of kilter (Mrs. Throgbottom appears to be nude, but that can't be true, so she must be wearing a beige dress). Tossing out bits and pieces that don't form patterns is essential to getting through life. The disadvantage is that sometimes the information we discard in this way is true. Many eccentrics have made great discoveries because they refused to ignore information that didn't fit.

SEEING WITH A SOUND TRACK

Imagine that you are watching a piece of film with no sound. A young man is running across a field toward a grove of trees. Now replay the film and imagine lilting, bucolic music in the background. The film is obviously showing us a happy young man, full of exuberance on a sunny day. Now run the film again and, this time, the music is thunderingly romantic. He is now on his way to a rendezvous with his love in the trees. On our third replay of the film, imagine an agitated theme. This time he is being chased by something menacing. If only he can reach the trees, he may be safe. And finally, the music is ominous. He is unaware that something *terrible* is waiting for him in the woods. What you see is always the same, but your mood or expectation creates your perception.

THE EFFECT OF LANGUAGE ON PERCEPTION

"How fast were the cars going when they *crashed* into each other?" A group of people were shown a film of two cars bumping. Those who were asked the above question estimated the speed at an average of 40.8 mph, while those who were asked "How fast were they going when they *contacted* each other?" estimated 31.8 mph. Their perception had been altered by the language of the question. The same people were quizzed about damage. Those who were asked "Did you see *the* broken headlight?" were twice as likely to say yes as those who were asked if there was *a* broken headlight. (There wasn't any.)

Linguist Benjamin Lee Whorf noted this phenomenon in his work as a fire investigator. Men who were working with *full* gasoline drums showed appropriate respect, but once the drums were *empty,* they were treated casually, even though the latter drums, now filled with gasoline vapor, were much more likely to explode. In another case, some distillation vats were encased in "spun lime stone." The word *stone* implied "fireproof" to those working with the material, but it wasn't. Result—poof!

Advertising takes full advantage of word associations. I recently bought a set of "professional" cookware. The fine print in the accompanying brochure stated that it was "not for commercial use." Can one be a "professional" cook and not a "commercial" one? Products are touted as "natural" (arsenic is natural), and "fresh" (well, they're certainly not rotten when they have a shelf life of two years), or "pure" (pure what?). We like to think of ourselves as too sophisticated to be taken in by slick advertising, but many of our everyday perceptions are deliberately or accidentally affected by language.

How to Retrieve Misfiled Information

Is it any wonder that we file information and then can't find it later? We are looking under the wrong heading. Sometimes the information is hopelessly lost to us, but occasionally we can retrieve it by letting our mind float high over the landscape, looking for random free associations that might provide a clue to where we put it. We may come across it accidentally as we search through another file, a delightful bonus for giving ourselves exploratory time.

Distraction Before We "Remember"

Funk and Wagnall's Dictionary defines *distraction* as a diversion. This sounds like a playful, refreshing interlude, and it may well be, unless you are being diverted when you don't want to be. Distraction can keep you from recording information or stop you from recalling it if you're interrupted in the process. No wonder being easily distracted gets a bad press. On the positive side, a distracted mind roves nimbly over a lot of territory or responds quickly to a variety of external stimuli. Just don't expect to remember much of it later.

Ironically, preoccupation can be just as effective in blocking memory. The mind is focusing totally on one thing and doesn't let other ideas get in the way. This is considered admirable if the thinker is concentrating on performing a heart transplant, less so if the thinker is absorbed in a fantasy about dating a movie star instead of listening to an economics lecture that is essential for the final exam. Whether our preoccupation is "good" or "bad," it is very effective at preventing us from noticing and storing new information.

Failure to Acquire and Record Information

A woman in one of my workshops wondered why she couldn't remember anything about the time she spent in Europe. As usual, I asked why she wanted to remember.

"Well, when I tell people I was there for two years, they want to know what I saw. I can't remember anything."

This seemed incredible until I dug a little deeper. I learned that she had lived on an army base, shopped only at the base PX, and associated only with other American army wives. The fact was that she *hadn't* seen Europe at all, only an army base identical to bases all over the United States. She couldn't remember Europe because she had never really been there.

Distraction during Retrieval

Another kind of mechanical loss is failure to complete the retrieval process. It frequently happens when we are juggling a lot of different activities instead of concentrating on one. A popular name for this is "overload."

Busy people are always wrestling with overload, trying to handle many unrelated activities without forgetting any of them. We may be thinking simultaneously about an important business letter, an errand we need to do on the way home from work, an upcoming social event, and an unpaid bill. Unless they are related in some way, they don't reinforce each other, and it is very easy for one to "slip through the cracks."

On the other hand, if a group of subjects are related—the many steps necessary to drive a car, cook an elaborate dinner, or run for president—we tend not to forget them because they represent progressive parts of a whole. Each step taken suggests another step, so we can remember an almost limitless number of bits.

The Price of Remembering

You probably could remember just about anything if you focused on it totally, excluding all other thoughts and activities. This can be effective, but it's not much fun.

An easier way is to build a structure, a kind of mental egg carton in which to arrange and count your odd bits. The simplest structure is, of course, the written list. The acts of conceiving, writing, and then reading back a list of objects or actions reinforces the information and gives us extra ways to retrieve it later, even if we lose the list. We'll talk about structures and reinforcement in part II, "How We Remember."

REMEMBERING IS HARD WORK

Keeping track of lots of things is work. During his years at Princeton University, Albert Einstein could never remember his own unlisted phone number, and once he had to call the switchboard to ask which house he lived in. When Paul Erdos, one of the world's foremost mathematicians, was lecturing at Washington University in St. Louis, he couldn't tell them his Social Security number. Each of these men was keeping his mind free of clutter for the important work at hand.

As long as the discomfort of forgetting doesn't get in the way, it may be easier for certain people to keep several spare car keys and house keys hidden around the neighborhood or simply to pay for forgotten dentist appointments. Some of this kind of disorder may even be your way of being in control, of setting yourself apart from "ordinary" people by creating a personal environment so distinctive that no one else will try to violate it. It's a little like a dog marking his own favorite fire hydrant so that other dogs will know it is a part of his private territory.

Some people can get as much real pleasure from their personal disorder as others get from controlling and creating order in their environment. If that works for you, that's fine. There's nothing wrong with disorder caused by forgetting as long as

- You don't mind.
- Others don't mind.
- It's not dangerous.
- It doesn't scare the horses.

When All Else Fails

You try and try and still forget things? That's okay. When all else fails, give up. It may be easier and more rewarding for you to tolerate occasional lapses of memory in order to be available to all the pleasant notions that flit through your unconscious mind. One price for being unusually disciplined is less spontaneity. By making friends with the way you already use your memory, you will actually remember more of what you want to remember. Self-harassment rarely improves memory because it sets up a system of negative stimuli that is, at best, distracting and, at worst, destructive.

Try This . . .

to See How Interference Thwarts Remembering

Interference can prevent you from remembering correctly or remembering at all. Glance at the figure below and then "remember" what you saw.

You could have seen any of the following words:

| bird | bans | bard | bind | find | fans |
| bins | band | bars | firs | fins | |

Much of the information you try to process each day is mixed with other information. Sometimes you will see it clearly because you're looking for it.

Other times it will be hopelessly muddled.

So keep your eyes open, maintain a sense of humor when information is garbled, and remember that self-harassment is optional.

4

Physical Blocks

Mental blocks are dramatic and frequently fascinating. Physical blocks are much less stylish, more common, and not nearly so arresting. In fact, the only nice thing to be said about them is that some of them are easier to overcome.

Matter Over Mind

Any physical condition that prevents our delightfully complex bodies from delivering information to the brain or storing it there qualifies as a physical block. Some physical conditions are permanent—blindness, color blindness, deafness, or tone deafness can effectively prevent a memory of colors or of melodies. Other conditions that interfere with memory may be temporary or reversible.

The pain of a stomachache or of hitting one's thumb with a hammer can effectively garble memory input or retrieval temporarily. These discomforts pass quickly enough, and you can probably postpone trying to remember the Table of Elements or your sister's address until you have recovered. (Of course, this is a good reason to have emergency phone numbers written down next to the telephone.)

Other physical memory blocks are long-term: nutritional deficiencies, some illnesses and/or the drugs used to treat them, recreational drugs, fatigue, tension, and lack of exercise. Some of these—poor nutrition, tension, and lack of exercise—we can correct ourselves. Other physical blocks, the ones caused by illness or prescribed drugs, may become less frustrating and frightening if we understand what is happening. The panic and depression that occur when strange things happen in our bodies and minds are effective memory blocks.

Let's look at some physical memory blocks.

Diet

You've heard the old joke about the elderly honey-mooner who disparaged oysters as an aphrodisiac: "I ate twelve of the things and only six worked."

Food is seen as a universal remedy for what ails us. In our search for health and well-being, we consume everything from mother's chicken soup to brewer's yeast to a hundred different hangover cures. Most of us would love to find a food or a vitamin that would "cure" our bad memory.

The bad news is that it's not that simple. Memory is so incredibly complex that, so far, no one has been able to prove that any single nutritional element will improve it. We do know that the *absence* of certain substances, especially thiamine, from the diet may be accompanied by a memory loss, but we can only suppose that the opposite might be also true—that the presence of these substances in the diet would promote a good memory. We certainly have no proof that increasing the intake of any nutrient, or combination of nutrients, would proportionately increase our power to remember.

However, one recent study may finally establish a direct link between specific nutrients and mental efficiency. The Brain Aging and Neuronal Plasticity Research Group at Ohio State University Medical Center has just completed a major collaborative study in which 11-month-old mice (comparable in age to human adults) were fed any one of 11 different diets for 11 months. The diets varied combinations of three substances: dietary choline, lecithin, and phosphatidylcholine. The last is a substance found in lecithin itself and is also a crucial component of the neuronal membranes. (Neurons are the information-sending cells that make up the brain.)

While the mice were on their special diets, each group was given behavior tests to compare their mental efficiency and memory capacity with that of mice on an average laboratory diet. The research group found that three of the diets notably increased the number of synapses, the connections between neurons that are necessary for memory. The study covered more than a third of the mice's life span, far longer than most previous research on choline.

The Ohio State mice were put in a two-chambered box with a door between the lighted front compartment and the darkened back. When a mouse walked into the dark section, the door dropped and the mouse was stuck in pitch darkness while getting a mild, but unpleasant electric shock for three seconds.

To test the mouse's long-term memory, it was put back in the box 24 hours later. The researchers then measured how long it took before the mouse forgot its previous unpleasant experience and returned to the darkened room. The mice who ate the standard laboratory diet waited an average of only 290 seconds before they wandered into the dark room. The mice fed the three most successful diets waited more than 400 seconds, indicating that they remembered their previous unpleasant experience longer.

The diets that resulted in this memory improvement were two rich in phosphatidylcholine and one rich in lecithin. On the basis of their study, Dr. Ronald Mervis says: "I would recommend lecithin or phosphatidylcholine [to enhance human memory]. Ingesting free choline itself produces no effect."

Does such a diet hold any hope for treating memory loss due to senility in later life? Dr. Mervis says that "lecithin or phosphatidylcholine, taken chronically, seem to be most effective when taken before the onset of memory loss. In other words, they have a prophylactic (preventative) effect. [But] we'll be running our tests on senile mice too, to see whether any improvement in synaptic connections can be induced."

Dr. Mervis suggests that previous testing of "precursor substances" (chemicals necessary for neurons to send out signals in the brain) may have been inconclusive because researchers were concentrating on choline. "Forty percent of the phospholipid found in neuronal membranes is phosphatidylcholine," he says, "so using its precursors on a long-term basis may preserve or help rebuild neuron membranes and thus offset or delay brain atrophy." (Alzheimer's disease, a cause of organic memory loss in older people, is known to attack the choline production of the brain.)

These findings are very exciting and may be a key to great advances in treating a variety of disorders. As with any scientific experiment, this one must be duplicated by other researchers who get similar results. When this happens, a theory becomes a fact.

While this lecithin/phosphatidylcholine theory still needs to be confirmed by further testing, it invites conjecture about possible applications. For instance, alcoholics are predisposed to early senility because their neuron membranes have become rigid. Lecithin therapy, suggests Dr. Mervis, might be able to improve brain functioning in former alcoholics. It might also aid children with certain nervous dysfunctions and forms of retardation by encouraging the development of more synaptic connections. Eventually even the common man might use it as a nutritional means to more efficient memory.

If you are tempted to start consuming quantities of lecithin, consider Dr. Mervis's warning: "It's important to emphasize that lecithin and phosphatidylcholine are most effective when used in low dosages. Larger amounts produce a bloating effect, among other undesirable ones."

WHAT THE FUTURE HOLDS

In the past, scientists thought of the brain as a protected organ, unaffected by the diet of its owner. Now we know that the food we eat can cause profound changes in brain output, affecting behavior in drastic ways. But since no one is certain exactly how the brain records information—whether by molecular changes, chemical changes, electromagnetic changes, or on a holographic basis—we are just beginning to discover how diet affects memory.

Some comforting news is that our knowledge of biochemistry is now doubling about every seven years. Lecithin researcher Dr. Ralph G. Walton is optimistic about this progress. "I think we'll see a real knowledge explosion over the next ten years."

A summary of nutrient sources that may be related to memory appears on the following page.

Summary of Selected Dietary Elements

Nutrient	General Functions	Good Food Sources	Relationship to Memory
Vitamin B$_1$ (thiamine)	Emotional stability. Energy. Memory.	brewer's yeast, dark-green leafy vegetables, lean meats, legumes,[1] nuts, sunflower seeds, variety meats[2] wheat germ, whole grain products	Necessary for good memory.
Vitamin B$_6$ (pyridoxine)	Production of antibodies. Elimination of excess fluids in premenstrual women. Emotional stability. Healthy skin. Central nervous system regulation.	bananas, brewer's yeast, buckwheat flour (dark), hazelnuts, peanuts, poultry, rice, salmon, sunflower seeds, tomatoes, variety meats,[2] wheat germ, whole grain products	Gives emotional stability. Provides central nervous system regulation.
Vitamin B$_{12}$ (cyanocobalamin)	Normal growth. Healthy nervous system. Normal red blood cell formation.	eggs, fish, meats, milk, variety meats[2]	Deficiency may cause poor memory and inability to concentrate. An alert sensory motor system depends on a good supply.

[1]Legumes include peas, beans, peanuts, and lentils.

[2]Variety meats include liver, heart, and kidney.

Summary of Selected Dietary Elements—*continued*

Nutrient	General Functions	Good Food Sources	Relationship to Memory
Choline	Prevents build-up of fat in liver.	Widely distributed in foods that contain fat	Deficiency seems to lead to confusion and memory loss. Increased levels appear to lead to clearer thinking and improved memory in older people.
Folic Acid (folate)	New red blood cell production. Found in the most rapidly growing tissues, such as bone marrow, alimentary tract lining, or tumors.	asparagus, brewer's yeast, broccoli, dark-green leafy vegetables, legumes,[1] liver, nuts, onions, tempeh, wheat germ, whole grain products	Deficiency may seriously impair learning abilities.
Niacin	Reduced blood cholesterol levels. Mental and emotional health. Aids metabolism of carbohydrates, fats, and amino acids.	brewer's yeast, fish, legumes,[1] poultry, variety meats,[2] whole grain products	Reduced levels cause nervousness, confusion, depression, hallucinations.
Vitamin C (ascorbic acid)	Formation of teeth and bones. Bone-fracture heal-	broccoli, brussels sprouts, cabbage,	Low levels can cause confusion, listlessness,

[1]Legumes include peas, beans, peanuts, and lentils.

[2]Variety meats include liver, heart, and kidney.

Nutrient	General Functions	Good Food Sources	Relationship to Memory
	ing. Wound and burn healing. Resistance to infection and other diseases. Collagen formation.	cantaloupes, cauliflower, citrus fruits and their juices, currants, dark-green leafy vegetables, green peppers, persimmons, pimentos, strawberries, tomatoes	depression.
Calcium	Blood clotting. Normal functioning of nerve tissues. Normal pulse and cardiac contraction. Formation and growth of bones and teeth.	almonds; brewer's yeast; broccoli; dark-green leafy vegetables; hazelnuts; milk, cheese, and most dairy products; salmon; soybeans; tempeh; tofu; watercress	Strengthens and stimulates neuronal growth and plays a crucial role in brain function. A severe deficiency may lead to memory loss.
Copper	Builds proteins that give blood vessel walls strength and flexibility. Protects myelin sheath around nerve fibers.	avocado, banana, beef, cod, legumes, mushrooms, nuts and seeds, oysters, pork, poultry, whole grain products	Promotes calm nerves and clear thinking.
Iodine	Regulates growth and development. Important in thyroid function.	saltwater fish, seafood	Deficiency slows thought processes.

Summary of Selected Dietary Elements—*continued*

Nutrient	General Functions	Good Food Sources	Relationship to Memory
Iron	Blood formation. Transportation of oxygen within the body.	apricots, blackstrap molasses, brewer's yeast, dark-green leafy vegetables, eggs, legumes,[1] nuts, sunflower seeds, variety meats,[2] wheat germ, whole grain products	Deficiency leads to irritability, dizziness, headaches.
Magnesium	Biological reactions within the cell. Conduction of nerve impulses. Normal muscle contraction. Healthy heart, muscles, nerves, brain, kidneys, liver, and other organs. Maintenance of normal basic metabolism.	brown rice, dark-green leafy vegetables, molasses, nuts, peas, soybeans, tofu, whole grain products	Essential for transmitting nervous system impulses. Reduced levels bring about hallucinations, mental confusion, disorientation, memory loss.
Manganese	Necessary for skeletal and connective tissue development. Fatty	bananas, corn, dark-green leafy vegetables, legumes, lettuce, nuts,	Aids central nervous system and muscle coordination.

[1]Legumes include peas, beans, peanuts, and lentils.

[2]Variety meats include liver, heart, and kidney.

Nutrient	General Functions	Good Food Sources	Relationship to Memory
	acid metabolism.	whole grain products	Necessary for precision between mind and body.
Potassium	Biological reactions within the cell. Healthy kidneys, heart, and skeletal muscles.	apples, apricots, avocados, bananas, beef, blackstrap molasses, brewer's yeast, broccoli, chicken, halibut, oranges, peanuts, potatoes, raisins, sesame seeds, sunflower seeds, tomatoes, tuna, wheat germ	Deficiency affects nerve functions.
Zinc	Production and growth of new healing cells. Healthy skin. Numerous enzyme actions throughout the body. Carbon dioxide exchange. Normal maintenance of levels of vitamin A in blood.	beef, cheese, eggs, fish, green beans, lamb, lima beans, meats, nuts, wheat germ, whole grain products	Is essential for synthesis of DNA and brain function.

HOW FOOD AFFECTS CHILDREN'S MEMORIES

When children don't remember well, we worry that they have what is now called "a learning disability." In other words, we wonder, is my kid stupid? Since most people (particularly teachers) equate intelligence with the ability to recall information, poor memories in children can be alarming.

Children respond quickly to many things they eat. They are especially susceptible to imbalances in their diets because their bodies need nutrients for growing. A number of studies have shown that iron deficiency in the mother during pregnancy and in the child causes a noticeable slowdown in memory functions and learning. The iron-deficient child can still learn, but not as efficiently or effectively.

Dr. Ben F. Feingold has shown that many people, especially children, react dramatically to food additives which may in turn create a sensitivity to natural salicylates found in many nourishing foods. Some of the symptoms of this sensitivity are an inability to concentrate, a short attention span, fidgeting, aggressiveness, excitability, impulsiveness, a low frustration threshold, clumsiness, and insomnia. Children with these problems rarely do well in school. The Feingold diet, designed to avoid additives, has shown some success in treating this problem.

Children's diets have been subject to even more food fads than those of adults. At various times in recent history almost every food group has been considered harmful to them. In the 1920s and '30s, for instance, many American mothers fed their offspring a diet low in protein to prevent "aggressiveness." The listless, hollow-eyed youngster fostered by such a diet was rarely aggressive, but frequently peevish and petulant.

Your child deserves the most nourishing diet possible within the limits of your income, food availability, and the current knowledge about nutrition. Special problems, including slow or erratic learning patterns, should get professional attention.

Your forgetful child also deserves as much understanding as you give yourself when you "just forget." Compared with adults, children have far fewer landmarks to use when they file information. Their experiences in learning the use of memory are similar to those you would have if you found yourself in a strange country, dealing with an unfamiliar language or customs. Children's discoveries and the new ways they develop for remembering what they see can be a constant delight to understanding, encouraging, loving adults.

EFFECTS OF REDUCING DIETS ON MEMORY

Most of the publicized reducing diets are deficient in nutrients. (The best thing to be said for many popular and bizarre diets is that they are so bizarre that very few people stay on them long enough to do permanent damage. Unfortunately this is not always the case.) While a person is dieting, the brain, like the body, has to make up any shortage of dietary nutrients by drawing on its reserves to function. When the reserves are used up, the dieter can become nervous and susceptible to suggestion, easily upset, and find it hard to make decisions—all conditions that can distort or block memory.

Experts warn that any diet providing fewer than 2100 calories a day for an adult is likely to be deficient in some vitamin, mineral, or trace element, unless the diet is carefully tailored by a doctor for the individual. In a study by Dr. Russell Wilder, Senior Physician at the Mayo Clinic, healthy subjects agreed to stay on a low-calorie reducing diet for an extended period of time. Within three months, they experienced a host of unpleasant symptoms: they became quarrelsome, hostile and anxious, felt persecuted, had nightmares and moments of extreme panic, became clumsy, had trouble paying attention, and *their memories became faulty*.

THE BIG PICTURE

Even the most unsophisticated person is likely to know about psychosomatic illness, but many well-educated people are totally unaware of its opposite, somatopsychic illness. These are simply two sides of the same coin. Psychosomatic illness is disease of the body that originates in the mind, and somatopsychic illness is disease of the mind that originates in the body. Sometimes mental problems, including forgetfulness, are caused by imbalances in the body's chemistry.

Many nutritionists are successful in treating illnesses with corrective diets and food supplements. Unfortunately, a few enthusiasts insist that almost every human illness is due solely to imbalances in nutrition, and they regularly encounter the skepticism of doctors and laymen. If you are feeling skeptical about this right now, just remember that a number of mental and physical conditions *are* caused by poor diet and *do* respond well to improved nutrition.

WELL-BALANCED DIETS

Doctors are fond of advising their patients to "eat a well-balanced diet." Patients presume the doctor has something specific in mind. Yet a study reported by Dr. Jean Mayer of Harvard University showed that "the average doctor at Harvard knows a wee bit more about nutrition than his secretary, unless his secretary has a weight problem, in which case the average secretary knows a wee bit more about nutrition than the average doctor."

If you think you have a nutritional deficiency, practice Disraeli's advice: "Moderation even in excess."

- Read as much as you can about recent discoveries in nutrition.
- If you decide you may be lacking a particular vitamin or mineral, increase your intake of foods that are rich in that nutrient but eat a *variety* of foods.
- Take moderate doses of supplements.
- If you feel a simple moderate approach isn't appropriate, see a nutrition-oriented doctor to work out a dietary program.

Good health is a great plus to memory. When you feel good, look good, and are bouncing with energy, your mind can process information faster and better, and remembering is easier.

Illnesses

The ravages of ill health, stress, depression, and serious injuries can have an adverse effect on our ability to concentrate or remember. In fact, memory loss and confusion are classic symptoms of some diseases. Here are some physical conditions that affect the memory.

AMNESIA

We are all familiar with the soap-opera version of amnesia. The victim-heroine forgets her name, home, and loved ones but is still able to dress herself (elegantly), talk (eloquently), and walk (gracefully). The unbearable personal portion of the victim's life is erased by the subconscious, but language, muscle skills, and general knowledge remain. Some people with this type of amnesia score just as well on I.Q. tests as they did before the illness struck. However, in other, more dramatic varieties of amnesia, the victim retains formerly learned language, motor skills, and knowledge, and is quite capable of acquiring new skills and knowledge, but doesn't know how these relate to activities of daily living.

Doctors generally categorize amnesia as either physically based or emotionally based. In a tragic example of the former type, pioneering brain surgeons erased the long-term memory of HM when they removed too much of the brain during an operation intended to control his epileptic seizures. Though he could reply to questions, he would forget the conversation within a few hours. He read the same newspapers over and over. The death of his father, which had occurred many years before, remained a fresh tragedy whenever it was mentioned.

Amnesia due to head injury can affect perception, language comprehension, and personality. Most patients of this type have a multitude of symptoms, and isolating memory loss from the other symptoms is difficult. Only in rare cases do amnesia victims have what laymen think of as "classic" amnesia, in which they experience memory loss but have no intellectual impairment.

Emotional amnesia is caused by stress, and memory usually returns in a few days. This pathological forgetting in response to emotional crisis is called "fugue." In a way, these amnesiacs design their own illness, but they have absolutely no voluntary control over it. They retain all memories except those of their personal lives. If they just ran away, they would have to bring their painful and overwhelming problems with them. Forgetting offers them the most complete escape short of death. But the release amnesia offers is only temporary. Once the person has forgotten those unbearable anxieties, a new anxiety soon appears—where is my memory?

Amnesia can erase memories imprinted either before or after the trauma. Physical injuries can result in either/or both kinds; however, amnesia due to emotional trauma is more likely to erase the causative events.

ARTERIOSCLEROSIS

When the blood vessels supplying the brain narrow or harden, the amount of oxygen delivered to the brain is reduced, resulting in memory loss. One theory is that the diminished oxygen supply, combined with older and fewer neurons, inhibits the electrical circuitry of the brain.

The effect increased oxygen has on the brain is heartening. Under the direction of Dr. Edwin Boyle, Jr., research director of the Miami Heart Institute, patients suffering from memory loss caused by arteriosclerosis breathed concentrated oxygen at three times normal atmospheric pressure. These patients were then able to remember recent events and learn new things, and the improvement lasted six weeks to six months.

ICU (INTENSIVE CARE UNIT) PSYCHOSIS

The trauma of injury or surgery can affect memory. About 25 percent of the patients in hospital intensive care units experience occasional bouts of confusion and forgetfulness which have been dubbed "intensive care unit psychosis." In the first weeks after receiving the first artificial heart, Dr. Barney Clark sometimes could not recall the surgery or why he was in the hospital. Doctors speculate that the initial trauma, plus the ongoing stress of the hospital routine—the constant beeping of electronic monitors and the necessary but exhausting routine of taking blood samples, giving medications, and changing intravenous tubes—caused this temporary memory loss.

SENILITY

Just as *consumption* was once used to describe any illness of the lungs, *senility* has become today's catchall term for a variety of physical and emotional conditions that can affect our memories adversely as we get older. Sometimes, the specific condition is recognized and treated, and the negative effect on memory is reversed.

Two professional men in their sixties who had similar symptoms—they forgot where they put things and had trouble remembering names, dates, faces, and recent events—were tested at the National Institute of Mental Health in Bethesda, Maryland. One man did poorly on the tests that required mental effort, but he could improve his overall memory when he was given clues for organizing material. The other worked very hard at the various tests, but when he was offered help in organizing, his score did not improve.

The first man was diagnosed as being depressed. When his depression cleared up, his memory problems disappeared. The other man, unfortunately, was diagnosed as being in the early stages of Alzheimer's disease, a degenerative illness that kept him from using his accumulated memories.

Commonly called "senile dementia," Alzheimer's disease produces loss of memory and is ultimately fatal. The exact cause is still unknown and much work is being done on this devastating disease. One interesting discovery—the degree of memory loss in Alzheimer patients is in direct proportion to the loss of cholinacetyltransferase (CAT) in the brain. CAT is an enzyme necessary for the formation of acetylcholine, the chemical which transmits nerve impulses from neuron to neuron. The less CAT, the fewer the transmissions.

Another preliminary finding is that women seem to lose brain material earlier than men. Two British pathologists say that most women lose two ounces of brain material between the ages of 40 and 50, while men don't experience this loss until their late 50s. After that, both sexes lose brain material at about the same rate.

Though senility, or the public image of senility, remains a problem, doctors and laymen both are beginning to recognize that memory loss in later years is rarely inevitable or irreversible when it occurs. Arteriosclerosis, malnutrition, depression, and the side effects of drugs taken for other conditions are a few potential contributors to memory loss, and they can happen at any age. (Huntington's chorea, similar to Alzheimer's disease, hits young adults.)

The picture is bright for older people today, and most of them *won't* experience real senility. Though we may castigate ourselves more at 60 than at 20 when we forget something, we are probably no more forgetful than we were 40 years earlier, provided we stay active, have lots of interests, exercise, and keep the circuits open. The motto, says neurologist David Krech, is, "He who lives by his wits dies *with* his wits." In other words—use it or lose it! For more about senility and what to do about it, see chapter 12, "Remembering—Young vs. Old."

"He who lives by his wits dies with *his wits."*

Injuries

Most people experience a good, hard crack on the head at least once during their lifetimes and recover with no ill effects. A few will find later that their intellect and behavior have undergone small changes, changes that may be irritating, frightening, or even dangerous. Memory, attention span, concentration, and abstract thinking may be affected. These people may be easily fatigued, impulsive, irritable, and no longer want to be with friends or socialize. Even worse, they may think they are going crazy; after all, the doctor has pronounced them "fine" since the original accident.

A study was made of 424 people who had been hospitalized for a day or two at the University of Virginia Medical

Center for head injuries and then released as neurologically "normal." Three months later, 79 percent experienced headaches, 59 percent had memory problems, and 34 percent had not returned to their former jobs. Many could not do math problems, had short attention spans, and were tired all the time. Some had trouble organizing their days, got bogged down in doing one thing, and couldn't maintain a routine for tasks. Naturally, they also experienced trouble on the job, loss of self-esteem, and depression. Some just sat around, lost track of things, and had difficulty learning new things and maintaining family and sexual relationships.

The common neurological tests used today aren't sensitive enough to detect the problems of these minor head injuries, says Dr. Leonard Diller, codirector of the head trauma program of New York University's Institute of Rehabilitation Medicine. He suggests having detailed neuropsychological testing and evaluation done by a neurologist, neuropsychologist, or rehabilitation medicine specialist. Recovery from even a minor brain injury can take years, and patients need to learn how to compensate in the meantime.

Allergies

Allergies play a very small part in memory loss, but anything that disrupts our physical and emotional well-being can make us forgetful. We now recognize that allergies can go beyond hives and hay fever. A few people are so sensitive to our twentieth-century world that they have been forced to retreat to sealed cocoons, free from hydrocarbons, plastics, pollution, formaldehyde in plywood and plasterboard, chlorine in water, and dyes and preservatives in food.

Drugs

Every drug, medical students are told, has two kinds of effects: the ones we know about and the ones we don't. Some drugs that are beneficial or even essential for treating physical problems have an unwelcome and unwanted side effect on the memory. Nervous-system depressants such as sleeping pills, tranquilizers, muscle relaxers, and antianxiety drugs can cause confusion and memory loss. So can arthritis drugs and cortisone.

Any drug that affects mood, perception, or alertness affects how you process information. Any drug which has depression as a side effect (and there are an awful lot of them) is bound to affect your memory. When you are profoundly depressed, you remember less. Even mild depression can make you *think* you remember less, although you still score well on an objective memory test. Among the drugs that can cause depression are blood-pressure drugs, boric acid, and ironically, antianxiety drugs.

Medications that produce drowsiness, such as cold remedies with their antihistamines, will probably have a temporary effect on your ability to remember. If the label says "Don't drive or operate machinery . . . ," plan on passing up heavy memory tasks too.

Another potential memory block, mercury, is found in a number of nonprescription medications. Prolonged use of such a product by a sensitive person could result in mercury poisoning, characterized by mental depression, irritability, fatigue, loss of appetite, anemia, and insomnia.

If you are taking a drug now and want to know if confusion, depression, or memory loss are recognized as possible side effects, you can get up-to-date information. Start by asking your doctor to check on the drug in his copy of the *Physicians' Desk Reference*. If the doctor is reluctant to detail the possible side effects of a prescribed medicine, and you are concerned that something you are taking may be fuddling your memory, talk to your pharmacist, read the fine-print brochure that may come packed with the medicine, or check out the medicine in the most recent edition of *The Essential Guide to Prescription Drugs: What You Need to Know for Safe Drug Use* (James W. Long, M.D., New York: Harper & Row) or the most recent edition of the more technical *Physician's Desk Reference* (popularly called "PDR") at your local library.

What about drugs specifically prescribed to improve the memory? Much experimentation is being done on substances that might improve memory affected by disease or injury. One of these, physostigmine, can cause a temporary improvement in memory when given intravenously in low doses. It temporarily inhibits formation of cholinesterase, an enzyme which breaks down neurotransmitter substances. However, psychologist Richard C. Mohs of the Psychiatric Service at the Veterans' Administration Medical Center, the Bronx, New York, warns that "higher amounts overstimulate the brain and block memory. Physostigmine is potentially toxic and not safe for casual or nonprescription use."

"My guess," says Dr. Mohs, "is that within ten years there will be drugs approved for treating certain memory disorders. They won't necessarily be so benign that one would recommend them for anyone off the street, and they'd have to be carefully prescribed and administered, but in the longer run I do see a variety of treatments being made available to improve memory functions for the aging."

Another prominent researcher that we spoke to is less certain. "If you knew mechanistically how the memory trace is laid down, you could then shoot something into the brain to enhance that trace; it would become a biochemical problem. But the work of Lashley showed that the brain does not localize memories in a mechanistic way. You end up with the holographic paradigm, which is much more evasive to approach medically. I don't see a research breakthrough as particularly likely."

Marijuana

Is marijuana a memory enhancer or a memory blocker?

Perceptions seem stronger and ideas seem to flow more freely when using marijuana. Sixty percent of American high school seniors have tried it, one-third use it at least once a month, and 7 percent smoke it every day.

Marijuana use is a highly controversial social and political issue. In this climate, test results, pro or con, about the physical effects of marijuana are easily politicized and dismissed by opponents as "propaganda."

The earliest experiments indicated that marijuana was harmless and had no effect on memory. An article by Lester Grinspoon in *Scientific American* (December, 1969) concluded, on the evidence available, that marijuana seemed to interrupt cognitive processes slightly, without affecting attention span or visual coordination, that it had no effect on long-term or short-term memory, and that it actually enhanced learning in regular users. Then there was a rush to *prove* that marijuana could cause everything from sore feet to senile dementia.

Recent experimenters have become more moderate in their assessments. The results, allowing for contributing factors, show that there is *usually* some memory loss with marijuana use. No recent tests show any memory improvement. The impression of memory enhancement appears to be only that—an impression.

As to how marijuana affects memory, one theory is that marijuana intoxication may make us process and remember different kinds of information in different ways. One group of experimenters predicted that marijuana would produce a greater loss of word recall than picture recall because marijuana is supposed to enhance imagery. However, they found just the opposite. As their cheerful volunteers became more and more stoned, they were less able to recall pictures than words.

Looking at words alone, a 1980 experiment indicated that marijuana use decreased the understanding and recall of all 42 types of linguistic information. In a different test, the volunteers lost their ability to recall information in a direct ratio to the strength of the joint they had smoked, and while their ability to recognize information, people, and things remained unchanged, it took them twice as long—an average of four seconds rather than the normal two seconds. One theory on why marijuana reduces memory is that it increases the number of intrusive thoughts—ideas that flit across the mind while the subject is trying to concentrate on a list of words or a group of pictures.

While I have said a lot about improving memory by expecting to remember, in this instance *feeling* you are remembering well doesn't help.

Alcohol

Few people think of alcohol as a memory booster, but how harmful to the mind is "social drinking"? Ernest P. Noble, professor of alcohol studies at the University of California School of Medicine, Los Angeles, says that even a few drinks—two to three drinks consumed four times a week—

will lower our ability to accomplish various thinking tasks including remembering.

Dr. Noble's studies revealed that people over 40 were most affected by alcohol in terms of memory impairment, and even young people, 21 to 30, experienced some memory loss. Dr. Noble theorizes that alcohol can lead to premature aging of the brain.

Another study done in 1979 at the University of Oklahoma Health Sciences Center showed that both young and middle-aged women who drank moderately experienced memory impairment that became greater as they drank more and as they aged. This impairment remained even when they stopped drinking.

People who are alternately drunk and sober experience "state dependency"—things learned in one state are difficult to remember in the other. This is why alcohol has a reputation for interfering with memory. You may have no memory of what you did at the party last night when you sober up the next morning, but if you got drunk again, it would all come back to you. What you learn when you are drunk is best recalled when you are drunk.

But even this has limits. One group of experimenters advertised for volunteers who could drink a (free) pint of whiskey in a few hours. They chose ten eager applicants who consumed their pint and then took simple arithmetic tests, answered questions about their early life, and tried to recall objects and a film they were shown.

All ten subjects could remember the objects and the film 2 minutes later, and five were able to recognize them 30 minutes later. These same five were able to recall 60 percent of this information 24 hours later, while sober control subjects could recall 80 percent. The other five, although still drunk, could *not* recognize objects after 30 minutes. They were all alcoholics and all had experienced frequent blackouts when they drank. Their memory loss was related to general brain damage, not to state dependency.

Smoking

Nicotine may start the day for a lot of cigarette smokers, but it doesn't necessarily start the memory mechanisms going. In Los Angeles, 23 smokers were divided into two groups by researchers at the University of California. People in the first group smoked a regular cigarette while members of the second group smoked a non-nicotine cigarette. All the volunteers then took a memory test, trying to recall a list of 75 items. After three tests, the non-nicotine group scored an average of 24 percent higher than the nicotine group.

Smokers who want to improve their ability to remember names have another good reason to give up the tobacco habit. In a British study, 37 smokers and 37 nonsmokers were asked to remember a list of a dozen names. Ten minutes later, the nonsmokers were able to recall significantly more names from the list than the smokers could. The Scottish psychologist who conducted the study suggested that smoking may impair the blood supply carrying oxygen to the brain, and this lowered oxygen level results in decreased memory efficiency.

Lack of Exercise

The brain is the most sensitive bodily organ. Deprived of oxygen for even a few minutes, it may be irreversibly damaged. We know that exercise improves general physical health and that good health is a powerful aid to memory, but research into the relationship of exercise and memory is just beginning. These initial studies indicate that lack of exercise may not block memory, but it significantly slows down response time; that is, it takes longer to call up the information we want.

One study at the University of Georgia in 1982 was limited to older women. Forty-eight volunteers (average age 65) were divided into two groups. The first group was made up of active people who worked out three days a week in an adult exercise program; the second group rated themselves as sedentary. The volunteers were tested on their ability to judge and predict the speed of a sequence of flashing lights. The active women recalled previous sequences better after ten minutes than the women in the inactive group. The retention was the same later, after one week, and again after 40 days. The researchers concluded that there is "some enhancement of cognitive processes, based on previous and present levels of physical activity."

In another study at Bowling Green State University in

Ohio, adult volunteers were divided into "fit" and "unfit" groups and asked to remember certain numbers. They then acted as contestants in a quiz-show-style game. The nonexercisers were beaten hands down by the exercisers on response time, although both had similar recall of the numbers. Members of the "unfit" group who participated in a ten-week exercise program were able to reduce the time it took them to perform memory tasks.

This indicates two things:

- If you are sedentary, you may be able to remember as much, but you won't be able to remember it as quickly as your active friends.
- If you become active, you can improve your speed of recall.

In other words, we increase our *speed* of reasoning and remembering when we increase our exercise level, even at an advanced age. We don't know exactly why yet, but certainly the extra oxygen for our brain cells and the extra awareness of our surroundings that exercise brings can't hurt.

Fatigue

When we're not talking, we're often hearing . . . but not always listening. Withdrawal is a very helpful and healthy activity, letting us shut out an overload of irrelevant information and renew ourselves in the midst of chaos. The trick is to be in control of when we withdraw so we can snap back into awareness when something important happens.

Fatigue has a strong effect on this process. Occasionally fatigue can be a friend to memory. We float in a rosy haze in which we can call up and idly cavort with an astounding variety of bits from our memory files. Scientists, philosophers, and artists have characterized this kind of dreamy state as the time when all the pieces of a lifetime puzzle come together in a few dazzling seconds.

"YOU NEVER LISTEN TO ME"—FATIGUE AND DISTRACTION

Fatigue can also numb us to a point where we perceive inaccurately, or don't consciously perceive at all. This depleted state of the body (a physical block) can easily combine with a self-protecting mechanism (an emotional block) to turn off anything that will frazzle us further. The tired child simply doesn't hear all the instructions of his bustling mother so he can't remember them. The exhausted student doesn't read the textbook correctly and therefore can't recall the information later during the test.

When people say, "You never listen to me," they may mean, "You never hear me" or, "You never do what I ask" or just, "I need your attention." Sometimes a minute of undivided attention is the best gift you can give anyone . . . and a valuable way to build happy memories.

Tension

We've all experienced this classic self-sabotage block, the frustrating "It's-on-the-tip-of-my-tongue" syndrome. We desperately want to recall a familiar fact, but we go blank. Our desperation to remember sets off a chain of physical responses that produces the opposite effect; we end up jamming our retrieval system.

First our heart rate speeds up, our muscle tension increases, and our digestive system knots. Naturally we concentrate on these unpleasant sensations, so we don't weave the usual web of rich sensory associations that will either let us recall an information bit from the past or file what is happening now for future use. Then, the more we try to remember, the more anxious we become, and the more we forget. It is the classic vicious circle.

OVERCOMING THE TENSION CYCLE

The hardest thing in the world to do at this point is to relax, but that is just what you need to do if you're going to remember. Eastern cultures have practiced body control for centuries, and now western medicine is teaching conscious techniques to control everything from migraine headaches to high blood pressure. Actors routinely learn to control tension to overcome stage fright and improve their performance.

Everyone has blanked out on a name or fact, then remembered it spontaneously hours or days later. You started by digging furiously in the wrong mental file drawer. As soon as you relaxed, your unconscious could continue going through other drawers until it found a cross-reference to the thing you were trying to remember.

If you relax and then try to remember, you will be able to begin the unconscious free association that lets you retrieve the connections that were made at the time of the original event. In other words, you will remember. *Forcing* yourself to remember bypasses this unconscious process. Encourage yourself to relax instead.

HOW CAN YOU RELAX?

Telling someone to relax is easy. It's usually done at the precise moment that relaxation is most difficult—You're taking the bar exam; a doctor or dentist has just inserted an icy steel implement into some part of your quivering body; you are about to address 4,000 delegates at a convention, and you left your notes in the taxi, and your zipper just broke.

Some long-term relaxation techniques that people find helpful include biofeedback, meditating, yoga, visualization, hypnosis, and an unsinkable sense of humor. Only the latter offers instant relief without some preparation.

As you struggle with stress, remember that it can be useful. There is strong evidence that the natural hormones produced when you are excited or under stress work to lock memories into the brain permanently. Adrenalin definitely increases the durability of memory in laboratory rats and blocking their adrenalin production interferes with their memory.

Try This . . .

Defense Against Tension-Induced Memory Blocks

To diminish stress and accelerate remembering, choose appropriate first aid measures from this list:

Take a deep breath, tense all your muscles, then slowly relax and exhale as you collect your thoughts.

Jot down a quick list of what you want to remember, adding to it as things come to you.

Visualize the adrenalin rush you are experiencing as energy for the task ahead, instead of fear. (Both these emotions show up identically when charted by an EEG.)

Play "once-upon-a-time." Go back and start over, rebuilding positive images and circuits to replace the negative ones that brought you to this impasse.

Try to see the humor in it *now.* Relish the details while they're happening as you imagine retelling this story at parties for years to come. (No, it's not possible to manufacture a sense of humor where none exists—you're born with it or not—but you can *arouse* a dormant one and refine and polish it throughout your life. Five-year-olds adore bathroom jokes, adults, Noel Coward. It's the same ability to laugh at ourselves, only more refined.)

5

When It's Okay to Forget

In general, we forget what we don't use, don't like, or fear. Also, we forget what we have never really learned to remember. What most of the famous memory books and systems seem to overlook is that forgetting can have subtle, yet substantial, benefits. Some of these benefits may be relatively frivolous—harmless little vanities that make our lives smoother and more fun. Others protect our very existence.

Forgetting for Self-Preservation

Not all protective memory blocks need to be discarded. When we forget hurtful and negative things, we may be enhancing our lives. Sometimes it can even be dangerous to remember. Consider the experience of a colleague of mine, a psychologist, who had been treating an especially difficult psychotic patient who suddenly missed three consecutive appointments. The patient telephoned several months later to set up a new appointment schedule, but the psychologist kept forgetting to return the call. Upon analyzing why he "forgot," the psychologist realized that he felt the patient was dangerous. He didn't want to see him because it might be unsafe to do so, but he was afraid of provoking the patient by being the one to terminate their relationship. His forgetting may have saved him from a risky situation.

A student who desperately wanted to go to art school had parents who insisted he attend law school. When he forgot to file some crucial forms for law school, his application was rejected. The young man's disappointed parents didn't know about the forms and assumed he had been passed over for other reasons. Forgetting enabled the son to pursue his real goal without facing his parents' anger.

Both of these people unconsciously used forgetting as a form of self-preservation, to get them out of a threatening situation. Forgetting actually made their lives better.

Sometimes we need help to accept the benefits of forgetting. A woman in her sixties came to me because she could not remember the details of an automobile accident 35 years earlier that had killed her husband, but left her unhurt. She had been pregnant at the time and a doctor on the scene had soothed her by saying: "You're alive, and your baby is alive. You're going to forget all this and have a happy, healthy baby." She had functioned very well ever since, and now, suddenly, she had an urge to relive the accident. Did she really need this knowledge to resolve her grief about her husband's death? If not, what was her purpose? She couldn't think of any positive results that would come from her remembering. I persuaded her that it was best to forget the experience, that it could only be a source of painful memories.

Forgetting Pain and Sorrow

Forgetting is a great pain killer. Watch a toddler learning to walk. He forgets the bump on his forehead, teeters forward, and falls again. A woman forgets the pain of giving birth and eagerly plans another child. A widow or widower forgets the pain of loss and decides to marry again.

To remember every pain clearly would immobilize us. To blot out everything unpleasant would condemn us to a life of burned fingers, picked pockets, and poison ivy. Choosing which pains to remember is an ongoing everyday task, accomplished by weighing each hurt against others in our memory bank. Many are better forgotten.

Romantic young men used to do it in droves. Laurel and

Hardy did it in a film. Workaholics practice a socially acceptable form of it, and it can be a lifesaver for the recently
bereaved. It's called "joining the French Foreign Legion" and
it's a valuable forgetting technique. We all resort to it
periodically, blocking out sad or disturbing memories by
immersing ourselves totally in a mentally and physically
exhausting regime. It can be a very valuable short-term solution to severe disappointment or sorrow.

Sometimes forgetting is essential. People faced with unbearable tragedy may block all memory by developing amnesia. Fortunately most of us can deal with painful memories
in a less drastic way, by moving them from our short-term to
our long-term memories. Once the raw and agonizing images
are filed in our total mental filing cabinet, we can mix them
with and evaluate them against other information. This way
of "gaining perspective" is important to survival.

A good night's sleep is one way to transfer strong short-
term memories to our long-term memory. Shakespeare understood this when he wrote about "sleep that knits up the
ravel'd sleeve of care." Some people resort to alcohol or
drugs to block painful memories, but this can have erratic
results. (See chapter 4, "Physical Blocks.") Fortunately for
humanity, the memory is adaptable, letting us keep what is
good and relevant while we discard what hurts and dimin-
ishes us.

Forgetting for Attention and Support

Harry's memory problem was unusual, among the odd-
est ever presented at one of my workshops. He frequently
forgot to shave in the morning, and said he felt embarrassed
at work because his boss and colleagues sometimes commented on his stubble. He forgot this basic grooming ritual
so often that he had to keep an electric shaver at the office.

"Do you occasionally remember to shave in the morning?" I asked.

"When my wife sleeps late, I shave and fix myself breakfast. But when we get up at the same time, she starts demanding things and I forget about shaving." He mimicked her and
her demands until the entire workshop roared with laughter.

He glowed with energy and enthusiasm as he described their morning routine and received a round of applause when he finished.

Slowly Harry began to see that he loved these morning dramas that deprived him of a shave. If he retired to the bathroom to shave in isolation, he would forfeit the stimulating encounter with his wife and miss out on some new incident to relate to his friends at the office. He also realized that on the mornings that he shaved, he missed the attention implicit in the teasing he got at work. For Harry the benefits of remembering to shave were far outweighed by those that came with forgetting.

When her husband died suddenly, 56-year-old Eunice had to take charge of paying the household bills. This new responsibility was terrifying to her. She frequently forgot to make the mortgage, insurance, and utility payments and that resulted in serious trouble. Her children had to come to her rescue repeatedly and soothed the pain of her loss with this demonstration of their concern and devotion. Finally they were forced to take over her financial affairs, freeing her to return to her daily bridge-playing where her phenomenal memory for numbers and detail made her a steady winner.

Neither of these people was deliberately forgetting, but subconsciously, they needed and relished the results that forgetting brought. A one-time memory lapse was reinforced by the response it brought out in others until it became an essential part of their self-image.

The need to be noticed and nurtured is primary in all human beings. But whenever we begin a sentence with "I always forget . . ." or "I can never remember . . . ," it's time to be wary. We are starting to form an image of ourselves as a forgetter. With enough of the right outside reinforcement, we can soon lose our motive to remember, and our self-enhancing forgetfulness turns into a self-destructive block.

Using Negative Memories

She: Darling, remember that quaint, inexpensive hotel we stayed at in Hawaii? The exotic food?

He: You mean that seedy, fleabag slum-within-a-slum? We had to walk two miles to the beach, and I got ptomaine poisoning.

He: Remember when my mother came to visit? I haven't had so much fun in years.

She: Yes. She criticized my cooking, my decorating, and my clothes. I cried for weeks.

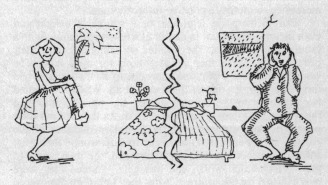

We can choose to remember experiences in different ways.

Both Sigmund Freud and psychological researcher Edward Thorndike suggested that people are likely to forget unpleasant things more quickly than pleasant ones. Though tests have failed to prove this, they do show that both pleasant and unpleasant things are remembered better than ordinary things. Also, results showed that some people tend to remember pleasant things more than unpleasant ones, while for others the unpleasant memories are stronger.

Can we choose between happy and sad memories? We all know an eternal optimist who sees only the bright side of a disaster, or an eternal pessimist who can always find something wrong. These people have a strong image of themselves and the world, and they choose to remember only the events and information that reinforce that image.

But most of us have a choice. Resourceful people can even use negative memories in positive ways. Consider the woman who dated three recently divorced men in a row and discovered that each was still so immersed in the mourning process that he was a poor companion. As a result, she decided to avoid dating recently divorced men. A movie star trusted his business affairs to a close friend who, though well intentioned, lost all the money due to poor decisions. The actor decided that in the future he would employ a well-established investment firm. Both these people used negative memories to motivate positive future actions.

Painful memories can also be a source of delight and even income. Paul went to dinner at a resort restaurant with a group of old friends. They waited 45 minutes before their orders were taken, then another hour for their food. The waitress dumped a plate of spaghetti in Paul's lap and had forgotten to order one of the meals at all. When they called her attention to the missing dinner, the waitress informed them that the kitchen was now closed. As they shared their poorly cooked dinners with the forgotten member of the party, a janitor appeared and began to mop around their feet. Instead of becoming angry or depressed, the men began to play "How much worse can this get?" Indeed they were overcharged by the waitress. After they left, they discovered that one man had forgotten his wallet at the restaurant so they had to return the next day.

A good raconteur, Paul told the story for years afterwards to appreciative friends. Like many well-paid comedy writers and performers, he was able to use negative memories positively for humorous purposes.

Forgetting Because We're Finished

Our minds love to play "School's out!" and discard information we're sure (or strongly hope) we'll never need again. It may be our identification number at a company we'll never work for again or the way to work a machine gun or an ancient, balky copying machine that we couldn't stand. It could even be our doctoral thesis on a subject we didn't select and never fully understood. We don't like the information and chuck it out of our mental library as soon as we can.

This is known formally as the Zeigarnick effect. Dr.

Bluma Zeigarnick of the University of Berlin gave her volunteers all kinds of simple tasks: stringing beads, learning poems, copying pictures. They were all allowed to finish half of these assigned tasks, but she prevented the volunteers from finishing the other 50 percent of the tasks, forcibly if necessary. Afterwards, her subjects could recall 68 percent of what they did or learned in the interrupted tasks, but only 42 percent of the substance of those they had been permitted to finish.

Not every experimenter has been able to duplicate this effect, but both Kurt Lewin and Alan Baddeley had similar results. Baddeley found that subjects who were given the answer to a puzzle before they had been able to solve it remembered the answer better later. Both he and Lewin reasoned that their subjects had unresolved tension because they had been frustrated in their task. (Since the obvious extension of this result would be to abolish most of our educational practices, let me add quickly that finding the answer yourself generally makes a thing more memorable— the attention, rehearsal, and pleasure of success lock it in your memory.)

Memory Misdemeanors

Learn that you needn't harass yourself when you forget something. If you need assurance that it is okay to forget, look over the true stories below. Do you think the people involved were successful in their chosen work?

A. Mr. A went to New York on business. After checking in to his hotel, he went out for a stroll. Sometime later he realized that he was lost and that he did not know the name of the hotel where he was staying. The police phoned all the major hotels in the area and learned that he was registered at the Waldorf Astoria, a half block from where he was found. He had simply been circling the block during his walk. Do you think Mr. A was successful and well regarded by his contemporaries?

B. Mr. B was a public official who went on a good

will tour of South America. Greeting the representatives of one large city, he said how happy he was to be in "_____" and named the capital of another country. When he realized his error, he said, "Oh, that's where I'm going next." The second city was not on his itinerary at all. Did Mr. B have a chance for advancement?

C. Miss C was a film actress who was always late and usually forgot her lines. Her lapses cost the studio lots of money and her coworkers many unhappy hours. Her director vowed never to work with her again. Did she make another movie?

D. The film director mentioned above expressed great affection for this lady. Miss D was always on time and always well prepared. She never forgot an appointment. Her life was one of neatness and order, exemplary in all respects. Did he make a picture with Miss D?

E. Efficiency was Mrs. E's middle name. Her home was spotless, and her closets had rows of neatly labeled containers holding all her possessions. At work her boss counted on her to remember where everything was, to recall the names of everyone he had contact with, and to remind him of every appointment, all of which she did without fail. What impact did Mrs. E have on the world?

I'll bet you have some pretty strong opinions on the relative successes of these people, but let's take a further look.

A. Albert Einstein *was* quite forgetful about ordinary things. There are numerous stories about his absentmindedness, but he possessed the two things necessary to do what he wanted to do.

    Energy—enough physical or mental energy to accomplish his goals.

    Focus—concentration on those goals, resistance to scattering energy in too many directions. (While good health is a definite asset for a high energy level, there are many examples of handicapped, chronically ill or elderly people who overcome their restrictions by focusing their limited energy.)

B. President Ronald Reagan, trying to remember a vast number of names, statistics, and places connected with his 1982 tour, forgot where he was. Interestingly, although he was well past 65, no one accused him of senility, and media treated the incident as an amusing anecdote, not a precursor of major mental decline.

C. Marilyn Monroe exasperated many people who worked with her. After directing her in *Some Like It Hot,* Billy Wilder *(The Seven Year Itch, Sunset Boulevard, The Apartment)* swore that he would never work with her again. In one scene Miss Monroe had to remember a three-word line, "Where's the bourbon?" as she rummaged through drawers. The line came out "Where's the whiskey?"—"Where's the bonbon?"—"Where's the bottle?" The frantic Wilder finally had the line written on the inside of the drawers.

Later he relented, saying: "She's not a parrot. Anyone can remember lines, but it takes a real artist to come on the set and not know her lines and give the performance she did." He suggested that Monroe play the title role in one of his later films, *Irma la Douce,* but the part eventually went to Shirley MacLaine.

D. Billy Wilder explained his change of heart about Marilyn Monroe by saying that he had an Aunt Ida in Vienna who was always on time and ready to do what was required, but he wouldn't put her in a movie.

E. Mrs. E is the aunt of a friend of mine. She lived a very useful, if unspectacular, life. Her chief contribution, a very necessary one, was to create order for people whose minds were hopping pell-mell past the details to the larger view of the project at hand.

This does *not* mean that you have to be disorganized to be creative. If you can remember how things worked in the past and can see how to make them work better in the future, you are way ahead:

remembering + evaluation = positive actions
positive actions + good luck = positive results

For instance, if you *remember* that you always underestimate the time it takes to do something, and then you *evaluate* this, you can take *positive action* by deliberately allowing more time than you think the project will take. With *luck*, your action will lead to a *positive result*—finishing the job on schedule. This is positive because you have saved time (for others who must mesh with your scheduled completion or arrival time), saved energy (less anguish and frustration), and probably saved money (yours and other people's).

Without lots of Mrs. E's, we would probably have to do without dependable electric service and running water, well-stocked supermarkets, brain surgery, air traffic control, and TV quiz programs. A memory for details is essential in all these things.

People who remember everything don't have any real advantage over those of us who *select* our memories. Recall the last time you did something that was important to you. What stands out in your mind? What were the *big* things? How can you use this information in planning for the future? If, as Ralph Waldo Emerson insisted, "a foolish consistency is the hobgoblin of little minds," then total recall without evaluation is the role of computers and the unfortunate few with perfect memories.

We use our memories to create a rich, meaningful landscape of information by *forgetting* some things. What is important steps forward. What is unimportant retreats or disappears. To remember everything equally would be to live in a flat, comic strip world without perspective.

Learning to Choose Your Memories

Selective forgetting is healthful. It's one of the big advantages that human beings have over computers. Instead of berating yourself over every memory lapse, learn to spot the ones that actually help you. Discover how to pick through your memories just as you pick through a bin of apples, looking for the crisp, unspotted nourishing ones that make your life better.

A healthy person doesn't need to eradicate unpleasant or tragic memories, but will choose more valuable memories in their place, "rehearsing" these other mental pictures until they are automatically called up in place of the negative ones.

Try This . . .

Quiz to Assess Your Ability to Forget Constructively

	Often	Usu-ally	Some-times	Never
1. I remember personal insults.	___	___	___	___
2. I fret about the inefficiency and pettiness of my coworkers.	___	___	___	___
3. When I am cheated or get poor service, I don't go back to that business if I can help it.	___	___	___	___
4. I get so mad at the crooked politicians that I don't vote anymore.	___	___	___	___
5. My motto is forgive but never forget.	___	___	___	___
6. When someone describes a situation in which someone I love was humiliated, I remember it clearly.	___	___	___	___
7. I forget to pay bills and to return library books.	___	___	___	___
8. When I am depressed, it's impossible to think about anything cheerful.	___	___	___	___
9. You have to keep your eye open for pickpockets and purse snatchers.	___	___	___	___
10. All in all, the world is a pretty nice place.	___	___	___	___

Score yourself below.   My Score

1. Often 0	Usually 2	Sometimes 6	Never 4	_____
2. Often 0	Usually 2	Sometimes 6	Never 4	_____
3. Often 6	Usually 4	Sometimes 4	Never 0	_____
4. Often 0	Usually 0	Sometimes 0	Never 6	_____
5. Often 0	Usually 0	Sometimes 2	Never 6	_____
6. Often 2	Usually 2	Sometimes 6	Never 0	_____
7. Often 0	Usually 0	Sometimes 2	Never 6	_____
8. Often 0	Usually 2	Sometimes 6	Never 2	_____
9. Often 6	Usually 6	Sometimes 6	Never 0	_____
10. Often 6	Usually 6	Sometimes 4	Never 2	_____

Total   _____

Score

50–60	Excellent—you are appropriately cautious and have a pretty realistic evaluation of the world, but it doesn't get you down.
40–48	Good—but you may need to be more cynical.
30–38	So so—too many things bother you.
20–28	Only fair—you need to forget more.
0–18	Poor—give yourself permission to do a mental version of artificial respiration: "Out with the bad memories, in with the good memories."

Now, study the following motto. You may write it in colored ink on shiny vellum paper or embroider it on a sampler or set it to music—anything that will lock it into your memory.

It's okay to forget—
    When you have to,
    When you need to,
    When you want to,
As long as what you don't remember won't hurt you.

How We Remember

PART **II**

How We
Remember

6

The Seat of Memory—Theories through the Ages

After a long journey hunting for saber-toothed tigers, the caveman snuggled down into his bearskin for a good night's sleep, while his mind prepared for another journey. As his leaden limbs sank into the soft fur, his brain filled with flickering images that soon carried his spirit to another place and another time.

Such experiences convinced ancient man that the mind could be quite separate from the body, free to wander during life and after death. He reasoned that memory, as one of the mind's major assets, must also be free to come and go. (When we recall something, we still say, "It came back to me.")

To their credit, ancient observers did notice that injuries to the head sometimes affected memory and personality. Fossilized human skulls have been found with small, neat holes cut into them, showing that their owners underwent repeated "trepanning," possibly to "let the devils out." The surgeons must have been skilled since many of these patients survived to undergo later surgery.

Aristotle and the Ancients

Aristotle, the Greek scientist and philosopher, concerned himself with the nature of memory more than 2,000 years ago. He concluded that thinking took place in the head, but that memory was stored in the heart.

Memory, said Aristotle, cannot occur in someone who is in a state of rapid transition. "It is like a seal stamped on running water." That is why young and old have trouble remembering, he said. "The former are growing and the latter decaying."

Aristotle also divided memory into two parts: a type of remembering common to all animals that he called "memory"; and a superior human action, involving a sense of time, deliberation, and the relation of a chain of experiences to a present experience, which can be translated as "recall" or "reminiscence."

Aristotle's teacher, Plato, conceived of thought as "an ideal form, existing separately from the sensible world"—the body. The more practical Aristotle decided that both thought and memory needed a home. What better place than the home of the soul, the human heart?

Whether he knew it or not, Aristotle was repeating a Chinese concept, then already several thousands of years old. The Chinese ideograph for both *remember* and *memory* is the same as the ideograph for *heart*.

Both the cavemen and ancient Egyptians performed brain operations but their learning has been lost to us. In the millenia since, the strong taboos against surgery and autopsies helped maintain many erroneous concepts about the brain. Only in the last few hundred years have these taboos diminished, allowing doctors and scientists to reveal the true nature of the heart and the brain. We now know that the heart is an active, enthusiastic muscle, capable of pumping blood around our bodies, while the brain is a silent, grey blob capable of exploring the universe.

Many ancient beliefs about memory were surprisingly accurate. Plato saw how one memory can lead to another when he described a lyre that made him think of its owner and then his friends, until a whole, rich picture of events and associations was called up from a simple stringed instrument.

Aristotle also considered the mechanics of memory. He listed four kinds of association that would stimulate memory.

1. Things near each other, like ocean and shore.
2. Things that happen at the same time, like adolescence and pimples.
3. Things that are similar, like roller skates and ice skates.
4. Things that show a contrast, like city and country.

Twentieth-century memory expert James D. Weinland adds to Aristotle's list.

5. Cause and effect, like fire and heat.
6. Part and whole, like nose and face.
7. Particular and general, like bee and insect.
8. Numerical contiguity, like five and six.

St. Augustine thought that Aristotle's four memory associations were unnecessary. Instead, he reasoned, the only thing necessary for one idea to suggest another is "coexistence," that the ideas must have been active in the mind at the same time, however unlikely the relationship. This two-ideas-at-once concept is now generally accepted—under the term *contiguity of experience*. Pavlov, the nineteenth-century Russian scientist, showed that even dogs could associate such unlikely things as bells and dinner.

Inventing the Brain

Let's invent a brain—or, at least, let's invent a model of how our minds work. Roger von Oech makes a sprightly analogy of man's continuing attempt to compare his mind to his most recent invention. In the seventeenth century, the mind was seen as a lens or a mirror, focusing thoughts and reflecting them back. In the Industrial Age, the mind became a vast factory, with Freud's image of the repressed, hidden unconscious occasionally bursting into the action-oriented conscious like steam from an engine. With the invention of the telephone, the brain was conceived of as a vast switchboard, sending and receiving messages. Now the computer is

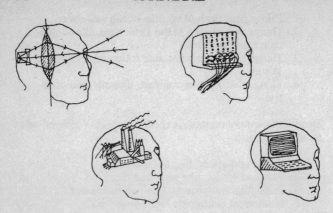

Man tends to compare his mind to his most recent inventions.

our model, with computer jargon describing many of our human exchanges—input, output, feedback, and programming. Our next brain model will probably be the hologram, a concept of matter in which the most minute particle contains a code for reproducing the whole. Indeed, the work of Karl Pribam of Stanford University indicates that the brain has many similarities to the hologram. We'll discuss this exciting holographic model of the brain in the next chapter.

Comparing Computers to the Human Brain

The computer has some big advantages over the human brain—speed, volume, flexibility, and lack of eccentricities . . . most of the time—but the human brain has more advantages. For instance, a human can beat a computer at chess. This is because there are 10^{120} (10 to the 120th power) different possible chess games. If the computer checked every possible move at the speed of one million moves per minute, it would take billions of years to play a game. Therefore chess-playing computers are taught basic chess patterns and groupings so they can discard illogical moves and speed up the game. Even then, a good chess player can beat them.

Another task that man can do better and faster than a computer is to figure the most efficient route for a salesman to visit 20 cities. The computer must compare distances between 20 to the 20th power locations, a task taking days. A child with a ruler could do it in minutes.

But if you are using them for something other than playing chess or traveling, computers are terrific for sifting quickly through mountains of information to find the one fact you want. In doing this book, we saved months, even years, of library research by doing computer searches of recent scientific literature for the latest studies on memory.

However, the key words the computer needed to start on its way were *retrieval* and *retention*—the computer didn't recognize the word *memory*. Thus, we were sometimes referred to articles on retrieval of foreign objects from the ear or articles on urine retention. A person knows instantly that these have nothing to do with memory, but the computer doesn't.

Ebbinghaus and Nonsense

Aristotle took memory out of the world of the spirit and brought it into the world of the scientist. A nineteenth-century German named Hermann Ebbinghaus (1850–1909) married memory study to modern science. He proposed three basic questions about memory.

1. How much information can we store?
2. How fast can we acquire it?
3. How long can we keep it?

In the 1870s Ebbinghaus addressed the latter two. With Germanic thoroughness, he set about a systematic search for answers, using himself as a guinea pig.

First he invented strings of nonsense syllables (wux, caz, bij, zol, etc.). Then he recited sequences of them aloud to see how many repeats were necessary before he could memorize them. He tested himself at the same time every day under the same conditions but varied all other factors such as the length of the lists or the time between memorization and recall. He also discovered that he could remember much better if he studied first thing in the morning than if he studied at 4:00 P.M., and concluded that fatigue affected memory.

Ebbinghaus described three possible ways that we forget.

1. Memories are buried (interference theory)—"the earlier images are more and more overlaid . . . and covered by the later ones."
2. Memories undergo changes (trace decay)—"the persisting images suffer changes which more and more affect their nature."
3. Memories fall apart—forgetting is caused by "crumbling into parts and the loss of separate components."

All of these theories seem to hold up in different situations, and forgetting is probably a complex combination of all of them.

Bartlett and Meaning

The next major studies of memory were done in the early part of this century by Sir Frederick Bartlett (1896–1969) in England. He felt that Ebbinghaus's pure approach was highly artificial. The brain stores information, he said, by using what it already knows, laying a new pattern over a similar old one. He designed experiments that were closer to how people usually use their memories.

Instead of memorizing nonsense, his subjects looked at pictures and read stories, summoning up their personal associations, prior experiences, and attitudes. He still needed strict controls to ensure a uniform basis of comparison, but at the time, many felt his work was too vague and complex. However, contemporary computers show that his theory is correct, at least as far as computers are concerned; using existing patterns *is* the most efficient way to store new information.

Twentieth-Century Debates

Memory research is subject to as many fashions and fads as any other science. Before the 1950s, memory was thought of as one system. Then a two-system theory became popular—a short-term memory for our immediate environment and a long-term memory for "facts": language, history, arithmetic, and the like.

In the '60s memory was regarded as a storage system. In the '70s it was looked on as a component in a larger information-processing system that included perception, comprehension, and reasoning. The '80s have brought new interest in nonverbal memory: visual, auditory, and kinesthetic.

Freud and Memory

Sigmund Freud (1856–1939) was a Viennese doctor who specialized in nerve and brain diseases. When some patients did not respond to physical treatment of their physical ailments, he found that treating their mental and emotional conditions—their *minds*—could result in a cure. Freud was not the first person to see this relationship between the body and the mind, but his theories about the powers of the human psyche were so forcefully described in his many books and papers that they became the basis of modern psychoanalysis and psychiatry.

THE CONSCIOUS AND UNCONSCIOUS MINDS

While Freud is probably best known for his theories on sexuality, he was fascinated with the concept of memory and why we forget things. According to his basic theory, people have conscious and unconscious minds, and the unconscious mind can have a tremendous effect on a person's conscious actions.

Of course doctors can't dissect the brain and locate these separate systems, neatly labeled. This is just a theory that attempts to explain the various forces that affect us, and as a theory it works pretty well. Freud decided that there is nothing accidental or arbitrary in our psychic lives. (If accepted unconditionally, this theory can produce a lot of guilt, so it is fortunate that Freud also did extensive theorizing about guilt.)

Aside from major memory loss caused by neurosis, Freud offered explanations for many everyday incidents of forgetting. He decided that temporary forgetfulness could be divided into both "forgetfulness" and "false recollection"— the latter substituting another name or word for the actual one. The memory process that should have produced the actual memory was interrupted; the memory was "displaced" by another. Displacement, Freud concluded, wasn't an arbitrary quirk. Instead it followed a routine as logical as summoning up the actual memory.

FREUD ON FORGETTING NAMES

In *The Psychopathology of Everyday Life* (New York; Random House, 1938), Freud analyzed a number of his own "Freudian slips." In one case he couldn't remember the name of a sanatorium, although he could remember the location, the doctor in charge, and the name of a patient who had been there. When his wife reminded him that the name of the place was "Nervi," Freud concluded that, as a nerve doctor, he, himself, had become weary of nerves. On another occasion Freud could not remember the name of a major railroad station, Rosenheim, which translates as Rose-home. Upon tracing the associations, he decided that the name was lost because he had just come from visiting the home of his sister, Rose (Rose's home). "This name was taken away by my 'family complex'."

Freud concluded that forgotten names are associated, however indirectly, with something painful and unpleasant. If you accept Freud's theory, you can decide that forgetting the name of your dear friend, Sue, may mean you are secretly angry at her, but it can also mean that the name reminds you of a nasty experience you had in *Sioux* Falls when you were *sued* by a *sewer* worker.

FREUD ON LOSING THINGS

Once Freud intended to order a book by a favorite author and could not find the book store catalog. He concluded that this was because he had at one time written this author of his admiration and received a cool reply.

Freud described another case in which a patient mislaid a book, a gift from his wife. The patient and his wife had been at odds for some time. Then about six months after he lost the book, they reconciled. He promptly found the book.

FREUD ON FORGETTING APPOINTMENTS

Neither lovers nor soldiers, Freud noted, can get away with saying "I forgot." Their preoccupation with the task at hand should be and is so overwhelming that there is no chance of forgetting. We can see many demonstrations of this in our own lives. If we are fleeing a burning building or rushing to present the winning raffle ticket, we rarely forget what we are about.

Freud explained his own lapses in everyday matters as a dislike of the task he had reluctantly agreed to do. He noticed with chagrin that he sometimes forgot to make calls on charity patients and colleagues, but never on paying clients. He saw the everyday forgetting of the many small promises we make as antagonism toward the demands placed upon us. (A reputation for forgetfulness can also discourage people from asking us to do things.)

Freud had no kind words for people who forget and then blame it on an organic defect ("poor memory"). "The motive is an unusually large amount of unavowed disregard for others which exploits a constitutional factor for its purpose."

FREUD AND YOU

If you are analytic by nature, you may want to explore some of your own common slips in a Freudian way. It's fun, usually harmless, and occasionally insightful.

But Freud was so successful at uncovering deep, psychological manifestations in what seemed to be utterly casual occurrences that you might find yourself ascribing every instance of forgetting or loss to some repressed hatred, latent psychosis, or psychic abnormality. Keep in mind that such all-pervasive self-analysis is usually erroneous and could be harmful to you and those around you. There *are* repressed hostilities, of course, but there are also holes in pockets, misunderstood instructions, mumbled introductions, and ringing phones that can interrupt a train of thought.

Once I fell down a flight of stairs. Afterwards I painfully contemplated all the psychological explanations for my accident. I decided that my life was in pretty good shape and I had had no subconscious reason to injure myself, so I went and measured the steps. They were several inches smaller than standard steps, actually illegally shallow. Sometimes there are very ordinary explanations for extraordinary events.

Remember, too, that Freud concluded that "no psychological theory has yet been able to explain the connection between remembering and forgetting; indeed, even the complete analysis of what we can actually observe has yet scarcely been grasped." After a hundred years of study, this is still true. Human memory is still slyly and shyly retaining its secrets.

Try This . . .

to See If You Forget for a Reason

Write down some things that you have forgotten recently that really bothered you: _____
_____.
Now go back and speculate on why you may have forgotten. _____
_____.
_____

7

How the Brain Remembers

Imagine sending three explorers into a strange land. One returns with an exhaustive report of the topography: the rivers, mountains, and deserts. Another deciphers the various languages spoken. A third describes the architecture but makes no attempt to relate it to the natural environment and resources or to political, religious, and cultural influences.

Until recently, the brain has been explored this way. Psychologists, biologists, and chemists looked at the brain independently, from the viewpoint of their separate disciplines. Now at last they are beginning to combine their studies.

Just as florists sort through masses of flowers to produce bouquets, scientists must pick through masses of sometimes conflicting facts and select the ones they want to shape into theories. Each works with a large variety of raw materials, and no two florists or scientists are likely to come up with exactly the same result. Sphinx-like, the brain quietly retains most of its secrets.

What We Remember With

To discover how we remember, we have to examine *where* we remember—the brain. The brain is a rather dull-looking grey mass, weighing about three pounds. Despite its mousy appearance, it contains the universe as each of us knows it. In fact, it contains everything we know. "If the brain were simple enough ever to understand," says Lyall Watson, "we would be so simple, we couldn't."

Scientists used to think that we use only a small percentage of our brain. This was because much of the brain remained uncharted. We now know that we use *all* our brain with differing degrees of efficiency.

The brain demands one-fifth of the body's blood and oxygen supply, but its energy output is equivalent to that of a 25-watt bulb. The brain can continue to function in the face of severe adversity—with several bullets in it or (once) even a crowbar; however, a few tiny crystals of a drug like etorphin can knock it out. One man lived a full, mentally competent life with only *one* cerebrum—half a brain. This amazing fact was discovered only through an autopsy.

The brain has changed little throughout our known history. Humans today are no smarter than they were 10,000 years ago, but they have a greater storehouse of knowledge to draw on, to *remember*.

A Brief History of the Brain

Join us for a diverting detour through the richest, most inscrutable galaxy of the universe—the brain. Let's look closely at our three-layered treasure.

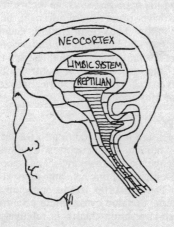

THE REPTILIAN BRAIN

Once upon a time there was a lizard with a perfectly good lizard's brain. It told him how to do all the essential things: look for food, defend his home, be sociable with other lizards, and reproduce. This simple brain has survived for 200 million years in all animals. We humans have improved on it, of course, but that primitive core is still there, controlling much more of our behavior than we might realize. It is responsible for much of our interaction with our fellow creatures and our need to follow leaders, everything from "keeping up with the Joneses" to "making the world safe for democracy." Scientists call this the R-Complex brain.

THE LIMBIC SYSTEM

As soon as our lizard ancestor stopped lying around on hot rocks and developed his own heating system, he added a more sophisticated brain to control it. One of the nice features of this new brain was love. While the old-style creatures ate (and continue to eat) their nearest and dearest without compunction, the new limbic-brained creatures were capable of all sorts of romantic notions. They could also smell and experience fear, pain, and pleasure.

You'll notice that we refer to this new, 150-million-year-old brain as a "system." That's because it consists of several parts including the *hypothalamus,* an inch-square organ that regulates sex drive, orders extra adrenalin during stressful situations, monitors body temperature, and lets us know when we're thirsty and hungry; the *pituitary gland,* our master producer of sex and growth hormones; and the *hippocampus*—shaped like a seahorse, it controls fear and rage, probably converts short-term memories into long-term, and regulates memories about place.

THE NEOCORTEX

The newest and largest addition to the brain is the part that makes us human. The neocortex is rational and lets us store logic, language, mathematics, and speculation about the future. (Dolphins, monkeys, and dogs also have large neocortexes.) The neocortex lets us consciously change the behavior patterns dictated by our more primitive brains.

This three-layer-brain theory is relatively new. It was

first set forth in 1972 by Dr. Paul MacLean of the Laboratory of Brain Evolution and Behavior of the National Institute of Mental Health in Maryland. Research and experiments since then seem to support it, and it is now generally accepted. This illustrates the process by which human imaginings, ideas, and speculations make the journey from fancy to demonstrable fact.

Could we add yet another more sophisticated layer? Maybe, in time. One basic problem—a larger brain would require a larger skull. Since the current size of a baby's head just fits (usually) through the circle of its mother's pelvic bones, we would either have to evolve bigger women or smaller babies or perhaps grow babies outside their mother's bodies. Ah, brave new world!

How Much Will You Remember?

How much you remember is determined by

- Your inborn capacity to remember.
- Your training for efficient collection, intelligent interpretation, and maximum storage of information (sometimes called "education").
- Your enthusiasm for remembering a particular thing.
- The effect of things you learned before (proactive interference) and things you learned after (retroactive interference) on the particular thing you want to remember.
- The effect of physical, mechanical, and emotional blocks.

Where Does the Brain Remember?

Is the brain a big library, with different subjects stored on different shelves? One way to test this is to study people who have lost part of their memory because of head injuries. If several people have suffered damage in the same part of the brain and they all experience similar memory loss, then presumably the affected part controlled that kind of memory.

However, attempts to catalog such relationships or to duplicate memory loss in animals have been unsuccessful.

Amazingly, people who have had large portions of their brain damaged can frequently remember most of what they knew before they were injured, although they may no longer be able to remember newly acquired information. In another type of injury—damage to the medial temporal cortex—the person can still learn readily on a short-term basis, but forgets the information almost immediately.

How Does the Brain Remember?

The brain is full of information-holding nerve cells called neurons. Neurons are all over the body, but the ones in the brain are especially sophisticated. We have billions of these brain cells (estimates range from 10 billion to 100 billion) and more than 20,000 of them will fit on the head of a pin.

Neurons come in different shapes, depending on their function. On one side, each neuron has a long tail (axon) ending in a brush. On the other side, the neuron has a set of short tails called dendrites. When the axon of one cell shyly reaches out and touches the dendrite of another cell, the connection is called a synapse. The synapse is actually a gap or open space, but it acts like a bridge between two towns or a street between two houses. Like a bridge or a public street, the synapse has a lot of traffic and this is where information exchange takes place. Synapses are found almost exclusively in the memory portions of the brain.

There are three major theories on how these synapses work.

- Information is physically coded on the neurons.
- Information is transmitted and stored as electrical signals.
- Information changes the chemical structure of the neurons.

It is also possible that memories are stored in the patterns of connections between neurons, rather than in the neurons themselves. Dr. Mark Rosenzweig, psychologist and memory expert at the University of California, Berkeley, suggests that whenever a person learns something new the neurons alter their areas of contact so that messages can get across the synapses more easily. New connections form, and old ones are removed.

To prove this, he put one group of rats in a dull, dreary cage. He put a second group in a veritable Disneyland for mice, with toys, mazes, ferris wheels, and merry-go-rounds. The brains of the stimulated mice grew larger and showed denser concentrations of neuronal connections. While there is no proof that fat, healthy neurons remember better than skinny, pale ones, we suspect they do.

THE HOLOGRAPHIC THEORY

Scientists once believed that memories were stored in neat little pigeonholes in different parts of the brain. If only we could find out which memory goes where, they reasoned, we would be able to fix defective memories and improve healthy ones.

They located parts of the brain that control sight, smell, taste, and hearing, but memory eluded them. Now we know that, even though certain parts of the brain let us remember certain things, they don't *store* the memory itself. They are just receivers for certain signals. Because memory can't be pinpointed in any one part of the brain, more and more experts are turning to a holographic concept of memory formulated by Dr. Karl Pribam of Stanford—that all memories are stored in all parts of the brain. In a holograph, any fragment can reproduce the whole.

PROFILE OF A RECEPTOR

To record a memory, the recording agent must be able to do two difficult things: respond within a fraction of a second to a stimulus and then keep the information indefinitely. Scientists at the University of California, Irvine, have tracked down such a wonder in the synapses found in the hippocampus.

Electrically stimulating this part of the brain or treating it with calpain, a protein-digesting enzyme, uncovers receptors and makes synapses in this region more active for months. Once these receptors are uncovered, they stay that way, passing information back and forth and keeping their neighbor neurons healthy and functioning throughout the life of the brain.

It's possible that some older people lose their memory abilities because their bodies have stopped producing the enzymes that keep their receptors receptive. Some laboratory work has already been done, showing that blocking norepinephrine production in animals keeps them from remembering new information—possibly why some people can clearly remember events from years before, but not what happened this morning. Stimulation of enzyme production in humans may (or may not) prove to be an incredible new way to enhance and extend memory throughout our lives.

Receptors are also "binding sites" for chemicals that affect mood and behavior. Sharks are one of the few animals that lack these receptors, which may explain why they have such boring personalities.

BRAIN CHEMICALS

When nerve signals are passed from cell to cell over the network of synapse bridges, they are helped by chemicals called neurotransmitters. There are four significant brain chemicals currently being studied: calpain, norepinephrine, Deamino-D-Arginine Vasopressin (DDAVP), and serotonin.

Calpain has the ability to digest protein and appears to clean up blocked receptors and let the neurons communicate more easily with their neighbors. Calpain is naturally released by calcium in the cells, and one possibility being studied right now is that calcium deficiency may decrease enzyme activity in older people, leading to memory loss.

Norepinephrine triggers long-term memory. Fearful memories are essential for survival, and we hang onto such memories unless production of norepinephrine is blocked. This was demonstrated by Dr. Larry Stein at the University of California, Irvine, who conducted an experiment in which he gave rats a shock whenever they stepped off a shelf. Weeks later they were put back in the same cage, and they still remembered not to step off the shelf. But when their production of norepinephrine was blocked, they forgot and got repeated shocks. Conclusion: norepinephrine is a trigger to long-term memory. When we have a strong experience, norepinephrine tells the brain to "print it."

DDAVP is used by the body to balance water content, but it can also temporarily improve the ability to recall in normal humans and some animals.

Serotonin is the fourth significant neurotransmitter. Changing the diet of laboratory rats can affect their production of serotonin, but so far this has not been demonstrated in humans. A 1983 study at U.C.L.A. made the intriguing discovery that very high levels of serotonin are present in dominant male vervet monkeys and in officers of college fraternities.

THE ROLE OF ADRENALIN

Adrenalin may be a key to locking memories in place. Psychobiologist James McGaugh of the University of California, Irvine, reports that rats that can't produce adrenalin have poorer recall ability than their normal adrenalin-producing kin. Rats that get a booster shot of adrenalin after learning something can remember it better. He and his colleagues theorize that hormones such as adrenalin act as "fixatives," locking memories of exciting, stimulating, or shocking events in the brain.

This fixing is a valuable sorting tool, a filter that lets us discard the trivial while retaining the important impressions in our lives. "If you were going to build a brain that emphasized thinking functions," McGaugh says, " . . . you would need a system that can tell exactly what is important to keep and what is not."

One of their most interesting discoveries was that injecting adrenalin into older rats after they had learned a maze improved their memory of the maze. This may support the theory that hormone deficiency in older people contributes to memory loss and senility.

Hormones may act directly on the brain, McGaugh says, or they may alter body chemistry so that some other substance can reach the brain and lock in the memory. Brain research is barely beginning, but someday we may be able to maintain and improve memory through subtle reinforcement of our body's natural memory-storing processes.

Brain Size

When it comes to brains, bigger is not necessarily better. The average brain is 1,349 grams (2.97 pounds). Nineteenth-century scientists, seeking a correlation between size and smarts, actually weighed the brains of famous men. Two writers, Jonathan Swift and Ivan Turgenev, weighed in as heavyweights, 2,000 grams (4.4 pounds) each. But Anatole France, no slouch as an author, had a brain weighing only 1,017 grams (2.24 pounds). The largest brain ever studied weighed 2,049 grams (4.51 pounds)—and belonged to an idiot! Brain size is no measurement of intelligence, at least in humans.

Relative brain size in animals can be confusing too. Many animals have larger brains than man. The elephant's brain weighs more than three times what a human brain weighs, but it represents only 0.2 percent of an elephant's body weight. Spider monkeys, mice, porpoises, tree shrews, and sparrows have a higher brain/body weight ratio than people do, yet only porpoises could claim similar intelligence. A horse's brain is only half the size of a human brain, yet a horse weighs ten times what a man weighs.

Between the time we are born and the time we reach adulthood, brain weight more than triples. From then on it decreases slightly, about a gram a year. Tall people have heavier brains than short people, but short people have a higher brain/body weight ratio. Eskimos generally have the largest brains of any ethnic group.

Can Memories Be Swallowed?

We can't leave the fascinating intricacies of the brain without mentioning one memory experiment that involved lowly worms. These little fellows, called planaria, were kept in a dark place by a scientist who periodically flashed a light and gave the poor things an electric shock. Whenever they got a shock, their bodies would naturally scrunch up. After a while, they would scrunch up whenever the light flashed, shock or no shock. Then the scientist ground up his unhappy worms, made a slurry, and fed them to a new group of planaria. After their cannibalistic breakfast, the new worms were placed in the darkened worm tanks, and a light was flashed. You guessed it; the new worms scrunched up.

Memory Pills

Is there a pill or medicine that we can take to improve our memories? Not yet, but experts are working on it. One candidate would be an "enhancer" that would increase the brain's protein synthesis or slow the synapse breakdowns, preventing or reversing memory loss. A kidney drug called Vasopressin may turn out to be such a natural substance. It's a pituitary hormone that constricts the blood vessels, raises blood pressure, and regulates the body's water content.

In experiments in the Netherlands and at the National Institute of Mental Health in Washington, D.C., both people and animals experienced enhanced memories after taking the Vasopressin. Human memory improved between 20 percent and 100 percent in different types of tests. Patients who had undergone electric shock therapy, which is frequently followed by temporary amnesia, improved by an astonishing 300 percent. The effects lasted about three weeks. However, Vasopressin has dangerous side effects on the body's circulation and water retention, so its use is still in the early experimental stages.

Another potential memory drug, adrenocorticotropic hormone/melanocyte-stimulating hormone (ACTH/MSH), is a combination of two pituitary hormones. Injections of ACTH/MSH seem to increase the power of concentration and may be helpful in treating some forms of retardation that result in inattention. Its effects on hyperactive children and adults with senile dementia are also being tested. But, like Vasopressin, it has dangerous side effects.

Another element that may improve fading memory is choline, a dietary substance that is the forerunner of acetylcholine, a brain compound necessary for transmitting nerve impulses. The major dietary source of choline is lecithin.

In one study conducted by the National Institute of Mental Health, a single ten-gram dose of choline significantly improved both memory and recall in normal, healthy volunteers. After taking the choline, the volunteers were able to memorize a sequence of unrelated words more quickly. Interestingly, those with the poorest memory at the start of the study were the ones helped the most by choline.

Other studies suggest that choline may also help persons with Alzheimer's disease. In numerous cases, the memory of patients increased significantly although it did not quite return to normal. The improvement lasted for up to 18 months.

Unlike the powerful drugs, choline appears to be completely safe even when as much as 20 to 25 grams is taken daily. Scientists stress that research on choline's effectiveness has just begun, but so far the results are very encouraging.

Things to Come

Most of the brain's chemistry has yet to be explored. One prominent chemist estimates that we understand less than one percent of the chemistry of the brain's nerve cells. He anticipates that chemical pathways for the major emotions will be mapped within the next 20 years. Of course, knowing where and how still won't tell us *why*.

Try This . . .

to Evaluate Your Personal Potential for Remembering

Here are five major factors that determine how much you can remember. Which can you develop?

1. *Your inborn capacity to remember.*
   You can't change your parents at this point, so you have to accept your inherited capacity as a fixed part of your memory equation. (Don't underrate it!)

2. *Your training for efficient collection, intelligent interpretation, and maximum storage of information (sometimes called "education").*
   Are you pretty good at this already, or would some practice help? The exercises in this book may show you where you need to do more work.

3. *Your enthusiasm for remembering a particular thing.*
   Think of three types of things that you rarely forget:

   _____
   _____
   _____.

   Are you enthusiastic about them, or have they become habits (like getting dressed in the morning)? Now think of three types of things you frequently forget:_____

   _____
   _____
   _____.

   Is there any way you could be more enthusiastic about them, or convert them to habits, or are they subject to the problems of number four and number five below?

4. *The effect of things you learned before and things you learned after the particular thing you want to remember.*
   Something that you learned earlier can keep you from recognizing or learning new things that are very similar. Imagine meeting people named Minninger, Benjanin, or Collingrood. You would probably convert them to the more

familiar Menninger, Benjamin, and Collingwood. If something is very similar to something you already know, it is easier—and harder—to remember.

The caveman spent much of his time noticing when things changed. His survival instinct constantly evaluated his shifting surroundings—can I eat it or will it eat me? When you encounter something that seems familiar, try playing caveman. What is the same? What is different?

Learning something new is a good reason to review related things you already knew. That incredibly boring school task was also a very useful way to lock into our memory things that might have been replaced by newer information.

Try playing "student" and give yourself lots of mental gold stars as you go over old information that you don't want to lose.

5. *The effect of physical, mechanical, and emotional blocks.* As a practice task for number four above, review the information in earlier chapters on physical, mechanical, and emotional blocks. Do you see new ways that you can improve how you remember things? Do you see memory blocks that have no immediate solution? Which blocks (such as ill health, fatigue, confused input) will you probably have to cope with throughout your life?

8

Three Stages of Memory

For generations scholars argued this classic question about memory: Is memory one system that is used in different ways at different depths, *or* is it two systems, one for what has just happened and another for the big picture of life—culture, language, science, mathematics, and the universe?

Memory goes through three stages: immediate memory (seconds), short-term memory (hours or days), and long-term memory (months or years).

Today scientists speculate that memory goes through not two, but *three* stages:

- immediate memory
- short-term memory
- long-term memory

We are constantly redrawing the "map" of how memory works, but here is the way most experts see it right now. Immediate memory lasts about two seconds and lets us do continuous activities—walk across a room or read a sentence.

Short-term memory is recent—the last few minutes, hours, days. You could probably say what you ate for breakfast yesterday and, just maybe, the day before, but asking you a week or a month from now would be fairly useless, unless it was a very special breakfast, or you always ate the same thing.

Long-term memory is the select filing cabinet where we would like all those pesky names, dates, and numbers to end up. When we talk about remembering, we are usually talking about long-term memory (although occasionally short-term memories like "Where did I put my glasses?" are more vexing).

All memory stages have two characteristics.

Capacity: how many bits of information can be held?
Duration: how long can they be held?

Each memory expert has slightly different figures for these categories, and some aren't sure that short-term memory must precede long-term memory. They argue that some information can go directly into our long-term memories.

Immediate Memory

Capacity: thousands, in terms of generalities (thousands of leaves on a tree, thousands of ants at the picnic)
Duration: two seconds or less
Instinct plays a big part in immediate memory (also called the sensory memory). Simple comparisons are made

between pictures: is this different than it was a second ago? Immediate memory notices a potential change and puts our short-term memories on standby.

Short-Term Memory

Capacity: seven things
Duration: 30 seconds to 2 days

The language of the Australian aborigine contains only eight words for numbers: one, two, three, four, five, six, seven, many. Seven seems to be the largest number of separate things we can remember. After that, things turn into groups, crowds, schools, herds, or congresses.

Seven is a mystical and popular number—seven days of the week, Seven seas, the Seven Hills of Rome, the Seven Wonders of the World, even the Seven Dwarfs. Seven seems to be the one real biological limitation on short-term memory. If there are more than seven digits in a phone number, most people won't remember it from the time they look it up to the time they dial it. They will have to read it off the page as they

How long does short-term memory last? How easily are we distracted from remembering?

dial. When more than seven things are needed from the supermarket, you write a list. And yet you can remember thousands of things by grouping them for storage in long-term memory. You remember more by remembering less.

Short-term memory lets us link things together, create contexts, assign meanings. Short-term memory is an active process. Reciting a phone number over and over until you can get to a phone is one example.

How long does short-term memory last? Again, the experts disagree. Some say only a few seconds, some say as long as two years. While the time period is probably several days for most things, you may find that a monthly event like a meeting brings back clear memories of the previous event, where you sat, what you heard and said, maybe even what you wore. An annual event, a holiday or birthday for example, may let you recall some surprising things: "Gee, Aunt Tootsie sent me this same card last year" or "I spilled gravy on my green shirt last Thanksgiving." This information has survived one year, but probably wouldn't last another, unless the Aunt Tootsie or the green shirt was very important to you.

Was this information still in your short-term memory? Or did it make it to long-term and then fade with time? Right now we don't know, but let's assume that you made no effort to remember it and that it was reconstructed from a quirky, lingering scrap of short-term memory.

During the entire time that something is in your short-term memory, bits and pieces are being transferred to long-term memory. Everyone agrees that anything in your short-term memory *can* get into your long-term memory. Studying is one way to do this. When you study, you also create a context for remembering by deciding what the information means and clustering it with similar information. It's the "handles" you build onto an information bit that help you retrieve it later. If you meet a charming fellow named Harry and associate him with an event coming up in two years and also with a dear friend whom you see regularly, you have a much better chance of remembering him than if you simply think of him as tall and dark haired.

It is important not to try to do too much in short-term memory. Remember, your capacity is seven things. Elementary school teachers are careful about this when working with students. They create learning structures with no more than four to seven units. Some classic learning structures are North, East, South, West; the four seasons; the four elements (air, fire, earth, and water); and animal, vegetable, mineral.

Long-Term Memory

Capacity: infinite
Duration: forever
Canadian psychologist Endel Tulving divides long-term memory into two kinds: episodic and semantic.
Episodic: remembering incidents, like what you had for breakfast, a presidential election, a book you read
Semantic: remembering knowledge—meanings of words and numbers, locations
Neurosurgeon Wilder Penfield probed areas of the human brain during surgery and discovered that patients vividly reexperienced events that happened as much as 50 years earlier. There seem to be no limits to how much we can remember and how long we can remember it.

But the transfer of information from short- to long-term memory can be blocked by any number of things. When rats find their way through a maze and are rewarded, they remember the route. When they find their way through and get an electric shock, they forget the route. It is not profitable for them to remember, so they discard the information. Similarly we choose our memories. The person who spots a newcomer across the room and asks, "Is he anybody?" really means, "Is he worth remembering?"

Most people think of long-term memory as a large dresser drawer that has to be emptied periodically to make room for new things. Wrong. There are no known limits to the storage in your memory. You can learn and remember new things all your life.

Try This . . .

Exercise for Recognizing Memory Stages

	Short	Long
Are the following examples of short-term or long-term memory loss?		
1. You lose your glasses.	_____	_____
2. You can't remember who was vice-president under Harry Truman.	_____	_____
3. You forget to put a dime in the parking meter.	_____	_____
4. There's a word starting with *m* that means some kind of road, "Mac . . ." something, but you can't think of it.	_____	_____
5. You get lost trying to find a restaurant in your old neighborhood.	_____	_____

Now consider whether these same incidents are also examples of episodic or semantic memory, as defined by Tulving.

	Episodic	Semantic
6. You lose your glasses.	_____	_____
7. You can't remember who was vice-president under Harry Truman.	_____	_____
8. You forget to put a dime in the parking meter.	_____	_____
9. There's a word starting with *m* that means some kind of road, "Mac . . ." something, but you can't think of it.	_____	_____
10. You get lost trying to find a restaurant in your old neighborhood.	_____	_____

Here are three actions that can help you convert information from short-term memory to long-term memory.

Intend to remember.

Rehearse the information.

File the information in several ways.

Decide which is represented by the following actions:

	Intention	Rehearsal	Multiple Filing
11. You recite a phone number over and over until you can dial it or write it down.	___	___	___
12. You set aside a time and place for studying and see that you aren't interrupted.	___	___	___
13. You want to remember that your child's new teacher is Mr. Post so you imagine him standing near the fence post on the school playground and also posting a sign on the class door with his name. His manners are so good he must be related to Emily Post.	___	___	___
14. You see yourself as a competent person who rarely loses things or forgets appointments.	___	___	___
15. You repeat a name when you are introduced.	___	___	___
16. You tie a big red ribbon on your keys, always hang them in the same place, and have duplicates at the home of a neighbor and at the office.	___	___	___

Answers

1. short-term
2. long-term
3. short-term
4. long-term
5. long-term
6. episodic
7. semantic
8. episodic
9. semantic
10. episodic
11. rehearsal
12. intention
13. multiple filing
14. intention
15. rehearsal
16. multiple filing

9

Three Steps To Remembering

As a child you learned your "three Rs"—Readin', 'Ritin', and 'Rithmetic, an illiterate but alliterative trio. Remembering also can be thought of as a "three Rs" process:

- Registration—you get the information.
- Retention—you file the information.
- Retrieval (recall/recognition)—you can find the information later, *or* it is familiar when you run into it again.

The three Rs of remembering.

Registration

You can't forget what you didn't get in the first place. We've already talked about overload and other distractions that prevent or confuse input. Trying to register information while the television is on, several conversations are taking place in the same room, the tea kettle is whistling in the kitchen, the phone is ringing, your head is aching, and the dog is barking at the door may be difficult or impossible.

Of course, if the information is *really* important, if the phone call is to tell you you've just won one million dollars, you will probably remember it. And some people thrive in just such an environment, letting the conflicting demands for attention cancel each other out until they blend into a soothing background noise like that of a waterfall. There are people who actually seek out crowded restaurants or bus terminals as ideal places to study.

Retention

Retention is "potential recall." You have noticed something and, hallelujah, it has made the trip from your short-term memory to your long-term memory, joining a billion other bits of information. You have filed it in your mental filing cabinet, put the book on the shelf of your mental library, and sent the carton off to your mental warehouse, or however else you want to envision the process. Now the fun begins.

Retrieval

There are two different ways to get the information back: recall and recognition. In recall, the memory returns to your consciousness. This can be either voluntary or involuntary. The face of a friend or the lyric of a song or an algebra formula is right there, center stage, for your use. You may have summoned it up or it may have drifted there unexpectedly, but it is there.

In recognition, you either haven't tried or haven't been able to summon up that memory, but when you run into the information again—the clerk who waited on you last week, a place you haven't visited in years, a taste long forgotten—you know you are reexperiencing it. You recognize it.

You can play a parlor game to illustrate this. Most of us have seen the back of a one dollar bill or a picture of the Eiffel Tower or a can of Campbell's Soup many, many times. We would all recognize them instantly. However, ask people to draw or describe them, to actively recall them, and few will come even close. (Interestingly, people are usually more accurate in recalling the Statue of Liberty, the Jolly Green Giant, or the Mona Lisa—perhaps because they are representations of people and therefore more worthy of recall.)

I'LL KNOW IT WHEN I SEE IT

If you've ever worked as a salesperson, you know the frustration of trying to help a customer who won't know what he's looking for until he finds it. "Why," you grumble, "can't he just describe it?"

Most of memory is recognition. We can recognize a lot more than we can recall.

Recognition sometimes seems like a weak substitute for the more vigorous recall, but most of memory *is* recognition. This is fortunate because we can recognize a lot more than we can recall.

You know those random lists of unrelated words that memory experts are so fond of: pizza, aardvark, espadrilles, etc.? Most of us asked to reproduce such a list would score only fair, but if we're shown a similar list, we would probably recognize most or all of the words that were on the original list. You can choose to think of your recall "failure" as a serious defect in your character, or you can be elated that you recognize so many millions of things. Much of the forgetting that people fret about is failure to recall, not failure to recognize.

Which Lasts Longer?

Here's a puzzlement: If we really never forget anything in our long-term memory as most scientists believe, then how can we talk about the length of memories? Some studies of learning retention seem to show that memory can fade.

According to these studies, we lose our ability to recall information much sooner than we lose our ability to recognize it. In one study, students who were tested a year after they completed algebra had forgotten two-thirds of the equations they had learned. Another study showed that half the psychology, zoology, and biochemistry learned in one school year was forgotten by the following October, although losses in recognition were less. A conflicting study showed that students never completely forgot what they had learned in elementary psychology classes during a five-year period. This study also showed slower losses in recognition than in recall.

Does this mean that we *do* lose things from long-term memory? Not necessarily. Much of the information that the students poured onto test pages in June may have been in their short-term memories, crammed there in the day or so before finals. The information that showed up as "recognition" five years later was certainly in long-term memory. If we think of our memory as a huge library, we can visualize these bits as books on high, dark shelves. We know where they are and can put our hands on them, but we haven't dusted them off yet and started to turn the pages. Numerous experiments show that we can re-learn what we have once learned in less time than was required for the original learning, even after many years' disuse.

Why Learn Anything?

"Ah ha!" some of you are muttering. "If I don't really remember all that dull stuff I had to learn in school, why did I bother?" If we broaden the definition of memory to "retained learning" or even "education," there are three good reasons.

First, you need to know something to learn something. All learning is comparing what's new to what's old. To make a simile, life is like a metaphor. A baby decides that its toes are like its fingers, except. . . . An adult decides that Einstein's theory of relativity is like riding a bicycle at the speed of light, except. . . .

Memory expert Alan Baddeley says:

> When we attempt to learn something new, we base our learning on already existing schemata. When these conflict with what is being remembered, distortions occur . . .

In other words, the more structure we already have to compare new information to, the less new information we are likely to discard because it is meaningless or to distort because we are trying to compare it to the wrong thing.

A second reason is that re-learning something you have already studied takes much less time. One doctor read his small son passages in ancient Greek every day when the boy was between the ages of 18 and 36 months. When the boy was 8, he phonetically memorized these selections plus some new ones. The previously heard passages took only 70 percent as long to memorize as did the new passages.

Once you have learned something, you can reactivate it much more easily than you can learn new material. With all the challenges that the world presents, would you really want to have to start from scratch at every turn? In our complex society, *knowledge* has come to mean knowing where and how to find out, not just knowing.

The final reason to learn is because *everything* you experience shapes your view of the world in some way. When you see order and purpose in even the most transitory experience, you come to expect order and purpose in life. Order is essential for people to function physically, and purpose is essential for people to function spiritually.

Try This . . .

to Compare Recall and Recognition

Try to *recall* the information on the quiz below. Then turn the page and take the multiple choice quiz with the same questions. Compare your score.

1. The heroine of *Gone with the Wind* is _____.
2. Harry Truman's second vice-president was _____.
3. A kind of road starting with "Mac" is _____.
4. The "tail" sticking out from a neuron is the _____.
5. Abbey Road is _____.
   Identify the following:
6. Hubert Horatio Humphrey _____.
7. Edwin Booth _____.
8. Elizabeth Bennet _____.
9. Bruno Hauptmann _____.
10. Kaiser-Fraser _____.

Now, without looking at the answers, try the same test for *recognition.*

1. The heroine of *Gone with the Wind* is (a) Melanie Hamilton, (b) Ashley Wilkes, (c) Scarlett O'Hara, (d) Prissy, or (e) Aunt Pitty Pat.
2. Harry Truman's second vice-president was (a) Richard Nixon, (b) Olveta Culp Hobby, (c) John Foster Dulles, (d) Alben W. Barkley, or (e) Henry Wallace.
3. A kind of road starting with "Mac" is (a) macadamia, (b) macadam, (c) macaque, (d) Macassar, or (e) Macruran.
4. The "tail" sticking out from a neuron is the (a) axon, (b) axiom, (c) axila, (d) axillary, or (e) axum.
5. Abbey Road is (a) the site of Westminster Abbey, (b) an alley in lower Manhattan, near Wall Street, (c) prison slang for visiting the chaplain, (d) an Australian pop singer who lost her vocal cords to cancer, or (e) the site of the Beatles' recording studio.
6. Hubert Horatio Humphrey was/is (a) the whaling captain who chases Moby Dick, (b) a nineteenth-century novel-

ist, (c) a Minnesota senator and presidential candidate, (d) a brand of chewing tobacco, or (e) the secretary of labor under Franklin Delano Roosevelt.

7. Edwin Booth was/is (a) an actor and brother of John Wilkes Booth, (b) the designer of the first motion picture camera, (c) the first doctor to do a heart transplant, (d) a first baseman for the old Boston Red Sox, or (e) the hero in Thornton Wilder's *Our Town.*

8. Elizabeth Bennet was/is (a) the heroine in Jane Austen's *Pride and Prejudice,* (b) the villainess in Donizetti's opera *Lucia de Lammermoor,* (c) the first woman secretary of the treasury, (d) the sister of actresses Joan and Constance Bennett, or (e) a tennis champion.

9. Bruno Hauptmann was/is (a) one of the founders of the Bauhaus movement, (b) a noted writer on psychiatry, (c) a Hollywood film director, (d) the man convicted of the 1932 kidnapping of the Lindbergh baby, or (e) the man convicted of running the World War II Auschwitz death camp.

10. Kaiser-Fraser was (a) a car company of the 1950s, (b) a pact between Germany and Switzerland in the 1880s, (c) a popular vitamin tonic in the 1920s, containing 60 percent alcohol, (d) a much-publicized society wedding in the late 1930s, or (e) the first company to patent a gene-splicing process.

Answers

Check your answers here and record your scores for recall and recognition.

1. The heroine of *Gone with the Wind* is (c) Scarlett O'Hara.
2. Harry Truman's vice-president was (d) Alben W. Barkley.
3. A kind of road starting with "Mac" is (b) macadam.
4. The "tail" sticking out from a neuron is the (a) axon.
5. Abbey Road is (e) the site of the Beatles' recording studio.
6. Hubert Horatio Humphrey was (c) a Minnesota senator and presidential candidate.
7. Edwin Booth was (a) an actor and brother of John Wilkes Booth.

8. Elizabeth Bennet is (a) the heroine in Jane Austen's *Pride and Prejudice*.
9. Bruno Hauptmann was (d) the man convicted of the 1932 kidnapping of the Lindbergh baby.
10. Kaiser-Fraser was (a) a car company of the 1950s.
   Recall: _____ correct/Recognition: _____ correct

Most people do significantly better on recognition than recall. When a group of volunteers were shown a list of 100 words five times, they could recall about 38 percent of them. But when they were shown the same 100 words mixed with 100 new words, they were able to recognize 96 percent of the original words.

Count the number of correct answers for each of the two parts of the test and enter the percentages below.

1 correct—10 percent	6 correct—60 percent
2 correct—20 percent	7 correct—70 percent
3 correct—30 percent	8 correct—80 percent
4 correct—40 percent	9 correct—90 percent
5 correct—50 percent	10 correct—100 percent

Recall: _____ percent correct
Recognition: _____ percent correct

Subtract your Recall score from your Recognition score for your Recall Quotient: _____ percent difference.

Score:
   0 percent difference—
      superb recall
   10 percent to 20
      percent difference—
      very good recall
   30 percent to 40
      percent difference—
      good recall

   50 percent difference—
      average recall
   60 percent to 70
      percent difference—
      fair recall
   80 percent to 90
      percent difference—
      poor recall

10

Three Kinds of Memory

There are three principal kinds of memory:

- verbal
- visual
- kinesthetic

In our literate culture, it is often difficult to separate verbal and visual memories from each other and from the memories provided by our other senses. Does the sound of the word *lion* call up the image? Does the image suggest the letters l-i-o-n written on a sheet of paper? Does the memory of the taste of strawberries make us name the taste, or does the word *strawberries* cause us to reexperience the sweet, gritty sensation on our tongue? Which is the lock and which the key?

Few of us worry about the third kind of memory, kinesthetic, unless we're trying to master tennis or a piano concerto. However, kinesthetic memory is essential to our everyday functioning and a valuable aid to reinforcing verbal and visual memory. Kinesthetic memory means remembering with our muscles, the sense of space around our bodies. Tying our shoes, walking down stairs, driving a car, and playing a piano are all the results of kinesthetic memories. But when we play the piano are we remembering just the placement of the keys, or are we also affected by the sound of the tones, the sight of the notes on the sheet music, the melody in our head, or a complex combination of any or all of these?

Taste, touch, and smell are potent tools for locking in or summoning other memories. We've all caught a whiff of an old, familiar smell and been flooded with nostalgic memories. Some people remember these sensations more powerfully than verbal or visual patterns. Even emotional states, whether we are happy, fearful, angry, or sad, are another access to things we experienced when we were in that state.

Are You Verbal, Visual, or Kinesthetic?

The average person tends to remember things better in one of two ways, either verbally or visually. If you get to the store and find you've forgotten your shopping list, do you recall it by hearing and seeing the names of the objects that you wrote down, or do you see the images of the objects themselves?

If you name things to remember them, if the sight or sound of the word conjures up the sight or sound of the object, you have a good verbal memory. You probably form rich images as you read and can come up with quotes for every occasion: "I do desire we may be better strangers," "'Tis safest in matrimony to begin with a little aversion," "I decline to accept the end of man," "I shall be irreproachably tender,/Not a man but a cloud in pants!"

Some people are better visualizers than others. Close your eyes and picture an orange. If that's easy for you to do, if you can see the texture and color vividly, then you're a visualizer. Another way to check on your visualizing ability is to recall the house you lived in as a child. Can you remember the furniture and how it was arranged? The wallpaper? The rug? If you can, you have strong visual recall. How about the address and phone number? If you remember those, you have good verbal memory. If you do well on both, congratulations, you have twice as many chances of finding things in your mental library.

Children usually remember visually until their language skills develop. Then they shift to verbal encoding. This is one reason that most of our earliest memories resemble snapshots rather than movies with sustained scenarios. We didn't have the verbal skills yet to write the script about what was happening. When we add both auditory and visual forms of verbal memory, we're able to start building our mental library, responding to all kinds of information around us.

There is even a communications theory that says you should listen to the imagery of someone you want to influence and respond in the same way. If the person says, "That doesn't look good," they are in a visual mood, and you can reply, "Let's see how we can improve it." If they say, "That doesn't sound quite right," they are being aural and you reply, "I hear it differently." And if they say, "That doesn't feel right," they are favoring their kinesthetic sensations and you can say, "I sense that we've touched on the problem but haven't come to grips with it."

One analyst, Ole Anderson, calls this "predicate usage." He classifies former President Jimmy Carter as auditory: "Those listening to my voice will have to make that decision," while Ronald Reagan is kinesthetic: "Do you feel that our security is as strong as it was four years ago?" Winston Churchill, says Anderson, used highly visual images, Gerald Ford was probably kinesthetic, while John F. Kennedy balanced all three well. Anderson estimates that about 20 percent of Americans are primarily auditory and about 15 percent are primarily kinesthetic. The rest are visual or a mixture. This, reasons Anderson, is why visual imagery is the most powerful.

Which Is Better?

The English memory researcher Sir Frederick Bartlett decided that visualizers tend to learn more quickly and be more confident about what they have learned. Visualizers are more direct, visualizing the whole without doing as much grouping or making comparisons as auditory learners do. Sound good?

He *also* found that visualizers tended to get the order of information mixed up more often, changed the information more often, and introduced more new, irrelevant material than did verbal learners. But they remained confident, despite their inaccuracy.

Verbal learners, on the other hand, captured more clues

and signposts as they went along, and gave them names. They used more associations and comparisons than did visual learners. They were less certain about the accuracy of their memories, even when they were correct.

Another experiment tested the verbal and visual ability of subjects to remember long lists of numbers. One group heard the numbers and the other read them; then both groups had to say the numbers back. People who heard the numbers could repeat the latter numbers with more accuracy, while the people who read them could remember the earlier numbers better. The earliest numbers seen made the strongest memory traces, but the last numbers heard are still in the *echoic memory,* a device that seems to let us remember the last thing we heard. ("Yes, yes, I heard what you said, dear, you said 'right now'!") Echoic memory seems to be limited to speech, because a random comment such as "Now . . ." will help block the memory of the number that went before, while a musical tone won't.

Even if your natural memory ability favors verbal over visual or vice versa, you can develop the other with practice and motivation. Airplane spotters during World War II had a powerful motivation for differentiating visually between friendly and enemy airplanes flying overhead. Chemistry students have little desire to confuse a bottle of water with a bottle of sulfuric acid:

> Johnny was a chemist.
> Johnny is no more.
> For what he thought was H_2O
> Was H_2SO_4.

Remembering Kinesthetically

Are you a good dancer, typist, pianist, or ball player? Then you have good kinesthetic memory. The movement of your muscles is stored in your brain. Many blind people routinely use kinesthetic memory to do complex tasks and negotiate complex routes for which sighted people would require instructions or maps.

How many times have you flailed your hands in the air, shaping an object you're trying to describe while you search for the word to name it? How many times has someone asked you for a key or other object and it seemed easier to get it yourself than to describe where it was? You were remembering kinesthetically.

Most people remember muscle skills longer and better than verbal or visual skills. The classic example is riding a bicycle. You may not have ridden one for 20 or 40 or 60 years, but you'll be able to wobble right off once you're back in the saddle.

Photographic Memory

The fabled photographic memory, popular in vaudeville and detective fiction, is strongest in childhood, and some people are able to retain it as adults. An example is the noted mathematician, John von Neumann, who could memorize and repeat the information in a column of the phone book on sight when he was eight years old. As an adult, he was able to do complex math problems in his head.

A photographic memory almost got one young law student in serious trouble when his exam paper contained lengthy quotes verbatim from his textbooks. He was accused of cheating, but proved his innocence by quickly memorizing pages verbatim in the presence of school officials.

Even if you have just a highly accurate visual memory, you may not be the best eyewitness. According to a Canadian study, witnesses who could remember all sorts of minute details such as the color of the suspect's socks were the least accurate in identifying the suspect himself. On the other hand, witnesses who could recall the main details were inaccurate on the trivia. Ironically jurors tended to discount the testimony of the latter group who were actually the most reliable witnesses.

Using Both Verbal and Visual Memory

Most visual memory uses the right half of the brain and most verbal memory uses the left half. When you use both verbal and visual cues to remember something, you are using your entire brain.

Since you are probably not reading this book in order to

remember the Highland fling or the skin of an orange, it is safe to say that most of what you want to remember can be verbally coded. Here are two rules about verbal memory.

- Naming something increases your chance of remembering it.
- *But* naming something can limit it.

If, like most people, you find that either your verbal or visual memory is dominant, you can improve your ability to remember by calling on the other system. For instance, actively picture what you just read. We do this all the time with fiction, but try it now with nonfiction. If you are primarily visual, play "Adam" and run around naming all the new things in the world. Let the image summon up the name, the sound, the printed word. Invent a word if none exists—a new name for a sensation, quirk, odd situation, or thing-a-ma-whatsis. Either the dictionary name will come later, or you may create a useful new term.

Where Does Kinesthetic Memory Come In?

Learning physical skills seems to follow the same patterns as learning verbal or visual things. Fortunately, once learned, we tend to remember muscular/spatial skills better and longer, as in the bicycle example. Kinesthetic memory can reinforce verbal and visual memory in valuable ways. Recently, schools that teach people test-taking techniques for bar exams, college-admissions tests, and the like, have become popular. One reason for their effectiveness may be that they use a classroom setting similar to the one in which the student will take the real test. Sitting in the same position, feeling the same type of pencil between his fingers, seeing a familiar test sheet, he may find the needed memories tumbling onto the paper.

Kinesthetic memories are frequently responsible for déjà vu, the sense of having already experienced something. If you have been comforted or frightened when you were in a particular position, you may reexperience the same sensations when you assume that position later. (This may account for the popularity of the fetal position for sleep.)

TAKE A PICTURE

Here's one valuable way to use kinesthetic memory to reinforce verbal and visual memory. Let's say that you must leave your car keys in a number of places because various members of the family use them, or you are lending an out-of-print book, or you are up on a ladder fixing something and decide to lay the screws on the top of the window frame. You suspect that you might not recall who, where, and what later on, so you "take a picture." Raise your hands to your eyes, miming a camera and click the button. As you do this, say out loud, "My keys are on the dining room table," or "Charles is borrowing my Aretha Franklin albums for his party on Thursday," or "The screws are on the window frame." You now have an aural and a visual image of what happened, plus the kinesthetic memory cue of physically snapping a picture of it.

Another way to use kinesthetic memory to jog other memories is to repeat a motion. (You may do this already.) Resume the position you were in when you originally had the experience you are trying to recall. Sit down at your desk or lie down in bed or backtrack and walk down the hall again. Recreating the sequence frequently lets you remember the verbal and visual parts.

You can have a visual and aural image of what happened, plus the kinesthetic memory of physically snapping a picture of it.

Try This . . .
to Determine Your Kind of Memory

Some people are good at all three kinds of memory: verbal, visual, and kinesthetic. Others are best at one kind. Rate yourself with this test. If your answer to a question is "yes" or "true," check the box that follows it. If no, leave blank. Then add the vertical columns of checks to compare your verbal, visual, and kinesthetic memory.

Think about what you had for breakfast this morning.

	Verbal	Visual	Kines- thetic
1. Do you have a vivid visual picture of it?		☐	
2. Did you just reexperience the tastes and smells?			☐
3. Can you list everything you ate?	☐		
4. Can you recall the brand names of the eggs, cereal, coffee, bread, jam, juice, etc.?	☐		
5. Can you remember the color of the plate and cup? The tablecloth? The shape of the spoon? Whether it was sunny or cloudy?		☐	
6. Can you recall where you ate? How you sat? The position of the food on your plate?			☐

Now imagine you are standing in front of the first house you can remember living in as a child.

	Verbal	Visual	Kines- thetic

7. Do you see the color clearly? Do you have a strong image of how many windows there are? The kind of steps? How many steps?   ☐ *(Visual)*

8. Do you remember the address and phone number? ☐ *(Verbal)*

9. Go up to the door. Can you remember whether the doorknob is on the left or right? Do you step up after you have opened the door? Is there a closet on the left or right inside?   ☐ *(Kinesthetic)*

If the answers to the questions below are "true," check the box at the right.

10. I am usually very aware of the furniture arrangement in a room.   ☐ *(Kinesthetic)*

11. If friends painted their living room a new color, I would definitely notice. ☐ *(Visual)*

12. I know whether the numbers on my watch are Arabic or Roman numerals. ☐ *(Visual)*

13. I know my Social Security number. ☐ *(Verbal)*

14. I'm good at sports and/or dancing.   ☐ *(Kinesthetic)*

	Verbal	Visual	Kines- thetic
15. I respond to the colors around me.		☐	
16. I always got good grades in English.	☐		
17. I didn't have much trouble learning to ride a bike.			☐
18. I love to do crossword puzzles.	☐		
Add up your scores.	_____	_____	_____

If you scored about the same in all three kinds of memory, you have three good ways to code and file each new memory. You can reinforce a primarily verbal, visual, or kinesthetic piece of information with two other backup memories (i.e., remember the three of clubs with a visual image of the card, the verbal memory of saying and writing the words, and the kinesthetic memory of sitting holding the cards and noticing that the three of clubs is the third card from the left).

If you are strongest in visual memory, you will remember better if you reinforce verbal and kinesthetic memories with a visual image. Write out names, addresses, and phone numbers and look at them. Make a visual image of the items on a list. See new people you meet with their names written on their chests or holding objects that suggest their names. When you learn a new physical skill, see yourself doing it, watch your body and hands as you experience the physical sensations in your muscles. Remember the colors and shapes of trees, signs, and buildings at the bus stop where you want to get off.

If you are strongest in verbal memory, you will help yourself remember better if you name things. Reinforce the memory of the faces of people you meet with private verbal descriptions—"Gladys Carpenter doesn't look like a glad carpenter, she looks like a sad carp." Make mental lists of the signs or the names of stores at the bus stop where you need to get off. You probably do much of this already without thinking, but expand it so you consciously reinforce visual and kinesthetic memories with a verbal backup.

If you are strongest in kinesthetic memory, you probably recall where you put things, but you may have trouble remembering written instructions or new people at parties or your shopping list. You will want to add strong kinesthetic memories to other information so you will have more ways to remember it. Shake hands with people you meet and repeat their name while you experience the texture of their hand, the feel of their muscles, your impression of their stature and movement. Feel the pattern when you punch or dial a phone number.

When you learn something new, study it in a situation that is physically similar to where you will need to recall the information. Read the driver's manual sitting in your car. Study the new postal regulations while you stand at the table where you will process mail. If you want to remember people's names at parties, practice them while standing or sitting in a rehearsal of the physical situation.

As you remind yourself to pick up your cleaning, feel the cold wire hangers and the slick polyethylene. Add the smell of the cleaning fluid in the store, the sight of the cheery clerk, the tinkle of the bell as you open the door, and the hiss of the pressing machines. See yourself turning off your regular route to stop at the cleaners and feel yourself doing it.

If you are good at two kinds of memory, use them both to reinforce information that is primarily of the third kind. If you are poor at kinesthetic memory, try visualizing your fingers on the typewriter keys and writing yourself instructions for operating simple appliances. If you are poor at verbal memory, make pictures and use your body to reinforce the words. If you lack visualization ability, write yourself a story about the thing and feel yourself handling it or responding to it.

11

Four Ways to Remember

Dividing memory in different ways often tells us more about our perceptions than about memory itself. The advantage of these divisions is that we can concentrate our attention on a small, manageable piece of a huge puzzle. The disadvantage is that labeling can limit our perceptions.

Episodic memories are personal, autobiographical reminiscences of experiences which occurred directly to you. Semantic memories are pieces of data about the external world, linguistic or mathematical for example, which you learn but which are not personal experiences.

Getting spanked by your mother for throwing bologna at your brother is episodic. Learning that bologna is spelled *b-o-l-o-g-n-a,* is pronounced "baloney," and when capitalized, is a city in Italy with a Communist administration, a reputation for efficiency, and a history of terrorist attacks by neo-Fascists, represents some subcategories of semantic memory—written and spoken language, history, and geography. Of course, this division is not absolute, since many tasks contain both episodic and semantic features.

Episodic Memory—"Where Did I Put It?"

Episodic memory is primarily emotional. Much of this book explores how emotions can block memory and how they can be used to stimulate it. Here's one example of how experiences can be recorded episodically (emotionally) but not semantically.

A woman in one of my workshops wanted to remember the names of restaurants she had visited: "I love going to restaurants! Later I describe everything in minute detail to my friends—the menu, the tastes, the smells, the decor. I rave. But when they ask me the name of the restaurant or where it is, I can't remember."

Her mistake was in thinking she had recorded all this information at the same level. She was emotionally involved with the food, emotionally stimulated by the decor, but not by the name and address. I suggested that she pretend she was a newspaper reporter and keep a notebook or diary of where and what she ate. Not only would this *aide memoire* help her recall her dining experiences later, but waiters might assume she was a restaurant reviewer in disguise and give her better service.

Because episodic memory is, by definition, emotional, it is subject to emotional blocks and emotionally enhanced retrieval. Of course, even the driest semantic facts can come with emotional overcoats—parental approval, society's messages, even the instinct for survival. William James, the early twentieth-century author and psychologist, said, "Memory requires more than mere dating of the fact in the past. It must be dated in *my* past." Fortunately we don't have to remember *where* or *how* we learned something to recall it later, although the emotional trappings may come along for the ride.

In the decade since a study on episodic and semantic memory by Canadian psychologist Endel Tulving, researchers have come up with literally hundreds of studies about semantic memory, but almost nothing about episodic memory. This may mean that such a division has not proved useful, or that our current explanations—emotional, mechanical, and physical blocks—are sufficient to explain why we lose our car keys and forget to mail the phone bill.

Semantic Memory—Naming Things to Remember Them

Lots of invisible things have names—"memory," for example. When we give names to objects and concepts and moods and ideas and then use these names to remember them, we are using "semantic memory." It's unclear and usually unimportant whether we are remembering the letters *h-a-p-p-y* or the feeling of happiness.

Semantics has several dictionary definitions, including the study of the meanings of words and symbols. "For the normal person, every experience, real or potential, is saturated with verbalism," said linguist Edward Sapir. He believed that language not only recorded experience, but could substitute for it.

When we name something, put a label on it, then we have a powerful handle for remembering it. But don't forget that naming something also limits it. The minute something is labeled and categorized, it is ready for convenient filing, but it is also unlikely to be reevaluated. Information that we have filed away and not used every day, such as "world's tallest building" or "Ted's skinny kid-sister," needs periodic reevaluation in the light of recent developments and discoveries.

Information we file away in our long-term memory needs periodic reevaluation.

Political factions frequently use emotionally charged, easy-to-remember slogans to make their points. "Fifty-four forty or fight," "Remember the Alamo," or "No forced busing" are examples. The presumption is that few will stop to analyze exactly *why* we should recall the Alamo or why we aren't also rebelling against forced taxes, forced zoning restrictions, and forced stop signs.

A CHICKEN—EGG DILEMMA CONCERNING LANGUAGE AND PERCEPTION

Here's the current debate:

- Does language shape our perceptions of the world around us by categorizing and labeling things?
- Or do perceptions shape our languages?
- Or both?
- Or neither?

Linguist Benjamin Lee Whorf argues that the language we speak determines our view of the world and how we sort, categorize, and evaluate the information around us so that we can remember it. He offers strong proofs . . . and so do researchers who hold the opposite view.

LANGUAGE AND MEMORY

If memory is categorizing and storing information and *if* each language divides the many natural variations of the world into different categories, then language and memory are totally dependent on each other.

Very roughly, the languages of the world can be divided (there we go again!) into:

Action languages
Languages (including all European tongues) that see the world as full of objects which then act or are acted upon. These could be called "physical" languages, conveying meaning by moving words around like blocks.

Condition languages
Languages that see the world as consisting of various states that are either transitory or permanent,

i.e., Indian languages that assign shape to all things (round like ball, round and flat like pancake, round like spiral, etc.) or condition (wet, dry, hard, soft) or, most basic of all, animate or inanimate. These languages construct meaning by a process that is closer to a chemical action than a physical one.

An example of a chemical-type language in which the words *verb* and *noun* become meaningless is Nootka, the language of Vancouver Island, in which a sentence is one compound word. The idea—

> He invites people to a feast

is represented in Nootka as the root *boil* or *cook* (tl'imsh) and five suffixes:

Boil-	ed	eat-	ers	go-for	he-does
Tl'imsh	- ya -	'is -	ita -	'itl	- ma

Similarly the Nootka sentence "He had been absent for four days" would be built around the root *four*, with *he, absent*, and *days* as suffixes. (If this sounds impossibly esoteric, consider our ancestral Latin which combines nouns and verbs into a single word—vini, vidi, vici. And some English words can act alternately as nouns, verbs, adjectives, adverbs, and prepositions, for instance the word *down*.)

Is it any wonder that Eastern and Western thought have taken such different routes when the road they traveled forked in such different ways?

LANGUAGE AND THOUGHT

The next time you are at a party, mention casually that other languages can be very different from English. I will bet you that someone replies that Eskimos have many words for snow. One of the most obvious differences in languages is the number of ways they divide natural phenomena. But do these vocabulary differences demonstrate a sharper natural perception on the part of the speaker, or do the additional divisions of information require the speaker to develop those perceptions? Memory expert Alan Baddeley slyly suggests that one way to test whether perceptions of snow are limited genetically and culturally to northern denizens would be to see if the polar bear can discriminate between more kinds of snow than the honey bear. He acknowledges, of course, that conducting and interpreting such a test would be "a challenge."

It may be impossible to resolve this argument either way, since experiments support both sides. In one study that was somewhat easier than leading bears to snow, a linguist tested speakers of Dani, a stone-age language of New Guinea. The only words for color in Dani are roughly *light* and *dark*. Yet she found that Dani speakers could readily discriminate between colors, although not as efficiently as American test subjects. This suggests that perception is not limited by language, although language can enhance perception.

"REAL MEN" DON'T SEE COLORS

Color names present a good way to compare perception and memory. There are probably millions of colors and even more names for them. Yet it is popular in our western culture for "real men" not to discriminate between shades of red, blue, or green unless they are in professions that require that discrimination. Industrial designers, printers, house painters, and fabric manufacturers can and do describe colors as *spider web, cumulus,* and *moccasin* without their masculinity being in doubt, but fashion designers, art directors, and fine artists who use words like *scarlet* and *vermilion* are questionable—and if they can actually distinguish between *cerise, fuchsia,* and *magenta,* they are definitely suspect! Yet it would be surprising if a western woman could not tell the difference between *buff, beige, camel,* and *tan.* Does this mean that women see more colors than men? (More men than women are color-blind but only a small percentage.) Or does it mean that culture has suppressed or enhanced a natural perception?

Language, declared Benjamin Lee Whorf, is "the best show that man puts on." Other creatures may communicate, but only man speaks. He added that, "thinking is most mysterious, and by far the greatest light upon it that we have is thrown by the study of language."

Can we have thought without language? Linguist Edward Sapir replies impishly that we *should* be able to, since he has observed that many people use language without thought. Theoretically it's possible, but close your eyes and try to imagine thinking and reasoning and remembering without language.

Skill Memory and Fact Memory

As you have seen, dividing memory in different ways to study it may tell as much about our own perceptions as about memory itself. There is one suggested division, however, that seems to have a definite physical basis. Before we tell more about it, let's look at some of the facts that the theorists had to work with in devising it.

HM had brain surgery 30 years ago in an attempt to cure his epilepsy. Now he cannot remember anything for more than a few minutes. Twenty-two-year-old NA was injured in 1960 when a fencing foil penetrated his brain. He, too, lost his ability to remember. In both cases, the hippocampus was severely damaged. Both men are now unable to remember any new material, that is, anything they have experienced since their brain trauma. In addition, NA cannot remember events that occurred just before his accident. Neither man can remember telephone numbers, words or shapes in a standard memory test, addresses, the current date, or even the identities of those who work with them every day.

Yet both men can work the tricky Tower of Hanoi puzzle in a minimum of moves, a feat that requires memory of previous moves. NA also drives a car and has no trouble getting around, but could not tell you the name of the street his home is on. What would you make of this? Let's look further.

Researchers noticed that other victims of severe organic amnesia (amnesia caused by injury to the brain and especially the hippocampus) also could not remember anything that has happened to them since they were injured. However, they *were* able to remember newly learned skills such as mirror writing or how to work a complex puzzle, although they frequently protested that they couldn't remember ever doing the task before. They also seemed to remember rules for games. Now, what theory can you come up with to explain this paradox?

Well, Richard Hirsh of McGill University considered all

these conflicting facts and suggested that we have two kinds of memory: "fact" memory and "skill" memory.

Fact memory, he concluded, is remembering information—names, places, dates, words, historical and personal events. Fact memories are easily acquired and lost, and your distress at misplacing them is probably why you are reading this book.

Skill memory is less consciously summoned up, and perhaps because so much of it is unconscious, it is harder to lose. Riding a bicycle is the classic example. Other hard-to-forget skills are tying a shoe, hitting a baseball, playing the piano, or taking a spoonful of soup from a bowl and placing it in one's mouth. As you can see, these are primarily examples of kinesthetic memory.

Fact memory seems to be a later development in man, supporting the theory that our brains have retained their original primitive memory system (skills) which now interacts with the newer, more recent outer layer (facts). Experiments with baby monkeys (and our own observations of human babies) show that skills are acquired much earlier than "knowledge." The more primitive skill memory seems to mature earlier than the more sophisticated and recently acquired fact memory. This would explain why we have so few memories of our early childhood. Our neuron connections simply had not matured enough to store factual information.

OUR PRIMITIVE SWITCHBOARD

The hippocampus is part of our brain's ancient limbic system. Along with the hypothalamus and pituitary gland, it forms our "second brain," the first step up and out from the simple reptilian brain that has served many species very nicely for millions of years. But man has added yet another layer on top of the limbic system—the neocortex.

Most theories about memory storage concentrate on our flashy new "third brains," but one group of researchers is concentrating on the more modest hippocampus. Neil Cohen and Larry Squire of the University of California at San Diego and Lynn Nadel of the University of California at Irvine theorize that the hippocampus is an invaluable switchboard. It assesses new facts and routes them to match up with and reinforce similar old ones in other parts of the brain. After enough similar memories accumulate, the neocortex learns to make direct connections, bypassing the hippocampus. The fact that NA could not remember events that happened just before his accident may mean that he had not processed them completely through his hippocampus and into his long-term memory.

We know that when a human hippocampus is damaged, the victim suffers from organic memory loss. However, researchers who tried to get the same results in rats were surprised that the rats without a hippocampus were still able to remember new things. Several theories were offered—that the hippocampus affects memory only in humans; that speech, exclusive to humans, plays some part in memory; or that injury to a neighboring part of the brain had actually caused the human memory loss.

The most recent theory was developed by John O'Keefe of University College, London, and Lynn Nadel of the University of California, Irvine. They found that rats that have had their hippocampi removed cannot learn mazes or perform tests that require spatial memory. They concluded that the hippocampus may be the storehouse for information about space, that the hippocampus makes maps.

Maps are essential for efficient memory storage. It *is* possible to store such information as lists in other parts of the brain, but maps do it much better. Imagine remembering the floor plan of your house as a list of directives: "Enter door, take two steps forward, turn right, enter living room, turn left, take four steps, turn, sit down." Map makers estimate that a map of the United States contains 100 million to 200 million bits of information. Much of that information is inferred by the viewer, for example, is Boise west or east of Chicago?

The Problem with Theories

Theories can (and should) offer an explanation for most of the known facts about a phenomenon, but there are usually a few niggling loose ends, colloquially if inaccurately known as "the exceptions that prove the rule." Have you noticed a basic conflict in these theories about the hippocampus?

Here it is. If the hippocampus allows us to draw mental

maps so we can negotiate our surroundings, and if rats without a hippocampus cannot find their way about a maze, then how is poor, injured NA able to drive a car, a skill assuredly, but one that should require a sense of space? As you can see, each answer brings us just a little closer to understanding our complex memory systems, and each answer also creates new questions.

Memory research used to be almost incomprehensible to anybody but the researchers, discussing such things as the "empirical relations governing acquisition, transfer and extinction of habits." Fortunately for us, today's researchers are more interested in learning how the mind registers and stores and uses information—studies that may give us more direct and practical clues to using our own memory more efficiently.

Try This . .

to See *How* You Remember

Episodic Memory

Notice *how* you try to remember these things, not *whether* you can remember them.

- What did you have for breakfast two days ago?
- Think of the bedroom you slept in when you were five years old. Were the windows on the north, south, east, or west side? Where was the doorway?
- Think about your first real job as an adult. Where did you hang up your coat? How often were you paid? By check or cash? What did you spend the money on?
- Where did you spend New Year's Eve ten years ago?
- What did you do the weekend before last?

Semantic Memory

An ancient Chinese encyclopedia divided animals as follows: belonging to the Emperor, embalmed, tame, suckling pigs, sirens, fabulous, stray dogs, included in the present classification, frenzied, innumerable, drawn with a very fine camel hair brush, etcetera, having just broken the water pitcher, those that, from a long way off, look like flies.

Semantic memory consists of comparing, pairing, opposing, and dividing information. One contemporary way to divide animals is mammals, birds, reptiles. Another is by the number of legs they have. A third is whether they are warm blooded or cold blooded. Let your mind float freely and come up with as many other ways as you can think of to divide animals: _____
_____.

A few of the many other possibilities are nocturnal or diurnal; by size, larger or smaller than X; by diet, herbivorous, carnivorous, or omnivorous; egg layers or non–egg layers; flyers or nonflyers; etc. Yours may be much better.

12

Remembering— Young vs. Old

It's not true that we forget more as we get older. We may take longer to make the search of our mental filing cabinets, but we have much more structure and more retrievable information to compare new things to.

We've already discussed the myth of senility, and we have considered the illnesses of old age that can affect memory, but what about the healthy older person who decides that his memory is failing because he forgot to mail a letter or stop at the cleaners? He's probably no more forgetful than he was at 18.

Edison, Goethe, Victor Hugo, Monet, and Titian did some of their best work in their 70s and 80s. George Bernard Shaw, Pablo Picasso, and pianist Arthur Rubinstein continued to work in their 90s. Composers particularly seem to have long productive careers—careers in which imagination and memory are essential tools. Handel wrote *The Messiah* when he was 56, and Haydn wrote *The Creation* when he was 67. Wagner wrote *Parsifal* at 69, and Verdi composed *Falstaff* when he was 80. Conductor Arthur Fiedler was active until weeks before his death at 88. Photographer Imogene Cunningham worked into her 90s. Grandma Moses didn't start painting until well after retirement, when arthritis kept her from crocheting. Though remaining active in your chosen field doesn't necessarily prove that your memory is good, it certainly shows that you can remember what is necessary.

Of course, some older people do become forgetful. This

can be caused by disease, by medication, by poor nutrition, by loneliness and isolation, by the attitude of those around them, or by their own expectation that they will become forgetful as they age. Older people also tend to use familiar, tried-and-true retrieval strategies and are less likely to try something else if the first approach fails.

Of course all of us get in problem-solving ruts. In *A Whack on the Side of the Head* (Menlo Park, Calif.: Creative Think, 1982), Roger von Oech describes creative solutions reached by playing "What if?"

> *First idea:* What if paint contained gunpowder so that it could be exploded off buildings when it got old and cracked?
> *Problem:* The building would blow up too.

Now many people would stop here, but von Oech shows how to use this first "what if?" as a stepping stone to further solutions.

> *Ultimate solution:* Put inert ingredients in paint that will react later when another solution is applied, causing the paint to drop off the surface.

Here's another example of creative thinking.

> *First idea:* What if we kept the streets clean by having public trash cans that pay people to put trash in them?
> *Problem:* No city could afford that.

Can you think of five new ways to get people to use trash cans?

> *Ultimate solution:* A city in the Netherlands rewarded people who deposited their trash in public cans with a tape-recorded joke, different for every can and changed every two weeks. Certain cans got reputations for having the best jokes, and people went out of their way to hear them.

Before you give up and decide that you're "getting old" when you forget something, try remembering in some of the new ways outlined in this book. Lots of older people see themselves as "forgetful," but tests have shown that people are poor judges of their own overall memory ability. (Ironically, most people are excellent judges of how well they will be able to remember any particular item on a list in relation to other items on the list.) But because more and more Americans are older than 65—there are 27 million right now and 35 million predicted by the year 2000—scientists are now ignoring the myth that older people are naturally forgetful and exploring the memory process in older people.

How Older People Learn New Things

Most people are no more likely to forget at 80 than they were at 20. People in their 80s and even 90s can go back to school and learn new things as well as their grandchildren. They just need to use different techniques for remembering the new material. Here are some valuable tips from the National Institute for Aging, plus some of my own.

- Give yourself plenty of uninterrupted time to learn new things. It may take longer than it used to, and you may have to concentrate more.
- Give yourself a good place to work. Be sure lighting is bright and your glasses appropriate.
- Ask questions. At your age you shouldn't let shyness keep you from understanding. Maybe the teacher isn't being clear, and the younger students in the class are afraid they'll look stupid if they ask questions.
- Don't try to do more than you can handle comfortably. Processing information at any age is difficult if you try to deal with too many elements at once.
- Don't expect to remember things as *quickly* as you used to. Develop tricks for giving yourself a little extra recall time. Smile, clear your throat, adjust your glasses, take a deep breath. These are all tricks used by accomplished actors to gain their

composure and get the audience's attention. Use
them.

How Children Remember

Children remember well because they use more of their
senses simultaneously to store their impressions. They also
haven't learned abstract thinking yet, so they store original
information rather than concepts. Indeed, this absence of
structure in the early years is probably why we have so few
memories of our childhood. We can summon up vivid full-
color images of particular moments, complete with smells,
sounds, and tastes, but we lack an overall view of our first
few years.

"WHY, MOMMY?"

Children are intensely curious about the world around
them. Keep your childhood curiosity with you all your life to
enhance your ability to remember.

To indulge our curiosity is to get closer, to become more
intimate. If childhood "why, why, whys" go unanswered,
curiosity soon withers. A child who is discouraged from
asking will have to start asking later as an adult. We must
begin noticing and prying if we are to absorb and savor the
infinite variety of the world around us.

Perhaps the reason children learn things like second
languages more easily than adults do is that they have an
abundance of synaptic connections, the tiny wires between
the brain's neurons that send information back and forth. The
average child under six learns a new word every two waking
hours.

Then why do we rarely remember our early childhood?
One possibility is that, although children have an abundance
of circuits, they haven't become sophisticated enough to
provide storage structures for everything they see. They have
no place to put much of the information, so they discard it
until they have built storage systems to hold it.

Losing Synaptic Connections

By the time we reach adulthood, we have lost half of our
synaptic connections. Most of these were never used and

withered away. Yet, the peak years for storing memories appear to be the late 20s. At 30, our brains start to shrink. Fortunately, by then we have so many mental structures for organizing and storing information that the lessened circuitry doesn't affect us.

Why do our brains shrink? One reason may be that we lose our ability to make the proteins and enzymes that activate the receptors for long-term memory. When protein synthesis in animals is blocked, the animals can still learn things, but they can't remember what they learned. Unfortunately eating a high-protein diet doesn't produce the necessary enzymes directly, so we're going to have to find other ways to keep our memories in top form.

Another theory of age-related memory loss is that we experience diminished blood flow and send less oxygen to our simultaneously diminishing neurons. This would then slow down our response time. Some doctors also think that environmental pollution is attacking the nervous system with harmful elements, weakening both our bodies and brains as we grow older. For example, today quantities of lead found in the human brain are higher than before. Obviously we need to work on the world without while we work on the world within.

"Am I Getting Senile?"

How can you be certain you're not getting "senile"? Senility in the past has been a catchall term for any memory loss in later years. We now know that memory loss in older people can be caused by hundreds of temporary and permanent conditions. Older people can be profoundly affected by the loss of work and isolation of retirement, by the deaths of spouse, friends, and relatives, or by failing health. They can also be victims of several debilitating diseases that cause memory loss. The most common of these is Alzheimer's disease, also known as senile dementia of the Alzheimer's type or SDAT. It results in memory loss, disorientation, severe behavior changes, and ultimately death. Vigorous and active people of all ages can be struck down by it. Approximately 1.5 million Americans have SDAT, and the disease affects about 5 percent of older people.

If you've ever observed an elderly neighbor or relative

with senile dementia, you may be concerned that you are next every time you misplace something or forget the name of an old friend. In some cases, the very fear of forgetting produces an emotional block that results in a self-fulfilling prophecy.

So, how can you tell if forgetfulness is caused by more than overloaded circuits or emotional blocks? Here are some clues that should send you to your doctor.

- You forget entire and important experiences, not just the details.
- Your forgetfulness limits your ability to function—your family, financial, social, and/or business responsibilities are suffering.
- You sometimes behave in uncomfortable, unfamiliar ways and are not sure why.
- Your forgetfulness is causing you distress.

Prompt medical testing can result in early treatment or, more likely, in assuring you that your memory lapses are not caused by disease and *don't* indicate the beginning of an inexorable mental decline.

About half of the older people who experience confusion and extreme forgetfulness have Alzheimer's disease. So far no one knows the cause or the cure, but it is being studied intently. Scientists know that the disease produces physical and chemical changes in the brain, and they are trying to find out if correcting or reversing these changes will reverse the disease. Possible causes may be heredity or a slow-acting virus. The fast-progressing SDAT that hits young adults tends to run in families, although the more common kind associated with advanced age does not.

The disease, first identified in 1906 by Alois Alzheimer in a 51-year-old patient, usually progresses slowly. The victim's early lapses can be attributed to normal causes. Those around him might begin to take over business and personal tasks on occasion. As the disease progresses, the victim may lose responsibilities at work or even lose his job. Friends may begin subconsciously withdrawing because of the behavior changes they see. When the victim succumbs, an autopsy will show a severely atrophied and distorted brain.

About 3 to 4 million of the 25 million elderly Americans

experience some kind of memory loss. Alzheimer's disease accounts for about half these cases. Another 30 percent are other forms of dementia, possibly in combination with SDAT. The remaining 20 percent may have any of a hundred reversible physical conditions that produce distressing but temporary memory loss. These include infections, fevers, cardiovascular and metabolic conditions, or toxic reactions to drugs. Some of these conditions need to be treated promptly or they can cause permanent damage or even death. So, if you're older than 35 and memory loss is a constant problem, get a physical checkup.

Competing Memories

Old and new memories are always jockeying for supremacy. The longer you live, the more you have to remember. Amazingly you are more likely to remember the names of childhood playmates than of people you worked with three years ago. This is because your brain was more efficient then, and you didn't have so many names to remember.

But collecting memories is essential for keeping the brain in order. Remember those synapses that withered because they were never used? This is a major clue to keeping your memory young. Stay active, stay interested, and keep your circuits open. In other words, use it or lose it.

Try This . . .

to Spot Abnormal Forgetfulness

Some of the following examples of forgetting should alert you to the possibility of disease rather than the normal reasons for forgetting that we have discussed: overload, fatigue, tension, emotional blocks, and the like.

1. You can't remember where you put your car keys.
2. You can't remember where you were married, no matter how hard you try.
3. You can't remember where you parked the car.
4. Your car is repossessed because you forgot to make the payments, even though you have the money.
5. You are demoted at work because you always forget where you put important papers, or you forget to return clients' phone calls.
6. You have almost started a fire two or more times because you turned on a burner on the stove and then forgot about it.
7. You often find your possessions in unusual places and don't know how they got there.
8. You fail to greet a neighbor or coworker on the street because you don't recognize him.
9. On several occasions, you have promised to meet a friend or relative and then forgotten all about it.
10. Your family has a joke about how you would lose your head if it weren't nailed on.

Score

If you answered yes to 2, 4, 5, 6, and 7, your forgetfulness may have a physical source. If you answered yes to 1, 3, or 8, remember that these things happen to all of us from time to time. They are only clues to a deeper problem if they happen consistently or disrupt your life in significant ways. The key word in example 9 is *several*. Everybody does double-think once in a while, planning to be two places at the same time, but if this happens repeatedly, something may be wrong.

If you answered yes to 10, that your family jokes about your forgetfulness, you can regard their teasing in several ways: (a) They are using humor to relieve their genuine frustration or concern over your actions; (b) They are using an out-of-date label for you—like calling someone "Skinny" who has become fat, or "Red" who has become bald—and you have a choice. You can go along with their expectations (a comfortable position) or point out their error (an uncomfortable position); (c) They are embarrassed by their own mental slips and relieve their frustration by pointing out yours—unfair, but a human weakness.

There are other reasons than these, of course, but these may start you thinking about how your family role affects your remembering. Do you get positive "strokes" for remembering or for forgetting? Does forgetting reinforce or undermine your position with your family, your friends, your job?

13

Does Anyone Have a Perfect Memory?

In the 1920s, the famous Russian neuropsychologist A. R. Luria studied a man he called S who seemed to have a perfect memory. S was a journalist named Shereshevskii who could remember everything said to him, word for word, without taking notes. S had never thought this was unusual until his fellow reporters commented on it.

When S saw the number 32, it had a kind of sound, smell, and color to it.

Luria found that S could remember 100-digit numbers, poetry in foreign languages he didn't know, and scientific formulas. S could remember a table of 400 numbers arranged randomly in a 20 by 20 grid pattern. Even after 30 years, he could recall all the numbers. His memory wasn't photographic. He had remarkably developed "synesthesia," the ability to code information in several sensory ways.

We all have synesthesia to some extent. It's what happens when we hear a favorite song and are flooded with poignant memories of a person, a perfume, a mood. When S saw the word *table* or the number 32, it had a kind of sound, smell, and color to it. This occurred automatically, and he had no control over it.

Ironically, S was not particularly successful in school. If someone said the same thing to him in two different tones of voice, he recorded it as two different messages. If someone coughed while S was reading, it was recorded as part of the story. The richness of his associations interfered with his solving mathematical problems. All sorts of sounds and shapes and smells would interfere with his functioning on an abstract level. To force himself to forget useless material, he taught himself to "write" it on a mental blackboard and then "erase" it. Eventually he went on the stage to support himself.

S shared one memory problem with the rest of us—he couldn't remember faces very well. To him the world was like a canvas by a primitive painter. All details were equally vibrant, equally detailed, and equally important whether they were near or far. He could not use the function of forgetting to separate important from unimportant details and therefore could not make value judgments.

VP and Professor Aitken

Before I leave you with the impression that people with super memories are generally misfits, I'd like to mention two "normal" people who practiced to develop their memory skills and used them to enhance their lives. One was VP who was born in Latvia, not far from where S was born.

At the age of ten, VP memorized 150 poems for a contest. As an adult, he emigrated to the United States and found work as a store clerk. He learned to speak all modern European languages except Greek and Hungarian, and loved chess, sometimes playing seven opponents simultaneously while blindfolded. Like S he could remember large grids of numbers; however, he did not appear to remember them as an overall visual image because he slowed down in recalling them when there were blank spaces in the grid. He appeared to rely mainly on semantic associations, aided by his knowledge of so many languages. He denied having any superior gift and said that his skill was developed by his traditional Eastern European Jewish upbringing which valued and encouraged memorization.

Another memory whiz was Professor A. C. Aitken of Edinburgh University. Aitken could recite the first thousand decimal places of pi, which he regarded as an easy if useless skill. He compared it to learning a Bach fugue. He was given several memory tests in 1933. In 1960, he was able to recall lists of words and stories that he had memorized 27 years earlier. Apparently numbers were so lively and interesting to him that he was not conscious of making mechanical associations between them, but when someone mentioned the year 1961, he immediately responded that it was 37 times 53 and also 44 squared plus 5 squared and also 40 squared plus 19 squared.

Idiot Savants

Some people with very low I.Q.s have remarkable memories. A blind young Frenchman in an asylum for mental defectives could give the cube root of any six-figure number in 6 seconds and the sum of 64 progressive doublings of a number in 45 seconds. You may wonder if this young man actually had a high I.Q.; it is possible. However, there are contemporary cases of people who have difficulty functioning, who can barely speak, and who cannot read or write, yet who have remarkable talents. The academic term for such people is "idiot savant"—learned idiots.

Dr. Bernard Rimland, director of the Institute for Child Behavior Research in San Diego, is an expert on this condition. Among the theories advanced to explain this phenomenon are extraordinary development of certain nerve cells or the division of functions between left and right cerebral hemispheres. However, Dr. Rimland believes that these people have a unique power of concentration, that their impairment lets them shut out everything else and put all their effort into one task.

For instance, mentally retarded twin brothers who lived at the New York Psychiatric Institute in the 1960s were able to do lightning calendar calculations into the next century, even though they could not add or subtract. Another fascinating case is that of a retarded young man in Milwaukee. Blind and suffering from cerebral palsy, the 19-year-old astounded his adoptive parents one morning by sitting down at the piano and playing Tchaikovsky's First Piano Concerto from memory after hearing it on the radio. He could not walk or speak a complete sentence, but he was able to remember and reproduce a large repertoire of classical, jazz, and popular music, and he even performed on television. Another mentally disabled boy can compute square roots in his head, play the piano by ear, and write songs.

About 1 out of every 2,000 retarded people seems to have this unique power of concentration that produces an extraordinary talent—usually for mathematics, art, or music, and frequently involving memory. This occurs more commonly in men than women, about a three to one ratio. "As we learn more about the mind and machines that work like the mind," says Dr. Rimland, "the savants become more and more intriguing. In the past there was a tendency to view these people as freaks with bizarre abilities. We now tend to view them as special people, as human beings who have unique and individual talents."

Famous People with Good Memories

Extraordinary memories and powers of concentration are not the exclusive property of misfits and idiot savants, however. Many famous people have used their memories to great advantage in their careers. Toscanini conducted long, complex symphonies and operas without a score. Napoleon could greet thousands of soldiers by name. American politician James Farley claimed he was able to call 50,000 people by their first names, and Charles Schwab, manager of the

Homestead Mill, knew all of his 8,000 employees by name. General George Marshall could recall almost every event of World War II, and English statesman and writer Thomas Macaulay could recite all of the epic *Paradise Lost* without error. Many of today's corporation heads have reputations for being able to call up thousands of names and figures at a moment's notice. And while we may find comfort in the tales of Albert Einstein's absentmindedness, he was certainly able to remember what he wanted to remember.

Napoleon and James Farley used the same strategies for remembering that you do. They just did it more efficiently, motivated by their ambition. Most of us go blank to some extent when we encounter a large group of strangers, but to a motivated person—a politician, a salesman, even a gregarious people-lover—remembering each new face and name can be a fascinating way to enhance himself. Toscanini was also motivated by a desire for power, but in a different way. He knew that if he had to keep looking at the score, he could not maintain eye contact with his musicians to control them.

Most people can remember all sorts of information about their hobbies, something that gives them great pleasure. It's hard to forget the details of our rich uncle's will or the winning score of our favorite team or the intricacies of a juicy scandal involving a long-time enemy. We remember what interests us, and people who remember "everything" are probably interested in everything.

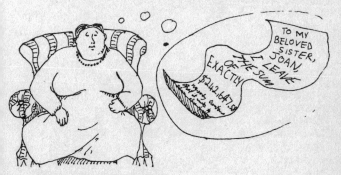

We remember what interests us.

Try This . . .
to Pinpoint What You Remember Easily

What do you enjoy remembering? What enhances you? Put yourself in a relaxed fantasy state.

You are on a platform before an adoring audience. You are filled with pleasure as you are introduced as the world's greatest expert on _____.

Or you pick up a newspaper, trade journal, or scholarly publication and see your photograph. The caption says that you are noted for your ability to remember all about _____.

Do you remember these things well in real life? If so, why? If not, why?

PART III

How To

14

How to Improve Your Memory

When people perform incredible memory feats, we assume that they have a unique and superior memory structure. "I could never remember that much!" Don't bet on it. The gulf between your memory and the kind of memory you envy is not so wide as you might think it is.

How do people with exceptional memories differ from "ordinary people"? The most obvious way is that they remember more. But are they just remembering more efficiently or do they use an entirely different method of remembering? Most of us make verbal "strings" to help us remember—words in a sentence, the days of the week, or the 1-2-3 sequence of numbers. People with a photographic memory, those who can remember huge charts of meaningless numbers after a few minutes of study, are assumed to remember visually; that is, they make a photograph-like mental image of the information. This is verified when they are able to repeat the numbers in any sequence—top to bottom, zig-zag, back and forth horizontally—as if they are reading it from the original chart.

The rest of us simply cannot remember that way, no matter how much we practice, but we *can* dramatically increase our ability to remember strings of information by using structures.

Rating Memory Capacity

Memory is too rich, complex, and elusive to be measured and weighed like a beef roast. This has never stopped scientists from trying. One early test, the "digit-span" measurement, was worked out by a London teacher in 1887. J. Jacobs wanted to find out how well his students could remember numbers, so he devised a system that has become a useful tool in psychology.

To test his students, Jacobs presented each with a sequence of digits and asked them to repeat it. He steadily increased the number until the student was able to repeat the list correctly only half of the time. This was the student's "digit span." A person's digit span seems to show the extent of his natural short-term memory ability.

Today, digit-span testing is a standard test. A series of numbers is read to the subject who immediately repeats them. An average ten-year-old can repeat three out of five sequences of six numbers. The average twelve-year-old can repeat backward at least one of three series of five digits. The average adult can repeat two out of three series of seven numbers, and superior adults can do eight-digit sequences forward and seven-digit sequences backward. As with any testing, the results could be affected if the person taking the test feels rivalry with, or hostility toward, the test giver. While a few people might improve their performance under these conditions, most of us would decrease our scores because of tension.

TEST YOUR OWN DIGIT SPAN

To test your own digit span, have someone read you lists of four-digit numbers and repeat them. If you can say them back correctly more than 50 percent of the time, move on to five-digit numbers. Keep going through six- and seven-digit numbers, increasing the amount of digits, until you are correct only *half* the time. That is your digit span. Most people have digit spans of about 7 and just a few surpass 10 digits. Until a recent digit-span experiment with a "normal" volunteer, the highest digit span ever recorded was 18 digits, scored by the German mathematics professor, Rückle Müller, in 1911. (That means that half the time he was able to repeat a sequence of 36 numbers from memory.)

The World's Digit-Span Champion

In 1981, Anders Ericsson of the University of Colorado and William G. Chase of Carnegie-Mellon University set out to discover if the digit span of the average person could be increased. They found a hardy volunteer with normal memory capacity, and they tested his digit span. They kept retesting SF, as they called him, without giving him any instructions. He soon began to invent his own methods to increase his digit span. When SF was first tested, he had a digit span of seven. When he was through, his digit span was eighty! Was he really a genius in disguise, or did he discover a new way to use his memory? Here's what he did.

For 1 hour a day, 3 to 5 days a week, for 20 months—230 hours of effort—SF was given a standard digit-span test. For the first four sessions, his digit span remained in the normal range, seven to nine. During this time, he either rehearsed the entire digit sequence or divided it into two groups and rehearsed each group. Sometimes he noticed patterns like 6-5-4 or 4-2-4, bu mostly he just tried to remember random numbers.

But things were about to change. SF was a competitive runner and had lots of running times in his long-term memory. At the fifth session he began relating the random numbers read to him with the known running times in his memory. Naturally, only a few numbers would match up, but he went on to construct additional pegs. For instance, 3,492 would be 3 minutes, 49.2 seconds, an excellent speed for running a mile. Following this would be 893 which he would interpret as 89.3 years, a very old runner.

Eventually SF contrived super groups of numbers divided into three or four smaller groups. His organization for 80 digits consisted of sets of three-digit and four-digit groups in this pattern:

4-4-4   4-4-4   3-3-3   3-3-3   4-4-4   3-3-3   4-4-4   5

SF was actually putting these numbers in his long-term memory because he was able to recall more than 90 percent of the 200 to 300 digits presented to him at each hourly session. After 100 hours of practice, he reduced the time it took him to memorize a given number of digits by half.

You don't have to be a runner to use SF's system. Think of all the numbers you have in your head: birthdays, historical dates, phone numbers, the years that your favorite classic cars or films appeared. Remembering random lists of meaningless numbers isn't something we do very often, but we *do* run into number sequences that would be useful to know—serial numbers, Social Security numbers of family members, new car license numbers, and endless phone numbers. Maybe SF's system will work for you.

Shortening the Trip from Short-Term to Long-Term Memory

You control your short-term memory. You've noticed something, and you want to get it into your long-term memory, in other words to *remember* it. You have a choice. You can work hard to develop new strategies (groan, too much work), or you can go on working hard, trying to remember the way you do now.

Familiar solutions are "safe" and comfortable, so we tend to try them again and again, even if they don't always work. It's like the terrified horse that runs back into a burning barn to reach the safety of his stall. Here are some new strategies.

STRATEGY 1: BE EMOTIONAL

Why can we remember batting averages and scores or lengthy melodies and stories, but not recall a phone number or the correct spelling of a six-letter word like frieze? It's because we can remember when we take things like names, numbers, or musical notes and surround them with emotional trappings as well as structures.

Like computers, people need structures for storing information, but unlike computers, the human mind loves novelty. Fascinate it with tricks and toys while you give it some storage boxes, and it will do whatever you want. Emotionally charged events are easily remembered, probably because they are intensely personal. If you can impose emotion on something, you'll remember it. Love it. Hate it. Fear it. Be mad at it. You'll also remember it at the same time.

STRATEGY 2: BE LOGICAL

Make structures for remembering. We'll talk more about that later on.

STRATEGY 3: REWARD YOURSELF FOR REMEMBERING

Any old reward doesn't work. You have to want it. Remember that "ought to remember" isn't the same as "will remember." Even "try to remember" is a cop-out because it implies that you might not succeed.

Use every means you have to help yourself remember.

If you constantly forget certain things—car keys, names, birthdays, appointments—you can go into analysis to figure out what they really signify to you, *or* you can decide how remembering them will enrich you, enhance you, make you feel good about yourself. Not wanting to feel stupid isn't enough. You may trap yourself in a self-punishing cycle— "I'm so dumb that I deserve all this pain." Instead, you need to impose a real rush of pleasure around remembering the object or event. That holds true, also, for remembering to do something genuinely unpleasant that must be done. As a last resort, you could allow yourself a ridiculously puritanical sense of self-righteousness for having remembered to do such a grim task.

STRATEGY 4: USE ALL YOUR SENSES

If you have "turn off copy machine before leaving office" in your short-term memory, you can form a multitude of sensory images around it that will help you get it into your long-term memory. Smell that copy fluid as you imagine holding your coat in one hand and flicking the switch with the other. See the machine and imagine it beckoning to you as you feel the sleek office doorknob in your hand. Listen to the hum of the copy machine as it purrs, "Turn me off, turn me off." If you routinely pop a breath mint, a cigarette, or a stick of gum in your mouth as you leave the office, you can even *taste* the copy machine's anxiety about being left on all night. Putting information in your long-term memory is an active process. Contrary to all laws of physics, you can speed up the trip by sending out more than one train.

The Uphill Struggle from Short to Long, or "How Scoop Flash Makes the Front Page"

Short-term memory is like a frame of photographic film intended for future use in a newspaper. Our fearless reporter, Scoop, has just gotten the news photo of a lifetime. He races back to the offices of the *Daily Blab,* clutching his precious roll of film, and hands it over to old Pop Slowpoke in the receiving room.

Pop sets it to one side while he answers the phone, then starts upstairs to the photo lab. His rheumatism is kicking up something terrible, so he is none too swift. Halfway up the stairs he is distracted as he stops to ogle Gloria Gorgeous, the *Blab*'s ace reporter. He finally reaches the lab, but the technician is busy. "Just toss it over there, Pop. I'll get to it when I can."

The film may roll under a table and be lost before it is ever developed; or it may be spoiled when the darkroom door is opened; or, developed, it may not be printed; or printed, it may not be filed in the right place with the right caption. If it finally makes it through all these steps, then it is in "Long-Term Memory," ready to be yanked out and put on the front page when it is needed. Long-term storage of material is an active process that *must* go through stages and *must* take time. If the process is interrupted at any point, we don't get the final photograph.

The Mind As a Library

Long-term memory requires a structure or framework so that you can retrieve the information later. The mind is like a huge, jumbled library. Sometimes we have difficulty finding the exact book we want, but it is there. We increase our chances of finding a book if we put a thousand copies of it in our library instead of one. We do this in our mind's library by repetition, repeating something over and over until we are almost certain to recall it when we need it. However, each repetition may be slightly different from the others, like different editions of the same book.

Remembering can be like a detective story. Let's say you read *Tom Sawyer* and get interested in the books of Mark Twain. You then read *Huckleberry Finn* and are fascinated with the character Jim. This leads you to reading about Black people before and during the Civil War. You read *Uncle Tom's Cabin* and then Bruce Catton's *Peace at Appomattox*. To remember an event in the Catton book, you might have to run through the chain starting with *Tom Sawyer*. It might also help if you read *Peace at Appomattox* in your uncle's vacation cabin by the lake when you were recovering from a broken leg. This gives you even more paths to lead you back to Catton. The more images, the more context you can put around a piece of information, the more likely you are to find it again.

Using Retrieval Cues

A thread is sticking out of your sleeve and you pull it. It may come off in your hand, or you may have grabbed the end of the master thread that holds your whole jacket together. Memories are similar. Sometimes we get a detached thread. "Pepys" leads to canaries and singing instead of Restoration London and diaries, or "Reuben" leads to sandwiches and dill pickles instead of Gen. 29:32, Jacob, and the tribes of Israel.

Word associations are a common way to retrieve information. For instance, fill in the missing words below:

_____ rampant   rant and _____
moot _____   diametrically _____
one _____swoop   _____ dudgeon

Most people will reply—run rampant—moot point—one fell swoop—rant and rave—diametrically opposed—high dudgeon. In learning abstract lists of word combinations, subjects remember "hot-cold" much more easily than "cold curtains." Following familiar word clues to the wrong conclusion is a hazard to successful remembering. When a key retrieval word may lead you astray, you need to build a new, stronger image. To remember the phrase "cold curtains," you can create a dramatic mental scene of ice-covered draperies, crackling as an Arctic wind howls through the shattered windows of an abandoned mansion. Similar arresting images can help you set up new ways to retrieve information that might not respond to everyday retrieval cues.

"Depth of Processing"

Do we really store some information bits deeper than others? In a 1972 study, Craik and Lockhart suggested that the amount of information we retain depends on how deeply we process it. They decided that information processed in a simple way offers us vague memory traces, and that this shallow processing would decrease our ability to remember later. Information that is judged, categorized, and sorted in a number of ways, they felt, is processed "in depth" and will be remembered better. Their "depth" concept could also be seen as "horizontal," providing the information with many associations or handles for later retrieval. You may go through life never quite sure of the meaning of *dialectic* or *pragmatic,* no matter how many times you look the word up in the dictionary, but if you write an essay, poem, or series of puns about the meaning of the word, you will probably never forget it.

Pleasant vs. Unpleasant

If you have ever suspected that the really grating TV commercials are *intended* to irritate you, you're right. Studies show that, while we quickly respond to positive images, we remember the negative ones longer. This is the opposite of Freud's theory that we would forget anxiety and pain more quickly than pleasant memories.

As with much of memory study, tests on this point frequently contradict each other. For instance, a test designed to rate the effectiveness of different painkillers also found that, as time passed, the patients remembered their original pain as less and less severe.

"We've Got to Get Organized"—Using Structures

There is little order or pattern to much of the world except what we perceive or impose ourselves. Our lives are spent in rating, sorting, and coping with a tumult of ideas and objects.

Everyone loves "organizers." We buy them in walnut for our walls and desk tops, plastic for our drawers and closets. We fill every corner with gadgets to keep our life in order. These are the *structures* of modern life. The trick is to *use* them.

The ability to create structures for ourselves, to set priorities and separate the important from the less important, is one of the keys to a good memory. A good way to do this is to use your memory. "Memory is a great abstractor," says memory expert Alan Baddeley. His own career illustrates this point. Before beginning his first book on memory he reviewed all the available literature to insure completeness. The result, five years later, was an all-inclusive specialist's text. For a second book, *Your Memory: A User's Guide* (Macmillan Publishing, New York, 1982), he let his memory abstract the material, racing over everything he knew to find highlights. He then wrote a delightful, readable book and checked the facts afterwards.

Anyone whose memory problems are caused by an inability to structure needs to learn mental organization. The optimum time to learn to structure things and ideas is between the ages 6 and 12. Given some encouragement and praise, children will involve themselves in how they want to arrange their rooms, their possessions, and even their time. However, if parents insist that children always conform to the parents' ideas of how things should be arranged, the children sometimes lose their incentive to experiment with structure. Parental help and recognition of the need for setting and keeping order encourages a child to learn to structure, if the help is judiciously given.

Fortunately, you can learn to structure at any age if you give yourself enough rewards for doing so. As you move about, notice what belongs to you and decide how you want to arrange it. Cook up convenient structures to retrieve your keys, wallet, eyeglasses, and checkbook. Then applaud yourself as you stick to your system. It is this sense of order, supported eventually by habit, that will give you the security that comes from knowing where your things are. They are in a familiar and chosen place, impossible to forget.

People who are always losing glasses, car keys, and important papers are either overloaded and need to slow down, or else they can't see a sufficient reward for giving up the anxiety and even attention they experience as they frantically hunt for the misplaced objects.

Sometimes people blame themselves for having a faulty memory when the problem really lies in how they structure their time and their lives. If we accept that we are as responsible for our mental clutter as for the physical clutter that surrounds us, we can take the next steps.

Organize
Create a structure for your possessions.

Use it
Put things where you decide they belong. (No structure works if you don't use it.)

Does this sound like that boring adage from your childhood, "A place for everything and everything in its place?" Do you immediately imagine yourself surrounded by a cold, sterile environment of grim, tyrannical order that will crush every bit of joy from your already overtaxed psyche? If so, perhaps your disorder is a delayed attempt to "show" your parents that you can structure your own environment, thank you.

Playing "Grown-up"

If the distant voice of a childhood critic is still ringing in your ears—"Hang up your coat," "Put away your bicycle," "How many times do I have to tell you to pick up your blocks,"—stop and decide if you still need to rebel or if you'd rather play "grown-up."

In this game, you have many more options than you did as a child. In addition to staying up late and eating as much candy as you want, you can choose between the deliciously naughty pleasure of tossing your things around or the comforting pleasure of finding them when you want them. Either way, when you play "grown-up," you're boss and *you* get to choose. You get to announce that "Setting things down anywhere I want makes me very powerful, but I think I'll skip the fun this time. It's more fun to find things the minute I want them. I'm even *more* powerful that way." (Logical considerations like wasted time, wasted energy, and emotional turmoil don't count when you're playing "grown-up." Go for the instant gratifications.)

Reinforcement—Writing Things Down or Rehearsing

We all know that writing things down helps us to remember. That's why we take notes and make lists. Writing is a form of rehearsing. You'll find an entire chapter on rehearsing later in this book, but let's look at everyday rehearsing right now.

You notice that you are out of mustard so you write *mustard* on your shopping list. You think "mustard," then you form the word with your pencil, then you look at the word after you've written it. You've just given yourself three copies of the thing to be remembered instead of one. You can also remember looking at the empty jar, smelling the fragrance, even licking a bit of mustard from your fingers after tossing the empty jar in the garbage. The more copies you have, the more likely you are to remember.

In rehearsing, you generally read aloud what you want to remember or you listen to it over and over. Here's something that may make your work more efficient. In one experiment, people were asked to either read or listen to a long sequence of numbers, then say them back. Those who *heard* the numbers remembered them longer than people who only saw them, which seems to indicate that auditory memory lasts longer than visual. However, this is an individual thing. If you hear and see the material at the same time, you more than double your chances of remembering.

In the Mood to Remember

We've already mentioned that when divers learn something under water, even if it is entirely unrelated to diving, they can remember it better under water, and that if people memorize something while they are drunk, they will be better able to remember it later if they are drunk than if they are sober. This is called "state dependency" and also holds true when people are under the influence of marijuana, amphetamines, or barbiturates.

But what about moods? Are you ever "not in the mood" to remember something? Tests show that people also remember things according to the mood they were in when they acquired the information. Gordon H. Bower, chairman of the Psychology Department at Stanford University, has found that information acquired in a happy, sad, angry, or fearful state is most easily recalled in that state. He calls this "mood dependency/congruity."

Interestingly, while depression ordinarily blocks memory, Bower's "sad" subjects learned just as well as the "happy" ones. However, their sadness was hypnosis-induced, brought about by thinking of a sad experience while in a relaxed state. Bower compares mood dependency to having "Happy" and "Sad" bulletin boards that are most easily read when you are in these respective moods. Emotions act as filters for information.

This may be one reason why it is so hard to remember

dreams. The dream state is unique and impossible to reproduce completely when we are awake.

Recall through Hypnotism

Does hypnosis really help people remember? Andre M. Weitzenhoffer found that people who had memorized prose or poetry and then were hypnotized remembered 50 percent more than they did in a normal state. He generalized that recall is improved by similar loose mental states: abstraction, free association, "twilight sleep," and simple relaxation.

Hypnosis may take away memory blocks, but it isn't foolproof. We can't retrieve what wasn't stored. Hypnosis simply removes distractions. Recently hypnotism has become a popular way to quiz witnesses of a crime. In a relaxed state they are sometimes able to visualize the scene clearly, recalling license numbers and physical details that were glimpsed only briefly while under great stress. One of the dangers is that people usually feel very cooperative with their questioners during hypnosis and may imagine details just to please. In July, 1983, the New York State Court of Appeals barred testimony induced by hypnotism. It held that, even if safeguards are used, hypnosis tends to produce "a mixture of accurate recall, fantasy or pure fabrication in unknown quantities."

Seven out of ten people can be hypnotized, and 10 percent of those can achieve a deep trance. People with dominant right brains seem to be better subjects. Fifteen thousand doctors in the United States now use hypnotism. So far, there has been no proof that studying under hypnosis can improve learning, but this is an area that will certainly be explored in the future.

"I've Got Rhythm . . ."

Rhythm as an aid to memory has fallen into disrepute, probably neglected because some associate it with nineteenth-century memory drills, but rhythm is an instinctive way to remember. Watch the toddler rocking and chanting a two-note song again and again. Listen to the sing-song voice of a kindergartner reciting a nursery rhyme. Or consider the cadences of most advertising slogans: "Not a cough in a carload," "See the U.S.A. in your Chevrolet," "Plop, plop, fizz, fizz, oh, what a relief it is!"

Rhythm is what makes poetry easy to remember. It can also help us to remember many other things. As we mentioned previously, Professor A. C. Aitken of Edinburgh University could remember pi to the first thousand decimals. It was easy, he said, because he simply grouped the digits in rows of 50 and divided the 50 into 10 groups of 5, "rather like learning a Bach fugue."

Misremembering

You've heard of Parkinson's Law and the Law of Gravity. In psychology there is a principle called Hodgson's Law: we often remember a thing in a way that we want to remember it. Once we have adjusted material to satisfy us emotionally, it remains in that form in our memory. This is one reason why witnesses rarely agree.

Sometimes people vividly remember things that didn't happen. The tabloids are always headlining stories like a housewife's journey to Mars or a bus driver's conversation with the spirit of Elvis Presley. Are these people crazy or just plain lying? Maybe neither.

Pioneer brain surgeon Wilder Penfield probed different parts of patients' brains during brain surgery and found that when he stimulated the cerebral cortex with an electrified needle the patient vividly recalled things that had happened as much as 50 years before. One woman remembered being at a parade when she was a child and hearing a band play. A girl thought that a phonograph had been turned on in the room, and a man heard his cousins talking and laughing. Penfield could also stimulate muscular movement with his probe. He concluded that he had caused a "ganglionic complex to recreate a steadily unfolding phenomenon, a psychical phenomenon . . ." Others quickly assumed that Penfield had proven that we never forget anything, and with proper stimuli, we should be able to summon up any information we have ever stored.

But Penfield's later experiments showed no consistency

in the brain's reaction to electrical stimulation. There seems to be no direct relationship between the area of stimulation and the response. The brain is not a switchboard with neatly labeled plugs and circuits.

Contemporary brain experts know that stimulating the hypothalamus can produce bizarre images that seem totally real. This may have been what happened to a highly respected forest ranger who went to check out a strange light in the woods. His companions saw an explosion and fled. He later reappeared and described in great detail a trip in a space ship. Scientists speculate that his hypothalamus was stimulated by ground lightning, an electrical charge caused by rotting vegetation. This decomposition also produces a strong glow.

These may sound like exceptional cases, but what about ordinary people who misremember? The big advertising agency, J. Walter Thompson, quizzed viewers following a major 1983 TV mini-series. They learned that 32 percent of the sample audience remembered seeing commercials for Kodak, 32 percent recalled Prudential Insurance, 28 percent—Budweiser, 28 percent—American Express, 19 percent—Volkswagen, and 16 percent—Mobil. *None* of these sponsors advertised during the mini-series.

Making Structures for Remembering

Researcher George Mandler claims that all learning involves organization. Well . . . *most* of the time. Organization can be very helpful to remembering. Mandler divides organization into three types:

Sequencing
Putting things in a series such as A-B-C-D, 1-2-3, birth-life-death. We tend to remember events in a once-upon-a-time sequence, in the order of happening or presentation. We could not look up a phone number or find a book in a library without seriation.

Categorizing
Putting things in groups of similar things. Subjects were given 100 word cards to memorize. Some were

told to divide them into categories. The more categories they created, the more words they were able to remember. (For instance, it would be harder to remember 25 animals than 4 birds, 3 farm animals, 6 reptiles, 5 fish, 3 house pets, and 4 zoo animals.)

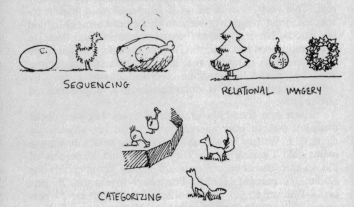

Try to structure information to remember it.

Relational imagery
Linking things that are visually similar—circular things, red things, sparkling things, things associated with Christmas, or sailing, or cooking.

Putting information in structures is essential to remembering it.

STRUCTURES CAN FOOL US

Our love of order can also play tricks with our memories. We love dramatic structure so much that we fill in stories to make them complete. If several unrelated events happen at about the same time, we *want* to find a cause/effect sequence. That's why we remember later that we "left a dull job to take a more exciting one," when we actually were fired from the first and found the second one several months later. Or the old joke: they fell in love, got married, and had twins . . . but not in that order.

Material that doesn't mean anything to us is frequently discarded. In one experiment, a very complicated story was passed from one person to another, mimicking the game of "telephone" that we played as children. As the story was retold, it lost its conflicting elements, and by the fifth retelling, its meaning had been reversed altogether.

We also love to "improve" stories by adding detail. A simple statement gets embroidered in the retelling. Think of Pooh Bah in *The Mikado* who lent "verisimilitude" to his lies by adding colorful details.

So as you work to improve your memory, be aware that some of what you remember just isn't true. As Will Rogers said, "It's not what you know, it's what you know that ain't so."

Try This . . .

Exercise in Grouping-to-Remember

Here are some groups of objects. Try grouping them in different ways.

Group I
  What categories could you make from these objects? Jot them down.

  small child   teenager
  hockey stick   cane
  candy cane   old lady

Group II
  What categories do these objects suggest?

  tire   diamond
  slice of loaf cake   champagne bottle
  license plate   dollar bill
  donut   limousine
  coin

Answers
  Group I—You could divide these things into child, teenager, old lady because they are all people; and candy cane, hockey stick, cane because they are all of a similar shape. You could also match the child to the candy, the teenager to the hockey stick, and the old lady to the cane.
  Group II—You could group the coin, donut, tire because they are all round; and the dollar bill, cake, license plate because they are all rectangular; and the diamond, champagne bottle, and limousine because they are all symbols of luxury. You could also cluster the coin, dollar bill, and diamond because they can all be used to buy something; the donut, cake, and champagne because they are all edible; the tire, license plate, and car because they are usually found together.

Now consider the 20 random objects below. If you try to "just remember" them, you will probably do fairly well. But try *grouping* them. There is no "right" answer. You have to make your own groups. Write them down on a sheet of paper if that helps, so you see the pattern you have made. Then start a fresh sheet and write down what you remember, using your clusters.

typewriter	baseball bat
gym shoe	top hat
stocking	football helmet
football	hot dog
dachshund	jar of mustard
book	cup and saucer
pencil	bicycle
cowboy hat	wheelbarrow
boxing gloves	automobile
tennis racket	horse

15

How to Use Memory Systems

Memory systems can seem overwhelming at first, but many people who approach them in a sufficiently playful manner discover that they can be invaluable tools for remembering.

"The advantage," says Dr. K. Anders Ericsson of Carnegie-Mellon University, "is that [mnemonics] relieves the burden on short-term memory because recall can be achieved through a single association with an already existing code in long-term memory."

What is mnemonics and how did it get such an odd name? Mnemosyne was the Greek goddess of memory and mother of the muses. Her namesake, mnemonics, simply means memory aids. A mnemonic can be simple or intricate, logical or silly. Sometimes the sillier or naughtier it is, the better we remember it. When I mentioned mnemonics to a room full of doctors, they spontaneously repeated a jovially vulgar memory aid:

On old Olympus' towering top,
A fat-assed German vaults and hops.

The first letter of each word is the first letter of the 12 cranial nerves. (A more genteel but less memorable version says, "A Finn and German viewed a hop.")

Many mnemonics are somewhat naughty and often not

170

very specific. For instance, several of the cranial nerves obviously begin with the letter *o*, but which is which? Gordon H. Bower, chairman of the Psychology Department at Stanford University, suggests that a better mnemonic for the cranial nerves would contain more information.

> At the *oil factory* (olfactory nerve) the *optician* (optic) looked for the *occupant* (oculomotor) of the *truck* (trochlear). He was searching because *three gems* (trigeminal) had been *abducted* (abducents) by a man who was hiding his *face* (facial) and *ears* (acoustic). A *glossy photograph* (glossopharyngeal) had been taken of him, but it was too *vague* (vagus) to use. He appeared to be *spineless* (spinal accessory) and *hypocritical* (hypoglossal).

Of course, a short, snappy, *and* exact mnemonic is best. The ones we remember are usually funny, naughty, or intriguing and have a rhyming structure. Children chant the names of the states as they jump rope:

> How did Wiscon-Sin? Stole a New-Brass-Key.
> What did Della-Wear? Wore a New-Jersey.
> How did Flora-Die? Died in Misery.

You probably remember:

> *i* before *e*, except after *c* or when sounded like *a*, as in *neighbor* or *weigh.*

A few of you may even have learned the sequel.

> Exceptions: "Neither leisured foreigner seized the weird heights."

And there's the very useful first aid advice:

> When the face is red, raise the head.
> When the face is pale, raise the tail.

Mnemonic devices are useful when you can't record information in writing, for example for the very young or in societies where many are illiterate. Tribal lore and nursery rhymes, prayers, political slogans, magic incantations, "Thirty days hath September," "*i* before *e,* except after *c,*" or even the sequential structure of numbers or the alphabet . . . all give us a map for remembering.

Numbering Things

Numbering or counting things can be an aid to learning. If you set out to name the 50 United States, you would probably do so in somewhat haphazard geographical or alphabetical order, checking yourself by counting how many you already had so you'd know how many were still missing. You probably don't associate numbers with states in a way that would let you "count" them. But if you wanted to name the elements or the amendments to the U.S. Constitution or the Ten Commandments, all of which are numbered, you'd most likely use their accompanying number as you went along, to make sure you got them all.

There are several counting systems that let you relate two visual images, one for the number and one for the object. If you tend to be verbal, try this one that uses rhyming words.

A Verbal Counting System

one	bun	six	sticks
two	shoe	seven	heaven
three	tree	eight	gate
four	door	nine	vine
five	hive	ten	hen

Or, if you tend to recall visually, here is a set of visual images described by popular memory writer Tony Buzan in his book *Make the Most of Your Mind* (New York; Simon and Schuster, 1984).

A Visual Counting System

one	pen	six	golf club
two	swan	seven	cliff
three	a pair of large breasts	eight	hourglass
four	sailboat	nine	pipe (hanging on a rack)
five	hook	ten	baseball and bat

A visual number system.

Having committed all those pens or hens to memory, you then match them to the new things you want to remember. For instance, you want to remember to do the following ten errands. You would list them mentally, matching them to either the rhyme number or the picture number.

1. *Buy stamps.*
   Rhyme: bun (A sticky cinnamon bun has stamps stuck all over it.)
   Picture: pen (Your pen pierces an assortment of stamps.)

2. *Buy tape at the hardware store.*
   Rhyme: shoe (Your shoe is wrapped tightly with tape so that it is hard to walk.)
   Picture: swan (A graceful swan is swathed in sticky tape. It is flapping about very inelegantly and squawking.)

3. *Buy washers at the hardware store.*
   Rhyme: tree (A Christmas tree is hung with rubber washers, like ornaments.)
   Picture: breasts (The doughnut-like washers are so big, they form the basis of a giant brassiere.)

4. *At the market you need bread . . .*
   Rhyme: door (A door won't shut because a big loaf of bread is in the way . . . it is getting crushed and scattering crumbs.)
   Picture: sailboat (A sailboat was unwisely baked out of bread. The foolish boatmaker is now sinking in his soggy craft as it sails in a sea of soup.)

5. *. . . and pickles . . .*
   Rhyme: hive (The bees have turned green as they tote pickle juice instead of nectar to their hive.)
   Picture: hook (Bait your hook with a pickle to catch a sourpuss catfish.)

6. *. . . and lightbulbs.*
   Rhyme: sticks (Smash burned-out light bulbs with a big stick as you anticipate your new ones.)
   Picture: golf club (Tee off with a lightbulb on your tee.)

7. *Go to the bank.*
   Rhyme: heaven (Imagine golden streets, angelic wings on the tellers as they run their hands through the coins in their drawers.)
   Picture: cliff (You are pushing wheelbarrows of money off a cliff, watching the dollar bills swirl down to the rocks below.)

8. *Pick up your dry cleaning.*
   Rhyme: gate (The plastic garment bags are draped over a gate . . . don't open it too fast or your best suit will fall in the mud.)

Picture: hourglass (Your dry cleaner is strapped into an old-fashioned hourglass corset. His or her eyes are bulging as he/she hands you your cleaning.)

9. *Buy a newspaper.*
   Rhyme: vine (Your paper is sprouting tendrils.)
   Picture: pipe (Dump the ashes out of your pipe into a newspaper, then fold the newspaper and put it in the garbage.)

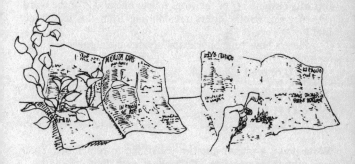

Nine/vine or nine/pipe—buy a newspaper.

10. *Get goldfish food at the pet store.*
    Rhyme: hen (Your goldfish is so hungry it could eat a hen. See her chasing one around her bowl.)
    Picture: baseball and bat (Your goldfish is playing baseball for the Galveston Goldfish. Watch him lob that can of fish food into the bleachers.)

As you can see, all this is *work,* and it only works for you if you enjoy games. Otherwise, just make a list and look at it.

In chapter 21, "How to Remember Dates and Numbers," I will show you a comprehensive number system. If you decide to invest the energy in learning it, you will want to use the images of that system as mental "pegs" for fastening your lists.

A Foolproof Fone Number System

Consider the Harvey Feinstein Foolproof Fone Number System. Harvey enjoys word puzzles, and one day, on the Illinois Central, he discovered that he could convert most phone numbers to words by selecting one of the three letters that share each number's hole or button. His own number became D-A-R-K-D-O-G (327-5364) while his girlfriend's number translated prophetically as Y-O-U-L-O-V-E (968-5683). Numbers with ones and zeros presented a problem since they have no accompanying letters, but he arbitrarily assigned *Q* or the word *one* to one and *Z* or the word *no!* to zero. (Both letters are missing from the telephone dial.)

Here's how your phone dial divides the alphabet:

1 (Q or *one*)	6 M N O
2 A B C	7 P R S
3 D E F	8 T U V
4 G H I	9 W X Y
5 J K L	0 (Z or *No!*)

Write down a phone number you'd like to remember. Then write the three possible letters under each digit.

Phone number   __ __ __ - __ __ __ __

Possible
Letters   __ __ __ - __ __ __ __

Now use your crossword puzzle skills to contrive a word or words.

Phone word   __ __ __ - __ __ __ __

Try some more to get used to the idea.

Not every phone number can be made into words, but enough can to make it fun to try. At various times, various cities across America have recited the time or the weather to people who dialed P-O-P-C-O-R-N, N-E-R-V-O-U-S, or W-E-N-C-H-E-S, and the Yellow Pages reveal businesses that have worked their name, product, or service into their phone number—B-U-G-D-E-A-D for an exterminator or D-I-A-L-C-A-R for a limousine service. Maybe custom phone numbers will replace custom license plates (and unlisted phone numbers) as a status system.

Abbreviations

Abbreviations are a quick way to say something complex, and they can also be a memory aid, furnishing the skeleton of the whole. You may not be sure what the initials stand for in TNT (trinitrotoluene) or UNICEF (United Nations International Children's Emergency Fund), but you probably know what they mean. See how many of the following you can identify.

U.S.A.	_____	IBM	_____
SPCA	_____	JFK	_____
E.O.E.	_____	M.I.T.	_____
YMCA	_____	E.T.	_____

Answers: United States of America, Society for the Prevention of Cruelty to Animals, Equal Opportunity Employer, Young Men's Christian Association, International Business Machines, John Fitzgerald Kennedy, Massachusetts Institute of Technology, Extra Terrestrial.

Here are some other abbreviated or acrostic memory aids:

Every good boy does fine
The musical notes on the lines of the staff.

PEWSAGL
Pride, envy, wrath, sloth, anger, gluttony, and lust (the Seven Deadly Sins).

Kings play cards on fairly good soft velvet
Kingdom, phylum, class, order, family, genus, species, variety (biology classifications).

P. Cohn's Cafe
Phosphorus, carbon, oxygen, hydrogen, nitrogen, sulfur, calcium (Ca), and iron (Fe) (the chemical shorthand for the elements most common in the human body).

Use Location to Help Remember

Remembering things by where they are placed is useful. The socks without holes are at the front of the drawer; the freshest milk is on the left side of the refrigerator shelf; the new batteries are in the glove compartment, and the old ones that might still work in an emergency are in the bottom shelf of the workbench.

The Greek poet Simonides is credited with first demonstrating this system of remembering by location. He was called away from the table during a banquet, and while he was outside, the roof collapsed, crushing the other guests beneath the stones. The bodies were unrecognizable, but Simonides was able to identify them by remembering where each guest had been sitting. Later he realized that location could be a clue to memory, and that objects with no location, such as abstract ideas, could be attached to locations in the imagination and thus be remembered more easily.

Four hundred years later, the Roman orator Cicero used this system to remember his speeches. He would write his speech and place each section in different parts of his house and garden. Then he would walk from place to place, memorizing what he had written. Later, as he delivered his speech, he imagined strolling through his home, finding his next topic waiting. The Romans called this system "topology" from the Greek word *topos* meaning place. Our word *topic* comes from this. We use this placement principle in everyday speech: "In the first place" . . . "in the second place."

The Peg System

Are you yearning to learn some party tricks that will let you dazzle your friends and coworkers with your brilliant new memory? Try the system that the Greeks developed in the days before TelePrompTers and three-by-five-inch file cards. They used the structure of something they already knew, their homes, to arrange and remember lists of things such as the main points they wanted to make in a speech. They called this system *lochi* meaning rooms, and the Greek word has given us the English word, *locution*.

Lochi is a "peg system" that uses a structure you know to arrange what you want to remember. You can use the rooms of your home, your body, the streets between your home and office, any series of objects that is firmly fixed in your mind.

Now project the new items onto this structure. Exaggerate them. Make them ludicrous, bizarre, even naughty, so the picture will stand out. The crazier the image, the more likely you will be to remember it.

WHAT USE IS IT?

Most stage memory experts ask their audiences to shout out lists of objects—watch, roller coaster, rhubarb—which they then rattle back. You can have fun repeating this feat at parties (it's embarrassingly easy), but the really practical use for *lochi* is to fix in your mind the random thoughts that flit through it at precisely the times you couldn't possibly write them down or act on them: when you're driving, in the shower, drifting off to sleep, or "paying attention" to a boss, relative, or lover. Or a great idea for one project comes to you when you are totally involved in another project. If what you want to remember is an abstraction, try to make it into a solid image—a face, object, or symbol. Then, instead of reaching for a pencil, reach for a peg—a *lochi* peg that will record that thought until you can play it back.

Memory pegs also are useful when you need to read the information back in a setting where writing notes is difficult, for example, when you're making a speech or asking for a raise, or if you are the type who can never remember where you left your list.

How to Remember 20 Things in Less Than 2 Minutes

To remember 20 or 30 or even 50 things, it is essential to divide them into smaller units of 5 or 10. (I discussed grouping in the last chapter.) Having several structures lets you use them for different purposes—your body, say, for what you have to do on the way home from work and your kitchen for the calls you want to make after dinner. Having a number of different structures also lets us use some for short-term memory and some for long-term—things you want to remember next week or next year. Also, several structures let you constantly insert new lists that won't get tangled. If you make five quick tours of the plant each morning, you may want five different structures to recall what you want to write down when you get back to your desk. That way, the information on location seven of the first structure—your belly button—won't collide with information stored minutes later in another location seven.

Let's start with ten always-available memory pegs on your body. Bodies are especially good for remembering objects—shopping lists—or things that have to be tended to—fix the *sink,* buy *stamps,* call *mother.*

1. *The top of your head*
   Make the first thing an incredible hat that perches or lurches there. Or the object you want to remember is running down over your face.
2. *Your forehead*
   It's a billboard or flashing neon sign advertising the second object.
3. *Your nose*
   It's a vending machine spurting out dozens of the third thing.
4. *Your mouth*
   It's a tunnel with the fourth item driving in or pouring out. Or your teeth or tongue become the object.
5. *Your throat*
   A transparent crystal cylinder that you think of as similar to Tiffany's window. The object it holds is very, very precious.
6. *Your chest*
   Here the object is stored in duplicate like a pair of lungs.

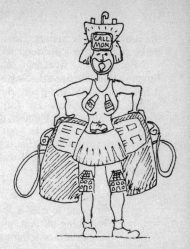

Your body has many always-available memory pegs for things that must be attended to (fix the sink, call Mom, buy gas, do laundry, get the kids at school, get shoes repaired, a shopping list—stamps, light bulbs, roast, nail polish).

7. *Your belly button*
   The object is glued there or flashing there.
8. *Your hips*
   A belly dancer's hip belt is strung with dozens of the eighth object, and they move, clank, twinkle as you dance.
9. *Your knees*
   You are kneeling on the ninth object. Is it pleasant? Comfortable? Awful?
10. *Your feet*
    You stand on the tenth object. What does it feel like? What are your feet doing to the object?

Experience a silly burst of pleasure as you pass down your body, finding your speech or your shopping list or a sequence of battles, presidents, or rock formations as you go. You are able to digress endlessly when you want, yet always return to the preplanned sequence. Having a playful trick like this can make studying less arduous and more fun.

For the next five pegs, choose a room in your house. Imagine that you are standing at the door of your kitchen. (If it has more than one door, choose one.) Kitchens are marvelous because they are full of objects: an oven, a refrigerator, a toaster, a blender, a garbage disposal, cabinets, a food processor, a sink. In your mind's eye, move clockwise, from left to right around the room. Pick out the first dramatic part of your kitchen. We'll walk you through an imaginary sequence.

11. *The table*

    You want to mail a letter so imagine sweeping everything off that table. Its surface becomes a giant letter, or letters are dancing on the top.

12. *The sink*

    You want to be sure to call someone, so put your telephone in the sink. Water is running all over it, and sparks are shooting all over the room.

13. *The refrigerator*

    You want to rewrite the letter to Mr. Jones and add three points. Three shelves of the refrigerator, or the freezer, butter drawer, and crisper hold each of those brilliant new thoughts, and the refrigerator door becomes Mr. Jones's face or the logo of his company.

14. *The toaster*

    You've got to get an important phone number you left at home and bring it to work tomorrow. See the slip of paper with the number on it popping up out of the toaster like a slice of toast; or see yourself burning with desire to get that number . . . or the numbers curling up like smoke from the slots.

15. *The stove*

    You told your boss you'd pick up something on your way to work tomorrow. See your breakfast cooking while that object nestles, sizzling in your frying pan. It is so important that it shoves your usual eggs aside. If you don't eat eggs, imagine it staring out of your coffee cup or bobbing in your oatmeal.

Don't be tempted to use ten things in your kitchen even if you could. You need "white space" to group information.

Now go to your bathroom door. Bathrooms are usually full of things that rush and gush and flush. You can float things in the bathtub, unroll things like toilet paper, rain down on things with the shower. Tour the room from left to right, pegging things on prominent objects around the room. Here is an imaginary sequence:

16. *The bathroom sink*
    It's probably different from your kitchen sink, maybe a different color and size. You want to remember to get gas for the car. Imagine gasoline pouring out of the faucets as you try to shave or wash your hair. Ugh!

17. *The toilet*
    Flush the thing. You want to remember to pay back the $1.51 you borrowed from Fred. Flush the money down the toilet as Fred hops up and down on the toilet tank, clapping his hands with glee.

18. *Toilet paper*
    The paper is printed all over with the next thing you want to remember. It unrolls and spills across the floor, till the room is full of colorful printed strips proclaiming your thought. You are engulfed with toilet paper.

19. *The shower*
    The object is pouring out over your bare body. Or it is under the shower, getting all wet. Your motor vehicle registration card is getting water logged, floating pathetically in the swirling water, and you won't be able to drive unless you renew it. Or the flowers for your mother-in-law's birthday are pelting your back as you stand under the shower. They pile up at your feet, smiling up at you for your thoughtfulness.

20. *The towel rack*
What you want to remember has replaced the towels and is hanging there. The steaks in the freezer that you have to leave out to thaw for dinner are right there on the rack. Or the check you promised to write and mail immediately is folded neatly, giant-sized, over the bar. If you want to remember an abstract idea, you could imagine yourself naked at the board meeting, drying yourself with a giant towel while you deliver your brilliant plan.

Using *lochi* to remember points in a speech makes your talk look and sound spontaneous. The audience watches you search for the next idea and sees it come to you.

Once, when the *New York Times* went on strike, its movie critic, Richard Eder, was invited to do his reviews on television. He carefully read the first one and then saw it played back. He thought it was deadly dull. He decided that, instead of knowing exactly what he was going to say, he would jot down a few points and think through the material as he went. This approach proved much more lively and wonderfully effective.

USING PEGS AS A BACKUP
Using pegs gives you two ways to remember things. One is rational—"Of course, I'll remember the five points of my speech or the eight things I have to do today." But if you block because of overload or nervousness, you have a second "list" to review. It's a marvelous backup, a way of putting ideas on hold.

Using Pegs to Learn New Things

You've just gotten a complicated new machine and have to do things in a certain sequence to make it work. For instance, imagine that you are learning to operate a new computer.

Step 1:
Turn on the green switch. (Imagine a green switch sticking out of the top of your head.)

Step 2:
Insert disc in slot. (Your forehead is a giant slot, opening to receive the disc.)
Step 3:
Hit the reset and shift buttons simultaneously. (Each nostril is a key with a huge sign sticking out of it. You must shove the signs back into the nostrils.)
Step 4:
Hit the "B" key. (Each of your teeth has a huge *B* on it.)
Step 5:
Hit the "return" key. (In the Tiffany's window of your throat is a golden key inscribed "Return to me.")
Step 6:
Type the name of the program you are about to do. (Make the alphabet soup of letters into a naughty brassiere. Remember, few people are mind readers and whatever connections you choose to make are strictly your property.)
Step 7:
. . . continue like this through all the steps.

You can use memory pegs to learn the steps to starting a car or opening a safe or any other sequence that must be done in order. It is simply another structure for storing information, temporarily or permanently.

It's Okay Not to Love Systems

If you've made a sporting try and you still feel frustrated and baffled by memory systems, that's okay. They work magnificently for some people and not at all for others. If you're one of the latter, you probably have many unconscious mental systems of your own that just don't mesh with outside ones. Try to keep a relaxed, open-minded, and playful attitude toward these external memory structures, and they may come in handy some day.

I prefer an approach to remembering that begins with what a person needs to recall. If you *need* to know it and *want* to know it, then you can usually find a way to remember it. The way may or may not include using a system, and the system may be a large, formal one (the alphabet, mathematics, the laws of physics), or it may be a ridiculous limerick. Both work.

Try This . . .

to Impress Friends with Your Ability to Remember

This is a great party trick. Get today's newspaper. You are going to memorize a key story or ad on each of the first 20 pages as your friends watch, or ask your friends to call the stories and ads out to you.

Your Peg	The Story or Ad	Your Silent Image (Make it funny.)
1. top of your head		
2. forehead		
3. nose		
4. mouth		
5. throat		
6. chest		
7. belly button		
8. hips		
9. knees		
10. feet		

Now enter your kitchen and, starting on the left, circle the room mentally and write down the five major things you see. Then choose a story or ad from pages 11 through 15 of your newspaper.

11.		
12.		
13.		
14.		
15.		

Repeat the process with your bathroom.

16.		
17.		
18.		
19.		
20.		

With a little practice, almost anyone can be a "memory whiz." If astounding your friends isn't your goal, use the above system to memorize a series of things you want to remember—the vice-presidents of the United States, the countries of Central and South America starting at the Mexican border, the operas of Verdi.

16

How to Study

"**A** student who changes the course of history,"
wrote humorist Franklin P. Adams, "is probably taking an
exam." We are always students. One way or another, we
never stop studying for exams. Even after surviving high
school physics tests, bar exams, and drivers' tests, there are
always things to remember that affect our job, our family, and
our society. That's why the way we remember as students is
so important. Poor memory habits start in school.

Cramming has a bad reputation, yet cramming can be
productive if you don't exhaust yourself and distort your
perception. Just remember that cramming makes the material maximally available during the test but minimally available afterwards. If that's what you want, it's okay. The most
efficient way to study, whether you cram or not, is to ask
yourself questions about what you've already read, instead of
rereading the material. Can you actively call the material
back? Then you've increased your chances of recalling during the test.

Be Sure to Make Mistakes

Studying isn't easy because failure and errors have gotten bad press. We are afraid not to be perfect, and therefore
we unconsciously avoid the many small evidences of our
"failure" during the learning process. As a result we end up
with the one big failure of flunking the exam, or not learning a
foreign language or the new skill. We exchange freedom from
small embarrassments for a major loss.

The Bad News

Here's some news you may not want to hear: studying requires concentration. If you work on seven things at once, you will get one-seventh of the total memory transfer for each that you would if you worked on one during the same time. It's like sharing time on a computer.

What is the benefit of flitting from one thing to another? If you stay with one thing until it is done, you may be judged by your product. The person who starts many new things and never finishes them delays this judgment.

To study successfully, you have to be inaccessible to external stimuli. The student, like the person who is beginning meditation, has to develop a spontaneous resistance to the enormous rush of distracting ideas, thoughts, and body sensations that greet him when he sits down to his task.

Why is it so hard? Well, reading and school work are very new ways to use a very old system, your mind. This system was designed millions of years ago to pay attention to what was happening at the moment. It was survival oriented.

The directed, focused way we use our minds today is a very specialized late addition. We always have a tendency to revert to the more spontaneous, less focused way of responding to new things. Like the caveman, we want to know, "Can I eat it or will it eat me?" This "mind wandering" is invaluable to us in terms of what we understand of the world, but mind wandering can make it hard to study.

Memorizing

Memorizing is done in two ways. We can learn mechanically by rote, or we can learn by understanding. Some things can only be learned one way or the other, but most memorizing benefits by a combination of both.

One example is the way people approach the computers that are flooding the world's business offices. One person, forced to deal with them, may say, "Don't bother me with details. Just show me which buttons to push." Another may want to know how they work, what they are capable of, and even how to take them apart for repairs and cleaning. The first person is trying to learn by rote, the second by understanding. Both may perform just as well in the short run, but the second probably has the long-term advantage.

Mechanical memorization may help you learn faster and perform better. This can be the best way to remember simple tasks. You don't need to know how a watch or a lock or an elevator works to use one effectively. Of course, you'd be helpless if one of them broke down in a crucial moment and you needed to fix it, but this happens so rarely that you really don't need to burden yourself with the intricacies of escapements, cylinders, or counterweights if you choose not to.

There are some drawbacks to mechanical rote learning. We may be mislearning the information. Children who learn so much by rote can be heard singing, "Land of the pills inside," instead of "Land of the pilgrim's pride"; or praying, "Lead us not into Penn Station." This can be charming and usually has no ill effects, but it may not aid later remembering unless the adult transposes pills and pilgrims.

Rote memorization, especially of something that has no meaning, rarely stays with us as long as information we truly understand. (An exception may be a particularly delightful bit of nonsense, such as "'Twas brillig and the slithy toves did gyre and gimble in the wabe" from *Alice's Adventures in Wonderland* or the popular song of the 1940s, "Mairzy Doats and Dozy Doats.")

The role of meaning in memory was tested in a study that divided students into six groups. Each was shown the same set of paintings, accompanied by varying degrees of information about the artist and the art. Those who received the most information were able to remember the most paintings later.

Adding meaning to memorization helps lock the information in place. This is why we can summon up poems and quotes memorized decades earlier in school. Much of what we learn by rote as children forms the basis of our adult knowledge when we add understanding.

To Understand or to Memorize?

The simplest way to remember anything is to understand it, but with the vast amount of information in the world, that isn't always possible. Sometimes we need to memorize information solely for survival—the battles of the Civil War for a history class, the towns on a commuter train so we don't miss our stop, the wives of Henry VIII to do crossword puzzles. Dr. Albert Schweitzer had his illiterate patients repeat his instructions ten times so he was sure they would remember them even if they didn't understand the medical reasons behind them.

If you're absolutely sure that surface knowledge is enough, that you really don't want to *know* the information, just remember it, then you can use a trick. For instance, convert the information to a readily remembered sentence with the first letter of each word representing one of the parts you want to remember. The popular mnemonic for the stations on the Paoli Local, a train that services many colleges and prep schools outside Philadelphia, is "Old Maids Never Wed And Have Babies Rarely." Students use this sentence to keep from missing their closely spaced stops at Overbrook, Merion, Narberth, Wynnewood, Ardmore, Haverford, Bryn Mawr, or Rosemont.

Memorizing Techniques

The bookstores are full of good books on how to study, and those books are full of good study techniques. Here are two offbeat ones:

- Write the information on index cards (an active process), and tape the cards around the house in surprising places. When you run into a card, repeat the information out loud (another active process).
- Tape-record the information, and play it back as you bathe, wash dishes, drive.

Conjuring Your Own Tricks

Let's say you want to remember the wives of Henry VIII. The easiest way would be to understand the rich and colorful drama of the time, the intense struggles between

Write what you want to remember on index cards and put them in unexpected places where you'll see them.

church and state, the heartache of a robust young king whose devoted, older wife bore him son after son, all stillborn, and of noble Sir Thomas More defying his king in the cause of his God. Understanding, in this case, would give you vivid, unforgettable pictures of the participants in this human historical drama. But you have neither the time nor the interest to do this. You just want to remember Henry's wives in sequence, with perhaps a few details on the side. How do you do it? Let's look at the list.

Catherine of Aragon (divorced)
Anne Boleyn (beheaded)
Jane Seymour (died)
Anne of Cleves (divorced)
Catherine Howard (beheaded)
Catherine Parr(survived)

Obviously you could make a quick rhythmic sequence of their fates:

Divorced, beheaded, died,
Divorced, beheaded, survived

193

But that's not much help if you don't know which was which. Let's look at the first letters of their names:

CAABJSACCHCP

Not very promising. The letters don't suggest a simple acronym (such as CREEP for Committee to Re-Elect the President or OPEC for Organization of Petroleum Exporting Countries). Maybe a verse could be contrived.

> The Spanish Princess said her prayers
> While pretty Anne leaped in bed.
> Catherine of Aragon
> Lost her paragon
> But Anne Boleyn lost her head.
>
> Lady Jane could see more (Seymour)
> But died in childbirth's fever.
> Then over the seas
> Came Anne of Cleves,
> Too smart for Henry's cleaver.
>
> Little Catherine Howard
> Thought she'd be his star.
> But she was discovered
> With more than one lover,
> And—chop, chop—Catherine Parr.

This is admittedly dreadful doggerel, but the five minutes or so you spend contriving something like it are far more *active* than five minutes spent reciting the names again and again, and this active process has a better chance of fixing the ladies' names permanently in your mind, even if you ultimately (as is likely) forget your poetic attempt. If your talents tend to be visual, rather than verbal, you could try a series of cartoons, logos, or caricatures to help lock your subjects in your mind.

How Long Should You Study?

In studying, as in everything, we get what we "pay" for, but there are ways to get the most for our money. Do you learn twice as much if you study twice as long? Or does the "rate of diminishing returns" apply? Or do you become more efficient as you study longer? Results of experiments have been somewhat contradictory.

One nineteenth-century study by Ebbinghaus, the first modern memory researcher, indicated that dividing study time into equal periods was more efficient. Those who alternate between long and short study periods will remember less than those who study in more equal periods.

A 1978 experiment tested the "Total Time Hypothesis" and found a direct ratio between learning and the amount of time spent. When British postmen had to learn to operate a complex number typewriter, it was the perfect opportunity for a study. The postmen were divided arbitrarily into four groups with four different study schedules. Here is how they did.

Those who studied one hour a day learned twice as fast as those who studied four hours a day in two two-hour sessions. The second group learned in half as many days but spent four times as many hours learning, a plus only if trying to meet a deadline. The other two groups studied either two hours once a day or one hour twice a day. They learned equally fast, and their speed fell between the first two groups.

This study indicates that if you don't have a deadline and want to spend the least number of hours studying, one hour a day is the most efficient way to study. Of course, if results are needed fast, like the famed 90-Day Wonders of World War II—officers trained and shipped to the battlefront in just 90 days—then the more hours spent each day, the fewer days or weeks needed to achieve the goal, even if many more hours are required.

Predicting Your Performance

People were shown a lengthy list of objects and asked to assign a number to each item, indicating how likely they were to remember it. It turned out that their estimates were very close to their actual performance on a test of recall. If you can do this kind of estimating, you can decide how much time you need to devote to studying something that you want to remember later.

Aural Repetition—an Inferior Study Aid

Recently the British Broadcasting Corporation had to change frequencies. In the weeks before the change, they broadcast the complex new channel information thousands of times. Surveys showed that almost no one could recall the information. When the change was made, most people referred to written instructions they had received and had few problems. The aural instructions failed because they were too complicated. Conclusion: complex information is better understood visually.

Forgetting and Restudying

We forget on a curve. It's rather like shooting down a steep slide that levels out at the bottom until we are scooting along on the level. At a specific moment we may have two memories at exactly the same spot on the downhill slide, but one started its trip long before the other. Jost's law, named after the nineteenth-century psychologist, says that if two memory traces are equally strong at the same moment, then the older of the two will be more durable and forgotten less rapidly. In other words, the older has already "leveled out" in its descent. Conclusion: spaced presentation enhances recall. Keep memories fresh by tracing over them periodically, and they will stay with you longer.

Theories about Forgetting—Fading vs. Interference

There are two basic theories about how we forget and neither can be proven. The first says that memory fades. If this is so, then time should be a constant factor, but it rarely is. The second theory says that memories are obscured or disrupted. Rugby players were asked to describe games in which they had played. Most could remember the greatest number of details about the most recent game they had played, no matter how many weeks had elapsed since they had played it. The elapsed time affected memory less than the number of intervening games.

The less that happens between learning and recall, the better. Subjects who learned just before going to bed remembered more 12 hours later than people who learned something first thing in the morning and had to recall it that night. (Of course, this is a generality . . . if you are bright and functioning first thing in the morning and a near-vegetable at night, this may not hold for you.)

Memories That Interfere with Memory

Memories can get in each other's way, just like people in a crowded corridor. When you are trying to remember a specific fact, older memories and more recent ones can both get in the way.

NEWER MEMORIES

Newer memories interfere because we tend to forget in reverse. New material pushes out old, so we can remember where we set something down today more easily than where we set it last week.

Lots of studies of this "overwriting," have been done. In 1900, two German researchers had volunteers memorize a long list. Then the volunteers were divided into two groups. One group relaxed while the other memorized a new list. Then both were retested on the first list. The ones who had been idle were able to remember 56 percent of the first list, but the ones who had been busy with a new list recalled only 26 percent.

OLDER MEMORIES

Older memories interfere when the older, more familiar material overcomes the new. The more similar two experiences are, the more likely we are to combine them. This may be helpful in strengthening a memory or it may not.

Husband: Remember that romantic weekend we
               spent in St. Louis?
Wife: (grimly) I've never *been* in St. Louis.

When more recent memories are blocked by earlier, stronger ones, we dilute the new information with lots of similar information. If we have only seen one baseball game or one opera or one airplane crash in our life, the details would probably remain fairly clear. But if we had seen dozens, even hundreds, the distinctions might begin to blur, unless we had a great interest in the information and formed structures to file it (as baseball fans, opera buffs, and crash investigators would do).

In another experiment in the 1930s, college students were asked to memorize lists of nonsense syllables. When their work periods were interrupted with such things as humorous readings, they remembered little of what they had been memorizing. The same experimenter did another study that indicated there is less interference between different kinds of information. In other words, if we have to study several different things in sequence, we can remember better when the subjects aren't similar. For instance, studying math immediately after history wouldn't erase much of the earlier history information, but studying American history after English history might blur the distinctions.

And, despite the accepted idea that good study habits are consistent, another 1930s study found that consistently using similar study habits also resulted in retroactive inhibition. This may mean that varying your procedure or schedule or even the place you study could help you remember better. You could try studying chemistry in one place, languages in another.

Studying Formulas

Sometimes it is absolutely essential to understand something to remember it. Of course, some people are always trying to come up with an easier way. In the book *How to Remember Anything* (New York: Arco, 1976) by David Markoff and Andrew Dubin, the authors say that remembering the classic formula $E = mc^2$ is easy if you translate it according to their memory table into "he, scale, ham, sea, and Noah." Then they suggest:

> See[ing] thousands of *he's* (men) weighing themselves on a *scale* . . . next we see a scale, or better a million scales being sucked into a steaming hot ham. Then we see the ham drowning in a sea . . . we now see thousands of hams dotting the sea

and they're all drowning. Finally there is Noah sipping up the whole sea through a straw.

Now, it is just possible that some of you may find this easier to remember than $E = mc^2$, but I am not going to tell you to remember that way. There are lots of tricks to get us through life's memory chores, and you should use any of them that work for you, but images of Noah sipping a sea full of hams and scales should not replace the elegance, power, and poetry of $E = mc^2$!

Maybe chemistry is a dark, miserable sea to you, something you have to get through just to graduate. The formulas are relatively meaningless, but you have to show the teacher you "know" them. S, the man with the incredible memory, knew no chemistry, but he could remember lengthy formulas by converting them to visual images. For instance, he was given this meaningless formula to memorize:

$$N . \sqrt{d^2 . \times 85 . \frac{}{vx}} \quad \sqrt{\frac{276^2 . \quad 86 \times n^2b}{n^2v . \quad 264}}$$

This is how he did it.

Neiman (N) came out and jabbed at the ground with his cane (.). He looked up at a tall tree which reminded him of a root ($\sqrt{}$) and thought to himself: "No wonder the tree has withered and begun to expose its roots. After all, it was here when I built these two houses (d^2)." And again he poked with this stick (.). He said, "The houses are old, a cross ($\times$) should be placed on them." This gives a great return on his original capital because he had invested 85,000 rubles to build them. The roof finishes off the building (—), and down below a man is standing and playing a harmonica (the $\times$). He is standing near the Post Office and at the corner is a large stone (.) to prevent carts from bashing the corner of the house . . .

This bizarre tale allowed him to remember it perfectly, both at the time and 15 years later.

To summarize, understanding a formula is best. Tricks are second best. And sometimes tricks get you through until real understanding comes.

Studying History

History has traditionally been structured chronologically by country—each culture standing apart from the others like separate columns. We may be able to rattle off lists of Chinese dynasties or English monarchs or American presidents, but we have to stop and think to relate them "sideways," to figure out who was King of England at the end of the Ming Dynasty (Charles I); who was President during the reign of William IV (Andrew Jackson); or who was the Russian Premier when President Kennedy was shot (Nikita Khrushchev); unless there had been an important interaction, such as that between Marco Polo and Kublai Khan.

Sometimes these relationships can strengthen our concept of the world as a whole in exciting ways. For instance:

1. Catherine the Great of Russia was a contemporary of:
   a. Queen Elizabeth I of England
   b. George Washington
   c. Abraham Lincoln
2. Beethoven was still alive when which of these people were born?
   a. Renoir
   b. Pasteur
   c. Gershwin
3. Which of the following things happened during Rembrandt's lifetime?
   a. The pilgrims landed at Plymouth Rock.
   b. Mozart was born.
   c. Leonardo da Vinci died.
   d. Molière wrote plays.
   e. The French Revolution began.

4. Which of the following people, chronologically if not geographically, could have met?
   a. Jane Fonda and Freud
   b. Sarah Bernhardt and Ernest Borgnine
   c. Thomas Edison and John F. Kennedy
   d. Abraham Lincoln and Henry Ford
   e. Shakespeare and Pocahontas
5. When the atomic bomb dropped on Hiroshima, which of the following things were true?
   a. American women were wearing ankle-length skirts.
   b. The countries of Tanzania, Estonia, and Montenegro did not exist.
   c. Betty Grable was a pinup girl.
   d. Most Americans had never heard of pizza or seen a television.
   e. There was no immunization against small-pox, and epidemics caused many deaths.

Answers: 1–b 2–b 3–a,e 4–a,b,c,d,e 5–b,c,d

Did these exercises stretch your mind and help you imagine history as a gigantic structure, full of relationships and "pegs" to hang things on? When you need to memorize a date, try summoning up all the things that happened on that date. Knit a web of horizontal associations to hold your vertical date in place.

Even though we are frequently taught to study history in neat sequential columns, events are never this tidy. History is a tumult, and it is only we poor mortals who try to make a story of it, to have beginnings and ends, causes and effects. Forcing a structure, a viewpoint, and a purpose on some-times-random happenings helps us to remember them, even though it distorts and occasionally falsifies them.

Studying Music

There was a vogue, some years ago, to teach music appreciation by having hapless students memorize the titles and composers of hundreds of pieces of music. The teacher reasoned that she could not test their true appreciation, but she could sure find out if they knew Schubert from Schumann. As a result, tens of thousands of Americans cannot hear the *Surprise* Symphony without muttering to themselves:

> Papa Haydn's dead and gone
> But his memory lingers on.
> When his mood was one of bliss
> He wrote jolly tunes like this.

(Haydn had the last laugh on that one, for this work is now attributed to another composer.)

About the only kind thing to say for a process that has left a generation of Americans putting doggerel lyrics to great music is that recognition *can* aid appreciation. A walk through the woods may be a pleasant experience, but if we can say, "Oh, that's a *Silene caroliniana* and that's a *Meleagrie gallopavo silvestris,* and over there is *Viola tricoleur,* also called Johnny-Jump-Up or Love-in-Idleness" and then launch into Oberon's speech from *A Midsummer Night's Dream:*

> . . . a little western flower,
> Before milk-white, now purple with love's wound,
> And maidens call it Love-in-Idleness.

our pleasant walk can become a sublime and memorable experience.

So, if you were spared the lyrical "learning" process, treasure each unencumbered moment of Mozart, ripple of Rachmaninoff, bar of Beethoven and thunder of Tchaikovsky. If not, seek out the wordless magnificence of Monteverdi, Scarlatti, Poulenc, and Stravinsky who probably escaped the degradations of this particular school of "memory training."

Auditory memory includes recognizing a friend's voice, the sound of glass breaking, or a piece of music. There has not been a great deal of auditory memory research, but two studies showed that people can remember a melody, even if the key and timing are different, as long as the "contour" is similar.

Both Eastern and Western music employ variations on a theme. The symphony form requires the composer to state his simple melodies and then elaborate and embellish them with great sophistication. Mozart once built an astounding tour de force of variations on the nursery melody we know as "Twinkle, Twinkle, Little Star." Jazz and raga take a tune and then dissect, enlarge, twist, and exhort it to sublime heights of reinterpretation. Yet the melody in all cases must remain recognizable or the exercise loses its purpose.

What changes can we tolerate before we "lose" the melody? One researcher played well-known melodies like "Auld Lang Syne" for his subjects with various distortions. They recognized the melodies 94 percent of the time when they were played "straight." This dropped to 80 percent when the pitch was changed and to 54 percent when the time between notes was changed. (Some relevant trivia: The estate of the opera composer Giacomo Puccini successfully sued Al Jolson and Vincent Rose because the first 12 notes of their song "Avalon" were identical to the first 12 notes of the tenor's third act aria, "E lucevan le stelle" from *Tosca*. The notes are the same, but the timing is so different that almost nobody, probably including Jolson and Rose, recognized the similarities. Something similar happened to George Harrison of the Beatles. He was successfully sued by the author of the Chiffons' hit "He's So Fine" which was judged to be too similar to Harrison's "My Sweet Lord.")

It seems that pitch and rhythm changes affect individual recognition of melodies to some extent and that music is a profoundly cultural experience. We learn to recognize patterns in our music, just as we recognize patterns in our language. Patterns that differ a little can sound fresh and exciting (I remember the fuss over Leonard Bernstein's dissonant score for *West Side Story* when it first came out, but now it sounds "normal" and even "traditional"), but patterns that differ too much can leave the listeners bored, confused, or angry (the riots that greeted Stravinsky's *Rite of Spring* or the ennui that engulfs most listeners of the works of Schönberg).

Studying to Music

Many of us put on a record or turn on the radio when we want to study. We're convinced that it soothes us, blocks extraneous noises, and helps us concentrate (especially if we did not have to memorize instructive lyrics to identify major composers). This may be wrong, according to a Bradley University study. Forty volunteers were divided into four groups of ten, with five men and five women each. All studied a passage from a law book and then were tested. Twenty of the students listened to their favorite "study" records while they studied, and the other twenty studied in silence. Afterwards, half of each group relaxed while the others did unrelated work.

Surprise! The silent group did slightly better than the group that listened to music, but even more surprising, the relaxation groups did about twice as well as the groups that did unrelated work between studying and taking the test. Here is a rundown on their scores, based on a maximum possible score of ten:

	Females	Males
music/relaxation	7.2	6.0
music/activity	2.8	3.2
silence/relaxation	8.8	8.0
silence/activity	3.6	4.0

Notice that women did slightly better than men in the same group if they relaxed before testing, and men did slightly better than women if they did an unrelated activity before testing. However, the relaxers are the big winners.

Some Laws for Learning

If you want a way to visualize the learning process, consider this equation:

$$readiness + frequency = learning$$

Edward E. Thorndike made groups of cats and chickens memorize things in order to eat. Later he repeated the experiment with college students. From their actions he decided there were key factors to learning including readiness, frequency, and effect. A hungry cat has readiness to learn. At first it tried many things to open the door of the cage to get to its food, but when it accidentally did so, it didn't connect the act and the door opening. But after the cause-effect repeated several times, the frequency impressed the cat. (Practice makes perfect.)

Frequency, however, isn't necessary if the thing being learned is so striking that it would be hard to ignore—your house is on fire; George makes more money than you do; Jupiter is about to crash into the earth. Anything that impresses you will go into your memory. An equation for this would be

$$\frac{\text{reward}}{\text{meaning}} = \text{learning}$$

Thorndike experimented with rewards for learning. People, he observed, will learn something that seems irrelevant at the time (like the alphabet, multiplication tables, or how to get along with a fussy boss) for an immediate reward. Occasionally the reward will be a personal sense of satisfaction. More often it is external—approval (including good grades, acceptance at college, degrees), power, fame, money, or personal possessions. The concept of reward can include avoiding punishment. Neurologist Richard M. Restak says that "novelty is a reward." I suggest tempting and charming yourself into remembering with the reward of novelty, rather than imagining all the terrible things that will happen if you forget (punishment).

Thorndike thought that people would remember pleasant things and forget unpleasant things, but other experiments and our own experiences show that this isn't always true. Thorndike amended his original theories to include the Law of Belongingness: meaningful associations are easier to remember than meaningless associations.

Experimenting with Rats, Cats, and College Students

Perhaps the ever-present rats, cats, and college students in memory experiments have you wondering, "What has all this got to do with *me?*" The answer is, not much and quite a lot.

When you read that a kangaroo learned to tap dance twice as fast when he was fed bananas while a red light flashed, you can easily dismiss it as nonsense. Much scientific study *does* seem like nonsense, but it's such delightful nonsense that makes up the building blocks of all human knowledge. To find out about the kangaroo, the experimenter had to design an experiment with strict controls.

For instance, was the kangaroo compared to a frog or only to other kangaroos? What were the variables? In other words, what was compared to what? Was it the task learned or the food ingested or the color of the light, or whether the light flashed or was steady? How was the speed of learning evaluated? Most important, can other experimenters duplicate the results?

If they can, then this bit of esoterica goes into the giant library of What-We-Know. Other researchers can try to apply its implications to other areas. If the implications prove to be broad enough, we could end up teaching every kangaroo in the country to tap dance, or we could increase the learning speed of school children by changing their diets, or we could change the lighting design of schools, or we could teach kinesthetic skills more quickly, or . . . Much of science is finding answers to questions that haven't been asked yet.

DISCOURAGING LEARNING

Some of us constantly rise to meet challenges, and others fold up under disparagement. If you often find yourself in the latter group, you have plenty of company. In one experiment, volunteers were asked to memorize lists of numbers. One group was arbitrarily criticized for not being as good as the others. These subjects remembered less than the uncriticized group.

A controversial experimenter, A. F. Zeller, also repressed learning with criticism in an experiment that has drawn some criticism itself. A subject who had learned a list of syllables was then verbally abused in this manner:

> Great concern was expressed . . . over [his] mental ability. He was asked if he had not considered the possibility that he could not get through college and was informed that he probably would not. On the other hand, it was pointed out his mechanical ability was so poor he probably couldn't succeed in any of the trades. Nothing was omitted which would serve to make [him] feel insecure and inadequate.

Subjects who got this kind of feedback remembered significantly less than their control counterparts. Then these abused subjects were told that the criticism had been part of the experiment. Their performances improved dramatically, but it never equaled that of the control group. Similar results have been obtained by other experimenters.

THE ETHICS OF EXPERIMENTATION

This experiment has some strong inferences for educators. It may have contributed positively to teaching philosophy, but the danger of such tactics to the lives and psychic health of the participants can't be overlooked. It is possible that some of the subjects were permanently damaged by the process, just as people in similar real-life situations can be damaged.

Risky experimentation is a constant moral dilemma for researchers. (In the 1930s, a syphilis cure was tested on convicts by letting a control group go untreated!) These abuses are usually criticized—Baddeley comments on "the dubious ethical status" of the Zeller experiment—but enthusiasm can sometimes cloud ethics when we are consumed with curiosity—"How does this work? Let's tear it apart and see!"

Darwin's Law for Studying

While we are seeking guidelines for effective studying, let's check in with a top-notch observer, Charles Darwin.

Darwin formulated what we have dubbed the Law of Contrariness. While collecting evidence for his theory of evolution, he forced himself to write down everything *contrary* to his theory because he knew he would forget the contradictions otherwise.

Try This . . .
to Determine Your Best Studying Technique

What type of fact—grammatical, historical, mathematical, general—is difficult for you to remember, no matter how often you study it? Or what concepts or what sequence, series, or group of things do you want to be able to recall? Go look up the information, if necessary, and write it down.

What studying technique might help you remember it? Look over the list below.

_____ repeating it over and over
_____ really understanding it
_____ studying it in a structured, regular way on a regular schedule
_____ studying it randomly, whenever time permits
_____ approaching it in an unusual, new way
_____ creating your own mnemonic about it
_____ drawing a picture of it
_____ being serious
_____ being silly
_____ being persistent
_____ being innovative

Check what you think will work. There are no right answers. Now test your predictions.

17

How to Remember Facts

It is easier to think, plan, persuade, and make decisions if you have the facts to back you up. What the diplomatic community calls "intelligence" is simply facts, facts to use or ignore in dealing with people and events.

Schools say that they teach people how to think, but usually what they want to hear back from their students is a list of facts. To pass those exams, you will need to remember facts, arrange them in a logical way, and interpret the whole constructively. This can be true of life too.

Learning is knowing how to locate data and analyze it, not storing it in your memory. We are overloaded with data, but the more we know, the easier it is to learn. Each new piece of information has more places to go in our large, structured mental filing cabinet. As we get older, we may take longer to retrieve a crucial bit of information, but we have more file drawers in action.

Much that we see and hear each day would be meaningless if we didn't recognize it and categorize it. Imagine a bushman dropped down in the Louvre or, the opposite, a cultured Frenchman whisked to the great Australian desert. Each would have little understanding of what he saw and therefore would remember few details. In his own territory, the bushman might spot an impression in the sand, note the angle of the sun, sniff the air, and draw a valuable conclusion about impending danger. The Frenchman might view the works of Flemish painters and draw valuable conclusions about life in Europe in the seventeenth century. The reverse would be unlikely.

Intelligence and Memory

The ability to express things precisely depends upon the depth of one's vocabulary. Memory, then, is really one of the building blocks of intelligence. By intelligence, we mean novel ways of using information, of putting things together in ways they have never been before. This is a creative act, not a repeat of something, and therefore not memory.

Do smart people remember better? No one knows because there is little agreement on what intelligence is. Is it how fast a person can process information? How long it takes to react? (This is inherited.) Or is it thoroughness which can be taught? If intelligence is defined as the "ability to learn," then all intelligence is based in some way on memory. However, I.Q. tests like Stanford-Binet and Wechsler-Bellevue test only portions of a student's memory.

Some superior memories are obviously built in and probably genetic. Chess masters are able to remember the arrangement of pieces on a chessboard more quickly than average club players, indicating that some people have more memory ability than others, no matter how much desire is involved. Most tests indicate that effort and training can't improve a person's memory capacity. Don't despair, though, because effort and training *can* increase efficiency.

And if anyone tries to persuade you that memory really is intelligence, tell them about the monkey in Texas who proved that monkeys remember just about as well as we do. In a test at the University of Texas Health Science Center in Houston, a five-year-old rhesus monkey competed against human volunteers. Both the monkey and the humans were shown a series of slides. Then they were shown a second set that contained some of the slides in the first series plus new slides. Both man and monkey were taught to hit a lever when a familiar picture from the first group appeared. (The monkey, we assume, got a reward for his trouble.) In a ten-item test, both monkey and humans were right 86 percent of the time, and in a twenty-item test, both succeeded 81 percent of the time.

Do You Understand?

It is much harder to learn something if you have no framework to organize and store the information that's coming in. In other words, the better you understand what it is, the better you can remember it. Understanding is an active brain process, and memory ability is high when the information comes into the brain in a way that is easy to retrieve. For example, to remember the table of elements, you can divide the list into classifications like metal and nonmetal. This scheme gives you an organized way to search for and recall information.

One instructor of a class on statistics tried to help his students by giving them a framework of philosophy about the material. The students simply wanted answers, not background. As a result they had no way of structuring the information and failed to learn it.

There is more than one way to organize information. You can classify it: apple belongs to fruit which belongs to growing things. This is a vertical scheme, going from top to bottom or bottom to top. Then there is the horizontal order: an apple a day keeps the doctor away, Eve gave Adam an apple, Winesaps make good pies. Both vertical and horizontal schemes enrich the context, the surrounding material that inevitably leads us to what we want to remember.

In any information system there is noise. When you listen to a radio program, there is static. Whether you can hear the signal through the noise depends on how strong the signal is and on how redundant or repetitive the information is. If the information is repeated again and again, we can lose part of the signal and still reconstruct the material we want.

You can increase your chances of remembering a fact by:

- classifying the fact in several ways
- making multiple copies—if one is lost, you still have others

- giving the fact so much context that outside noise can't block it

More memory benefits come from spending an hour trying to recall what you've read than by spending the same time rereading the material. By recalling, you are actively involved in trying to retrieve the information.

Try This . . .

to Test and Enhance Your Powers of Recall

A few seconds ago you read about three ways to remember facts. Without looking, *actively* recall them by writing them down.

Compare what you wrote to the list on the previous page and make any corrections. Now, read over what you wrote. Then shut your eyes and repeat it out loud. You have just reinforced the information three ways: writing, seeing, hearing. Think you'll remember it?

Just the Facts

Remembering facts doesn't have to be a "grind." For a bit of fun, try this "Tribute to the Mystery."

"I can discover facts, Watson," said Sherlock Holmes, "but I cannot change them." In *The Problem of Thor Bridge,* Sir Arthur Conan Doyle put forth one of the most perfect of the great sleuth's cases. All the facts the reader needs to solve the cases are clearly presented. Try to remember each fact as you read it. Then match your solution to Holmes's.

1. Neil Gibson, "the Gold King," was once an American senator of a western state. He now lives on a large country estate in England with his middle-aged wife and their two children who are tended by a pretty young governess.
2. The wife was once a great Brazilian beauty, but her charms have faded. Although she adores her husband, he no longer loves her. He is cruel to her, and there are rumors that he loves the governess.
3. At 11:00 one evening the body of the wife is found a half-mile from the house, in the middle of the roadway a few yards from Thor Bridge.
4. She has been shot at close range in the right temple.
5. No gun is found.
6. The road is hard, and there are no footprints.
7. Clutched tightly in the wife's left hand is a note. "I will be

at Thor Bridge at 9:00." It is signed by the governess who admits writing it. She also admits that she met the wife at the bridge at 9:00, but that the woman was alive when she left her.

8. The next day a gun of the same caliber as the murder weapon is found on the floor of the governess's wardrobe under some dresses. One bullet has been fired from it.

9. Neil Gibson owns many guns. The gun found in the wardrobe is one of a pair, but the other gun cannot be found.

10. The estate manager says he suspects that Gibson, an attractive but ruthless man, has murdered his wife so he can marry the governess. The servants all love and pity their warm-hearted, passionate mistress, while distrusting their cold, arrogant master.

11. The governess says that she found a note on her school desk signed by the wife, asking to meet her that evening at Thor Bridge. It also asked her to leave a reply at the sundial so that Gibson would not know of their meeting. The governess says she left such a note at the sundial, and it is the one found in the murdered woman's hand.

12. The governess says that when she met the wife at the bridge, the woman began screaming jealous accusations at her. The governess put her hands over her ears and fled back to the house. She heard no shot.

13. The governess says that the gun could not have been in her wardrobe the previous day, because she would have seen it.

All this is known to the police. The governess is arrested for murder. She seems to have no chance of acquittal until Sherlock Holmes discovers an additional fact.

14. Sherlock Holmes finds a fresh chip in the underside of the bridge railing, about 15 feet from where the body was found. Although he strikes the rail repeatedly with his heavy cane, he cannot make a similar mark. The stone is too hard.

At this point, Holmes has solved the case. Watson, not so swift as his friend, requires more hints. Here is Watson's final clue.

15. Sherlock Holmes asks why the governess would carry out a carefully premeditated murder and then leave an incriminating note in the dead woman's hand? Why, too, would she carry the gun back to her room, rather than tossing it in the bulrushes below the bridge?

Now stop and decide what conclusions could be reached from the above facts. Have you solved the case? There is another fact that should make everything clear.

16. Sherlock Holmes asks that the area immediately below the white chip on the bridge be dragged. Searchers find the twin to the gun in the wardrobe. It is tied to one end of a 20-foot cord and a heavy rock is tied to the other end. One shot has been fired.

Do you have a final solution now?

Answer

The wife, in a jealous rage, committed suicide after planting evidence to make it look like a murder by her supposed rival. First she took a pair of identical pistols from her husband's collection. She fired one shot from the first gun, probably in the woods where it would not be noticed, and hid it in the governess's wardrobe. Then she met the governess as planned.

After the young woman had fled her jealous outburst, she tied a heavy rock to one end of a cord and tied the other end to the gun. She stretched the cord across the road with the rock hanging over the side of the bridge. She then held the note in her left hand and shot herself in the right temple. As she fell, the gun dropped from her hand and was pulled over the edge of the bridge and into the bulrushes. The metal gun hit the rail with a sharp blow, causing the chip.

The first step to deciding and solving is to remember the facts. The second step is to use them.

18

How to Remember What You Read

Do you ever find yourself reading and rereading a page without knowing what you've read?

If it's fiction and you're not remembering it, then you and the author are probably a bad match. Don't bother with each other. We read fiction either to experience something strange and new or to learn another perspective from someone with very similar experiences to our own in dealing with life.

It's nonfiction that most people want to remember. Whether you are reading for business or pleasure, it helps to recognize five basic patterns that authors use to organize their material.

Structures for Nonfiction Books and Articles

When you walk into a strange house, you can usually find the kitchen or bedroom because you recognize a familiar structure. When you buy a new TV set or a new car, you can usually figure out how to operate it, even if the controls are in a different place than on the one you owned before.

Nonfiction is similar. When you learn to recognize the structure of what you are reading, you can find what you are looking for quickly and easily, and recall the parts that make up the pattern of organization.

As you begin reading, look for the structure. Make a guess and then see if you are right. You can change your mind and try another structure if the first doesn't fit. When you find the structure and then arrange the information bits on that structure, you will have a much better chance of remembering than if you stack all the information up like old magazines in the garage for sorting later.

Speed Reading—Good or Bad?

Some people think that speed reading means skipping over the printed words without really absorbing them. You *can* skim through a book, sailing high over the landscape until you spot what you want and swoop down on it. But that's skimming, not speed reading.

We remember more if we concentrate. We concentrate more if we read at a speed closer to the speed at which we process information—in other words, very fast. When we take in more ideas instead of lingering over each sentence, it is actually easier to notice the information. The difference between casual reading and speed reading is the difference between driving on a flat highway in the desert and on a twisty mountain road. Our concentration rises on the twisty road, and we process much more information. Like mountain driving, speed reading is *work,* but it gives us back much more than it asks.

Misreading

You're sitting on the bus or subway and someone in front of you is holding the latest newspaper with part of the headline obscured. You may be able to fill in the missing part quickly, or you may remain tantalized, needing the missing letters to complete the message.

    RAPE IS
    NO SIN
becomes
  GRAPE IS KING AT
  VINO SINGFEST

when the paper is straightened and unfolded.

Much of our reading (indeed much of life) is filling in the blanks. They can be letters in words or words in sentences. We also fill in meaning, tying things together so they form patterns. Sir Frederick Bartlett used complicated stories to test memory. He found that several kinds of changes occurred when the subjects tried to recall the story later.

Omissions
Parts of the story that were hard to understand or which did not fit the reader's expectations were dropped.

Rationalization
New features were added to explain difficult or confusing parts of the story.

Dominant detail
The reader usually selected a key point to "anchor" the story.

Transformation of detail
Unfamiliar words and concepts were changed to more familiar words or concepts.

Transformation of order
The order was changed. This happened more often with material that was a series of random descriptions than with a tightly organized narrative.

Importance of the subject's attitude
Readers tended to recall their attitude toward a story before they recalled the story. The recall of the story then tended to be a justification of that attitude.

So what we read, like what we hear and see, is subject to misremembering. Let's explore some ways to remember more and remember it better.

The Patterns

Listed below are five main structures for nonfiction: problem, opinion, thesis, information, and instruction. A few pieces of nonfiction are combinations of two or more of these structures, but most of what you read falls into one of these structures.

THE PROBLEM PATTERN

Problem: I need more money.
Effect: outgo exceeds income. Bankruptcy is imminent.
Causes: unemployment.
Solution: find a job, steal, join the army, shoot my rich uncle.

THE OPINION PATTERN

Opinion: the next president should be a woman.
Reasons: women are better business managers, less likely to start wars, and have more compassion for people.
Significance: you should support a woman candidate.

THE THESIS PATTERN

Thesis: alcoholism is caused by a metabolic difference.
Proofs: results of recent experiments.
Significance: testing blood samples from children might prevent alcoholism in adults.

THE INFORMATION PATTERN

Facet 1: location and description of Easter Island.
Facet 2: discovery by early explorers.
Facet 3: current inhabitants.
Facet 4: etc. . . .

THE INSTRUCTION PATTERN

Step 1: place egg in saucepan of cold water.
Step 2: place saucepan on stove.
Step 3: turn burner on to medium heat.
Step 4: etc. . . .

A Need to Know

When you want to remember what you read, but you haven't decided exactly what you'd like to get from your reading effort, try analyzing the structure or organization of the piece. Unless you have a particular purpose or a "need to know," it's easy to fall into your old habit of just passing your eyes from left to right over each word or phrase. Then you end up with a random collection of miscellaneous ideas. This can be very pleasant if you are reading for pleasure only, but when you are reading to remember, you need to sort the information into structures.

Buckminster Fuller said that only 20 percent of a book can consist of new ideas, or the book won't be popular. We need that familiar 80 percent as our structure or framework for positioning the new 20 percent. The trick is to be aware of what you don't know and then use your natural predicting skills and your new knowledge of nonfiction structure to dive in for the new 20 percent.

Start reading with a purpose. It's okay to be tantalized into side-trips if you wish, and you can change your destination along the way, but at least you start out with an itinerary. Having a purpose increases your memory of what you are reading.

Distraction is the enemy of memory. When you look for the organization and the pattern parts, it's like taking an X ray or looking at a map. Have you ever found your mind wandering when you were lost and examining a road map? It's unlikely. You had a purpose (figuring out where you were) and a structure (a map full of streets, highways, and landmarks). Reading to remember requires the same two things. The structure has an added bonus: by organizing the material you read into the nonfiction pattern, you *pay attention* to it and probably remember it better.

Is all information arranged logically? Of course not! There are miserable writers, misguided editors, and inept publishers. If you run into any of these, you may have to rewrite the information in your own head in order to remember it.

Try This . . .

to Test Your Memory of What You Read

If remembering what you read is important to you, you might like to take the following quizzes on material in this book.

The Problem Pattern

Reread chapter 2, "Emotional Blocks," looking for the problem, effects, causes, and solutions. Then fill in these sentences.

The problem is_____.
Some effects are_____.
Some causes are_____.
Some solutions are_____.

The Opinion Pattern

Reread chapter 5, "When It's Okay to Forget," looking for the opinion, reasons, and significance. Then fill in these sentences.

The opinion is_____.
The reasons are_____.
(List supports for each reason if you wish.)
The significance is_____.

The Thesis Pattern

We don't have a classic thesis-pattern chapter in this book, but you can learn how to look for working hypotheses by spotting the theories in chapter 7, "How the Brain Remembers." Skim this chapter, looking for the four current theories on how the brain stores information. Now list the theories on how the brain remembers.

The Information Pattern

Turn to chapter 11, "Four Ways to Remember." Get a pencil and read through the chapter fairly quickly, making a pencil slash wherever the facet (the subject being discussed) changes. Then go back and write a heading for each facet, describing the contents. Compare them to the answers.

The Instruction Pattern
　　　Turn ahead and read chapter 20, "How to Remember Names and Faces," stopping on page 239. Then list the five steps to remembering names.

Answers

The Problem Pattern—chapter 2, "Emotional Blocks."
Problem: Emotions can block memory. (Memory blocks can be a casual annoyance, a major inconvenience, or a life-threatening disaster.)

Effects:
　　　People "go blank."
　　　Negative feelings about self: frustration, embarrassment, disappointment, guilt.
　　　Blocks threaten job, personal relationships.
　　　　　Also:
　　　　　• Gisela couldn't remember men's names at work.
　　　　　• Mary couldn't remember lyrics of songs.
　　　　　• Louise couldn't remember first names.
　　　　　• Dan couldn't remember police station phone number.
　　　　　• Barbara couldn't remember addresses and phone numbers.
　　　　　• Rose could not remember how to read.
　　　　　• Leslie misplaced things.

Causes: caring, conflict, self-protection.

Solutions:
　　　Discard blocks because you don't need them anymore.
　　　Develop new strategies for dealing with them.
　　　Accept blocks.

The Opinion Pattern—chapter 5, "When It's Okay to Forget."
Opinion: It's okay for forget some things.

Reasons:
　　　Forgetting can be safer (forgetting for self-preservation)—protecting ourselves from danger.

- Doctor forgot to return call to avoid disturbed patient.
- Student forgot to file crucial forms and avoided being accepted at law school.
- Woman forgot husband's death to concentrate on baby.

Forgetting painful experiences—enables us to function despite pain.

- Toddlers forget bumps and learn to walk.
- Women forget pain of childbirth and have another child.

Forgetting sorrow—enables us to survive tragedy.

Forgetting for attention and support—gets us needed help.

- Harry got attention at office by not shaving.
- Eunice got help of children by forgetting insurance.

Forgetting because you are finished.

Significance:
Forgetting can be healthful.
- It's okay to forget—when you have to . . .
  when you need to . . .
  when you want to . . .
  as long as it doesn't hurt you.

Also:
Negative memories can be used for humor, future income, and to reinforce positive future actions.

Healthy people can choose their memories.

Healthy people can "rehearse" positive mental images to replace negative ones.

The Thesis Pattern—chapter 7, "How the Brain Remembers."

Theories on how we remember

1. *Holographic theory*—memory occurs in all parts of the brain simultaneously.
2. *Mechanical theory*—information is stored physically on neurons.
3. *Electrical theory*—information is transmitted by electrical signals.
4. *Chemical theory*—information changes the chemical structure of the neurons.

The Information Pattern—chapter 11, "Four Ways to Remember."

Facet 1:	paragraph 1	Introduction
Facet 2:	paragraphs 2–3	Differences between episodic and semantic memory
Facet 3:	paragraphs 4–8	Episodic memory
Facet 4:	paragraphs 9–22	Semantic memory
Facet 5:	paragraph 23	History of skill and fact memory
Facet 6:	paragraphs 24–26	Evidence of skill and fact division
Facet 7:	paragraphs 27–30	Current research on skill and fact division
Facet 8:	paragraphs 31–37	Role of hippocampus in skill and fact memory
Facet 9:	paragraph 38	Importance of research into memory

The Instruction Pattern—chapter 20, "How to Remember Names and Faces."
How to remember names.

1. Decide to remember.
2. Be impressed before you hear the name.

3. Listen to the name, then match the name to your impression.
4. Repeat the name.
5. Lock the name to the face.

Also: Make a survival kit of things to say when you can't remember immediately.

19

How to Remember What You Hear

Remembering what you hear requires the same structuring tools you use to remember what you read, with one important exception—what is said is not always what is meant.

When we "listen," we interpret more than just the words we hear. We hear the tone of voice, see the body posture and facial expressions (unless we are on the telephone), get subtle or not-so-subtle inferences from the context and atmosphere.

For instance, here is what was *said*. What do you think was *meant*?

- "Oh, I couldn't possibly have any dessert. I'm on a diet."
- "I'm sure you have much better things to do than waste an evening playing checkers with your old grandpa."
- "Of course, if you want to have an affair with your secretary, go right ahead. We don't *own* each other . . ."

Did you "hear" anything in those statements that wasn't actually stated? Rightly or wrongly, we often hear things that aren't said. Criticism is an especially delicate area. A child who is criticized in moderate tones may respond, "Don't shout at me!" "My boss really yelled at me," is another commonly heard phrase, although the boss may have spoken softly.

As in reading, you often hear what you expect to hear or want to hear. A carefully phrased refusal may leave a lover or job applicant still hopeful if he chooses to overlook the negative whole for the positive tone.

Understanding what you hear is the first step in remembering it. This may be a skill you were born with. Just as some people most clearly understand and remember things they see, others need to hear it before it is locked in their memory. A good example of this was the experience of Stella, the head of the publications department of a major corporation. She found that much of her day was spent on the phone, *reading* portions of the company's *Manual of Procedures* to puzzled employees. It wasn't that the written description wasn't clear. These employees simply didn't understand the information until they *heard* it.

Fortunately, most of us absorb information both visually and aurally and can use one to reinforce the other. Students who take notes while listening to a lecturer are doing this and so are the people who read important instructions out loud to themselves. They are hearing and seeing the information at the same time.

Speed Listening

Processing the information we hear presents the same problems as processing the information we read, only more so. No one can talk as fast as we can listen, even those salesmen on television. The split second left over after we have absorbed one word and are waiting for the next gives us lots of time for mind wandering. Probably you have been at a lecture or at church or a meeting and found that your mind "took off" from something that was said. You miss several minutes of the speaker's comments while you mentally elaborate on or rebut an earlier remark.

Sometimes this can be very valuable—your conclusions outshine the speaker's and give you a new insight into the problem. But if you really need to hear what is *said,* you can set up a system to keep you anchored during the spaces between words.

- Predict what the speaker will say next.
- Confirm that prediction.
- Note your success or failure on a mental tote board. Fill in the listening gaps with this activity. *Don't* let your mind drift off into wondering why your prediction "failed," or you're back where you started.

Recently a process has been developed that will permit speed-recording for the blind. In the past, blind people have had access to magazines and newspapers through recordings. This is a slow, tedious method—imagine reading every word of your morning paper. But now it is possible to clip milliseconds out of a tape, speeding up the voice without rasing it to a Minnie Mouse pitch. This is indeed speed listening and may find many uses among sighted listeners also.

Mishearing

I estimate that about 40 percent of spoken communication is either not heard or misheard. This may be a low guess. The wonder is that the other 60 percent gets through.

An incredible amount of talk is just friendly noise, a sort of social glue acknowledging that other people are present and letting them know you are there too. "How are you doing?" "Have a nice weekend." "Lovely weather." "Boy, are these buses slow." Much of what you hear is unimportant, uninteresting, or unrelated to you.

The chances of mishearing in English are great. We have homonyms: tide/tied, die/dye, plane/plain. We have poor pronunciation: use/youse, go on/gone, grandma/grammar. Simple words have multiple meanings: bill, check, let. Poor grammar can sabotage meaning. Hear are three real examples:

- Our tuxedos are cut ridiculously.
- Police kill six coyotes after mauling girl.
- Shoes are required to eat in the dining room.

Analyzing What You Hear

Remember the people who were shown a film of two cars running into each other (page 23)? Half were asked, "How fast were the cars going when they *contacted* each other?" The other half were asked, "How fast were the cars going when they *smashed* into each other?" Guess which group thought the cars were going the fastest?

What we hear can easily be colored by the emotions of the moment, by the skills of the speaker, by the power of the words themselves. Shakespeare was good at writing crowd-motivating speeches. Think of Mark Antony in *Julius Caesar* who turns all Rome against the hero Brutus with a few sentences. Or the incredible St. Crispian speech in *Henry V* that changes Henry's dispirited rag-tag troops into invincible warriors. John F. Kennedy is said to have quoted this speech to his advisors during the Cuban missile crisis when the world seemed a hair's breadth away from nuclear destruction.

Listening to Silence

Neurologist Richard M. Restak tells of a professor leaving a faculty meeting. He remarked to several of his colleagues that the matter they had discussed was certain to be approved. "Why do you say that?" one of them asked. The professor listed the distinguished speakers who had spoken in favor of the proposal. "Yes," replied the other, "but the meeting arrived at the opposite conclusion, and the motion was defeated. You heard the words spoken, but you didn't understand the silences between them."

Giving Directions

Psychologist Douglas Kingsbury stopped people on the street and asked them how to get to a nearby place. He found that when he dressed and acted like a "local" the instructions were brief but adequate. When he assumed the air of an out-of-towner, people gave much longer, more detailed instructions. He concluded that we base our communication on how we perceive the knowledge and background of the listener. A cook who seems experienced will be told, "Sauté the chicken." An obvious novice will be told: "Get out a heavy iron skillet and put it on the stove. Turn on the burner. When the pan is hot, put in some butter or shortening . . .”

When Everyone Talks at Once

Everybody is excited and everybody starts talking at once. Since no one responds to what you have said (the others are too busy talking), you repeat yourself . . . only louder. The result is bedlam and wasted time.

Sound familiar? Try this trick. Create a diversion to provide a moment of silence—drop something or sprawl full-length on the floor—then say, “Let's take turns, starting with the youngest.” While everyone tries to figure that out, order is restored, and a one-at-a-time approach allows each speaker to feel *heard*. Constant repetition in a conversation usually means that the speaker doesn't feel he has made his point, that he is not being listened to. You can save lots of precious time by *listening*.

Inadmissible Evidence

Ear-witness testimony may be more suspect than previously supposed, according to one study by University of Florida anthropologists. They found that most people can't remember with whom they talked the previous week. People were able to estimate correctly how many conversations they had had, but half the time they couldn't remember with whom they spoke. This indicates that courtroom reconstructions of conversations may be less than accurate.

Structuring What You Hear

Structuring what you hear is similar to structuring what you read, only harder because the most organized person rarely speaks in a straight line from A to B. Speech is a “hot” medium, easily deflected by the response of the listener and the rushing thoughts of the speaker. “I don't know what I'm going to say, until I hear myself say it,” said semanticist Wendell Johnson in his book *People in Quandries: The Semantics of Personal Adjustment* (New York: Harper & Row, 1946). And sometimes, even then, neither the speaker nor the listener knows what was said.

Try This . . .

to Sharpen Your Listening Memory

Let's do some exercises to structure what is being said. Have someone read the following passages aloud to you and try to arrange the information logically, just as you did in reading.

Your wife says:

We have a lot to do before the party tonight. I don't know if we have enough glasses. Could you call your brother, George, and ask him to bring ice when he comes if he's coming before 7:00. If he won't get here until later, ask Harriet to pick it up on her way home from work. The tablecloths are still in the dryer, and the folding chairs have to be brought up from the basement. I suppose George can do that if he comes early. I don't know if we have enough glasses. I better go get those tablecloths out of the dryer before they get wrinkled. Do you think your brother and Harriet will hit it off?

You just got a lot of extraneous information. Your goals here are to decide what you were being asked to do and arrange them in proper sequence.

Here's what you should have "heard."

Call George and see if he is coming before 7:00 P.M.

If yes: (a) ask him to bring ice; (b) tell your wife he will be early, so he will bring the ice and can help carry the chairs up from the basement.

If no: (a) call Harriet and ask her to buy ice on her way home from work; (b) tell your wife that Harriet is bringing the ice, and you will have to carry the chairs up from the basement.

Optional: count the glasses.

That was a typical family situation. Now try one that you may have run into in your business life. Your boss, Mr. Fickle, also likes to "think out loud."

Mr. Fickle says:

I need some cigarettes from the drugstore downstairs. Get me a carton of Camel Lights and charge it to my wife's account. Try to get Steve to take care of you because the older guy may give you a hard time. Before you go down, take this report to Mr. Samson on the 13th floor in the annex and give it to his secretary. If she's not there, get somebody to sign for it. Last month some jerk lost the report and I got my tail chewed. Make two Xeroxes of it just to be safe. One of those copies has to go to headquarters today, so drop it off at shipping, but tell them to send it book rate. Mr. Samson says we're spending too much on postage, so if it takes longer to get there, that's his sweet problem. Do you think something's wrong in his department? He's been crabby as the devil lately.

This was a hard one, but typical of many busy offices. Most of what was said was instructions, spoken and implied, but it certainly wasn't in order. You might even have had to grab a pencil and write down what was wanted to be sure you got it all.

Here's what you were being asked to do.

1. Address an envelope to headquarters (implied).
2. Make two photocopies of the report. Place one copy in the envelope you just addressed.
3. Deliver the original report to Mr. Samson's secretary on the 13th floor in the annex. If she is not there, leave the report with someone else and get a signed receipt.
4. Deliver the "headquarters" envelope containing the photocopied report to shipping and ask them to send it by U.S. mail at book rate.
5. Buy a carton of Camel Lights at the drugstore and charge them to Mrs. Fickle's account. Try to be waited on by the younger clerk.
6. File the second photocopy of the report as a backup, in case one of the other copies is lost (implied).

Remember that the skills acquired in the mail room will serve you equally well in the board room. Getting instructions from a teacher, coworker, or salesperson can be tricky. See how much of the following you actually need to remember, and try to organize it into a sequence.

The paint store salesperson says:

Put the stain on with a soft cloth and really rub it in. If you try to use a brush, it will be too thick, and the surface will dry while the underneath part is still wet. Then you'll get a rippled surface because the hard top skates over the wet bottom. Did I tell you that you have to thin the stain with alcohol? Don't use turpentine, or it will separate. The lighter colors really look good in this finish, but I think the dark color you've chosen will be okay. You have to seal it afterwards with two or three coats of clear plastic, otherwise the rain will soak in and warp the wood. Oh, but you're using it inside, so that's not a problem, but be sure you wash the wood with alcohol first to open the pores.

You had to discard some of the information you got here. If you put the remainder in a working sequence, it should come out like this:

1. Wash the wood first with alcohol.
2. Thin the stain with alcohol if necessary.
3. Rub the stain into the wood thoroughly with a soft cloth.
4. The salesperson doesn't like dark stains.

20

How to Remember Names and Faces

What's the worst thing that can happen when you forget a name or a face? In a Hollywood thriller it might mean getting shot at sunrise or losing the million dollar inheritance. In real life it is rarely so devastating.

What *is* the worst thing?

- "I might get fired."
- "I lose important business contacts."
- "My employees think I don't care about them."
- "I feel like a nerd."

If someone walked up to you and said, "I'll give you $1,000 if you can remember that my name is Fred Jones," you would probably be able to remember "Fred Jones." First of all, he has made himself memorable. Secondly he has given you a way to enhance yourself personally by remembering him. This what's-in-it-for-me is important, though the reward doesn't have to be monetary or even a social advantage. It can also be the joy of curiosity rewarded.

People who don't remember people may be protecting themselves.

- Some people are trying to avoid overload and may be acting sensibly—"Why remember the 50 people at that party or all my child's classmates when I probably will never encounter them again?"

234

- Some people may be enjoying a bit of egomania—
  "I am much too important to bother remembering
  people."
- Some people may see themselves as helpless to
  control the comings and goings of those around
  them. They avoid bereavement by deciding, "I
  won't miss you if I don't give you a name or a
  face."
- And for some people all of life is threatening—
  "The world is full of dark and terrible creatures
  ready to zap me, so I won't give them any more
  power over me by allowing them names and
  faces." (This is a popular device of little kids that
  can extend into adulthood if we're not careful.)

People who don't remember people should consider whether
they still need to protect themselves or whether the method
has outlived its usefulness.

People who *remember* people are usually those who
retain their sense of wonder. Once my friend's three-year-old
daughter opened the door and stared in astonishment at the
visitor on the porch. "Oh, mommy," she cried, "come see
how much makeup the lady's wearing!" When the child in us
is struck with the novelty of those we meet, we can approach
each new person with the same enthusiasm and percep-
tiveness.

Sharing a Common Weakness

People rarely disclose their true shortcomings to other
people. Instead they expose their subtle vices, assuming that
the perceptive listener will see them as the virtues they are.

- "I have such a weakness for emeralds."
- "I guess I'm hard to work for—I'm such a perfec-
  tionist."
- "I have a terrible memory for names."

In fact, when someone says, "I can't remember names
(or faces)," he is usually doing something very close to
bragging. He may think he is establishing a sense of cama-

raderie by showing he shares a common weakness. He is also warning you in advance that he is not responsible for remembering you or anyone else he meets.

Do we have a choice about forgetting or remembering people? Yes. Here are two sets of "How To's" for you to choose from.

HOW TO FORGET PEOPLE
WHEN YOU'RE INTRODUCED

Be preoccupied—worry about what they think of you.
Be distracted—think about what you will say.

HOW TO REMEMBER PEOPLE
WHEN YOU'RE INTRODUCED

Decide to remember. How many names and faces have you forgotten when you really made an effort?

Be impressed . . . before you hear the name. Use the first three seconds to notice a person's characteristics. Pick something positive or negative. Look with the eyes of a child. You can change your mind later if you want.

What if the person has no outstanding characteristics, is mousy and almost invisible? Then play "Knock, knock, who's there." Make up a story to dramatize the person in your mind. "She works for the CIA" or "He's really a male stripper" or "Where's the last place in the world I'd expect to meet this person?"

Exercise: talk to someone you plan *not* to remember and, as you remain passive, be aware of what is passing through your mind when you *don't* focus on the name. This awareness will help you to be in charge of forgetting or remembering, two very different behaviors.

Listen to the name. Then ask yourself if this name matches your initial impression. It doesn't matter if your answer is yes or no. The point is you've made a decision that will affect your memory. Have you met a beautiful girl named Euphemia? A straightforward young man named Marmaduke? A man named Carol or a girl named Sydney? We tend to define the aptness of names by people we know. Sheilas should look a certain way. Unless you decide *why* this

Ask yourself if the name matches your initial impression.

Sheila is different, you may forget her because she doesn't match your template.

Memory lecturer Hermine Hilton suggests that we categorize names as we meet new people. The energy spent mentally filing a name under one or more of various headings helps us retrieve it later. She recommends the following categories:

- The same as someone I know?
- The same as a celebrity?
- An occupation (Singer, Shoemaker, Smith)?
- A thing (Cane, Woods, Car)?
- A brand name (Campbell, Kellogg, Ford)?
- Can you rhyme it?
- Can you convert it to a familiar word or words (Askew to ask-you)?
- Can you make a euphonious description (Jovial Jones, Smiling Smith)?
- Can you translate it (Morgenstern is morning star)?

Perhaps you can devise your own system for categorizing names that will make them memorable to you.

Repeat the name. Is it Dan or Don? Joan or Joann? When meeting a lot of people at once, slow down and try to lock on each one. Ask a question. "John? How do you spell your last name? Are you from New York, too?" Say your name so they can get an auditory image of you. Shake hands.

Maybe that's one reason why shaking hands has stayed in fashion. It's an excellent slowing-down process and can work as a kinesthetic reinforcement.

It's also very flattering to turn to someone you've been chatting with for a few minutes at a party and say, "Tell me your name again." This helps you and lets them know you are interested in them.

Lock the name to the face. As the song from the musical *Gypsy* says, "Ya gotta have a gimmick." Her name is Joan. Imagine her on a horse as Joan of Arc. Does the name translate into another language? Boulanger—the baker? Verdi—green? Schwartz—black? Can you use that to remember them? Mr. Boulanger has French bread for ears. Miss Verdi is eating great strings of green Italian pasta. Mr. Schwartz has blond hair, so he belies his name—imagine black dye pouring over his handsome hair as he looks distressed. Pick an image—silly, bizarre, even obscene. Here's a typical workshop group.

Peggy Lindsay
Linseed oil? Imagine oil poured over her peg-like head. One student imagines Lindsay Water Softener—she's soft and cuddly. Or you might summon up images of former New York mayor John Lindsay or the bionic woman, actress Lindsay Wagner. Peggy's freckles might remind you of a pegboard. How about "Piggy"? Do her mannerisms suggest the bravura style of Miss Piggy, or is she shy and modest?

Nancy Smith
"Antsy?" Are ants crawling all over her face? Smith—imagine two horseshoes around her eyes. Or she has muscles like Longfellow's Village Smithy who stood under the spreading chestnut tree.

Al Fredericks
A free derrick? Alley for "Al"? Make a mental bowling alley out of his nose. Alexander the Great and Frederick the Great? A great guy, Al!

Giles Langlois
Foreign names can be hard because we have no

preconceived notions. Here's where reading *The Three Musketeers* proves helpful. If you aren't a Dumas buff, try rhyming Giles with heel and Langlois with Bang-Wah. Imagine him hopping about in pain after banging his heel.

The more far-fetched the images, the more likely you are to remember them, but try to be specific. There may come a day when you call Mr. Lambreth "Mr. Ramsbottom."

Ask if you don't remember. Sometimes we forget names when we run into someone because we are so anxious to remember them that we panic. Try saying, "Where did we meet last time?" or, "How long has it been?" which gives you a few extra seconds and may furnish the clue you need. Or say, "I know we've met and I am not remembering your name . . ." Or, "We've had such good conversations, but your name has slipped right out of my head."

Memorable Names

A lovely red-haired woman waited on me in a New York store. I overheard her name as "Bridgit O'Keary" and complimented her on her "fine Irish name." "Actually my last name is 'Okuri,'" she replied. "My husband is Japanese." That's a name I've never forgotten.

Names that mix nationalities can be memorable. The Nanette Kennedy Laundry used to be a source of amusement to my friends . . . until Jacqueline Kennedy graced the White House. Ming Toy Epstein, Boris Lopez, or Sean Giacometti would be hard to forget. As the global village becomes smaller, such international mixings will be more common, but right now such names are pure gold for name-rememberers.

"Naughty" Names

Some people have memorable names through no fault of their own. People named "Gay," "Pratt," "Knocker," or "Tush" face unfair snickers because their very proper names have at one time or another been appropriated as slang words.

A friend of mine grew up in the state of Washington where few people knew Yiddish. When he went away to college in New York, he was astonished that his name was greeted with laughter when a professor called the roster. He didn't know that *Putz,* literally "clean" in German, had quite a different slang meaning in Yiddish. In fact, a Yiddish dictionary warned that, "*putz* is worse than *schmuck,* and should not be used by anyone unfamiliar with the martial arts."

Sometimes it's pronunciation, not translation, that gets giggles. Fine names like Lipschitz, Pissi, and Foq have unfortunate connotations in English.

During World War II, I went to school with a boy named Adolph. It was a fine family name, but the poor boy was teased mercilessly by his classmates who constantly gave him the Nazi salute. He was wild and unruly and did poorly in school until his parents changed his name to Franklin. Obviously names are very powerful stuff, one of the most intimate things we possess, and we can use that power to remember other people's names.

How to Remember Faces

Have you ever murmured, "Nice to have met you" to someone you encounter with a friend and found out later you had met him many times before? He had just never made an impression on you, or you didn't recognize him when you ran into him away from his usual setting. If you plead that you lack a strong visual memory, then the trick is to convert what you see at the moment into verbal information. Try pinpointing physical characteristics, not necessarily flattering ones, and locking them to the names. Warning: weight, beards, and hairstyles (even hair color) are all subject to sudden changes. Use them, but back them up with the shape of the eyes, nose, mouth, ears, and hairline.

Overall impression seems to be more important in recognizing faces than any particular feature. Notice—

- physical characteristics
- posture and attitude
- mannerisms

Most portraits show a three-quarter view of the face, giving the best impression of the relationship of the different features. Front and profile views are dramatic, but less informative. (This may be one reason that those Post Office mug shots rarely look like anyone we know.)

Most people would have trouble identifying a friend or a well-known person from just their eyes, ears, or nose unless that feature were outstanding and unique—Barbra Streisand's nose or Joan Crawford's eyes, for instance. But used as part of a bigger framework, they can be valuable clues to recall.

Start with the eyes. Are they round like an owl's? Perhaps they are triangular or oval. Do the brows slant, arch, march straight across? Now that you've noticed (half the work), try making up silly shorthand names for the characteristics, names that will stick in your memory. Repeat this with other features. Then lock them to the name. Let's try it with our original workshop group.

Peggy Lindsay
Linseed oil pouring over a peg-like head. The peg is a round one in a square hole because her eyes are round, and her jaw is square. The oil is golden like her eyes. It will pour off quickly because her eyebrows slant down at the sides.

Nancy Smith
Ants are crawling on her face which has two horseshoes around her eyes. The ants will be especially attracted to her mouth which is tiny and sweet like a gumdrop. The horses will want to drink from her lake-blue eyes and graze in the thick lashes surrounding them.

Al Fredericks
His nose is a bowling alley owned by an Italian because it is a Roman nose. His chin is a free derrick, his square jaw the shovel. Bulging tendons run up his neck to manipulate the derrick. The alley continues over his high forehead to his receding hairline, where—strike!—he sports a toupee.

Giles Langlois
He is hopping about from pain in his heel (heel bang-wah!), and his eyes are squinty with pain. His nose is a bulging one like a sore heel, and his ears have shrunk to a small size, so they won't hear his shouting.

All of the above is utter nonsense, of course, and much of it may be totally useless to you. The point is that you will make your own images, meaningful to you, and the effort you put into it will probably lock that person in your mind for good. You may even decide that all the tricks are too cumbersome, and it is easier just to remember.

How Well Do You Remember?

Some people say, "Oh, I never forget a face," or "I can never remember names." While most people are relatively good at predicting how successfully they will remember different items on a list, few people are accurate judges of their overall memory ability. In England, 100 housewives were asked to rate their memory for faces. Then they were tested with a series of slides. There proved to be no relationship between how well they did and how well they thought they would do.

Memory for faces may depend on a particular system located in the brain. Patients who suffer from prosopagnosia, a rare neurological condition, can't recognize faces, but can recognize other objects. Memory for faces is still being studied. Doctors have found that babies recognize their mothers from a small portion of their total face. Large portions of the mother's face could be masked and the baby would still recognize her, but when the crucial area—containing an eye and cheek area—was covered, the baby would respond as if she were a stranger.

Even newborns can recognize face-shaped designs. Dr. R. Fanz projected two designs on the ceiling over the cribs of infants only hours old. One design resembled a human face. The other contained the same features, rearranged into an abstract pattern. The infants preferred gazing at the face-like design.

Most people have trouble recognizing faces when the face is upside-down. However, patients with right brain damage were tested on ability to recognize faces and buildings, both right side up and upside-down. These patients did poorly on upright faces, compared to the control group, but they could recognize upside-down faces more readily. Both groups did almost equally well with famous buildings.

Divide and Conquer?

One theory is that dividing faces into parts helps us recognize them. In a treatise on painting, Leonardo da Vinci described dividing the face into four parts horizontally for classification. Recently Jacques Penry developed the "Photo-fit System," a set of pictures of noses, chins, ears, etc. He said that study of these parts would improve ability to recognize and remember faces. Students learned how to "read" faces by abstracting and categorizing types of features. But when students who had taken intensive Photo-fit training were tested against a control group by impartial observers, both groups did just as well, except in one photo-recognition test. In that test, the untutored group did *better*. One interpretation of this experiment is that the principle of dividing the face to recognize it is faulty. It's the relationship of the whole that we recognize, not separate parts.

Misnaming

"When I'm in the same house with my wife and sister," said a man in one of my workshops, "I start calling each by the other's name. My sister doesn't mind, but my wife gets mad as hell. Why do I do this?"

"What sort of things are you saying when you mix up their names?" I asked.

"Oh, stuff like, 'When do we eat?' or, 'Have you seen the paper?' Nothing heavy."

"Do you like your sister?"

"Sure."

"And do you like your wife?"

"Yeah!"

Now, it's possible to make a great deal of misnaming

people. Pure Freudians might suggest everything from repressed incest to open hostility. But in this case, the answer seemed simpler.

I suggested that he really didn't care which of them he asked, that these were neutral exchanges, and it really didn't matter whether he was talking to his wife or sister. "You chose your wife partially because she had qualities you liked in your sister, mother, and other women you knew as a child. She may even have unpleasant qualities you associated with the other women in your life, but they were faults that you felt 'comfortable' dealing with. It doesn't matter that you mix them up in these neutral social situations. What *does* matter is that it upsets your wife. Your goal is probably to make a 'present' to your wife of never calling her by your sister's name."

I recommended that when he found himself in the company of both women, he pause before addressing either and concentrate on the name. Or if that concentration took too much enjoyment out of the situation, he could always fall back on the Hollywood trick:

> Get into the habit of calling them 'dear'
> For it not only sounds very sweet,
> It helps to avoid the continual fear
> Of calling 'Louise' 'Marguerite.'

Children sometimes call mommy "daddy" and vice versa. This is not because the child can't tell the difference, but because both are providers of things wanted. A mother may be crushed when her little darling calls her "Teacher" after returning from school or "Grandma" after a vacation with grandparents, but this is perfectly natural. If, in a moment of passion, a husband calls his second wife by his first wife's name, this *may* be significant and is *definitely* dangerous.

Why Fictional Names Are Unforgettable

The names of fictional characters can stick in our memories better than the names of real people. This is because we may have few associations with the real people—we don't really "know" them well—while the fictional characters have rich personalities and, frequently, deliberately memorable names. Most people would recognize the names of Romeo and Juliet, Simon Legree, Camille, Captain Bligh, Dr. Frankenstein, Sadie Hawkins, King Kong, Mary Poppins, and Mildred Pierce.

Consider the colorful characters of Dickens: Ebenezer Scrooge, Uriah Heep, Mr. Bumble, Mr. Pickwick and Mr. Fezziwig, Tiny Tim and Little Nell. Or Tennessee Williams's way with names: Mrs. Wire, Stanley Kowalski, Amanda Wingfield, Alexandra Del Lago, Chance Wayne, and Heavenly Finley. The names stand out before we learn anything about the characters, and when we have added something about their physical appearance and character, they are locked in our brains.

Stage Names

Actors need memorable names. (Rosemary Clooney said she knew she had become famous when people began accusing her of changing her name—"*Who* would change [her] name to 'Rosemary Clooney'?") In the old days, many proudly used their own unusual names and endowed them with the magic of their personalities—Humphrey Bogart, Francis X. Bushman, Una Merkel, and Ida Lupino, for example. Others, rightly or wrongly, opted for name changes. Several used their middle names. Just plain Bill Gable became Clark; Eldred Peck became Gregory. Their new names were probably easier to remember. Then there were the manufactured names: Rock Hudson (Roy Scherer), Tab Hunter (Arthur Gelien), and Troy Donahue (Meryl Johnson.)

We can regret the loss of the highly memorable and colorful names of Eunice Quedens, Archie Leach, Joe Yule, and Tula Ellice Finklea. These sprightly monikers were tamed to the bland (Eve Arden, Cary Grant), the cute (Mickey Rooney), and the exotic (Cyd Charisse). Today there is a simultaneous resurgence of "real names" (Meryl Streep, Tovah Feldshuh, Dustin Hoffman) and conjured ones (Engelbert Humperdinck, Sid Vicious, Alice Cooper). The purpose of a performer's name, whenever it was acquired, is to make him unforgettable and to reinforce his public image.

Maybe if we could choose our own names upon reaching our majority (as is done in some cultures) so that they reflected our adult selves, names would be much harder to forget.

Strategies for Coping with Memory Lapses

The mayor of a large university town was well known to most of the residents, but there was almost no way he could have remembered the 40,000 or so people who "knew" *him*. However, he developed a useful technique for the times he appeared in public. When someone approached him with a smile of recognition, he would peer at them over his glasses and then extend his hand—"Well, *hello* there, I didn't recognize you for a moment. How have you been?" This got him over the first moments of the encounter and probably got him some votes besides.

One doctor has practiced for 30 years, training thousands of students. When they come up to him to say hello, he usually says jovially, "Well, who the hell are you anyway?" His wife is less flamboyant. She says, "I remember you very well, but your name has slipped my mind."

Give yourself permission to say one of the above. (I recommend the latter.) Otherwise, you're playing "Let's pretend"—"Let's pretend I can remember the name of everyone I've ever met."

Make up a survival kit of things to tell yourself and to tell other people. Suffering is optional when it comes to remembering names. Taking good care of yourself and keeping a sense of humor are the important things.

The people who are going to think that you're a creep for not remembering their names are probably not the kind of people you want in your life anyway. Who do you have fun with? Usually people with high nurturing and low critical attitudes.

Some of us are in the habit of harassing ourselves. We may have been brought up by very critical parents who wanted us to be perfect. Perfection comes in handy when you are flying a plane or building a nuclear reactor, but it is a nuisance most of the time. People who had a "do your best" upbringing seem to remember better than those who were told they had to be perfect.

NEW STRATEGIES FOR REMEMBERING PEOPLE

You're so shy that you want to drop through the floor when someone says "hello." Or you're so involved in your own thoughts that you're rarely aware of the people around you. If you're not interested in people or if you're basically shy and feel you need to protect yourself from confrontation, involvement, or unwelcome requests, you won't remember the people you see. This can be valuable when striding down a crowded city street. Not noticing leaves your mind free to think of other things. But not noticing can become a bad habit that haunts you when it would be better to notice.

Here's a way to start noticing again. Begin a writer's notebook, real or imaginary, to write down characteristics of strangers for a novel you will write some day. Note quirks—bitten fingernails on a beautiful woman; dangling earlobes on a jogger; chipped front teeth, indicating perhaps a seamstress who bites her thread; an elegantly dressed man with raw, red, workman's hands or a laborer with soft, white hands unaccustomed to work; an old woman who walks like a ballet dancer; a teenager who alternately swaggers and scurries like a scared rabbit. Make up stories about total strangers on the street, across the aisle on the bus, or ahead of you in line at the bank. Once you can do this with strangers, try it with someone you want to remember.

YOUR LAST OPTION

You have one last option: choose *not* to be embarrassed when you forget. Feeling mortified or guilty or stupid is a choice. If you choose to be comfortable despite your lapse, you will have a much greater chance of recalling the name or the face.

Survival Kit

What to say if the name won't come to you:

"It's been so long. When was the last time we met?"

"I remember you so well . . . your name has slipped my mind."

"I loved your speech at the meeting last month. Tell me your name again."

Introduce an old, but temporarily nameless, friend to a new acquaintance with, "This is Mary Jones," and hope he replies by saying, "Hi, I'm Harvey Smith."

And behaviorist B. F. Skinner proposes a conspiratorial strategy in his book *Enjoy Old Age* (with Margaret Vaughn, New York: W. W. Norton & Company, 1983). For this you need a congenial partner (mate, friend, business associate, etc.). When a familiar stranger approaches you at a gathering, shake his or her hand and turn to your partner saying, "Of course you remember. . . ." Your partner immediately extends a hand and replies, "Of course! How *are* you?" (If you are the conspiratorial partner, you may be able to fill in by adding the person's name. If you've never seen the person before, you are free to approach him later alone and say, "Tell me your name again. I didn't want Sam to know it had slipped my mind.")

Try This . . .

Exercise for Remembering Names and Faces

The Name Game

Here's a game that may tell you something about how and why you remember names. Read over the list below.

Bob Baker	Molly Quinn
Rosanna Calcese	Sue Wong
Lazarus Hennenberg	Mary Foster
Marie DuBois	Horst Egensperger
Juan Lopez	Vincent Yoshihiro
Rose Cohen	Clyde Wyndham
Riordan McIlhenny	Eva Weber
LaTonya Robison	Jackson Davis
Cynthia Petherbridge	Etienne Giradoux
Gino Romano	Imelda Hermosilla

After you've looked them over, close the book and write down as many of the 20 names as you can remember, in any order you wish.

Check your answers, and note the number you got correct.

That was probably very hard. I'll make it a little easier for you. Try the quiz that follows.

Below are the original 20 names combined with 20 new ones. Take your pencil and check off the ones that look familiar.

_____	Lisa Dupree	_____	Joella Vincent
_____	Molly Quinn	_____	Bob Baker
_____	Sid Goldstein	_____	Jim Jordon
_____	Edward Temby	_____	Rosanna Calcese
_____	Sue Wong	_____	Benito Bustamente
_____	Mary Foster	_____	Lazarus Hennenberg
_____	Leticia Long	_____	Fifi d'Orsay
_____	Horst Egensperger	_____	Marie DuBois
_____	Fleyda Vetch	_____	Max Glotzbach
_____	Rhonda Weber	_____	Juan Lopez

_____ Vincent Yoshihiro	_____ Rose Cohen
_____ Clyde Wyndham	_____ Riordan McIlhenny
_____ Maryalice Mayberry	_____ LaTonya Robison
_____ Eva Weber	_____ Pedro Hernandez
_____ Jackson Davis	_____ Jeff Marshall
_____ Gordon Clark	_____ Cynthia Petherbridge
_____ Benjamin Bridges	_____ Gino Romano
_____ Humphrey Doxstater	_____ Jacob Jasinski
_____ Etienne Giradoux	_____ Crystal Clark
_____ Imelda Hermosilla	_____ Edward Taft

Check your answers with the original list, and note the number you got correct.

Was recognition easier than recall? Did you find yourself better able to recognize names of one sex or one ethnic group? Did simpler names seem simpler to remember, or did the unusual ones fix themselves in your mind? These can be valuable clues to your perceptions of others.

So far, you've been trying to remember names in a vacuum. Without the flesh and blood people attached to them, or at least a literary facsimile, it's pretty difficult to form images around the names. Now we're going to give you more information about our cast of characters.

- Bob Baker was your best friend in college. He has red hair and laughs a lot. He lent you $100 when you were broke and refused to let you pay it back. This bothers you, but you can't complain, so you get back at him by addressing your letters to him, Bob "Big Bucks" Baker.
- Your sister's roommate, Cynthia Petherbridge, has been telling vicious lies about you, and you are not sure why.
- The car that sideswiped you was driven by Gino Romano, a short, fat teenager with no insurance.
- Since Rosanna Calcese's big dinner party, everyone has been trying to get her recipe for chopped liver, but you are the only one she will give it to.
- The famous writer, Lazarus Hennenberg, is lecturing on Thursday.
- Rose Cohen has brown hair.
- When you got home, you found that you had accidentally

taken Riordan McIlhenny's briefcase, and he was on a plane for Calcutta with yours at that very moment.

- Molly Quinn has got to be the hottest new TV star of the season. With her Kewpie doll face, red curls, sea-green eyes, and sultry singing voice, she has 70 percent of the nation's viewers glued to their sets on Sunday night. Golly-Molly clubs are springing up all over the country.

- You weren't going to get the big promotion, but Sue Wong, the regional manager, put in a special plug for you. After she talked to several vice presidents, the top man changed his mind, and you got the job. You call her true blue Sue.

- Your parking space by the main entrance is always grabbed by Vincent Yoshihiro, the lazy slob, so he can sleep late and still get to the coffee machine before your boss gets in.

- You can't stand that Clyde Wyndham. His jokes are terrible, and he laughs like a hyena whenever he tells one. Oh, oh . . . here he comes now. You duck out.

- Did you hear that Mary Foster is expecting triplets? She and her husband tried to have a baby for years, and then she went on fertility drugs. Now they're going to have a houseful!

- Our company's financial future hangs on a phone call that will come this morning. Horst Egensperger is calling from Switzerland, and if we can persuade him that the deal is sound, he will approve the multimillion-dollar contract.

- That snooty bank teller who always wears lavender nail polish, what's her name . . . Eva Weber . . . ever since you took in the change from your piggy bank and asked her to count it, she shuts her window when she sees you coming.

- Jackson Davis is the elevator operator's brother.

- When you go to Paris, Etienne Giradoux and his wife would love to put you up and show you around. They share your interest in art and theatre and speak perfect English.

- Our neighbor, Imelda Hermosilla, accepted delivery of your package of live lobsters, but she's so dizzy, she forgot to give it to us before she left for the weekend. The box sat on her sun porch for three days and boy, did *she* have a surprise when she got back. The neighborhood kids were chanting "Imelda smelda!" She was so embarrassed.

- Marie DuBois is trying to get you fired.

- One of the scholarship candidates is LaTonya Robison, a
  prelaw student. LaTonya is an orphan with 11 brothers and
  sisters. Without the scholarship, LaTonya will have to go to
  work at a menial job.
- Juan Lopez has offered to buy out our foundering restaurants. We'll make a nice profit, and he'll merge it with his
  successful Juan's Weenies chain.

Now fill in the blanks.

1. The lady with smelly lobsters on her sunporch is_____
   _____
2. In Paris, you are invited to stay with_____.
3. The elevator man's brother is named_____.
4. Your best friend in college was red-headed_____.
5. The coveted chopped liver recipe came from_____.
6. The wimp who nabs your parking place is_____.
7. The snooty teller with lavender nails who hates pennies
   is_____.
8. The woman with brown hair is_____.
9. Your briefcase is on its way to Calcutta with_____.
10. The regional manager who got you the promotion was
    _____.
11. Your sister's lying roommate is_____.
12. The famous writer who is lecturing Thursday is_____.
13. The lady expecting triplets is_____.
14. The scholarship candidate is_____.
15. Our restaurants are being bought by_____.
16. Your car was sideswiped by_____.
17. The beautiful new TV star is_____.
18. The man who tells terrible jokes is_____.
19. The important caller from Switzerland is_____.
20. The woman who is trying to get you fired is_____.

    Check your answers on the chart below, and circle the
letters that follow each correct answer. Then add each vertical
column.

	Positive	Negative	Male	Female	Common	Uncommon
1. Imelda Hermosilla		N		F		U
2. Etienne Giradoux	P		M			U
3. Jackson Davis	—	—	M		C	
4. Bob Baker	P		M		C	
5. Rosanna Calcese	P			F		U
6. Vincent Yoshihiro		N	M			U
7. Eva Weber		N		F	C	
8. Rose Cohen	—	—		F	C	
9. Riordan McIlhenny		N	M			U
10. Sue Wong	P			F	C	
11. Cynthia Petherbridge		N		F		U
12. Lazarus Hennenberg	—	—	M			U
13. Mary Foster	P			F	C	
14. LaTonya Robison	—	—		F		U
15. Juan Lopez	P		M		C	
16. Gino Romano		N	M		C	
17. Molly Quinn	P			F	C	
18. Clyde Wyndham		N	M			U
19. Horst Egensperger	P		M			U
20. Marie DuBois		N		F	C	
	of 8 positive	of 8 negative	of 10 male	of 10 female	of 10 common	of 10 uncommon

Did you remember more names with positive or negative associations? More men or women? More common or uncommon names? Notice that four of the names had neutral associations. Did that affect your ability to remember them?

Several of the descriptions repeated the person's name and connected it to something else like a nickname or a business. Did you remember them better? If you did, notice that adding information to a name makes it more memorable.

Of course, these questions are highly subjective. You may regard having triplets as negative rather than positive, or think the name Gino Romano very unusual and hard to remember, rather than common. This small sampling can't give you a true picture of your memory patterns, but it may offer clues that you can follow up on your own.

Chaining Names

Here's a name-chaining game that may make you stretch the way you associate names for recall. The idea comes from a *New York Magazine* competition of several years ago, designed by Mary Ann Madden.

Start by writing down a name—a movie star, politician, historical character, your aunt, anyone—on the top line. Then make an association with another name. Continue making associations until you have chained ten names. Ready for the trick? Your assignment is to make the last name the same as the first, that is, to come full circle.

Here's a sample list:

1. Richard Nixon
2. John Mitchell
3. Margaret Mitchell
4. Scarlett O'Hara
5. Red Buttons
6. Santa Claus
7. Monty Woolley
8. Cybil Shepard
9. Richard Crooks
10. Richard Nixon

Do you see the connections between each descending pair of names? If they are too obscure, here is a rundown. Richard Nixon was President and his Attorney General was John Mitchell. John Mitchell and Margaret Mitchell share the same last name. Margaret Mitchell created the literary heroine, Scarlett O'Hara. Scarlet is a shade of red, so Red Buttons. Red Buttons would be found on the clothing of Santa Claus. Santa Claus has a white beard and so did Monty Woolley. Woolly sheep might be guarded by a Shepard.

Shepherds carry hooked sticks called Crooks. Richard Crooks, the tenor, shares the same first name with Richard Nixon who, to avoid confusion, proclaimed, "I am not a crook."

Want to try? Make up some ten-line game sheets. While you have fun, notice the association tricks you use. How could these tricks help you remember the people you meet?

21

How to Remember Dates and Numbers

You may think that you simply can't remember numbers, that they have no emotional trappings to help you recall them, but that's not true. Read the story below and see how much you understand.

> 007, dressed to the 9s, sauntered off the 747. He yearned to spend the evening at 21 with a 36-26-36, but recalled the 86 he had experienced on his last visit. Instead, he hopped in his 911 and drove to a 7-11 where he bought a 17 and some 409. Dropping them in his flight bag next to his .44, he drove off to see 2001 for the 10th time.

For those who need a translation: special agent James Bond, superbly dressed, sauntered off the airplane. He yearned to spend the evening at a famous restaurant with a shapely woman, but recalled that he had been thrown out on his last visit. Instead he hopped in his car and drove to a convenience store where he purchased a teen fashion magazine and some spot remover, put them in his bag alongside his gun, and went to see a movie.

Now James Bond would *never* have done some of the things described above. Also some of the trademarked numbers above are spelled out in their regular form (i.e., *Seventeen* magazine, 7-Eleven stores), but I wanted you to see how much personality plain numbers can have.

Using Your Life as a Calendar

Many people date recent happenings by where they were living or working at the time. Women with several children frequently date an event by recalling which child they were pregnant with. It is a rare individual who can't tell you where he or she was when Pearl Harbor was bombed or when President Kennedy or John Lennon were shot.

These dates are signposts in our lives. Like the numbers on a clock, they give us markers so we can figure out the time in between. In the larger context of history, most people can identify key dates: A.D. 33, 1066, 1492, 1776, 1929, the Fourth of July, *Cinco de Mayo,* the Ides of March.

The Easiest Way to Remember

How do you remember a specific date? Your mother-in-law's birthday or an important meeting? The simplest way is to write it down and then acquire the habit of checking your calendar weekly or daily or hourly.

But what if you need to remember dates or numbers for business purposes or an exam? Students have to process and play back an incredible array of numbers to satisfy their teachers. Lawyers need to recall case numbers, and salesmen want to know model numbers. Librarians must memorize the Dewey decimal system, and a musician may want to memorize the Koechel listings for all of Mozart's works.

Since most people remember words better than numbers (that's why telephone exchanges used to be MUrray Hill 9 instead of 689), you may want to try a memory system that turns numbers into words. We'll tell you about one in a moment.

Reciting and Grouping

Saying numbers aloud seems to give better results than reading them silently to yourself, and grouping digits in clusters greatly improves your ability to remember them. If you think of a number as 386-54-36 or 38-65-436, rather than 3865436 or even 386-5436, you'll remember it better. Indeed, that's how most European phone numbers are written. Our high rate of errors in reproducing phone numbers might be reduced if we divided them that way.

Of course, there *was* a time when phone numbers had *names* instead of prefixes, an effulgent era, redolent with shy "SUsquehanna 7" and mighty "MUrray Hill 9," with haughty "BEekman 3," and humble but hard-working "CHelsea 2." The phone company decided that numbers were better, and now we have to remember anemic 736 or bland 258, instead of potent "PEnnsylvania 6" or lyrical "ALhambra 8."

When Should You Try a Number System?

S, the man with the incredible memory, said that numbers possessed colors, shapes, sounds, and personalities for him. Two, for instance, was a high-spirited woman, rectangular, whitish in color. He could remember long strings of numbers because each was as memorable as an interesting person he had met.

If you also feel that numbers have personalities, work to develop this perception. Forget number conversion systems and give each number a color, shape, size, texture, a musical theme, or a mood. Then strings of apparently arbitrary numbers will become parades of old friends, constantly rearranged into fascinating patterns.

Learning a letter/number conversion system is *hard work*. You should only do it if:

- You see numbers as just so many dreary squiggles—perhaps even slightly threatening in their incomprehensibility—and absolutely can't remember them.
- You have a strong verbal memory and enjoy word games and puzzles.

Otherwise, learning charts of words to replace numbers will just be another baffling, frustrating task that will leave you worse off than when you started.

Most numbers that you use every day—the combination of the office safe, the code that opens your garage door or lets you take cash out of a sidewalk machine—get locked into your memory pretty quickly. You don't need a system to remember them.

But there are numbers that you only use once in a while that can be invaluable. For instance, being able to come up with the Social Security numbers or insurance policy numbers of every member of your family or the registration number of your car or the numbers of all your bank accounts and credit cards can save you lots of time and aggravation in an emergency. You may have this information written down in a safe place, but having it at the tip of your tongue can be mighty handy in our red-tape society.

Or you may need a complex number only several times a year, but when you need it, you really need it—pi or a code number that lets you operate your company's computer or the number that turns off the burglar alarm in a friend's apartment, even your automated teller number if you don't use it often and are afraid to carry it around with you. If remembering numbers is hard for you, you may want to use a system that converts them to more memorable words or sentences.

Don't Be Scared

Most memory books have huge charts of word equivalents for numbers. Most people look at these charts and turn to jelly; "How can I possibly remember that 'carob' is 749 if I can't even remember 'carob'!"

What I'm going to show you now is a guaranteed terror-free way to create *your own* system, using letters and numbers in ways that are comfortable for you. Like Adam, you will name the animals, and if someone says, "Why did you call that animal a hippopotamus," you can reply that it looked more like a hippopotamus than anything else around. However, the beauty of making your own system is that *no one* will know anything about it. Like the mantras of Eastern religions, it is absolutely your own. Let's look at how most number/letter exchange systems work.

Exchanging Numbers for Letters

Memory instructors have evolved a more-or-less standard system of number/letter exchanges. Here is a suggested table. If you find yourself saying, "But that's not how *I'd* remember it," you are free to adapt it. It is strictly your private toy.

Notice that all the equivalents are consonants.

0 = s or z (for *zero*)
1 = t (one vertical bar)
2 = n (two vertical bars)
3 = m (three vertical bars)
4 = r (its last letter)
5 = l (your left hand, thumb extended, forms an *L*)
6 = b (6 and *b* look alike)
7 = k (prop up two 7s to make *k*)
8 = d (script *d* has two loops)
9 = p (*p* backward looks like 9)

This exchange system has two uses:

- By mixing these consonants with "free" letters— *a, e, i, o, u, y*—you can convert hard-to-remember numbers into easier-to-remember words and sentences.
- You can also substitute images inspired by the number/letter exchange as a peg system for remembering shopping lists, speeches, etc.

USING THIS NUMBER SYSTEM AS A PEG SYSTEM

Earlier in chapter 15, "How to Use Memory Systems," we told you about two number/word exchanges that could help you recall a long string of objects or actions by relating them to the *images* of the numbers. One of these was verbal (rhymes: one-bun, two-shoe, etc.), and the other was visual (pictures: one-pen, two-swan, etc.). By visualizing these buns or pens interacting with a list of things you wanted to remember, you could recall them all quickly and easily.

If you decide to learn this comprehensive system to convert numbers to words, you can (and should) substitute the images below for the buns and pens of the other systems.

Number	Letter	A Key Word
0	S	Sea
1	T	Tea
2	N	N.Y.
3	M	Ma
4	R	aiR
5	L	eeL
6	B	Bee
7	K	Key
8	D	Doe
9	P	Pie

This works just like the peg systems described in chapter 15. Let's say that either ketchup or milk is on your shopping list among other items. Depending on numerical position, here are images that would "peg" them for you.

1 = Tea   (A Tea cup is poured full of ketchup to everyone's astonishment; a cow is giving milk into an elegant silver pitcher at a formal Tea party.)

2 = N.Y.   (Even if you have never been to New York, you probably know something about it. Here, the Empire State Building becomes a giant red ketchup bottle; the Hudson River runs with white milk. You could also use Broadway, the Statue of Liberty, the United Nations, Madison Square Garden, Central Park, etc.)

3 = Ma   (Ma is a grey-haired little old lady. She is pouring ketchup into bottles with a funnel and slopping it all over; for milk, a grey-haired lady is shampooing her hair in milk to make it white.)

4 = aiR   (Ketchup bottles are floating everywhere in the aiR—you can't *catch up* with them; the aiR is white with milky rain pouring down—try to catch it in milk buckets.)

5 = eeL   (A wiggly, squiggly eeL wraps itself around a ketchup bottle—you take off the cap, and more eeLs pop out and slither onto your hotdog; a group of eeLs are laying eggs in a stream—each

little egg looks like a milk carton, and you try to scoop them up.)

6 = Bee   (The Bees live in a hive shaped like a giant ketchup bottle—they are red and black and red ketchup oozes out of their hive; the milk case at the supermarket is surrounded by circling, buzzing Bees—everyone else is afraid, but you walk through and pick up your milk because the Bees are your friends and have been protecting the last carton until you got there.)

7 = Key   (A ketchup bottle forms the handle of a large Key that you must use to unlock your front door—try not to get the drippy red stuff on your clothes; you turn the Key in your front door, and a wall of white milk gushes out, carrying you along—the Key inflates and helps you keep afloat in the sea of milk.)

8 = Doe   (A Doe is suckling her fawn—her underside is covered with teats that look like ketchup bottles, and Bambi is covered with dripping red ketchup; the milk carton on your breakfast table suddenly sprouts antlers and hooves and begins running around the room.)

9 = Pie   (Ketchup Pie—yuck!—imagine the faces on your guests when you serve it; people are throwing Pies at an old-fashioned milkman—the street and all his bottles are covered with whipped cream Pies.)

10 = ToeS   (Your ten little ToeS are covered with ketchup; you try to make shoes out of milk cartons, but your ToeS stick out—you need another milk carton to cover your ToeS.)

Try This . . .

if You Want to Learn a Number System

Most number systems turn numbers into words by giving each digit, 0 through 9, a consonant equivalent. Then you write down the number you want to remember, using consonants, and fill in with vowels—*a, e, i, o, u, y*—to make words, or you contrive a short sentence using the consonants at the beginning of each word. Words beginning with vowels can be used freely in the sentence method without affecting the number. To show you how this works, let's try an arbitrary list of consonants and see if you can make words or phrases out of them.

Consonants	Write Your Word(s) Here	Possible Answers
L D N S	_____	LouD NoiSe
		LeaDeN Sea
		Lazy Dogs Never Sit
B R M L	_____	BaRe MaLe
		beau BRuMeL
		Banks Rarely Make Love

Some Don't-Panic Number Charts

We are about to turn numbers into words on a systematic scale. Don't be intimidated. You're going to learn a *tool* for memory, not create another massive thing to memorize.

Some number systems use the *sounds* of letters to replace numbers. I think this just adds to the confusion. For instance, in one system, 6 can be represented by *shoe, chair, judge,* or *George,* while the letters *s* and *c* can be used for 0 if they are pronounced as in *soap* and *cipher,* and *c* can also be used for 7 if it is in *cow.* Are you following all this? Probably not.

In this system, a consonant is always exchanged for the same number, no matter how it is pronounced. The purpose of this exchange is to let you make words, sentences, rhymes, or riddles out of numbers that you would otherwise have a hard time remembering. The system assumes that you remember words more easily than you remember numbers.

You don't have to stop in the middle of your conversion to ponder whether *c* is 6 or 7 or 0. In this system, you always exchange the same letter for the same number.

How to Use the System

Here's how you do it. Each number is represented by a consonant.

1. Write down the number you want to remember.
2. Write the letter equivalent underneath.
3. Fill in vowels to make words. Or construct sentences in which each word starts with the number-equivalent letter.

Use this system or plot your own. (Hint: avoid using extra consonants—ToSs and DoLI, for instance—because later you won't be sure which letters represent numbers and which are "silent.") If you decide to create your own exchange system, notice how the active, physical process of writing out the chart locks your code in your memory.

In the number/letter conversion system below you *don't* have to memorize a word substitute for every number up to a hundred. (If you could do that, you probably wouldn't need a system!) Instead, you memorize just ten digit/consonant combinations, then form words and sentences as memory hooks.

Examples

Phone number:	381-1470	MaD aT TuRKeyS
Social Security number:	947-25-0028	PaRK iN LooSe SaND
Safe combination:	73-21-1	Key Me iNTo iT

Learn the system as you practice making words out of the key letters.

Numbers	Letters (Fill in a word.)		Possible Words
0	S		Sea, Say, So, iS
1	T		Tea, Tie, aTe, eaT
2	N		N.Y., No, Nee, Nay
3	M		Ma, Moo, May, aM
4	R		aiR, Ray, Rue, Rye
5	L		eeL, aLe, Loo, Lie, Lay
6	B		Bee, Be, aBe, oBoe
7	K		Key, oaK, a.K.a.
8	D		Doe, Do, Day, iD
9	P		Pie, Pea, aPe, Poo
10	T	S	ToeS, iTS, oaTS
11	T	T	ToT, TaT, TooT, iTTy
12	T	N	TaN, TiN, ToN
13	T	M	TaM, TaMe, TiMe (etc.)

You are probably asking what you can do with all these clue words. One thing would be to rehearse with a partner so you can amaze your friends at parties with your "mind reading" ability. But you can also use your hard work for more practical applications.

You want to remember the full citation for

Abrahamson v. Fleschner, 648 F.2d 862 (1977).

6 4 8	F.2d	8 6 2	1 9 7 7
B R D	FND	D B N	T P K K
BiRD	FouND	DuBiN	ToP CooK

Fortunately I have a friend named Dubin who is a good cook. (Personalizing your memories helps rivet them.) For this one, I might relate the "flesh" of Fleschner to a succulent roast chicken cooked by my friend. You might prefer an "idea ban" or a "doe bone." Silly? Of course. That's why it takes energy to create and why that energy lets you recall it later.

Try these famous cases on your own.

Plessy v. Ferguson 163 U.S. 537 (1896)

1 6 3	U S	5 3 7	1 8 9 6
T B M	U S	L M K	T D P B

Make some words or sentences here.

———————   ————   ————   —————————
———————   ————   ————   —————————

Plessy v. Ferguson established the "separate but equal" rule for schools and public accommodations in the United States. It took 58 years to reverse this with the *Brown v. Board of Education* decision.

> *Brown v. Board of Education 347 U.S. 483 (1954)*

3 4 7	U S	4 8 3	1 9 5 4
M R K	U S	R D M	T P L R

Make some words or sentences here.

———————   ————   ————   —————————
———————   ————   ————   —————————

Let's say you are very anxious to remember pi to the 20th decimal point. Write your letter equivalent under each number below.

3 . 1 4 1 5 8 2 6 5 3 5 8 9 7 9 3 2 3 8 4 6

— . ———————————————————————————————————————

Now convert your consonants into words by adding vowels. Divide the words anywhere you want.

Here's how it would work with the standard conversion system, customized to my needs with a 6-b and 8-d combination.

3 . 1 4 1 5 8 2 6 5 3 5 8 9 7 9 3 2 3 8 4 6
M . T R T L D N B L M L D P K P M N M D R B

This is a toughy, but perhaps you could use the first letter of each word in a verse:

May Tempestuous Roamed The Land
Delighting Naughty British Lords.

May Lured Dukes,
Princes and Kooks.
Presently a Majesty
Noticed May's Diversity:
Royal Board.

Another classic mnemonic for pi is the following:

Pie
I wish I could determine pi.
Eureka cried the great inventor.
Christmas pudding, Christmas pie
Is the problem's very center.

This gives you pi to the 20th decimal if you count the number
of letters in each word. (As you can see, these "systems" are
a lot of work and only help people who are great with words
and terrible with numbers.)

Coding Dates
    A student must remember the birthdates of Franklin
Delano Roosevelt, Harry S. Truman, and Dwight D.
Eisenhower. Here's how he does it.

Roosevelt   1 - 30 - 82   T M S D N
                                    TiMeS DoNe
                              Roosevelt - the one,
                              hero of TiMeS DoNe

Truman   5 - 8 - 84   L D D R
                                   LaDDeR
                          Feisty Harry climbed the LaDDeR
                          of success. His foes got madder.

Eisenhower   10 - 14 - 90   T S T R P S
                                   T-STRaPS
                          Maybe Eisenhower used STRaPS to
                          carry his many golf Tees.

    You are about to say that these are pretty bad, and you
are right. The reason they work is that *you* figure them out,

you write them down and *you* read back what you wrote, actively locking them in your memory three ways.

Write down some dates you want to remember here, family birthdays or anniversaries.

Event	Date	Letter Code	Word or Sentence
_____	_____	_____	_____
_____	_____	_____	_____

Use What Works

If some of these techniques for remembering numbers seem harder to remember than the numbers themselves, you may find that your poetical ear prefers the repetition of a number sequence until its cadences sing automatically in your memory. If that works for you, that's great. You're a natural number person. The point of these varied suggestions is that you select what works for *you* and forget the rest.

22

How to Rehearse

Rehearsal comes from the Middle English word *rehersen* which means to reharrow or redig the earth. Rehearsing something over and over until you have memorized it is a lot like hoeing a row. It's boring, exhausting, demeaning work, and it frequently results in very welcome fruit.

Memorizing a Script

Professional actors aren't the only people who must memorize scripts. You may also need to know something word for word so you can make proper introductions, do an effective business presentation, act in an amateur stage production, make a TV commercial about your company, or even stage an elaborate effort to persuade your boss to give you a raise. The many things that need memorization—words, stance, tone, gestures, emphasis—can be harder to master than just one component, but once you've meshed them, they reinforce each other.

> Step forward, pick up the wrench, scratch ear,
> and say, "The problem with cantaloupes is . . ."

It would be difficult to take a step forward or encounter a wrench or scratch your ear without going right on to cantaloupes.

Actors use two basic methods to memorize scripts—to "learn their lines." Some memorize all the lines and then explore their meaning in rehearsal. Others prefer to get a sense of the whole script and then memorize the specific words as they work on individual sections.

Actress Julie Harris says she likes to begin with the part fully memorized. "I prefer not to worry about the mechanics of the part when rehearsal starts. This allows me the freedom to concentrate fully on the meaning." She starts by reading the script over two or three times and underlining her part. Then she divides the amount of material she must learn by the number of days she has to do it. Each day she tackles the predetermined chunk, reading five lines and then repeating them and repeating them until they are memorized. She constantly backtracks and reviews material already studied, adding it on to the new chunk.

Christopher Plummer uses the second technique, beginning with the meaning and adding an exact reading of the text later. The great film actor, Paul Muni, used a tape recorder, listening to the lines over and over and hearing his own voice in different "readings"—emotional approaches—to the material. Sir John Gielgud writes his parts out in longhand two or three times, like a schoolboy writing, "I will not chew gum in class" on the blackboard. This is a valuable technique, as we have noted before, because it combines an *active* process (writing), a *visual* process (reading), and an *aural* process (saying it back).

CUES

All recall is based on "cues." Scripts consist of a series of responses, each triggered by what went before it. When you learn a script, you learn to respond to these cues. A cue can be something another person says or a sound or an action.

As you memorize your script, trigger your response with appropriate cues. If they are actions, act them out. If they are sounds—bells, clapping, music—simulate them. If they are words, mumble the preceding line to yourself or, better yet, have someone read it to you so that you respond automatically with what comes next. Once you're feeling cocky about knowing your "part," have your friend mix up the cues and see if you can respond correctly. (When you do this, you will come to appreciate the angst of professional actors when one

of their stage fellows gives them the wrong cue.) Notice
where repeated phrases or similar cues may lead you astray.
If necessary, make up a mnemonic or numerical framework
to keep them in order.

Some soap opera actors have to memorize more di-
alogue each day than most stage and film actors do in a week.
They can be forgiven if they go for the sense of the scene,
memorizing only key transitional lines that cue another actor's entrance or a change of scene. Probably few lines of
deathless prose are lost to the world. However, an actor who
tried to be similarly cavalier with the words of Shakespeare
or Molière or Calderon would quickly be hooted off stage.
Imagine a Hamlet who intones, "The question is whether to
be or not," or a Rhett Butler who sneers, "Frankly, Scarlett,
I couldn't care less." The "real" lines sing in our souls, and
while we may accept unusual readings of them, we want each
and every word as we remember it.

Should We Practice Memorizing?

Is memorization a skill that you can improve with practice? Some experts say no. For instance, in 1890, William
James recorded how long it took him to memorize 158 lines of
Hugo's *Satyr*. Then he memorized *Paradise Lost*. Then he
memorized the next 158 lines of the *Satyr*. It took him longer
than to learn the first 158 lines. He decided that the ability to
memorize could not be improved by practicing.

But most actors advocate memorizing for the fun of it as
an everyday exercise, just as a pianist would practice scales.
Julie Harris suggests learning one Shakespearean sonnet a
day and then going on to famous speeches.

Children used to memorize long poems in school to train
their minds, just as they now do calisthenics to train their
bodies. Then the idea that memory capacity was genetic and
unchangeable made such practice unpopular. Today, even the
most curmudgeonly expert will usually concede that training
improves the efficiency with which we use our inherited
capacity. Memorizing just for the sake of memorizing has not

yet made a comeback in our educational system, but many people get great pleasure from knowing long, complicated sequences of material—poems, songs, quotations, laws, chemical formulas, or equations—by heart. They savor both the usefulness of the information and the pleasure that mastering it gives them. It becomes a form of play.

Like the rest of us, some actors are "easy studies," committing lengthy parts to memory with little effort, while others agonize over every sentence, repeating it hundreds of times before they can remember it. Stage and film actor John Barrymore was famous for forgetting lines. He solved his problem by writing them down and placing them all about the set. Speeches were pasted on the back of chairs, penciled in the pattern of the wallpaper, even inked on his cuffs. Then he practiced his own mnemonic technique by literally walking to where his next lines appeared, reciting them and moving on. His delivery was so impressive that his audiences neither knew nor cared.

Memorizing a Speech

A mnemonic technique for remembering speeches is described in chapter 15, "How to Use Memory Systems," but here is a way to polish your presentation. First of all, I highly recommend memorizing *what* you are going to say, not the words that say it. You want to remember your ideas, your key phrases, your main points, but unless you are delivering someone else's speech in his absence or making a critical press statement after a disaster where your every word will be weighed by the press and the victims' lawyers, you don't *want* to read a speech or even say it word for word so that you sound like you're reciting *The Face on the Barroom Floor*. What you want to remember is the thought process.

Here is a technique that may help you do that. The following steps are adapted from the Lessac system devised by Professor Arthur Lessac of the State University of New York, Binghamton. He has applied his techniques of kinesthetic feedback not only to vocal presentations, but to body movement and relaxation.

Your written speech is a gem, beautifully phrased and

polished, with each idea following the last like a string of pearls.

1. Write an outline of your speech, listing main points.
2. Divide the written speech into logical sections, not too long or short. Then stand in the middle of the room and read the first section to an imaginary audience. They are bright-faced students who will be tested on what you are saying as soon as you stop.
3. Done? Okay, now put down your script and look at all those eager faces. You see questions in their eyes, so you repeat what you have just said naturally, in your own words, emphasizing and elaborating on points that they may not have understood. How do your gestures, facial expressions, pauses, emphases make your message clearer? What new ways do you find to strengthen what you want to get across? (Don't be afraid to ad lib. It may give you some of your best material.)
4. Look at your written speech again and see if you've left anything out. If you did, write it down on your outline.
5. Pick up your written speech and deliver it again, but look at the page *only* when you have to.
6. Now set down the written speech and deliver the section again, using only your outline. Don't be afraid that your imaginary audience will get bored. They're still there, hanging on your every word.
7. Repeat these steps with each section of the speech, until you are completely comfortable with the material.
8. Deliver the entire speech without notes. If you get stuck or realize that you left something out, stop and note it on the outline sheet. If you have trouble keeping the segments in order, try the techniques described in chapter 15, "How to Use Memory Systems."

9. Keep the outline sheet as a backup during your speech. (I'll bet that you won't need to look at it.)

Memorizing Movement

Did you ever watch a stage full of ballet dancers doing complex movements to the crash of garbage cans, the cries of whales, or total silence? Do they really know what they are doing, or are they just making it up as they go along? Yes, they *do* know what they are doing because in silent accompaniment to "Concerto for Chevrolet Engines" or "Fugue for Tin Cans and Roller Skates" they are *counting:* a-one-and-a-two-and-a-three, dip, twist, six, kick, kick, slide, ten. You probably did the same thing when (or if) you learned the waltz—*one* two three, *one* two three, *one* two three.

Dancing is a fugitive art. Choreographers can write out a dance in any of several systems of dance notation or even in their own shorthand, but dancers can't move about the stage holding a script, and so they count.

Counting is a useful way to lock any movement into memory. Dancers count in variable units, depending on the music. The most common counts are four, eight, sixteen, or thirty-two, corresponding to common musical segments. Each set of counts is called a "combination." The counts within a combination can be thought of as words in a sentence. Each "sentence" follows the last until a "paragraph" is formed. Unless the dance is an incredibly complicated contemporary piece, the counts are soon locked into their muscles and become kinesthetic memory. No more conscious counting is necessary. The *music* becomes the *cue*.

How can dancers' counts help in nondance pursuits? Well, music or other sounds can serve as cues for motion. An assembly-line-type process could be "choreographed" to music so that you know exactly where you should be in relation to the music. You could time getting out of the house in the morning to songs from the musical *Annie*. ("Oh, oh, I'm late, I should be brushing my teeth by 'You're Never Fully Dressed Without a Smile' and I'm only putting on my shoes." "Hard-Knock Life" reminds you to take your wallet and keys off the dresser and put them in your pocket.) You could wash the car to a Michael Jackson album ("The Girl Is Mine" means don't forget to scour the whitewalls). Clean the house to *The Marriage of Figaro* (scrub the refrigerator and set out the meat to defrost for dinner when "Se a casa Madama" comes on). Music keys action.

You may want to use counts to divide a complicated activity into simpler units. Five steps for a tummy-firming exercise before breakfast or changing the blades on a food processor, seven steps to threading a projector or booting up a computer.

Even Professionals Can Goof

The late pianist Artur Schnabel once got utterly lost in the midst of the *Brahms Piano Concerto in B Flat*. With great dignity he rose from the piano, walked to the podium, and studied the conductor's score, then returned to finish the piece.

Another master pianist, Andre Watts, played *Chopin's F Minor Fantasy* at 12 different concerts and 12 times forgot his place. He finally "conquered" the piece by scheduling it for the second half of a concert. During the intermission he rehearsed it over and over, and finally succeeded in playing it through correctly. "I said afterward, 'Right, I'm never playing this piece again'," Watts recalls. "I refused to play it for a long, long time."

Rehearsing for Life

The methods professionals use to memorize their very special material can be applied in many ways in our day-to-day memory projects. Professionals have the advantage over the rest of us—they *want* to remember, *need* to remember, and *enjoy* remembering. When you add those three conditions to any memorization project you have a winning combination.

As you struggle with memorizing a few pages or paragraphs, think of this: Under the Chinese emperors, no one could become a civil servant until he could prove in a national examination that he had memorized several books of classical literature and poetry. The reasoning was that in order to serve wisely, you had to be wise in the history, morality, and beauty of the world. We can only imagine what it would be like today if all postal workers were also Shakespearean scholars and if every meter maid could recite T. S. Eliot and e. e. cummings as she wrote out our tickets. What a lovely thought!

Try This . . .
to Celebrate Memory

Pick out something you would enjoy remembering—a poem, saying, song, or speech—and memorize it for sheer pleasure.

23

A Bag of Miscellaneous Memory Tricks

Now you know how to dazzle your friends and how to solve most of life's major memory problems. How about some simple tricks for coping with the pesky nuts and bolts of everyday remembering? Here is a collection.

The Old Watch-on-the-Wrong-Wrist Trick—You need to do something before you leave your home or office, or you need to remember to take something with you or to stop on the way and do an errand. Switch your wristwatch to the other wrist. Most people automatically check their watches

The old tie-a-string-to-your-finger trick for remembering.

whenever they make a transition. Your bare wrist will trigger the memory of what you want to do.

The Rubber Band/Safety Pin Trick—This is a variation of the string around the finger, much easier in these days of package tape. (When was the last time you owned a ball of string?) If you lack a watch or want to remember *two* things, try slipping a rubber band around your wrist or pinning a safety pin in the little metal loop that holds the handle on your purse or briefcase. If you're incredibly forgetful or have lots of things to remember, make your left hand "home" and your right hand "office" (or any other suitable division) and assign fingers to different areas, then slip rubber bands around the appropriate fingers. You may look silly, but it beats burning the house down or arriving at work without the day's mail that you were supposed to pick up at the post office.

The Tipped Lampshade Trick—An important thought floats into your mind as you drift off to sleep. If you leap up and get a pencil and paper, you will spend an hour getting back to sleep. If you don't, you'll have forgotten it in the morning. Try tipping the shade on your bedside lamp to a sharp angle. Or set the alarm clock on the floor. Or pull open the drawer of your bedside table, or toss a pillow across the room where you will have to step on it when you get up. In the morning you'll see what you've done and rebuild the memory connections.

The Billboard Trick—This only works occasionally. Like all good things, if you do it too much, it loses its effect. Simply write yourself a big note and stick it on the bathroom mirror or the front door, or your typewriter, someplace where you will have to physically remove it to go about your business.

The Phone Call at 10:35 Trick—Hardest of all is when you absolutely must call Mr. Bludgett at 10:35, not 10:30 or 10:40. Otherwise, Worldwide Widgetts will be bankrupt and you will be out in the street. Actually, if it were that important, you would probably sit staring at your watch from 8:30 on, so let's pretend that failing to reach Bludgett would only cause massive inconvenience and loss of money. You could count on the arrival of the coffee wagon to prompt you, but this may be the one morning it's late. You could trust your secretary, but she might get tied up on the phone and forget. Or you could set an alarm clock or timer to ring. My recommendation is to try all of them. Give yourself three ways to remember, then forget it and get on with your work.

The Step-On-It Trick—easiest of all. If you have to take something with you when you leave the house, set it in front of the door. If someone else might step on it first, have a special (and it *must* be special) place where everything that goes with you is laid out. If everything gets dumped there, forget it. A really organized person might even have a set of shelves labeled Monday, Tuesday, Wednesday, Thursday, Friday to lay out things for the whole week.

The Siamese Twins Trick—Behaviorist B. F. Skinner suggests remembering something you should do regularly by relating it to a similarly regular activity that has become habit. For instance, if you have to take pills twice a day, attach the pill bottle to your toothbrush with a big rubber band. When you reach automatically for the toothbrush, you will be reminded to take your pills. If you promise to wake up a friend each morning until he can find a new answering service, set the phone (or a note) on the toilet seat. Attach objects or notes to coffee pots, refrigerator door handles, shower heads, typewriters, mirrors, dog leashes—anything you use at regular intervals. Try to attach them in a way that will hinder the use of the regularly used object. For instance, if you put a note on the bathroom mirror, make it a big one. Cover the mirror. Otherwise you might shave, comb your hair, and stumble off to work without seeing it.

The Make-Life-Simpler Trick—an unattainable goal, but still worth the effort. Keep your brain cells free to ponder life's mysteries by doing most of your more boring remembering outside your head. Make lists and use them. Have a place for everything and everything in its place. Have a schedule for paying bills, ordering supplies, going to the dentist. If all this sounds impossibly idealistic, think of the energy you spend on chaos. We can't control how we spend every dime and every minute, but we do have a lot of choices in our expenditures.

24

How to Be Happy Though Forgetful

John went out on his lunch hour to pick up his shoes at the repair shop. On the way he stopped to fill a prescription, buy the new issue of his favorite magazine, deposit his pay check, and pick up the key for his new locker at the health club. When he got back to the office, flushed but on time, he realized he had forgotten to pick up his shoes.

Now if they were his only pair of black shoes and he was due to be best man at his brother-in-law's wedding that evening, a good case could be made for deliberate forgetting. But he probably just overloaded himself.

Clara went down to the basement for a jar of pickles. On the way, she stopped to toss a load of laundry in the washer and rinse out the plastic laundry basket that had gotten coated with detergent. As she hung up the basket, the hook came off the wall, so she got out the screwdriver and fixed it. While she was at it, she tightened some loose screws on the door hinges and got out the oil to lubricate them. Just then the phone rang and she raced upstairs to answer it. Twenty minutes later she realized she had never gotten the pickles.

Pretty dumb, huh? If the pickles had been *that* important, if she craved a pickle so intensely that she would have cheerfully knocked over ten linebackers in her rush to get one, then she wouldn't have stopped. And if the pickles were for her husband's lunch and they had just had a fight . . . but maybe the pickles were just as important as the other things.

Now Clara and John could spend a great deal of time berating themselves and their terrible memories. They could form strong images of themselves as useless, feebleminded failures, incapable of a simple task. If Clara's husband or John's brother-in-law subscribed to the theory that there are no accidents, John and Clara could have resonated with guilt for months or years to come. But let's look at the other side.

Both accomplished several useful tasks, worked off some extra calories, and enjoyed what they were doing. The fact that they had started the action that would result in the desired effect probably caused them to check it off their mental list. How often have you gone to the store for one particular thing and come home with everything else but?

You probably could train yourself to focus totally on the task at hand, denying any extraneous thought, and repeating your mission in mantra-like fashion. You *could* . . . but so far this is not your nature.

You may find it easier and more rewarding to tolerate occasional lapses of memory in order to be available to some of the pleasant notions that flit through your unconscious mind. The price for being unusually disciplined is less spontaneity. By making friends with the way you already use your memory, you will actually remember more of what you want to remember. Self-harassment rarely improves memory because it sets up a system of negative stimuli that is, at best, distracting and, at worst, destructive.

Buy a Memory Insurance Policy

Most people buy health insurance and accident insurance. Treat yourself to some memory insurance. When forgetting turns out to be expensive—when you forget to make a payment and are charged a penalty or when you forget to buy gas and have to be towed—you can either make yourself sick with regret and self-abuse or you can draw on your memory insurance policy.

A memory insurance policy is simple. At the beginning of each year, budget a certain amount of money for memory lapses. Forgetting that costs money is painful. If you plan for it, then expensive slips of the mind can be tolerated without self-recrimination.

Try the same technique with cost-free forgetting. When enough good things are happening in our lives, one or two low moments don't usually get us down. If you forget an umbrella, birthday, or appointment, remind yourself of all the essential things you *did* remember. Remedy the situation as best you can and then . . . forget it.

Three Things You Should Never Forget

1. We remember what enhances us and gives us pleasure.
2. We forget what doesn't enrich our immediate lives.
3. Anyone with a belly button is allowed at least a 20 percent margin for error.

Bibliography

Anderson, John N., and Hubbard, Barbara M. "Sex Differences in Age-Related Brain Atrophy." *Lancet,* 25 June 1983, pp. 1447–48.

Baddeley, Alan D. *The Psychology of Memory.* New York: Basic Books, 1976.

———. *Your Memory: A User's Guide.* New York: Macmillan Publishing Company, 1982.

Baddeley, Alan D., and Hitch, G. J. "Recency Re-examined." In *Attention and Performance VI,* edited by S. Domic. Hillsdale, N.J.: Lawrence Erlbaum Associates, 1977.

Baddeley, Alan D., and Longman, D. J. A. "The Influence of Length and Frequency of Training Sessions on Rate of Learning to Type." *Ergonomics* 21 (1978): 627–35.

Bartlett, F. C. *Remembering.* London: Cambridge University Press, 1932.

Bower, Gordon H. "How to . . . uh . . . Remember!" *Psychology Today,* October 1973, pp. 62–70.

———. "Mood and Memory." *Psychology Today,* June 1981, pp. 60–69.

"Brain's Record of Past: A Continuous Movie Film." *Science News Letter,* 27 April 1957, p. 265.

Brody, Jane E. "Head Injuries and the 'Silent Epidemic.'" *New York Times,* 23 March 1983.

Burtt, H. E. "An Experimental Study of Early Childhood Memory." *Journal of Genetic Psychology* 40 (1932): 287–95.

Butler, Robert N. "Alzheimer's Disease: An Examination." *Ambassador Magazine,* November 1982, pp. 69–83.

Buzan, Tony. *Make the Most of Your Mind.* New York: Simon & Schuster, 1984.

Carroll, John B., ed. *Language, Thought and Reality: Selected Writings of Benjamin Lee Whorf.* Cambridge, Mass.: MIT Press, 1956.

Cheraskin, E., and Ringsdorf, W. M., Jr. *Psychodietetics.* New York: Bantam Books, 1974.

Clark, Ronald W. *Einstein: The Life and Times*. New York: World Publishing Company, 1971.

Craik, Fergus I. M., and Lockhart, Robert S. "Levels of Processing: A Framework for Memory Research." *Journal of Verbal Learning and Verbal Behavior* 11 (1972): 671–84.

Del Rey, Patricia. "Effects of Contextual Interference on the Memory of Older Females Differing in Levels of Physical Activity." *Perceptual and Motor Skills*, August 1982, pp. 171–80.

Dembart, Lee. "Mathematician [Paul] Erdos: In the World of Numbers, He's No. 1." *Los Angeles Times*, 26 March 1983.

The Diagram Group. *The Brain: A User's Manual*. New York: Perigee Books, Putnam Publishing Group, 1982.

Dowling, W. J., and Fujitani, D. S. "Contour, Interval and Pitch Recognition in Memory for Melodies." *Journal of the Acoustical Society of America* 49 (1971): 524–31.

Drachman, David A. et al. "Memory Decline in the Aged: Treatment with Lecithin and Physostigmine." *Neurology* 32 (1982): 944–50.

Eisenson, Marc. "Parents: Get Smart about Drugs . . . and Drug Abuse!" *Family Circle Magazine*, 16 November 1982, pp. 195–99.

Ericsson, K. Anders, and Chase, William G. "Exceptional Memory." *American Scientist*, November-December 1982, pp. 607–15.

Etaugh, Clair, and Ptasnik, Patricia. "Effects of Studying to Music and Post-study Relaxation on Reading Comprehension." *Perceptual and Motor Skills*, August 1982, pp. 141–42.

Fanz, Dr. R. "The Origin of Form Perception." *Scientific American* 24 (1961): 66.

Feingold, Benjamin F. *Why Your Child Is Hyperactive*. New York: Random House, 1974.

Fernstrom, John D., and Wurtman, Richard J. "Nutrition and the Brain." *Scientific American*, February 1974, pp. 84–91.

Finn, Robert. "Amnesia: Case of a Fragmented Past." *Science Digest*, November 1983, pp. 72–74.

Foucault, Michel. *The Order of Things: An Archaeology of the Human Sciences*. New York: Vintage/Random House, 1973.

Freud, Sigmund. *The Basic Writings of Sigmund Freud*. Translated and edited by Dr. A. A. Brill. New York: Random House, 1938.

Goodwin, D. W.; Othmer, E.; Halikas, J. A.; and Freemon, F. "Loss of Short-Term Memory as a Predictor of Alcoholic 'Blackout.'" *Nature,* 11 July 1970, pp. 201–2.

Goulding, Robert L., and Goulding, Mary McClure. *Changing Lives Through Redecision Therapy*. New York: Brunner/Mazel, 1979.

Graedon, Joe. *The People's Pharmacy-2*. New York: Avon Books, 1980.

Green, Blake. "What Their Eyes Tell Us." *San Francisco Chronicle,* 3 November 1980.

Greene, E. B. "The Retention of Information Learned in College Courses." *Journal of Educational Research* 21 (1931): 262–73.

Grinspoon, Lester. "Marijuana." *Scientific American,* December 1969, pp. 17–25.

Harris, Julie, with Tarshis, Barry. *Talks to Young Actors*. New York: Lothrop, Lee and Shepard Books, 1971.

Heider, Eleanor Rosch. "Universals in Color Naming and Memory." *Journal of Experimental Psychology,* April 1972, pp. 10–20.

Hilton, Hermine. *A Head Start to a Better Memory* (Los Angeles: Kessler Management, 1982) is of great value.

Houston, John R.; Schneider, Nina G.; and Jarvick, Murray E. "Effects of Smoking on Free Recall and Organization." *American Journal of Psychiatry,* February 1978, pp. 220–22.

Hunt, E., and Love, T. "How Good Can Memory Be?" In *Coding Processes in Human Memory,* edited by A. W. Melton and E. Martin. Washington, D.C.: Halsted Press, John Wiley & Sons, 1972.

Hunter, I. M. L. "An Exceptional Talent for Calculative Thinking." *British Journal of Psychology* 53 (1962): 243–58.

Jacobs, J. "Experiments in 'Prehension.'" *Mind* 12 (1887): 75–82.

James, William. *Principles of Psychology*. 1890. Reprint. New York: Henry Holt & Company, 1950.

Johnson, Wendell. *People in Quandries: The Semantics of*

Personal Adjustment. New York: Harper & Row, 1946.

Jones, Marilyn K., and Jones, Ben Morgan. "The Relationship of Age and Drinking Habits to the Effects of Alcohol on Memory in Women." *Journal of Studies on Alcohol,* January 1980, pp. 179–86.

Killworth, Peter D., and Bernard, H. Russell. "Informant Accuracy in Social Network Data." *Human Organization,* 35 (1976): 269–86.

Laird, Donald Anderson, and Laird, Eleanor C. *Techniques for Efficient Remembering.* New York: McGraw-Hill, 1960.

Layton, E. T. "The Persistence of Learning in Elementary Algebra." *Journal of Educational Psychology* 23 (1932): 46–55.

Lessac, Arthur. *The Use and Training of the Human Voice: A Practical Approach to Speech and Voice Dynamics.* 1960. Reprint. New York: Drama Book Publishers, 1967.

Lieber, Charles S. "The Metabolism of Alcohol." *Scientific American,* March 1976, pp. 25–33.

Loftus, E. F., and Palmer, J. C. "Reconstruction of Automobile Destruction: An Example of the Interaction Between Language and Memory." *Journal of Verbal Learning and Verbal Behavior* 13 (1974): 585–89.

Luria, A. R. *The Mind of a Mnemonist.* New York: Basic Books, 1968.

McGaugh, James L. "Role of Hormones and Adrenalin in Memory." Paper delivered at the Western Psychological Association, San Francisco, April 27, 1983.

McKean, Kevin. "Memory." *Discover,* November 1983, pp. 19–27.

MacLean, Paul. "The Brain's Generation Gap: Some Human Implications." *Zygon/Journal of Religion and Science,* June 1973, pp. 113–27.

McWhirter, Norris, ed. *Guiness 1983 Book of World Records.* New York: Bantam Books, 1983.

Mandler, George. "Organization and Memory." In *The Psychology of Learning and Motivation,* edited by K. W. Spence and J. T. Spence, vol. 1. New York: Academic Press, 1969.

———. "Words, Lists and Categories: An Experimental View of Organized Memory." In *Studies in Thought and*

Language, edited by J. L. Cowan. Tucson: University of Arizona Press, 1970.

Mandler, George; Pearlstone, Zena; and Koopman, Henry S. "Effects of Organization and Semantic Similarity on Recall and Recognition." *Journal of Verbal Learning and Verbal Behavior* 8 (1969): 410–23.

Markoff, David, and Dubin, Andrew. *How to Remember Anything.* New York: Arco Publishing, 1976.

Martinez, Joe L., Jr.; Jensen, Robert A.; Messing, Rita B.; Rigter, Hank; McGaugh, James L. "Endogenous Peptides and Learning and Memory Processes." *Contemporary Psychology,* September 1982, p. 727.

Mazer, Eileen. "Five Proven Ways to Sharpen Your Memory." *Prevention,* February 1982, pp. 58–62.

Miller, L. L. et al. "Marijuana: Effects on Free Recall and Subjective Organization of Pictures and Words." *Psychopharmacology,* 29 December 1977, pp. 257–62.

Penry, J. *Looking at Faces and Remembering Them: A Guide to Facial Identification.* London: Elek Books, 1971.

Pribam, Karl. *Holographic Theory of the Brain* (San Francisco: New Dimensions Foundation, 1980) is of great value.

Restak, Richard M. *The Brain.* Garden City, N.Y.: Doubleday, 1979.

Sagan, Carl. *Cosmos.* New York: Random House, 1980.

Sands, S. F., and Wright, A. A. "Primate Memory: Retention of Serial List Items by a Rhesus Monkey." *Science,* 22 August 1980, pp. 938–40.

Sapir, Edward. *Selected Writings of Edward Sapir in Language, Culture and Personality.* Edited by David G. Mandelbaum. Los Angeles: University of California Press, 1963.

Schmeck, Harold M., Jr. "The Biology of Fear and Anxiety: Evidence Points to Chemical Triggers." *New York Times,* 7 September 1982.

———. "How Does Memory Work?" *New York Times,* 26 October 1982.

Schmidt, William E. "Gifted Retardates: The Search for Clues to Mysterious Talent." *New York Times,* 12 July 1983.

Simpson, Christopher. "World Brain." *Science Digest,* May 1982, pp. 52–54, 95.

Skinner, B. F., and Vaughan, Margaret. *Enjoy Old Age.* New York: W. W. Norton & Company, 1983.

"Social Drinking Tied to Cognitive Impairment While Sober." *Internal Medicine News,* 16 April 1983.

Sorabji, Richard. *Aristotle on Memory.* Providence, R. I.: Brown University Press, 1972.

"Tips to Making Learning Easier." *Modern Maturity,* June-July 1983, pp. 4–6.

Tulving, Endel. "Episodic and Semantic Memory." In *Organization of Memory,* edited by Endel Tulving and Wayne Donaldson. New York: Academic Press, 1972.

Underwood, Benton J. "Forgetting." *Scientific American,* March 1964, pp. 91–99.

von Oech, Roger. *A Whack on the Side of the Head: How to Unlock Your Mind for Innovation.* New York: Warner Books, 1983.

Watson, Robert I. "An Experimental Study of the Permanence of Course Material in Introductory Psychology." *Archives of Psychology* 32 (1938): 3–64.

Weeks, David J. "Do Chronic Cigarette Smokers Forget People's Names?" *British Medical Journal,* December 22–29, 1979, p. 1627.

Weingartner, Herbert et al. "Effects of Vasopressin on Human Memory Factors." *Science,* 6 February 1981, pp. 601–3.

Weinland, James D. *How to Improve Your Memory.* New York: Barnes & Noble Books, 1957.

Weitzenhoffer, Andre M. *Hypnotism.* New York: John Wiley & Sons, 1953.

Wells, Gary L., and Murray, Donna M. "What Can Psychology Say about *Neil v. Biggers* Criteria for Judging Eyewitness Testimony?" *Journal of Applied Psychology,* April 1983, pp. 347–62.

White, B. "Recognition of Distorted Melodies." *American Journal of Psychology* 73 (1960): 100–107.

Wilson, Jeanie. "The Amazing Brain." *Town & Country,* August 1982, pp. 73–84.

Woodworth, Robert S. *Experimental Psychology.* New York: Henry Holt & Company, 1938.

Wright, Jonathan V. *Dr. Wright's Book of Nutritional Therapy.* Emmaus, Pa.: Rodale Press, 1979.

Zailian, Marian. "A Genius Who Eschews the Title of Prodigy." *San Francisco Examiner,* 4 September 1983.

Zeisel, Steven H. "The Effects of Dietary Components on Brain Function." In *Advances in Human Clinical Nutrition.* Littleton, Mass.: John Wright/PSG, 1982.

Zeller, Anchard, F. "An Experimental Analogue of Repression: Ill the Effect of Induced Failure and Success on Memory Measured by Recall." *Journal of Experimental Psychology* 42 (1951): 32–38.

Zolotow, Maurice. *Billy Wilder in Hollywood.* New York: Putnam Publishing Group, 1971.

Index

THE
BOOKS THAT
SOLVE
ALL YOUR PROBLEMS

"I'm marrying someone else."

"I'm not disagreeing with you," Blade said. "But I still think you're settling. You have passion, verve."

"What do you know about me?"

"I know enough." His voice was quiet, cutting through the kitchen like a knife.

Cassidy whirled away from him and gripped the granite countertop.

"Cassidy."

Something in the tone of his voice softened her.

"Yes?"

"Are you afraid to turn around and look at me?"

Actually, at that moment she was. All she had to do was stand in the room and she wanted him. He tempted her like chocolate cake, but she needed to remain true to her diet of bland. Slowly Cassidy turned around and looked at him, sensing the mistake the moment she did so.

Dear Reader,

This month we have a wonderful lineup of stories, guaranteed to warm you on these last chilly days of winter. First, Charlotte Douglas kicks things off with *Surprise Inheritance*, the third installment in Harlequin American Romance's MILLIONAIRE, MONTANA series, in which a sexy sheriff is reunited with the woman he's always loved when she returns to town to claim her inheritance.

Next, THE BABIES OF DOCTORS CIRCLE, Jacqueline Diamond's new miniseries centered around a maternity and well-baby clinic, premieres this month with *Diagnosis: Expecting Boss's Baby*. In this sparkling story, an unforgettable night of passion between a secretary and her handsome employer leads to an unexpected pregnancy.

Also available this month is *Sweeping the Bride Away* by Michele Dunaway. A bride-to-be is all set to wed "Mr. Boring" until she hires a rugged contractor who makes her pulse race and gives her second thoughts about her upcoming nuptials. Rounding things out is *Professor & the Pregnant Nanny* by Emily Dalton. This heartwarming story pairs a single dad in need of a nanny for his three adorable children with a woman who is alone, pregnant and in need of a job.

Enjoy this month's offerings as Harlequin American Romance continues to celebrate twenty years of publishing the best in contemporary category romance fiction. Be sure to come back next month for more stories guaranteed to touch your heart!

Melissa Jeglinski
Associate Senior Editor
Harlequin American Romance

ABOUT THE AUTHOR

In first grade Michele Dunaway knew she wanted to be a teacher when she grew up, and by second grade she wanted to be an author. By third grade she was determined to be both. Born and raised in a west county suburb of St. Louis, Michele recently moved to five acres in the rolling hills of Labadie. She's traveled extensively, with the cities and places she's visited often becoming settings for her stories.

Michele currently teaches high school English, raises her two young daughters and describes herself as a woman who does too much but doesn't want to stop.

Michele loves to hear from readers, and you can visit her Web site at www.micheledunaway.com or write to her at P.O. Box 45, Labadie, MO 63055. Please enclose a SASE.

Books by Michele Dunaway

HARLEQUIN AMERICAN ROMANCE

Don't miss any of our special offers. Write to us at the following address for information on our newest releases.

Harlequin Reader Service
U.S.: 3010 Walden Ave., P.O. Box 1325, Buffalo, NY 14269
Canadian: P.O. Box 609, Fort Erie, Ont. L2A 5X3

A Bride-to-be's Do's and Don'ts

Do...

...listen to everything your busybody future mother-in-law has to say.

...go to dress fittings even though your wedding attire makes you look like a cumulus cloud.

...have fun with girlfriends before the wedding (especially to encourage them to find their own Mr. Perfect).

...write your future married name repeatedly.

Don't...

...stare at the good-looking contractor who's working on your house.

...even think about wearing his tool belt.

...contemplate long walks on the beach with your good-looking contractor.

...believe everything your fiancé says. Looks can be deceiving.

Chapter One

Mistake number one had been letting Lillian Morris, neighbor from hell and her future mother-in-law, in the front door. Yes, it would have been much better to have just ignored the doorbell and pretended she wasn't home. But Cassidy Clayton had been waiting for the city building inspector, and when she'd opened the door, unfortunately he hadn't been standing on the other side.

Cassidy looked at her fiancé's mother and grimaced. Once again, this time within five seconds after Lillian's arrival, Cassidy had been hit up to set an exact wedding date.

"I'm not sure," she said slowly, for it was always wise to choose your words carefully around Lillian, "exactly, if Dan and I want to marry this June. We haven't discussed it. After all, we've only been engaged two months. I was thinking more like October. That's eight months from now."

Lillian Morris peered over her horn-rimmed glasses

and with a dismissive wave brushed off Cassidy's concerns.

"Darling Cassidy, engagements should be short. Yours can be even shorter than normal, given that you've known my son all your life. Besides, a June wedding is perfect for you and Dan. Even Ed," Lillian mentioned her husband, "agrees with me. He's going to announce Luke's candidacy for senate right after the best man's wedding toast. Of course, Dan already agreed that his brother, Luke, would be best man. It's only fitting."

Great. Before Cassidy could even fully open her mouth to remind Lillian whose wedding it was supposed to be, Lillian went right on. After all, Dan was her baby boy.

"Besides," Lillian said, "Dan and I discussed it just last night and he agreed that June is perfect. Of course he wants to see his older brother win the senate race and keep the seat in the family. Luke would be the third generation you know. And we'll hold the reception at the Diamond Country Club. I've already contacted the manager, booked the room and arranged the menu. We'll be starting with roving waiters carrying trays of appetizers that are—"

If only for a brief moment, the doorbell's ringing interrupted Lillian's prattle. The older woman blinked, as if startled, as she glanced at Cassidy. "Are you expecting anyone?"

Even the devil himself was welcome at this moment. "City building inspector," Cassidy replied as she rose from the overstuffed armchair that had been her mother's latest attempt at redecorating.

Lillian nodded. "Oh, that makes sense. I had wondered why you were here. Usually you're at work by now." Lillian waved her hand dramatically around Cassidy's family home.

"You must be so grateful, Cassidy, to have sold this albatross. I'd imagine it gives you terrible memories, especially with your father divorcing your mother clear out of the blue like that after what, thirty-seven years of marriage? No wonder she took off for Cannes. I'd do the same. Not that my Ed would ever leave me. Some marriages are just meant to last. But I've always been lucky. I hope your mother isn't taking too much of a loss on the property. She should have fetched quite a price for this neighborhood, especially selling it furnished like that."

Cassidy's smile tightened. Next-door neighbors for almost twenty-five years, Cassidy's mother had always said that if Senator Ed Morris had thought divorcing his wife was less of a liability than was keeping her, then the tactless Lillian would have already been history.

Cassidy opened the front door. The elderly inspector standing between the columns looked like a smaller version of Santa Claus. Cassidy sighed. He seemed harmless enough. Grateful for the welcome diversion from Lillian and the already insane wedding planning, she bade him to come in without shooing Lillian out.

Right after that, Cassidy discovered that not getting rid of Lillian was mistake number two.

FOUR HOURS LATER Cassidy tossed her handbag onto the wooden bar. It landed with a thump, nearly knocking the half-empty bowl of peanuts off the other side. She ignored the curious look crossing the face of the man seated to her right.

"Bud Light." The words coming from her lips sounded foreign to her own ears.

But the bartender simply nodded as if dodging flying peanuts was the norm, and without a word of judgment, she took a beer from the cooler, removed the top and handed over the longneck bottle.

Cassidy placed the cold brown glass to her lips and took a long slow slip of the golden liquid. Normally she avoided beer, but today an ice-cold one sounded like just the medicine she needed. Besides, it would serve her fiancé and his silly mother right. When she was with them she only drank wine, for in their "crowd" domestic beer was frowned upon as something bourgeois. As if millions of Americans who tossed cold ones back every night could be wrong.

Oh well, drinking beer could be mistake number three in her perfectly ordered world. With satisfaction Cassidy mulled over that thought. After all, what else could happen?

Thanks to Lillian's inane prattle to the building inspector, which caused him to find even more code violations to cite, Cassie now had a multitude of problems all needing to be repaired by the home closing date in just two weeks' time. If the code violations weren't fixed, the house sale couldn't be completed, and she couldn't take a well-deserved vacation and close on her cute new condo in Clear Lake.

Cassidy took another long sip. The building inspector hadn't missed a thing. She had to do everything from painting to fixing a cracked concrete pad under a screened-in porch.

Closing her eyes, Cassidy again let the cool liquid slide down her throat. Perfect. She opened her eyes. At least this one thing was what she needed, which was good because right now the rest of her life was absolutely falling apart.

And, of course, Sara wasn't on time, and that was after Cassidy, preparing for her former college roommate's perpetual lateness, had arrived fifteen minutes past their designated meeting time of seven o'clock. There was nothing Cassidy hated more than sitting in a bar by herself.

Making the best of it, she took another long swallow and drummed her manicured fingernails on the bar as she surveyed the place Sara had picked out. "No one will know you there," Sara had said after Cassidy had called her in the throes of desperation. Now after seeing the place for herself, Cassidy couldn't agree more. As an image consultant, she'd helped some of Houston's elite refine their images, and this wasn't where anyone worth their salt would ever be caught dead.

At least it wasn't smoky, although that was about

all it had going for it. There was no question that the
place was a dive. The wooden tables had seen better
days, the chairs were vinyl, and the waitress sported a
tattoo under her Harley-Davidson T-shirt. All that was
missing was sawdust covering the floor and musicians
behind chicken wire.

"You know, most people at least try to relax when
they come into a bar."

Cassidy turned toward the deep silken tone coming
from the man seated to her right. Her eyes narrowed
slightly. "Excuse me?"

"Perhaps, as long as you relax a little," he said, his
drawl rolling over her in waves. He grinned, and inwardly Cassidy groaned. Not another one.

Ever since she'd been a cheerleader in high school
she'd attracted the wrong type of men like a refrigerator door attracted magnets. But at least this one was
attractive. More than attractive.

From where he was sitting on the stool, he looked
as if he would tower over her by at least a foot. His
body was lean and wiry, and his shoulders were wide
and broad. She liked that. Too bad his upper body was
covered by a T-shirt that looked as if had been laun-
dered too many times.

He twisted his beer in his hand, and Cassidy shivered despite herself. Maybe the air-conditioning inside
the bar was set too high.

"Can I buy you another one?" Without waiting for
her answer, he gestured to the bartender.

As he smiled again, Cassidy immediately gave him

credit for having wide sensual lips, twinkling dimples and a roman nose that wasn't too long. Too bad she wasn't interested in men with dark-brown eyebrows and eyelashes, no matter how deep and sensual his greenish-blue eyes. Bedroom eyes. For that's what they were, given the blood racing in her body. She made a show of studying her fingernails.

No, she told herself, as she tried to ignore the man's magnetism, her fiancé Dan suited her just fine. At five-eight Dan only stood two inches taller than she. She could look Dan right in the eye. Plus he was always impeccably tailored, and his profession allowed him to keep his hands clean, unlike the man next to her, whose cuticles looked as if they'd recently seen some hard washing with Fast Orange.

Besides, she rationalized, she'd been dating Dan for more than two years now, and that was after they'd been friends forever. He'd been the boy next door of her childhood, and no one had been surprised when he'd proposed to her with a flawless diamond in the middle of the annual Morris New Year's Eve party. Even better, Dan was easy, comfortable, not at all unsettling like the man seated next to her.

She hadn't been this unsettled since— She brushed that thought aside. In college she'd learned that burning passion did just that—burn you and leave you singed.

Still, Cassidy had been raised in the spirit of Texan hospitality, and the man had just bought her a beer.

She gave him a courteous smile and made her tone politely neutral. "Thank you."

"No problem." He shrugged, as if it were a gesture he made all the time. "You look like you had a hard day."

It had been hard, but Cassidy was loath to tell him that. She'd learned long ago not to engage men in bars with idle chitchat. It always gave them the wrong ideas. Besides, would the man really care about her problems?

Doubtful. Even Dan didn't think the fact that Cassidy's parents were divorcing after thirty-seven years of marriage was a big deal. After all, her well-to-do parents had been estranged for years. Her mother just hadn't looked the other way this time.

"Cat got your tongue," he observed. He signaled the bartender. "Bring me my regular, okay, Dee?"

"Sure, Blade," she replied with a warm smile.

"My dinner," he offered, seeing Cassidy's look.

Cassidy nodded benignly and pinned her gaze to the door. Just where was Sara, anyway? She was never this late.

He ignored her nonverbal cue.

"Say, would you like something to eat? The food here is actually pretty good. I can personally recommend the strip steak. It's the best around."

She drew herself up and chilled her posture, sending down her nose the ice maiden look she'd perfected long ago. "No thanks," she replied. Perhaps now he'd get the idea.

At her change in posture, Blade Frederick almost wanted to laugh at the irony of it. For once he hated being right. For once, why couldn't he be wrong?

Nope.

Not this time. He'd pegged her from the moment she'd arrived in his bar. One of those upper-crust women, slumming in an environment not her own, for reasons she felt like keeping to herself. Perhaps she was having second thoughts about her perfect life. Maybe wedding-day jitters?

His beer tasted stale in his mouth as he studied her left hand. Judging by the Rock of Gibraltar diamond on her third finger, no wonder she didn't want to be noticed, or bothered, either.

Although not noticing her was damn near impossible.

Her suit, especially its short skirt, showed off her figure perfectly. With her long blond hair she could rival a Barbie doll for perfection. Being raised around the fake stuff, he could tell natural color when he saw it, and she had it. He'd wager money on it, and nowadays that was something he had plenty of to spare.

Since she'd walked into his place, she'd judged and juried him into a neat little box, a box he'd long ago broken out of. He didn't like her assumptions of who he was, but what the hell. When whoever she was waiting for finally arrived, she'd be gone. Just this once he might as well act the part she'd already assigned to him, a persona he'd long ago shed.

"You know, darlin'," he drawled, "you really

should eat something if you're going to be slamming those beers down that fast.''

That got a rise out of her. He grinned. Yep, she was one of those high-and-mighty ones. She may have him pegged wrong, but he hadn't made a mistake. He sure had her number.

"Excuse me?" Those golden eyebrows of hers arched again, and despite himself, Blade felt a bit of glee at getting a rise out of her.

He knew he shouldn't delight in it, but after being looked down upon by the high and mighty of Scott Creek while he grew up, it was fun to toy with a woman of her class knowing that he wanted absolutely nothing to do with her. No matter what, he knew her type and her game, and never again would he let a woman out of her perfect world slum with his heart.

She continued to glare at him, and he found himself staring into her baby-blue eyes. Damn, she was pretty. But they always were.

God built them that way just to torment men. Blade shifted, trying to get that image out of his head and his now tightening jeans.

"Look, I didn't come here to eat but to meet some-one," she said in a haughty tone that bordered on in-dignation. Blade bit the inside of his cheek to keep himself from chuckling at her. She was too cute. "And since we do not know each other, and I'd like to keep it that way, please refrain from stating your opinion on my activities."

The smile he'd been trying to restrain cracked open.

"You almost sent the peanuts flying with your purse, honey. I was just concerned for Dee's safety. She's the best bartender around."

"Thanks, Blade," Dee called from where she was wiping up a residual beer ring.

Cassidy swung around toward him, her hosiery-clad legs connecting with his. She didn't seem to notice, but he did. Immediately.

Her baby blues flashed fire. "You think I'm dangerous after two beers? Since you have no idea who I am or what I can do or how much I can drink, your opinion is best kept to yourself."

Worrying about her drinking was now the last thing on his mind. His mind had headed south, and he wondered if she could feel the heat rising from his jean-clad thighs simply because of her touch. He suddenly hoped not. He hadn't gotten this much of a rise from a woman in a long time, and despite himself, he wanted to prolong it.

"Most people value my opinion," he drawled, giving her his best wink. If he'd worn his Resistol, he'd have tipped the cowboy hat's brim to her.

She recoiled as if she'd seen a snake. "I am not most people."

He could agree with her there. Actually, she was different from the others he'd met of her class. She had spunk, style. Perhaps his first impression of her had been wrong. He didn't mind being wrong, not in this case.

A slow smile edged across his face. She'd said she

wasn't most people, meaning she didn't value his opinion. He had the perfect reply. "Then that makes you one of the few that don't know better."

If she weren't waiting for Sara, Cassidy would have shown him her beer up close and personal by dumping it in his lap. She bit her tongue from the barbaric reply that sprang to her lips, and instead replied through clenched teeth.

"I see your mother forgot to raise you with manners."

He had to give her credit. She was fast on her feet. But so was he, and he was enjoying this challenge way too much. It had been a long time since he'd met a woman who could match wits and spar with him. "What I lack in manners, ma'am, I make up for in other areas."

"Really." Those areas were not something she wanted to think about, but unable to resist his bait, she exaggerated her Texan drawl to match his. "Too bad I'm so unimpressed with any of the areas I see."

The electricity between them sizzled. His voice silky, he drawled, "Then perhaps you should investigate the areas you don't see. I'm sure you'll find something to your liking."

Her legs pressed even more into his, and she deliberately allowed her gaze to rove over his body. "Nah. Those don't interest me, either."

He arched an eyebrow at her and laughed. He hadn't seen this much spirit and spunk in a woman in a long time. He had to admit, it intrigued him. Better, she intrigued him. He had judged her too quickly, and now he wanted to peel off her layers in more ways than one.

Besides, he would remain in control. He was all grown-up and practiced in the art of womanly wiles now.

Cassidy bristled, annoyed at his obvious ease. Still she maintained her outward composure as she dug a little deeper. "What, a woman not being interested isn't a reply you hear every day?"

"Can't say that it is." He signaled for another round of longnecks and his expression sobered. "Seriously, though, why don't we make peace and then you can tell me what's got you in such a foul mood."

Cassidy blinked at him, her suspicion obvious at the sudden shift of conversation. Oh, what the hell. It could be mistake number four, or was she now on five? She'd lost count, and all she knew was that she needed to vent, and Sara sure wasn't around.

Suddenly noticing that her legs were touching his, she moved herself a safe distance away. Her body immediately missed his touch, and Cassidy frowned. That wasn't a feeling she should be having. She found her safe topic. "I had the house I'm selling inspected by the city today."

He nodded his understanding. "I should have guessed. Hit you hard, did he?"

"Four pages worth of predications," she replied, reaching for the bottle of beer the waitress deposited in front of her.

He whistled low. "Not good."

"You're telling me," Cassidy replied, her comfort level with him escalating.

Finally, here was someone who actually understood. Dan had been too busy with some project to talk to her. Not even her real estate agent had been sympathetic, and she stood to make a huge commission from the deal. Blade's roast beef sandwich arrived, and it did look good. Cassidy's eyes glazed as she stared at it. Maybe she should eat something. "I thought you recommended the strip steak."

"I do, but my usual is roast beef." He dipped the French bread roll in the juice, and Cassidy's mouth started watering as he raised the morsel to his lips.

He gestured with a French fry. "So you were saying, about the house?"

She blinked as the French fry disappeared. Darn her. She'd been staring at his lips! "Oh. Right. It's all Lillian's fault."

"Lillian?" His dark-brown eyebrow shot up and Cassidy again noticed his eyes. Those bedroom blues had turned boardroom. He was actually interested in what she was saying. Danger signals went off in her head. Whoa, she thought. Time to stop drinking beer.

She reached for the plastic dish holding the remaining peanuts. She should at least eat something. "Lillian's my mother-in-law. Well, she's not my mother-in-law. Not yet. Not ever if I could help it. She means well, but…"

Cassidy shuddered. Immediately forgetting her resolve, she took another sip of her third beer. She tried to gather her thoughts and retrench. Had she just criticized Lillian aloud? "She kept talking and the more she talked, the more he wrote."

The inspector certainly hadn't been impressed that Lillian had been the wife of Senator Ed Morris of Texas, or that she lived next door, or that she could get him fired. He'd just kept writing, turning the paper over, filling the back, and then beginning a new sheet.

Even worse, Lillian had remained calm about the whole thing.

"You'll just need to build a new house," Lillian had said. "I'll talk to Ed and Dan about it tonight. If you contracted for one now it might be ready when you come home from your honeymoon. A month in Alaska, doesn't that sound wonderful? June is the perfect month to see Alaska. It'll be Ed's and my gift to you both."

At that moment Cassidy was glad she'd never taken advantage of Texas's concealed carry law.

"Sounds pretty bad," the man next to her sympathized as she finished the story.

"It is," Cassidy said. He finished his sandwich, and her mouth went dry. What had gotten into her? She'd just told him everything. She never did that. She never drank beer, either, or held conversations with strange but attractive guys in a bar. She blinked. He was gorgeous, enough to be a calendar pinup. She shoved another handful of peanuts into her mouth. Sober. She needed to be sober.

"Look," he began, "I know some handymen who can help you out. I can call them and..."

"Oh no," Cassidy managed through the mouthful of peanuts. She shook her head firmly and cut him off. Do not accept favors from strangers in bars. Especially good-looking men like him that would break your heart. Rule number thirteen or something like that in the *Single Woman's Guide to*...something or other. "No. No." She couldn't believe she sounded so nervous. "Thanks for offering, but I'll take care of it."

Somehow she would, although frankly, she had no idea how. Maybe one just looked up handymen under the letter *H* in the yellow pages.

"Here." Cassidy almost jumped out of her skin as he handed her a small card. Why was he making her so nervous? Even she could see that it was only a business card. People handed her business cards all the time.

"Uh," she stammered, suddenly feeling the urgent need to flee and get out from his magnetic proximity. It was either that or kiss him. Where had that thought come from? She would never drink beer again. Ever.

"Take my card," he said. Then he reached forward and uncurled her fingers. Never had a man violated her personal space like this.

But the rage at his invasion of her space didn't come. Instead Cassidy felt heat flow through her. Underneath his touch all rational thought evaporated as he closed her fingers around the card. "Call me if you need me."

Oh, I do, she thought, heat rising into her face. At least the words hadn't been voiced.

Wait! What was she doing? What was she thinking? Dan. Think of Dan. That's right. Think of nice, safe Dan who never made her quiver like this. The thought evaporated as Sara walked in the door. Relief filled Cassidy. Finally.

"Look, there's my friend." Cassidy jerked her hand away from his, her fingers instantly missing the heat of touching his. She shoved his card in her purse and edged her way off the bar stool. "Thanks for the drink. Enjoy your dinner." Grabbing her beer, she tottered over to meet Sara.

With a mixture of relief and frustration Blade watched her walk away. Relief filled him because she had been one of those women and he'd actually found himself enjoying the conversation with her. Frustration filled him for just about the exact same reason. She was one of those women, and he'd been enjoying the conversation with her. Would he never learn?

Dee came over and stood for a second as they both watched the two women take a seat at a back booth.

"How was the food?" Dee asked.

"Fine," Blade replied.

Dee's expression, as she looked down her nose at him, said it all. "Just fine?"

"You know it was great, like always." He shoved the empty basket toward her, his concentration still on the woman he'd just been sitting next to.

"Pretty thing," Dee observed, following his gaze.

She could take those liberties. Blade had hired her four years ago when he'd bought the place from the elderly man who owned it. Greg had wanted to retire, and Blade, flush with money, had seen the need to own something that wasn't just concrete and steel.

"So did you get her phone number?"

"Please, Dee. I don't even know her name."

Dee dropped the basket on a tray beneath the bar. "You sure looked like you were getting friendly with her."

Blade gave a short, bitter laugh. "Please," he said, denying the attraction he'd felt, that he still felt. "She's not my type. Heck, she doesn't even belong here. Can you see her in the back room shooting pool?"

Dee cocked her head and watched as the other waitress, Lisa, took the women's order. "Maybe not," Dee replied. "But looks can be deceiving."

He turned back around so he couldn't see the women, especially her, anymore. "I've never discovered that to be true," Blade protested, already knowing that whoever she was, she'd gotten under his skin.

At that lie, Dee simply shook her head and walked away.

"SO WHO'S THE GUY?"

Cassidy's fork hovered over her strip steak. "You mean Dan?"

"No, not him." Sara said. She pushed a dark hair off of her face. "The guy at the bar who keeps staring at you every few minutes. You were sitting by him when I arrived.''

"I don't know him," Cassidy said, spearing her cut piece of meat with such a force that Sara leaned back.

"Well for not knowing him, he sure got under your skin.''

"He did not," Cassidy said with a vigorous shake of her head. "He's just a guy sitting at the bar, that's all. If you'd been on time, I wouldn't have even been talking to him. You weren't even your usual fashionably late self.''

"No, but my extremely late self got you next to him," Sara said. She let her gaze rove over him, and Cassidy found herself bristling. "Man, he's hot. I'd do him.''

"Sara!"

"What?" Sara looked taken back, as if surprised at the force of Cassidy's reaction.

"You're married.''

"Only until the divorce paperwork's final," Sara said. "Believe me, I'm allowed to look.''

Cassidy knew that. Never had she been so rattled. It had to be the beer. She stared at the empty bottle in front of her. She'd stopped at three, thank goodness.

Sara turned slightly so she'd have a better view. Cassidy watched as Sara put the end of her pinkie finger in between her teeth and gazed over toward the guy again. "I mean, he's hot. And you know what they say, that you can tell a guy's size by the distance between his thumb and pinkie. From the look of his hands..."

"Sara!" Cassidy put her fork down.

Sara's brow furrowed. "Come on, Cass. Lighten up. You were never this prudish in college."

"I wasn't engaged then," Cassidy said.

"Yeah, well you shouldn't be engaged now, either."

"Sara!" Cassidy realized she'd shouted that last one at her former roommate.

"Sorry, Cass. You know me. I call them the way I see them. All your friends are married, and now you're settling down just because it's the right thing to do. Believe me, I settled, and look what happened. He cheated on me right from the start."

"I am not settling," Cassidy protested. "I love Dan."

"Dan is dull," Sara said. "He's like dishwater. You need it, but you don't want to keep it."

"I love Dan."

"Yeah, as a brother," Sara said. "I think that you've waited so long for Mr. Right you're settling for Mr. Wrong. Come on, you can't tell me that you don't think that guy over there is to die for."

Cassidy couldn't get her lips to voice the lie. Instead she found another argument tack. "Yeah, but look where passion got me last time. Jeff the jerk."

Sara nodded, but didn't concede. "I'd forgotten about good old J.J. No offense but he was a loser."

"Yeah, but passionate. He swept me off my feet and burned me bad."

"True." Sara thought for a second. "But we all go through the bad ones to find the good ones. Consider J.J. a learning experience."

Cassidy shook her head. "I don't have time for more learning experiences. I want children and a family. I'm twenty-eight. Dan is perfect."

He was. She jutted her chin forward stubbornly.

Sara simply shook her head. "I hope for your sake you're right."

"I am," Cassidy said. *As long as I don't run into that guy again.*

She'd throw his business card away as soon as she got home.

IMAGE CONSULTANTS were not supposed to have hangovers. In fact, no one was supposed to have a hangover after only three longneck bottles of beer, then dinner and then another two hours of conversation with only water to drink before either she or Sara had done any driving home. Even that guy had left long before she had.

Cassidy rolled over and shielded her eyes from the bright sunlight pouring in her bedroom windows. Lillian's mantra suddenly filled her mind. "Today is the first day of the rest of your life. Make the best of it."

With that annoying thought, Cassidy sat up straight in bed. Today already sucked, and if today was a crystal ball of the future then she wanted no part of it. She blinked and glanced at the alarm clock—7:00 a.m. Great. Her alarm wasn't scheduled to go off for at least another fifteen minutes.

Figured. She hadn't even slept in.

Cassidy flopped back on the pillows and covered her eyes with her arm. Not that she could go back to sleep, anyway. The only concession was that she'd slept soundly, with no dreams of said men to haunt her.

Begrudgingly she rolled out of bed, hit the shower and within forty minutes had seated herself at the breakfast table with the yellow pages.

As she munched a grape-jelly-covered bagel, she frowned. By the time she'd finished the last of the bagel, she was sure lines ridged her brow, as well, creating a look her mother had always chided would give her premature wrinkles.

The yellow pages listed hundreds of contractors, and Cassidy had no clue whatsoever who to call.

Three hours later, after dialing for over an hour, she faced failure.

"Your problems are too small," one contractor had said. "We don't handle residential," another's haughty secretary had replied. "We can't put you on the schedule for at least three weeks," most had told her.

She was already at the *H*s. She rose and faced her nightmare. Two steps took her to the stainless steel trash compactor. She'd run it last night when she'd gotten home.

Grimacing, she opened it up. Gingerly she picked through the remnants, finally finding the tiny cardstock paper she was looking for.

Glad the sauce had been white not red, she brushed off a leftover fettuccini noodle and read the words embossed.

J & B Construction. Blade Frederick, President.

Rather a fancy title to disguise what was probably a sole-proprietorship. She shivered as her gaze swept over the card again. His name was Blade.

She'd briefly heard it once or twice at the bar, but it hadn't really registered. It did now, and his name fit. Sara's prophetic words came rushing back, and Cassidy dropped the card back into the trash compactor.

She couldn't call him.

She stared at the card, lying faceup on the congealing fettuccine Alfredo. She had to call him. She had no choice. Besides, he said he would recommend a handyman, not do the work himself.

Inaction paralyzed her, and finally anger overtook her. She was being silly. Last night had just been too much beer and too much of feeling sorry for herself because of her home situation.

She grabbed the card back out of the compactor and kicked the stainless steel door closed.

She'd simply make it clear to…Blade that she needed his help and that she wasn't interested in any of his other services.

Besides, over the phone she wouldn't be tempted to look at his hands and wonder if...

She brushed that distracting thought aside as she swore never to drink beer again. I can do this, Cassidy whispered the pep talk to herself as she reached for the phone. She dialed the number for J & B Construction. Besides, it'll be fine, she told herself. After yesterday I deserve a break.

Chapter Two

Blade needed a break, and not an endless coffee break like his secretary still seemed to be on. Bidding on— and winning—the job to build the state's newest revenue office should have been a piece of cake. But it wasn't turning out that way, and Jake was annoyed.

Blade hated it when Jake, his best friend and business partner, was annoyed. It always spelled trouble.

"We're up against D. W. Braun, and it's down to just us two," Jake said.

Blade sat forward, letting the back of his leather chair thump him gently in the back. He knew there was more. "What do they have on our bid?"

"I'm not sure." His partner, and technically the company co-president, paced the room anxiously. "I've heard on the street that D.W.'s put money into some political campaigns."

"Figures." Blade gritted his teeth. "So much for the lowest bidder."

"Come on, Blade, we know it's rarely the lowest bidder. It's the bidder with the longest tentacles who can justify all the expenses and pad the congressmen's pockets. That's why public projects always run over budget.''

''Not with our company.''

''Of course not.'' Jake knew Blade was as honest and ethical as they came, and their company had a reputation for the same. ''But we've only been bidding on public projects for the past two years. We're new in this arena. We usually do private, like the renovation of the old Caferelli warehouse into an upscale hotel and lofts.''

''I want this project,'' Blade said. ''We have the best design and the best company for the job. I want to see us diversify from just office buildings and 200,000-square-foot retail developments.''

''Exactly,'' Jake agreed with a short nod. ''We want to diversify. To do that we've got to get out there on the social scene. Make some political contacts. Show them we're serious about running with the big boys.''

''That's your job.'' Blade took a mechanical pencil and tapped it, top down, on the mahogany desk. ''I may own a half dozen custom suits, but I don't wear them unless I have to. You win jobs—I work the field and make sure we come in under budget and on time.''

''Yeah, but we want to continue to grow, don't we?''

''Grow?'' Blade snorted his disbelief. ''We're the fastest growing commercial contractor in the nation. We did two billion in revenue last year.''

''Exactly. Two million less than the year before.''

Jake sounded as if two *million* was the end of the world. "Come on, Blade. I want this company to be one of the top in the country, and so do you. Right now we're number ten in Houston and thirty-third in the nation."

"And we're not satisfied with that?" Blade asked. Their growth had been so phenomenal they'd passed companies in business for generations, not a mere eighteen years.

"Of course we're not satisfied," Jake replied. "We made a goal when we graduated high school that we'd never settle. Remember?"

The ringing of Blade's desk phone interrupted the conversation. He frowned. He'd left orders not to be disturbed. Obviously the temp at the front reception desk had screwed up again. Already this morning she'd disconnected three important calls.

Blade checked his tone. No use scaring the temp. He could replace her tomorrow. Better yet, he'd have his secretary do it. "Hello?"

"Hello," the female voice on the phone said slowly. Blade stopped tapping the pencil. Not the temp, and not one of his former girlfriends. He would have recognized one of their voices. Still, the voice sounded oddly familiar.

"I've gotten lost in the phone system twice now. I want to speak with Blade Frederick about fixing some code violations."

Great. The temp had screwed up. J & B did not do code violation repairs.

"Lady, we're—" Blade began, but she cut him off before he could finish.

"Please," she said, her voice a breathy rush. "I need Blade Frederick. He said he could help me and I've tried everyone else. I have four pages of predications. You should have seen the guy. He just kept writing. If it weren't for Lillian I never would have been in this fix."

On the other end of the phone Cassidy bit her tongue. Had she just said that, again?

In his office Blade waved off Jake's curious look and silent whisper of "Who is it?"

It was the girl from last night, and no, Blade himself couldn't believe it. She'd called. Last night he'd left the bar long before she had, and he'd spent a sleepless night dreaming of her. He hadn't woken up in a hot sweat like that since he'd been a randy teenager.

And she'd called. Unbelievable. He'd certainly lost that bet with himself.

He steadied his tone before speaking. No use giving away too much yet. "You do know we're a commercial contractor."

Sitting in her home office, Cassidy had no idea what that meant. "No," she said. "Look, I need to talk to Blade. I need him."

Blade shifted. That was not an image he needed at 11:00 a.m. Didn't she know what a seductive voice she had? He should tell her she had him. "You've got him."

"Oh." Cassidy never felt so out of her element.

"Look, I'm a little busy right now, but how about you fax the list to me and I'll take a look at them?"

Cassidy shifted the cordless phone to her other ear. So much for worrying about him hitting on her. Far from it.

"All right," she replied, her ego just a bit dented that she'd worried for nothing. She fingered the list that sat on her desk. "What's your fax number?"

Blade gave it to her. "I'll send it right over," Cassidy said. "I can't thank you enough. My neighbor Lillian, I told you about her, she kept telling the inspector she was a senator's wife. The more she talked, the more he wrote."

He'd heard all that before. "Fax it over and give me a number where I can reach you."

"Okay," Cassidy replied. "Oh. By the way, I'm Cassidy."

"Great, Cassidy," Blade said, deliberately keeping his tone professional. "Send it over and I'll get back to you."

"Uh, thanks."

"No problem." Blade set down the phone before she had a chance to say anything else. He chuckled.

"What is it?" Jake asked.

Blade leaned back in his swivel chair and linked his hands behind his head. "I met this woman in the bar last night. Pretty thing, one of those rich women who live around the medical center and Rice University. The building inspector hit her up for four pages of violations."

Jake gave a low whistle. "And she called you?"

Blade stretched and shook his head before he sat forward. "Well, I gave her my card."

Jake looked impressed. "You dog. I didn't think you still had it in you. You've been out of the scene awhile."

"Yeah, well, I told her I'd find her a handyman. I really didn't think she'd call."

"She probably figured out how much you're worth."

"That's the funny part. She has no clue. She wants me to find someone to fix her home predications. She thinks I'm some redneck, not a CEO."

"But you didn't correct her. You told her to fax you." Suddenly Jake laughed as Blade grinned. "You're a devil, Blade. Just wanted to know if you still had it, huh?"

"Yeah, well," Blade changed *that* subject, "besides it really isn't her fault. I kind of feel sorry for her. Her fiancé's mother kept telling the city inspector she was married to a senator or something. So don't get your hopes up. I'll help her find a contractor, but that's all."

Jake's ears perked up, and he ignored the last part of Blade's explanation. "Senator? Did you say senator?"

Fire alarms pealed in Blade's head. "Don't look at me like that. We've been friends for too long. You should be warning me off. She's set to be married."

"That's irrelevant. I like married women. They don't want to settle down, just play. Which senator?"

Blade had long ago given up on Jake and his morals of an alley cat. "I don't know. All I remember is that his wife's name is Lillian."

Jake's jaw dropped and he stared at Blade. "Lillian Morris?"

Blade arched an eyebrow. "You know her?"

"Everyone knows Lillian whether they want to or not. She's a firebrand who gets her way because she'll just run you over if you don't move."

Blade shrugged. "Whatever. She didn't make much of an impression on the building inspector."

Jake blinked in surprise. "That's because he hasn't learned better. I bet he'll never make that mistake again."

"Anyway, I'll look at the predications, and I'll call her and find someone to fix them for her. I offered to do it last night in the bar. My mother raised me to be a gentleman."

"Yeah, when she was home. Anyway, while you're being so ignoble, why don't you just hit the lady up for an invitation to meet the infamous Lillian. Senator Morris has a lot of pull in this town. We could use the connection."

That didn't sound good. "How about *you* meet the famous Lillian?"

Jake's smile turned wicked. "Maybe I will. You described the girl on the phone as a pretty thing, but I know you. She's hot, isn't she?"

Blade shifted. Sure he'd describe Cassidy as hot, but

that sounded so cheap. She was beautiful, an image of perfection, just as he'd thought last night.

Jake's gray eyes gleamed at Blade's silence. "I think I want to meet her. After all, it is my job to make contacts."

The idea of Jake, whom he liked a lot but wouldn't set up with his sister even if he had one, didn't sit well at all. No, the idea of Jake meeting the lady from the night before, Cassidy, didn't sit well at all.

"I'll do it," Blade said simply, his decision instantaneous. "I'll get you a meeting with Senator Morris, and you take it from there." There, that solution sounded just fine.

Sending Jake after Cassidy was like sending Christians to the lions.

Jake grinned. "Blade, my man, we are now on our way into Houston old money society, and I have just the plan to get us there."

Blade frowned. Jake's ideas involving women and Blade often backfired. "Yeah, well let's hope it doesn't leave a bad taste in my mouth."

"Money never leaves a bad taste, Blade," Jake chided. "It's time you learned that. Yep, high time you learned that, especially when the babe is hot. Now you listen to me, and I'll tell you what we are going to do."

CASSIDY COULDN'T BELIEVE her luck. A man named Jake from J & B Construction had called and told her that his company would do her work. Even better, he'd told her that J & B was licensed by the city and oversaw a crew that would do the job.

She pushed a loose strand of blond hair back off of her face. Jake had told her someone would come over at four-thirty. She'd be his last appointment of the day.

The doorbell rang, and she threw it open.

"I saw your car and since I knew you were home, I came over to discuss the flowers."

"Lillian!" Cassidy managed to step out of the way before Lillian barged right in. "I'm meeting with the contractor."

Lillian stopped and peered over her glasses. "Is he here?"

"Not yet. Any minute."

Lillian didn't look too concerned. "Well then, you have plenty of time."

"No, I don't." Cassidy tried anyway, but as always, protests with Lillian were useless.

"I talked it over with Dan this morning and he agreed with me."

Of course he had, Cassidy thought. He'd just smiled and nodded, just like his father did when Lillian got her teeth into something.

"Orchids. We'll be doing orchids. I think that's the perfect flower, and we'll get them at Estelle's. All I need to tell her is the color, although honestly I think we'll be sticking with pure white. You do agree white is best, don't you?"

"Sure," Cassidy said in resignation, giving Lillian

a smile and a nod. Anything to get Lillian out of the house.

The last thing Cassidy needed was Lillian scaring off the contractor. She'd done enough damage with the city inspector.

"Excellent. I've also booked the church for 3:00 p.m., June 10. An afternoon wedding is best, and your rehearsal dinner is the night before. I'm still choosing the location. I can't decide between The Ryan Room or Gillamaine's." Lillian stopped to draw a rare breath. "We also have a private appointment tomorrow evening at Monica's Boutique to find you an appropriate wedding dress."

"I thought I'd wear my mother's dress," Cassidy said. "It's in a box in the attic, and…"

Lillian's mouth dropped open in surprise and she looked as if Cassidy had grown another head. "That won't do, dear, especially with your parents getting divorced. Heavens, no." Lillian shook her head vehemently. "Tomorrow evening at six. We'll be the only ones in the shop. I'll pick you up at five. You know how traffic can be."

Cassidy gave Lillian another smile and nod before panic struck. Was that a truck pulling into the driveway? It was. Not good. Somehow Cassidy managed to usher Lillian to the door and got her through it. "See you tomorrow, Lillian."

Cassidy leaned back against the door and took a moment to sigh with relief. Home safe.

"Oh, you must be the contractor," she heard Lillian say.

Nope, out at third. Cassidy threw open the front door and walked out. The Ford 350 truck now sitting in her driveway looked as if it had known better days. Red with faded black lettering on the passenger side door, it proudly proclaimed to be from J & B Construction.

"You are the contractor, right?" Lillian asked.

"That would be me, ma'am."

Great. Lillian was already engaging the contractor in conversation. Did the infernal woman ever stop talking? Cassidy bit her lip and sped up. Wearing heels didn't help.

Worse, once again she'd had a mean thought about Lillian. That was so unlike herself. She usually had such good manners and polite thoughts.

And just when had the front walk gotten so long? Finally Cassidy reached the back of the truck. The contractor had his back to her, with Lillian facing him. He stood about six-six and had a nice posterior. Great, Cassidy thought. One night with Sara and now she was looking at everyone.

Cassidy paused just a moment, turning around to take a second look at something she'd at first only caught in the periphery of her eye.

Just what did that homemade back license plate say? *Power Strokers do it better?* Dear Lord. Don't let Lillian see that.

"What's that license plate mean?"

Too late.

"It's the engine. Ford has a diesel power stroke."

Cassidy saw Lillian nod as if she understood. "I see," Lillian said. "But shouldn't you have a real license plate?"

"Trucks over a certain gross vehicle weight don't need back plates. We pull trailers."

"Oh. So that plate really isn't a sexual thing at all."

"Uh, well," the contractor began.

Cassidy rolled her eyes and stepped closer. Time to interrupt before someone got himself in deep trouble with the matriarch of the Houston morality police. "Hi, I'm Cassidy Clayton. I believe you're looking for me."

As he turned around, she gasped. He wasn't supposed to be here. Jake had said...

Mistake number five didn't look surprised to see her. Instead he gave her a wide smile.

"Hello again," he said. "I'm here to do your work."

LILLIAN GLANCED over her glasses, her gaze speculative. "You two have met?"

"Yes," he said, his gaze never leaving Cassidy's.

"No," she said, wrenching hers away.

Lillian's head turned from one to another as if she were watching a championship Ping-Pong match. "So which is it?"

"No, we haven't met," Cassidy inserted quickly. She gave the man a wide smile that didn't reach her eyes. She had never thought she would see him again! After all, wasn't he a president? He really was a one-man, well, a two-man operation. After talking to a receptionist, and then Jake, she'd hoped otherwise.

"We just talked on the phone today. This is my contractor, uh…" After rolling his name on her tongue all day, now she couldn't get his name out.

"Blade," he finished smoothly, returning her fake smile with an infuriatingly real, and extremely sexy, one of his own.

"Blade," Cassidy repeated. She shot him a warning glance and hoped the man had enough brain cells upstairs to figure out what she meant—keep quiet.

Seemingly satisfied with the explanation, Lillian broke into a small smile. "So, you're doing all the repairs on Cassidy's house?"

"That's what I intend on doing," he replied. His tone insinuated to Cassidy that there might be more to his plan. Cassidy shifted on her feet.

"Oh, good," Lillian said, seeming not to notice the sexual undercurrents as she warmed to a topic she knew way too well. "Cassidy needs to get rid of this house quickly. Thank goodness it closes in two weeks. I mean, you heard why she has to sell it didn't you? Her philandering father left her mother for a younger woman and…"

Great. One more complication to her already hectic life. Now the infernal contractor, Blade—she got his name right this time—knew her personal business.

First things first. Time to get Lillian moving toward her own home.

"I doubt he really cares about my parents' problems, Lillian," Cassidy said. Relying on her training as an image consultant, she froze her smile in place and hoped that Lillian would get the subtle message. Instead Lillian looked confused.

Cassidy wanted to scream. Did no one around her understand body language? This was her career, and she was good at it. Somehow she managed to keep her voice calm. "I'm sure he's on the clock, and I'm sure he wants to go home soon. I'll see you at five tomorrow."

"Five," Lillian repeated. She let her gaze rove over Blade one last time. Cassidy bristled. Did every woman stare at him like that? Then Lillian straightened as if the moment hadn't occurred and gave Cassidy a stern look of warning. "We need to be on time tomorrow. Monica's is open only to us, so don't forget. Five."

"As if you'd let me forget," Cassidy said under her breath after Lillian slipped through the gate in the hedge between the two side yards.

His voice was right by her ear. "So I take it that's the infamous mother-in-law-to-be."

"That's her." Cassidy whirled around and found herself facing Blade's chest. Whoa. She took a step back "Would you care to explain what you are doing here?"

"I'm the contractor."

Why did he upset her equilibrium so? "Yes, well, your card said you're the president."

He grinned, and Cassidy wished she'd never called him. "Oh, that's a little joke Jake and I have. We own the company together. He's also a president. But I can assure you, I'm a contractor."

She struggled to regain control of the mess she was now in. "Well I can see that. You have a truck, and you're dressed in—"

"They're called carpenter whites. Whites for short."

Cassidy swallowed. Never had a pair of dirty white pants and a dirty white T-shirt looked so good. They hinted too well at what lay beneath. And just when had he gotten so tall? And his chest so broad? She gathered her wits, and rallied.

"Well, why didn't you say something on the phone when I called?"

His greenish-blue eyes twinkled, drowning her. "And ruin the surprise?"

She found a life preserver. "I don't like surprises."

His cheek dimpled as his smile curved upward. "I do, especially when it was a phone call from you. Imagine you calling me, especially after insisting you didn't need my help last night. I thought you'd just throw my card away."

She had, but she wasn't going to let him have the satisfaction of knowing that.

His voice washed over her. "Ironic isn't it, how fate works?"

"Look, this is a business arrangement." She stressed the word *business.*

He shot her another infuriating grin, as if he knew exactly what she was really thinking. "Never said it wasn't." He sobered his expression for a second. "Look, do you want me to do this work or not? Or would you rather hire someone else?"

Cassidy drew herself up. As if she could find another contractor on this short notice, and he knew it. After all, she only had ten business days until closing. "Fine, then. Come inside and I'll show you what that infernal city inspector is referring to."

With a huff she turned and walked toward the house.

IT WAS ALL BLADE COULD do to stop from humming to himself. He'd made one change to Jake's misguided plan.

He'd borrowed one of his foremen's trucks for the occasion, and from the expression on Cassidy's face, it had been worth it. While Jake wanted him to reveal who he was, Blade didn't. Why spoil her preconceived notions? No, his plan of appearing like the everyday Joe that Cassidy had pegged him for had gone off perfectly.

Blade grinned at his success. Earlier that day he'd considered Jake's suggestion of driving his own truck, but the more he thought of it, the more he had decided not to.

She already thought he was just a blue-collar workingman. While Blade had a diesel Ford 350 himself, he knew it didn't look like what Cassidy thought a contractor's truck would look like, not with leather seats and being loaded with every known option.

Besides, she'd never believe his truck cost almost as much as a Corvette.

So, instead he had borrowed Frank's truck, and of course, the forty-year-old Frank had been only too happy to exchange his work truck for Blade's new BMW convertible, which, too, had cost a few hundred less than Blade's truck.

"I'll even take the wife on a date," Frank had said with a grin. "I'll tell her I sold the truck. It'll pay her back for my license plate."

Blade had laughed. Everyone knew Frank's wife was a practical joker, and she'd gotten him the plate as a gag gift for his fortieth birthday.

Blade snapped to attention as Cassidy began talking. "This is the first predication," she said as she came to the front steps. "He said something about needing some new boards, plus he wanted the entire front porch painted."

"I saw that on the fax you sent," Blade said. He reached into the pocket of his pants. "I brought it with me."

Cassidy's lips thinned into a slight smile. "You're so efficient."

"That would be me," he replied, ignoring her slight sarcasm. Heck, he'd be a mite upset if someone had just pulled this surprise on him. However, he rationalized, he was going to fix her house, so in the end that made it all okay. And despite how pretty she was, he wasn't going to hit on her the way she obviously thought he was.

His gaze scanned the porch. She did need a few new boards, but nothing really major. "Why don't you show me the rest?"

"Front door needs painting," Cassidy said as they walked through it. "All the windows need to have working sashes. Something about the springs being broken. When the city inspector lifted the one in the bay window, the whole window fell out."

Blade nodded. "That's not difficult. I know where to get the parts."

"Good." And with that, Cassidy was on a roll. Twenty minutes later Blade was certain of two things. One was that the city inspector had been overzealous in citing things that he really didn't need to have cited. The other was that Cassidy Clayton had grown up with every possible advantage in life.

His bedroom, which he'd shared with his two older brothers, would have fit in the master bedroom closet. The master bathroom of the house, which needed all new plumbing fixtures, was bigger than the living room and kitchen where he'd grown up.

Sure he had a house about the same size now, but he'd worked and sweated for every brick. Cassidy had simply been born into it.

"That's all of them," she said. "Think you can have all this work done in a week?"

Blade stared at her. She'd pushed her hair behind her ears and was peering earnestly up at him. Darn, but she was pretty.

"I'm going to have to work nights to get these all finished," he said. Where those words had come from, he would later decide that he didn't know. They'd just slipped out. He was the boss. He could do what he wanted, and he could work days.

"You want time and a half?" She seemed shocked.

"I didn't say that," he replied, trying to backtrack. "Jake gave you our bid already for all hours worked. No matter what time of day, fixed hourly rate. You only have about twenty hours of work."

"So what's the catch?"

Was there a catch? He thought about it a second and dismissed what Jake wanted him to do out of his head. "No catch. It'll take me about four days of about five hours each. I'll get here at four and leave by nine."

She frowned. "Look," he said, "That's the best I can do. I've got other jobs in the queue, as well, and somehow I'm going to have to balance everything. So I won't get here until four. But I will get your predications done and have them done before your deadline."

The thought of him in her house at night seemed so… "I sometimes have to work at night," Cassidy said, pushing thoughts of Blade in her house at night out of her mind. That was not a path she should tread. He raised an eyebrow, encouraging her to explain, and she felt the need to. "I'm an image consultant, and depending on the day I attend dinner functions and..."

Suddenly he didn't want to hear about her social life. He cut her off. "If you aren't here to let me in, then I'll need a key and your alarm code."

He almost wanted to laugh at her horrified reaction. "We are licensed and bonded, ma'am."

"Cassidy," she corrected automatically. She hated being called ma'am. It made her feel old.

"Cassidy." He rolled her name on his tongue and decided that he liked it. "Well, Cassidy, since I'm here, shall I get started?"

Her mouth puckered. "You're starting the job tonight?"

He folded his arms across his chest. "Is there a problem with that? I'm already here, and I need to make a list of stuff I need. Plus, you don't have time to spare."

He was right.

Cassidy gulped and tore her gaze off Blade's chest. Last night Sara had said something about stroking it and discovering if his chest was smooth or covered with dark whirls of hair.

If he took off his shirt when he worked in the Texas heat she'd know.

Whoa! Wait right there. Those were not thoughts she should have. Think of Dan, think of Dan.

Oh, God. Dan. He'd be over in less than an hour to take her out to dinner. He had some clients to impress. That meant she needed a shower, and she needed to redo her makeup and… Then again, she also needed to have her predications fixed. What was it Blade had asked?

Normally she wasn't so scatterbrained. Maybe it was the stress of everything. Her parents had dumped the selling of the family home and moving the few belongings they wanted to keep into her lap.

"No problem," she said after finally remembering his question about whether he should get started tonight. "Just stay on the first floor."

The last thing she needed was for him to be in her bedroom. Thankfully that had been one room that hadn't needed any repairs.

"I'll try," Blade replied, his gaze sweeping over her.

"See that you do," she said, suddenly feeling the need for a long, cold shower. She now knew the truth. She couldn't blame her physical reaction to him on beer.

Turning, she disappeared up the stairs. She had the distinct impression that he stared at her legs the whole time.

Chapter Three

As Cassidy walked away, Blade let himself take a long look at her legs as she walked upstairs. Nice and slender. He liked that. A lot.

Too bad he couldn't let himself really like her. Liking Cassidy would be a mistake. She was engaged, and he, unlike Jake, didn't tread on another man's domain.

But he could look. That was acceptable, no harm done, and it could be his job perk.

Jake could get Lillian as the job perk. That would serve him right.

Humming to himself, Blade began an inventory of what materials he would need in order to do the work. About a half hour later he looked at the long list he'd made and compared it with the city inspector's predications. He frowned. He'd missed something.

Blade shook his head as he realized what it was. How had he missed something so obvious? He needed ground-fault interrupters for one of the guest bathrooms upstairs.

He thought for a moment, trying to remember how the house had been wired. Newer homes often had one GFI circuit breaker that had all the outlets wired to it. Older homes often had individual circuits and each receptacle needed a GFI.

He strode toward the back staircase. He'd just have to go test them and see. It would only take a second.

Blade paused on the upstairs landing, but he wasn't interested in the original Monet hanging on the wall. Instead, it was the muffled sound of water that had caught his attention. Cassidy was in the shower.

He stood there a moment, unable to stop from visualizing the rushing water streaming down her back, over her breasts and down her legs. He shook himself. That job perk vision was off-limits. He moved down the hall and into a spare bedroom. This had to be the right one. He'd just check the outlet and be on his way....

He paused, stricken, remembering that Virginia Woolf line, "People shouldn't have looking glasses in their houses."

For it was true.

For there, reflected in the mirror, he could see Cassidy, clear as day, through the shower door.

God, she was gorgeous. The steam hadn't yet covered the see-through glass, giving him a perfect glimpse of her high, firm breasts. And her legs...his mouth dried as she worked a mesh sponge over her body. His earlier fantasy about her legs had been nothing compared to the reality.

The reality was much better.

He stood, transfixed, as if someone had frozen him in time. Her voice drifted into his consciousness. She was singing some old Madonna tune about being a virgin touched for the very first time.

He attempted to move his feet. He wasn't a Peeping Tom. He didn't look on unknowing women, especially engaged ones. His feet refused to budge.

Another part of his anatomy was refusing to follow directions, as well, and Blade swallowed a groan. He had to admit the truth.

Despite himself, he wanted this woman.

Damn it, man! A voice cut into his brain, overriding the desire paralyzing him. You know better than this! First off she's engaged, and most important, she's not your type.

The sound of Cassidy turning off the water jolted him to action. He fled before she could see him.

Quickly he headed down the back stairs. The GFIs could wait until tomorrow. He'd just bring a half dozen and be on the safe side.

He could replace all of them if need be. He jerked a hand through his chestnut-brown hair. Why hadn't she been using the master bathroom? After all, she was alone in the house.

Dumb mistake, Blade, dumb. He strode through the kitchen so fast that he almost didn't see the smaller man standing in front of him.

"Hey."

"Sorry." Blade checked his movements in order to stop from body slamming the man by accident.

"Who are you?" The man looked surprised, and he drew himself up. At five foot eight he failed to dwarf or intimidate Blade's six-foot-six-inch frame.

"Contractor," Blade said, irritated with the question and the man's obvious ease in Cassidy's kitchen. So this was the beloved fiancé.

The man brushed a piece of lint from his perfectly tailored suit. "Contractor? Cassidy hired a contractor?"

Did the man not know what his fiancée did? "She did. Can't you tell by the whites and the tool belt?"

The man frowned, as if trying to remember something. Finally he spoke. "Why does Cassidy need a contractor?"

Blade wondered if the man was dense. Maybe he should have body slammed him, but he doubted that would have knocked any sense into him. Besides, didn't people in love share everything? Have discussions?

Then again, it had always been one-sided between him and Clara. He'd never really shared anything with her, and he'd almost married her, which would have been totally unfair. She was now blissfully happy with someone else.

"Cassidy needs a contractor to fix her home predications, the violations the inspector cited."

"Predications." The fiancé mulled that over for a moment. "I guess she did tell me about that."

For a moment Blade felt sorry for Cassidy, especially if this was her ideal man. "I'm starting work today, Mr...." He paused to let the fiancé fill in the blank.

The man blinked, and Blade wondered if his mind really was a million miles away. "Oh, yes. I'm Dan. Dan Morris. I'm Cassidy's fiancé. I live next door."

Blade already knew that.

"Well, Dan Morris, I'm Blade Frederick. The contractor."

"Um, yes. We've established that."

"Exactly," Blade said, taking control of the conversation. "I'm fixing her home predications. Since it's such short notice I'll be working nights to get the job done. She does have four pages of predications you know."

"Yes, I guess she does." Behind his wire-rim glasses Dan blinked again. "She did tell me, it's just that I've been busy working on a new exhibit at the museum. I'm trying to get a life-size dinosaur skeleton, like Sue at the Field Museum in Chicago, only much better. It would be the highlight of our new wing and—"

"Dan!" Cassidy stood in the doorway wearing a silken robe that knotted at her waist. Her blond hair hung loosely around her shoulders. "I thought I heard your voice. What are you doing here already?"

Dan frowned. "I'm picking you up. We're meeting the Schmidts for dinner. You couldn't have forgotten.

You know how important this is, and you never forget anything.''

"No. Of course not." Cassidy shook her head, sending the damp strands flying. The action caused Blade's breath to lodge in his throat. "I didn't forget. It's not until eight."

"No, we're meeting them at seven. Cass, love, you did forget," Dan chided. At Dan's response, Blade decided Dan really was the absentminded professor type who fit in well at a museum.

"I guess." Cassidy ran her fingers through her hair, causing a lump to form in Blade's throat. She was too pretty. "I'll just go get ready. I'll only be a moment."

"We can't be late," Dan told Blade as Cassidy darted back upstairs. "The Schmidts are important investors, and I'm hoping that they'll contribute generously to the new wing we have under construction. In case you haven't gathered, I'm the curator for the science center that's being expanded downtown."

"That's nice," Blade said. That had been another job J & B Construction had lost out on to D. W. Braun.

"Yes. Cassidy knows how important financing is to the various exhibits. I'm trying to convince the Schmidts to donate a large sum of money. It won't look good if we're late."

"I said I'll be ready," Cassidy called down the stairs.

Hearing her voice made Blade wonder what Cassidy saw in Dan Morris.

The man was boring. Couldn't she see she was settling? He'd been bored with Clara, and she with him.
Clara had just been there, almost like a doormat. She
had been a constant in his life, someone safe and secure. It had been almost too late when he realized that
both he and Clara deserved more, and that settling for
safety didn't mean you'd found love.

With Clara there had been no passion, and after last
night and their verbal sparring, Blade knew Cassidy
had loads of passion.

Couldn't Dan see that? The image of Cassidy in the
silken robe was already imprinted on Blade's libido,
and knowing what was under it made the illusion of
covering it even more seductive. Way past time to get
out of here.

"Cassidy, I need a key," he called up the stairs.

"Dan, give Blade your key and the alarm code."

"Are you sure?" Dan called.

"Yes," Cassidy shouted back. Dan reached into his
pocket and pulled out a small key chain. He removed
a key from the fob and passed it to Blade.

"The code, too?" Dan called.

"The code, too," Cassidy said, and Blade heard her
feet on the hardwood stairs. "He's licensed and
bonded," Cassidy said, adjusting an earring as she entered the kitchen.

Blade's heart skipped a beat. He'd been wrong. She
wasn't just pretty. She was gorgeous.

Lingerie models couldn't hold a candle to her. His
eyes drank in the way the red slip dress curved over

her figure to layer just above her knees in small, loose ruffles.

Blade wondered what was wrong with Dan.

He wasn't even looking at Cassidy, but rather the afternoon daily.

Was the man blind? Maybe he needed to have his glasses checked.

For if Cassidy were Blade's fiancée, he sure wouldn't be treating her this way. No, he'd never complain if she'd forgotten the time, especially if she greeted him looking like that and wearing only a silk robe. He'd be thinking, the heck with the Schmidts. They could eat by themselves while he and Cassidy made passionate love upstairs.

Or that short dress would just lift up, and he would lean her back on the kitchen island and see whether lace or silk was hiding underneath.

Instead Dan was now checking his watch.

Blade shook his head, clearing his erotic and disturbing thoughts. Cassidy's choice of a husband was her problem. He just didn't think she should be settling, as Clara had tried to do.

What he had to do, though, was check his lust for her. That was his problem.

He had to admit it; he lusted for her. He had from the moment she'd sent the peanuts flying across his bar. But he knew his lust would be just a temporary phase he'd go through. He'd given up phases long ago; he could outlast this one, too. As a grown man he knew that you didn't get everything you wanted.

She belonged to someone else.

"Blade," Cassidy said.

To get his attention, her hand touched his briefly. The small gesture sent a shock ricocheting through him. He quickly removed his hand, breaking the electricity sparking through him.

For an instant he wondered if she'd felt it, but the smooth facade had returned. "The alarm code is 4321. Not very original, I know, but my mother couldn't remember numbers."

Blade repeated, "4321." Even though he knew he wouldn't forget, he reached up and took a flat carpenter's pencil out from behind his ear and wrote the number on the thigh portion of his white pants.

He glanced back up at her and caught her watching him, her guard down. "How much time do I have?"

"Oh, right." She again regained composure. "You'll have forty-five seconds to get from any of the doors to the box. It's right here in the pantry." She moved to a door and opened it.

Blade didn't bother to look inside the pantry. Instead he stared at Cassidy, watching the dress cling and swish as she moved.

Suddenly he needed to leave fast. "I'll be here tomorrow." With that he took a step toward the door.

"I won't be here."

"I know." Despite himself and his overpowering need for escape, he turned back and smiled at her. She was so lovely standing there, a vision. He found his voice. "I overheard. Monica's at five."

"Right," Cassidy repeated. She smiled back at him, and Blade felt a stirring in his soul at her next words. "Thank you. I appreciate your helping me."

He'd somehow lost control. This was a business deal, that was all it was supposed to be. All he needed to do was fix her work and get to Lillian. That was it. Right? "No problem. It's my job."

"But still." Her baby-blue gaze gutted him and he edged to the door. Damn. Dan Morris was a lucky man, and the fool didn't even know it.

Blade fired up Frank's truck and turned the country music on as loud as it could go, which was pretty loud given Frank's speakers. Even that didn't make Blade feel better.

He wanted a woman who was engaged.

"STRANGE CONTRACTOR you hired," Dan said the moment Blade left the house. "I've never seen anyone write on his pants like that before. And what is it with flat pencils? Interesting. Oh, speaking of interesting, we're getting a machine that demonstrates how sedimentary rocks are formed."

"How nice," Cassidy said, staring at Dan as if she were seeing him for the first time. Why had she never noticed before that his job consumed his life? Sara's prophetic words haunted her. Dull.

A shrill alerted Dan to an incoming cell phone call. He reached into his jacket pocket. "Yes?" he said. He listened for a moment. "It's not a good night for this."

He listened some more. "All right. By ten-thirty." He pressed the end key and faced Cassidy.

"I've got an emergency crisis with one of the night crew. I need to leave right after dinner," he told her. "I'm sorry, love, but it can't be helped."

"Really, it's fine," Cassidy replied, for once not really caring about what Dan did. In fact, had she ever? "I have some work to do anyway."

Dan reached forward and touched Cassidy's face. Unlike Blade, whose touch was fire, Dan's fingers felt clammy. She pulled back. "That's what I adore about you, Cass. You're so understanding. That's why we're so perfect together."

For the first time in her life, Cassidy had doubts.

Chapter Four

"So how did it go?" At 9:00 a.m. the next morning, a perky and freshly shaved Jake leaned over Blade's desk.

"Fine." Blade kept his voice noncommittal. He'd been in the office for only about fifteen minutes and was surprised Jake had waited so long to show. Of the two, Jake was always the early bird, the morning man.

"Only fine?" Jake's voice revealed his skepticism. "No way, Blade, old buddy. You came into the office humming. Everyone heard you. Word around the watercooler is that it looks like you got lucky last night."

Blade glanced up at his best friend and business partner. "I did get lucky." He saw Jake's face light up. "That is, if you consider that I finally beat the Falcon at a game of pool."

Jake's face fell. Then he whistled, impressed. "You've been trying to beat him for a while."

"Yeah, ever since he walked into my bar quite a few months ago. Last night I finally did." Blade pushed the blueprints to the side. "And the best part is that he wasn't off his game, either."

"Something must have gotten you hyped up. A special lady maybe?" Jake's eyes gleamed.

Blade refused to bite. "Oh, you mean Lillian Morris? I met her. You're right. She's worse than a Texas twister."

Jake slammed a fist onto Blade's desk, and Blade steadied his coffee cup. "Blade, you are a devil. Did you make any progress with her?"

Blade feigned dumb. "Who, Lillian?"

"Yeah, of course her. And the other one. The hot one. Cassidy Clayton."

"She's engaged."

"So?"

Blade's features clouded over. "Unlike you, I don't move in on any man's property."

"Women are their own property, Blade, my man. You know that as well as I do. Even afterward they're never faithful. Look at the string of married ones I've run through."

"I'd like to believe that some of them are faithful."

"Our mothers certainly weren't." Jake shrugged. "I'm never marrying. Just give me a warm body in bed that I can replace when necessary, and I'll be fine."

Blade swiveled his chair and looked out the window. For a moment he studied the Houston skyline. From his office he could see right down the ship channel and all the way to Galveston Bay. One had to appreciate the true beauty in chemical plant spires. This area was a boomtown.

Would Cassidy be the faithful type? She'd certainly seemed submissive to the fiancé last night. He frowned. She'd had much more spirit and verve when he'd met her in his bar. Faithfulness wasn't about submission but partnership.

She was settling; he knew it.

"Earth to Blade."

"Sorry." Blade swiveled around again. "Did you need something specific?"

Jake waved a hand in front of Blade's face. "Yeah, I need you to focus. When will you see Lillian again?"

"I don't know. Probably tonight or tomorrow. I'm working over there starting around four. I'm doing the job at night."

"Isn't tomorrow your scouting night?"

Blade nodded. "I won't miss that." For the past ten years, ever since he'd turned twenty-six, Blade had been a scoutmaster for a troop of low-income boys living in his former neighborhood.

Jake's eyebrow arched. "I sure hope you know what you're doing. We've got to get this job."

"I'm working on it."

Jake straightened and stared at Blade for a long moment. He grinned wickedly. "Yeah, you know, I just bet you are."

"No, THAT WON'T DO AT ALL." Lillian shook her head with absolute disapproval. "I don't like that one."

Cassidy threw her hands up in the air and turned toward the woman who was becoming a daily menace. "I like this one." At least more than the others, Cassidy didn't add. The whole evening of trying on dresses hadn't been very much fun at all, and was fast becoming a horrific ordeal.

"The bodice is too low cut. You don't have enough chest to do justice to the dress."

"Lillian, please. I'm getting tired." Cassidy glanced at her watch. "It's eight already. I'd like to go home."

Lillian's shoulders rose in a dramatic sigh as she turned to the saleswoman. "We'll take the first one."

Cassidy's jaw dropped. She'd hated that dress on sight and hadn't even wanted to try it on. Even the cost, seven thousand dollars, didn't redeem it. The designer creation was hideous. It had made Cassidy look like a bloated marshmallow covered with white cotton candy.

"You've made an excellent choice, Mrs. Morris," the saleswoman said, relief evident. "Now, let's get Cassidy's measurements so we can contact the designer."

"No." Cassidy put her hands on her hips. "I'm going home now. We can do it tomorrow."

"We need to do it now." Lillian's jaw shot forward.

"I'm in this part of town tomorrow. One more day won't hurt." Looking for support, Cassidy turned to the saleswoman.

"Uh," the saleswoman said, clearly not knowing

whom to side with. Incurring Lillian's wrath was dangerous.

"Tomorrow," Cassidy asserted. She fingered the white silk she was wearing.

"I guess one day won't hurt. But tomorrow," Lillian conceded with pursed lips. Cassidy knew Lillian wasn't pleased to have been thwarted. "I'll expect you to make it by here tomorrow."

"Thank you," Cassidy said. She gestured to the relieved saleswoman. "I'm going to go change now."

Twenty minutes later Cassidy opened the gate between the Morrises' and her property. She blinked for a moment. Light beamed from almost all the windows of her house. Blinded, she almost walked into the red truck sitting in a shadow of darkness.

Blade was here.

A fluttering captured her heart and she straightened and walked toward her kitchen door. Of course he was here. He was fixing the predications. As she entered the kitchen she saw him, well at least part of him, the moment she walked in. He was working under the kitchen sink.

"Nice legs." Her hand flew over her mouth. Had she actually said her thoughts aloud?

"Thanks."

Oops. She had.

He slid out from under the sink and stood up, grinning. "Could say the same about yours."

Automatically Cassidy glanced down. It was an unseasonably warm late-February day, and while Blade was in cutoff carpenter whites, she wore pleated trousers. "I saw them last night," he added, referring to her legs. "Got a good view of them when you were in the robe."

"Oh." She blushed and then regained control. "Consider it a job perk."

"Believe me, I did."

"Uh-huh." Unsettled by the veiled intensity of his words, Cassidy laughed to lighten the moment as she went to the refrigerator.

Oddly, she had a six-pack of beer. Where had that come from? Blade? At this moment the devil himself could have brought it. Dismissing her resolve never to have another, she grabbed one and took a seat at the center island.

Blade made a magnanimous gesture. "Help yourself."

"I will," she replied, twisting off the top. "If it's in my refrigerator it's mine."

"Of course. Does that mean if it's in your house it's yours, too?"

"Absolutely." Cassidy missed his expression as she closed her eyes and let the cold liquid slide down her throat. Beer had never tasted so heavenly. She must be developing a taste for it. She opened her eyes and found him staring at her. His greenish-blue eyes had darkened almost to a solid blue. What exactly had she said?

His eyes lightened and Cassidy's unease at remembering her words disappeared. "Hard day?" he asked.

"The worst," she admitted.

"Dress shopping not quite what you expected?"

"Lillian purchased a dress that will make me look like a seven-thousand-dollar marshmallow covered with white cotton candy."

He wiped his hands on his pants before he leaned his hip on the center island. "That bad, huh?"

"I hate it." Cassidy took another sip of her beer. She needed food. She'd missed dinner again.

"So why did you get it?"

"I had no choice."

Blade arched an eyebrow as if contradicting her. "We always have choices."

"Oh, no, not with Lillian. It's just easier to let her do what she wants than fight her, believe me."

As if sensing Cassidy needed to talk, Blade took a break from work. He reached in the refrigerator for a beer. "You don't strike me as the type of person who backs down from a fight."

"Normally I don't," Cassidy replied. "But I guess I've grown up living next to Lillian so I know better."

"She caused all your predication problems, you know," Blade said, removing the top off the longneck bottle.

"Yes, and the guy got a two-week suspension without pay for having the city truck out of city jurisdiction. Whether he did or not is irrelevant, but in the end she got him. Her tentacles are long."

Blade shook his head. "And yet you're choosing to marry into her family."

"At twenty-eight it's hard to find an appropriate man. I mean, appropriate men don't come around very often."

"So." Blade crossed his arms over his chest.

"It's easier for men," Cassidy insisted. "How old are you? Thirty?"

"Thirty-six."

"See? No one cares if you're still single or wonders if you're gay. I'm an image consultant. I should be married by now. If not, women don't trust me to school their husbands in business etiquette or proper attire unless they think I'm gay."

"So you're marrying Dan because you need a husband for your job?"

"No. I love Dan. I mean, I've known him all my life. We grew up together."

"I grew up with Jake. We're business partners, but if he were female I wouldn't marry him. If I had a sister I wouldn't let her marry him, either."

Cassidy exhaled a long sigh. "Whatever. I couldn't expect you to understand."

"Why? Because I'm not in your social circle?" Blade's eyes glittered dangerously.

"No." After dealing with Lillian, Cassidy was too tired to argue with anyone else. "You wouldn't understand because you're a man. You don't have a biological clock ticking."

"So?" Blade asked. "That doesn't mean I want to be sixty watching my kids graduate from college."

"I meant—" she began.

He interrupted her. "I know what you meant, but what about passion? How does that figure into your equation?"

Cassidy dragged a hand through her blond hair. "You mean that stuff of romance novels? Please. Passion just burns you and then burns out. Look, I'm really exhausted."

Instantly Blade's attitude changed as he saw she really was tired. "What was I thinking? Your blood sugar is probably low. What you need is food."

Despite herself she smiled. "Not that again."

"That again." Blade said with a low chuckle.

"You're always trying to feed me."

His eyebrow shot up. "Did you eat anything while on your terrible quest for marshmallow froth?"

"No." She shook her head, and a pounding began behind her left temple.

"Then come on. We're leaving because you have nothing worth foraging for in your refrigerator."

She blinked. "How do you know?"

"I put my beer in there. I had one of those days, too. I hoped you wouldn't mind."

"I don't." And oddly, she didn't, although she probably should. It was a pretty big assumption to place beer in your client's Subzero.

He laughed. "Let's go."

Cassidy scooted off the wrought-iron stool. "I must be crazy because I'm agreeing to this."

"No, you're just hungry, and no offense, but you are a lightweight."

"I am," Cassidy said, for she knew she must be. She was following him out the door without a clue as to where they were going. "By the way, where are you taking me?"

"To the place with the best strip steak in town."

TWO HOURS LATER Cassidy found herself having one of the best times of her life, and she wasn't drunk, either. Far from it. Except for glasses of water, she hadn't drunk anything else since leaving her house with Blade.

She couldn't believe she'd ridden in a truck. It had actually been fun. Being in the inside of his truck was almost like being in the inside of a small office.

Cowboy hats hung upside down from racks on the inside of the roof of the truck. A CB radio blared from its perch next to a center console. Blade had tossed a 128 CD binder onto the full-size back seat as Cassidy had climbed up, and then in.

The ride certainly wasn't smooth, but it wasn't bad, either. The diesel engine had an odd, soothing rumbling sound.

When he'd parked, he left it in gear. "Emergency brake isn't working right," he told her. "Gotta get around to getting it fixed."

"So, how long have you had this truck," she'd asked as they'd walked toward the bar entrance.

"Awhile," had been his answer. And then they'd talked about other miscellaneous things.

He'd been a fantastic listener, and Cassidy had

laughed, and shared. So had he. He'd told her about growing up poor, and striking out on his own at eighteen. Then he'd challenged her to a game of pool.

"See that guy over there?" Cassidy brought her attention back to the present and followed the point of Blade's cue stick.

"The one with the cowboy hat," she confirmed.

"That's the Falcon."

Cassidy watched him play for a moment. With one click of the cue ball, three solid balls entered various pockets. "He's really good."

"He is," Blade agreed. "He's one of the best at pool I've ever seen."

She turned her attention back to Blade. She waited until he brought his gaze back to hers. "So have you ever beaten him?"

"Not until last night."

"You did?" Surprised joy caused a wide smile to spread across her face.

"I did." Blade gave a modest nod. "It took me a month or so, but I finally won one."

Cassidy was impressed. She'd seen how good Blade was, and she couldn't imagine anyone being better except a professional. They'd been playing themselves in the bar's back room for a little over a half hour. When she'd gone back there with Blade, Dee had shot Blade a strange look. When she'd asked him about it, Blade had assured her it was nothing.

Now Cassidy knew why. Blade played pool, a lot, and Dee had probably been worried about Cassidy being hustled. Not to worry. She had lost every game, but thanks to Blade's patient instruction, Cassidy had been learning all sorts of shots she'd never tried before. Next time she played pool in the Morrises' billiard room she'd be able to really show them a thing or two.

"Hey, Blade." The man known as the Falcon ambled over, and Cassidy was surprised to see how young he actually was. The goatee made him appear older. "Followed your lead on the construction job. I start next Monday."

"Great." Blade nodded as the man moved on by.

"You got him a job?"

"I heard of a place that was hiring," Blade replied noncommittally. "It's your turn to break."

Cassidy twirled the custom cue stick Blade had lent her. "That was a nice thing to do."

Blade shrugged his broad shoulders. "What can I say? I'm a nice guy."

"I'm discovering that," she said. She saw the surprise on his face. "I wasn't very impressed with you when I first met you."

"You judged me on appearances," Blade told her. Cassidy approached the table, lined up her shot and sent the cue ball flying.

"No," she said as she straightened back up and decided what shot to take. "I judged the bar on its appearance. I judged you on attitude." She circled the table and sent another striped ball into a corner pocket. "You seemed, well, just a bit cocky."

"I am," he told her.

"Yes, but I've seen your softer side." She missed the next shot.

"I don't have a soft side," he told her. He leaned over and she got a great view of his rear. His wearing shorts should be outlawed. The view was dangerous.

"Certainly you have a soft side," she argued, pulling her gaze from his fantastic backside. She really needed to stop staring at it.

He didn't turn around as he lined up his shot. "Everything I do is always to my advantage."

Assuming he wasn't serious, Cassidy laughed slightly. She took her pool cue and touched the point to the bare skin on the back of his knee. His concentration thwarted, Blade missed the shot.

"I work things to my advantage, too," she told him. Blade reached for his glass of water and lifted it up in a mock salute.

Cassidy grinned as she made another shot. She never would have teased Dan like that. Sara was right. Dan was dull. Blade had simply taken it in stride.

In fact, Blade took just about everything in stride. Compared to Dan, he was pretty laid-back about life in general. He was easy to talk to, and even better, he was a good listener who actually was interested in what Cassidy had to say.

Perhaps she and Dan had known each other too long. Perhaps they didn't even really know the people they'd grown up into, the people they'd become. Perhaps they'd simply gotten too comfortable with each other to really care about finding out.

Cassidy didn't know the answer to that conundrum and decided she didn't want to find out. At least not now. Not while she was having too much fun. Tonight she wanted to discover the enigma that was Blade Frederick.

And that enigma had just cleared the table leaving only her striped balls. "Eight ball in the corner pocket," he told her as he gestured with his cue stick.

Cassidy shook her head in mock disappointment as he made the perfect shot. "One of these days I'll have to see if I can beat you."

"Keep practicing," he told her. Cassidy laughed as she handed him the cue stick she'd been using. She watched as he wiped it down with a terry-cloth towel, took it apart and put it away in its case. Then he did the same with the cue stick he'd been playing with.

"That time already?" Cassidy asked. She glanced at her watch. "Oh my! It's after eleven!"

Blade lifted the cue stick case. "I figured we'd call it a night. I'm more of a night owl than a lark, and I've got to be on a job site at 6:00 a.m. tomorrow."

"I'm so sorry. I kept you out too late!"

Blade sent her a strange look. "Stop apologizing. It's not your fault. I know how to tell time, and I know how much sleep I need. I'd rather stay up, especially with you."

"Sorry. It's just that Dan always says—"

Blade cut her off. "I'm not Dan."

Cassidy took a sip of water as she tried to retrench her thoughts. "No," she said slowly. "No, you're not." Definitely not.

Standing in the bar where she'd first compared the two men, she wondered how she'd ever found Dan more appropriate. Blade was a breath of fresh air. He was a diamond in the rough, a gem in hiding. Cassidy knew that hidden under his steely, worn exterior was a heart of gold.

While he claimed to do things only to his advantage, Cassidy knew that wasn't true. Dan was the perfect example of someone who only did things when he would reap a benefit. Blade was reaping no benefits from helping Cassidy. He wasn't even making time and a half.

She contemplated that as they left the bar. He must need the money, she realized. Maybe to get that emergency brake fixed or something.

Why else would he take on a job at night? Sure her job often required after-five hours, but she was well compensated for it. Contractors surely didn't work after hours without overtime.

As she studied Blade's profile she decided not to ask him about it. A man like him would be offended if she brought up the subject. His type hated charity, hated those who depended on it instead of working for a living.

Cassidy suddenly realized they were listening to a country music station. They hadn't listened to the radio on the way to the bar. Blade must have turned it on. The song playing sounded familiar. "What's the name of this song?"

"'How Do You Like Me Now' by Toby Keith," he replied.

"Oh. I thought I'd heard it."

"Probably. It was the number-one country song of the year a few years back."

"That's probably it," she said, although she rarely listened to country music herself. After all, not every Texan liked country music. "So you like country?"

"The radio only gets one station," Blade told her.

"Seriously?" Cassidy couldn't believe it. Houston had dozens of radio stations.

"It's broken, and this is all it gets. The CD player works, though."

"You should get the radio fixed." Oops. That was out before she could retract it.

Blade turned onto her street. "Why?"

Quickly she searched for a good reason, knowing that he probably didn't have the money. "Because then you'll have more choices."

"What if this choice is fine? Why have more if I'm satisfied?"

Why indeed? He had her there, and Cassidy couldn't fault his logic. "We're here," she pointed out unnecessarily. His fingers gripped the steering wheel lightly as he let the diesel idle in her driveway. Cassidy was sure the truck's puttering could be heard at least three houses over.

At that moment the inside of the truck seemed to

shrink. In the moonlight beaming through the untinted front truck windows Cassidy saw Blade, sitting there in his white T-shirt, his dirty carpenter white cutoffs and his battered tennis shoes. Never before had an evening ended so strangely, or with her feeling so lavishly wanton.

"Thanks for taking me out to eat," she said. Her gaze locked onto his, and right then, time screeched to a stop. His lips were so close, so full. Her blood boiled. She didn't want the night to end.

She wanted him to kiss her. She wanted to taste that delectable mouth, the one that edged into a cheeky grin that made his eyes twinkle. She leaned forward slightly, until that thought again hit her like a thunderbolt.

She wanted him to kiss her!

He was her contractor for goodness sake! He was being paid to fix her house, not fix her other "needs." And she shouldn't be having those needs, anyway. She was engaged. And she couldn't use beer as an excuse tonight, either. She had only had one, hours ago.

As if sensing her recoil, Blade broke the spell by turning his head and unlocking his hypnotic gaze from hers. "I better get going before this truck wakes up your whole neighborhood. It's pretty loud."

"Probably a good idea," Cassidy said, willing her voice not to sound so breathy with desire. "We wouldn't want Lillian to come over and begin asking questions."

"No, that wouldn't be good."

"I doubt she'd believe we were at the twenty-four-hour Home Depot," Cassidy said with a shaky laugh.

"No," Blade agreed.

She still wanted a kiss, but that was impossible. She knew she should go, she had to go, but she couldn't get herself to reach for the door handle. Somehow she managed to get her hand on the metal lever. "Thanks again for dinner and pool. I had a great time."

His lids dropped down, hiding his expression. Still, she heard the truth in his voice. "I did, too. I'll see you tomorrow night."

"Tomorrow," Cassidy echoed. She opened the truck door and stuck her leg out.

"Watch your step, it's a long way down. Here. Wait a minute. Let me help you." He made a move to open his door.

"No, I've got it." Cassidy said quickly.

Without waiting for him, she stepped down onto the running board. If he helped her out of the truck now, as he had in the bar parking lot, she'd be lost. He'd touch her, she'd melt, and that would be bad. Very bad.

One touch, as simple as his hand on her arm, would be her undoing.

She reached the ground and shut the door. Her heels clicked on the driveway as she fled for the safety of her house, relieved and yet strangely troubled to hear the rumbling of the diesel as it sped off into the night.

Chapter Five

"Excellent," Mrs. Diane Rothchild said with an approving nod. "I'm glad we had this conversation, Cassidy. You will come to Austin three weeks from now, and we'll begin."

"Yes," Cassidy said. Beneath her desk she wiped her hands on the terry-cloth towel she kept hidden there. It was a small trick, one designed to keep sweaty hands and palms at bay.

"Fantastic," Diane said with another nod. "We have such high hopes for this political campaign, and in four years I want to see my Bert Rothchild as the next president of this country. He is the best man for the job."

"I understand," Cassidy replied. She stood up and shook Diane Rothchild's hand. After showing Diane to the door, Cassidy sat down in her office chair and gave it a spin.

Elation filled her. She'd just landed her biggest client yet. Formidable as Barbara Bush, yet known as well for her kind heart, Diane Rothchild, wife of the current Texas governor, had visions of herself as first lady of the United States.

Now, according to "be sure to call me Diane, dear," all that had to occur was a bit of polish to Bert's good-ol'-boy image and public speaking skills.

While the deep drawl worked well in Texas, Diane wanted Bert to be absolutely perfect and more "global" for a presidential run, and her hiring of Cassidy Clayton was just one part of the process.

Cassidy glanced at her watch—4:00 p.m. Diane Rothchild had been an unexpected client, but when the governor's wife just "drops in" after a political luncheon, everything else gets rescheduled.

"You've come highly recommended," Diane had said, "from Rachel Dempsey. She said you did wonders with Jack."

Jack had been a vice president who wanted to be a president of a major oil firm. He'd gotten the nod shortly after some sessions with Cassidy.

The ringing of the phone caught her attention. She pressed the button. "Dan is on line one."

"Thanks, Jennifer," Cassidy said to her secretary. "Send it through."

"Hi," she said. She couldn't wait until she told Dan her news.

"Hey, Cass," Dan said from the other end of the line. "How's your day been?"

That was the opening she'd been waiting for. "It's been great. You won't believe who dropped in and hired me."

"You've got a new client. That's super," Dan said instead. "You can tell me more about it later. I've got only a few seconds. The Schmidts are coming by and they'll be here any moment. They want to see the dinosaur models. I think they're going to donate, Cass, but they want to see what they'd be sponsoring first. Anyway, about dinner tonight, we'll have to reschedule. You don't mind, do you?"

Cassidy sat there, feeling as if someone had punctured her balloon. "Of course not," she rallied.

"You are such a sweetheart, Cass," Dan said. "I won't be too late, want me to come over when I get back?"

"No," Cassidy said. Blade would be there, and for some reason, seeing him sounded much more appealing than Dan whose dinosaurs were much more important than his fiancée.

"Okay," Dan actually sounded relieved. "You're such a good sport, Cass. By the way, did you get your dress measurements done? Mom told me about the dress over breakfast. Says you'll be the belle of the ball."

Yeah, of a carnival costume ball, Cassidy thought. "I didn't get to it yet," she said. She glanced at her watch again. "I'll probably have to get it done on lunch tomorrow. My client was—"

"As long as you get it done," Dan said. "I don't want Mom breathing down my neck any more than she already is. You know how she is. She would have made a great drill sergeant with all of her military precision.''

Cassidy didn't say anything. Whereas Dan could say it, if she agreed with him he'd say she was criticizing the oh-so-perfect Lillian Morris.

''Anyway,'' Dan continued, ''I think Mom has the wedding plans under control, so just be sure to get your dress done. Don't forget.''

''I won't,'' Cassidy replied. She gritted her teeth.

''Good.'' Dan's voice faded, and in the background she could hear ''They're here? Send them in.'' Suddenly Dan was back. ''They're on their way in. I'll talk to you later, Cass. Love you.''

And without waiting for her to reply, or to say it back, he was gone.

Cassidy set the phone down. Then, angrily, she picked it up again. ''Sara Burgoyne,'' she said when the receptionist answered.

''Hello?''

''Sara, it's Cassidy. Are you free for happy hour? Different place this time, though?''

Cassidy waited barely a second for Sara's answer. ''Five-thirty,'' she said. ''Don't you dare be late this time, either!''

WHEN CASSIDY PULLED into her driveway three hours later, her house was dark.

At first she didn't think anything of the everyday occurrence, for after all, since her parents' exodus the house remained dark when Cassidy wasn't home. Then Cassidy remembered. Blade should have been here.

But the driveway didn't contain a big diesel Ford 350. She went inside and turned off the alarm. Four beers were all that filled the empty refrigerator. She stuffed in her take-home containers containing her dinner leftovers. No, a quick look around revealed that he hadn't even been there.

Panic filled her. She'd just lost a day on her predications. Then her terror increased. What if he wasn't planning on doing the work? What if he'd just strung her along, and now he wasn't going to do it?

No, Blade wasn't like that. She shook her head and tried to erase the fear threatening to consume her. She went and checked the answering machine. Nothing.

The insistent ringing of the front doorbell sent her scurrying. She tossed it open. "Blade, I—"

Lillian, like a bad penny, again had turned up and stood on the other side.

"Contractor didn't show?" Lillian said, her voice more of an insinuation than a question. She arched a gray eyebrow. "He certainly worked late last night."

"He came back from Home Depot with supplies." The lie left Cassidy's tongue before she could stop it.

"I see." Lillian stepped past Cassidy. "I'm sure that's all it was."

"What else would it be?" Cassidy asked.

Lillian shrugged. "You could tell me."

"I would if there was something to tell," Cassidy replied tightly. Her spine prickled, and her sixth sense told her that Lillian was miffed about something. She just hadn't spit it out yet.

"Dan tells me you didn't get your dress measurements done," Lillian said slowly, her disapproval evident.

"Is Dan home?" Cassidy said brightly. "I thought he'd still be with the Schmidts."

"I talked to him over the phone," Lillian said. "I thought I made it very clear that you needed to get by Monica's today. Not tomorrow."

Cassidy's ire flared, and only her years of training kept it from becoming evident. Lillian Morris did not, and would not, run her life.

"I had an unexpected client drop by today," Cassidy said.

"Nothing is more important than getting your dress measurements done. Really, Cassidy, this job of yours is sweet, but you need to also concentrate on becoming a wife. Wives support their husbands."

"Wives in this day and age also have their own careers," Cassidy returned.

At this statement Lillian's eyebrow arched its disapproval once again. "Surely you don't think you can raise a Morris child and work, too?"

"Why not?" Cassidy retorted. She turned and strode into the kitchen, leaving Lillian gaping after her.

Oh, what the hell. She'd had nothing but iced tea to drink for dinner, and right now some of Blade's magic might ease her foul mood.

Besides, it should create the rebellious look she was hoping for.

"Oh, my God. You're drinking beer!"

Success. Cassidy lifted the bottle to her lips again and took another swallow. "It's pretty awesome stuff, too. I've got more. Want one?"

Lillian looked suitably horrified. "I never touch that blue-collar beverage."

"Come on, Lillian. As if millions of Americans could be wrong." Cassidy twisted the bottle and took a long swallow.

"I don't know what has gotten into you," Lillian huffed. "It must be this disaster of your parents' marriage. Have you sought professional help yet? My friend Enid knows a wonderful therapist that specializes in helping children through divorce."

"Chill out a bit, Lil," Cassidy said. Lillian's expression appeared even more mortified. Cassidy almost snickered. After all, Lillian had taken over her entire wedding, what else could the dynamic Mrs. Morris do to her future daughter-in-law? "Seriously, I don't need a therapist. What I need is some space. I will get my measurements done. You don't need to be breathing fire down my back constantly. I'm a grown woman. I can take care of it."

"Well you haven't managed so far." Lillian sniffed her disapproval. "This wedding is important. Luke Morris needs to have a successful launch, and all of our friends and political allies will be at this wedding.

I told you the guest list is approaching one thousand people, didn't I?''

That caused Cassidy's quest to irritate Lillian to waver slightly. "No."

"Well, it is. Luke is young enough that if he wins his father's seat he could go on to be governor, or even president. You know how many presidents have come from Texas, especially in the twentieth and twenty-first century.''

"I think I heard that somewhere today," Cassidy said. Diane Rothchild had mentioned about the same thing.

Of course, now was probably not the time to bring that up. Diane Rothchild's husband and Lillian's husband were in different political parties.

While that one would be fun to hit Lillian with, suddenly the adrenaline had worn off. Cassidy had simply tired of the game. "Look, Lillian, I said I'd get my measurements done. I'm grateful for all you've done with the wedding planning. You've done a fantastic job and it'll be just a fantastic June event. The event of Houston, I'm sure.''

Lillian eyed her skeptically. "You think so?"

"I know so," Cassidy said, maneuvering Lillian toward the kitchen door. "You always have the best parties, Lillian. I'm sure my wedding won't be an exception.''

"I'm glad you agree," Lillian said. She put her hand on the doorknob, somehow sensing she'd been outmaneuvered but not quite sure how. "By the way, where is your contractor?"

Cassidy got Lillian out the door and shut it behind her. That last question was one she'd love to have the answer to herself.

"HOW'D I DO?" Rick held out the eye splice he'd made. Blade took it, turned it over, and admired the teen's workmanship.

"You did a great job."

"Cool!" Rick beamed. "That's my last requirement. I'm hoping for a tap out at camp this summer. I want that Order of the Arrow."

"I think you've got a pretty good shot at it," Blade said.

"Man, I hope so," Rick replied as Blade checked off the requirement.

Blade stood and stretched. Few understood his commitment to the Boy Scouts of America, but it had been a troop like this that had shown him that there was more to life than just living in a hovel. Through Scouting he'd discovered goal setting, determination and perseverance.

Few people also knew that Blade himself had achieved the rank of Eagle Scout, a feat accomplished before his last year of high school.

It had been one of the few times his mother had bothered to sober up and attend a ceremony. She'd even missed his high school graduation. Instead she'd been on a trip to Reno with an over-the-road trucker she'd met at the bar where she worked.

As for his father, Blade didn't even know where the man was. When the manufacturing company where his dad had worked had moved the factory to Mexico, his dad had lost his job. Faced with unemployment, Chad Frederick had hit the road for work. He'd been home sporadically ever since, picking right back up with his wife as if neither of them had ever seen anyone else.

The thought of their marriage, or lack of it, still curled Blade's stomach. His marriage, if he ever married at all, would not be "open." It would be about commitment and understanding. It would be about love and tenderness and family. All those things he and his older brothers had never had.

For a moment he wondered if Cassidy had all those things growing up. Had her parents been loving? They'd put a roof over her head, but from Lillian's cryptic remarks about Cassidy's father's philandering behavior, it didn't sound as if her family's money made the problem any better. She'd just had better food and shelter. The emotional scars were probably the same.

Maybe that's why she was settling for Dan.

Blade pushed those thoughts out of his head. He didn't need to contemplate her reasons, or tread into that dangerous territory. What Cassidy did with her life wasn't his concern, right? While he might want her with an intensity he hadn't felt in a long while, he couldn't do anything about it. No, she was off-limits, for he certainly didn't plan on taking Dan's place in her life.

He helped the last of the boys clean up. The troop consisted of boys of various grade levels, and this next weekend they were all going camping at the Boy Scout camp located near Lake Houston State Park.

He reminded two of them to bring their permission slips with them Friday night, and saw all of them to the school door. Within moments he and the other scoutmaster were leaving the custodians to lock up for the night.

"See you Friday," Blade told him. He walked the short distance to his truck. He'd switched it back with Frank that morning.

As he climbed in and fired up the power stroke diesel engine, he retrieved his cell phone from the visor. A frown crossed his face. He had told Cassidy he wasn't going to be there, hadn't he?

The thought of forgetting to let her know bothered him. He punched in the number he'd memorized the moment Jake had handed it to him and hit Send.

EVEN A LONG, HOT BATH in her mother's Jacuzzi tub hadn't calmed Cassidy down. Was it just her imagination, or was it that everyone had just the nerve and gall to simply walk all over her?

Sara had said something to that effect earlier during dinner, and while Cassidy had blown it off with a brush of her hand, she found herself mulling over it now.

As for Lillian Morris, Cassidy wanted to wring her neck.

She would wring her own neck if it helped get rid of Lillian. At least, in less than two weeks Cassidy would be out of this house and out of walking distance. She flipped the switch, turning off the bubbling jets. She stood, grabbed a plush towel and stepped from the tub.

Twenty minutes later, her body tired and just about ready for bed, she straightened up the kitchen. She poured the remainder of the beer from the open bottle down the drain. She smiled, remembering Lillian's reaction. Wasting the beer had been worth it. She'd not even had three ounces.

The shrilling of the phone made her jump, and before answering it Cassidy looked at the clock. Almost nine-thirty. Maybe Dan had decided to at least call.

"Hello?"

"Cassidy."

The warm drawl that was almost second nature to her ear washed over her. Definitely not Dan.

"Blade," she said, trying to make her voice sound calm and not too hopeful.

"How are you?" His voice warmed her, relieving her of the fear that had plagued her earlier. She knew she should be angry at him, but the emotion refused to enter her body.

"I'm fine," she said, mentally telling herself not to sound eager or chastising. After all, he was only her contractor, right? "I thought I'd be seeing you tonight."

"I just realized that," he said. "I'm so sorry I didn't make it clear I wouldn't be working today. Tonight's my Boy Scout troop meeting. I never miss a night."

"You're a Boy Scout?"

His chuckle at her disbelief filled the receiver. "Yes. I'm a troop leader."

Cassidy racked her brain, trying to reconcile this side of Blade Frederick. "I don't think you told me that story."

"What, the one where I'm an Eagle Scout or the one where I'm taking twenty boys camping this weekend?"

"Either of those," Cassidy said. She strolled into the salon and tossed herself across a comfortable chair.

"Both true," he insisted. She heard him chuckle again.

"You're not lying?"

"Would you like to go camping this weekend and see for yourself?"

"No, that's okay," Cassidy said quickly.

"What, not a camper?"

"Can't say that I am," she replied. Not that she'd ever been camping. Her mother's idea of vacation included nothing short of five stars.

"Ought to try it," he said. "You'd probably love to camp."

"You mean with a tent and a fire?"

"Exactly that," Blade challenged.

"Uh," she began. She stared at the Picasso on the wall. In two days Christie's was coming to pack up the paintings. To finance her parents' new lifestyles, those magnificent works of art were all being auctioned off.

"I tell you what," Blade said, "you're an image consultant, right?"

"Yes," Cassidy said slowly. There was a catch coming, that she was sure of. But like a moth to a flame, she had to know what it was.

"How about giving a consultation to the boys? These guys don't have some of the skills. Could you help them with say, Communication 101?"

"As in?"

"Elimination of slang from their everyday speech. They're learning that there's a world out there besides just what they see in their neighborhood, and I want them to be welcomed into it."

"They don't teach communication and oral presentation in school anymore?"

"Cassidy, most of these guys have attendance records that would make a truant officer cringe. Boy Scouts is one of the best, if only, things they've got."

"What about their parents?" As soon as she said it, she knew the truth. Right then and there, Blade's character rose in her esteem. Blade was giving back to people less fortunate, people like he had been. No silly fancy charity functions for him that simply raised money, this man lived it. He volunteered. He was on the front lines making a difference.

"I'll do it," she said. The words slipped out, but once out there, she realized that she didn't want to take the words back. After all, it would only be a Boy Scout meeting. How difficult could that be?

Besides, she wanted to see Blade Frederick in action. She wanted to see all sides of this man, this man she simply accepted unconditionally.

In fact, everything about him seemed perfect. She knew he wasn't, but she'd simply accepted him the way he was, for who he was.

Lillian Morris would have a conniption fit if she knew what Cassidy planned to do.

"We'll talk about it tomorrow," Blade said. "I'm going by the hardware store first for some supplies and then I'll be over."

"Okay." Cassidy shifted the receiver to the other ear. "You know what you're doing."

She heard him laugh, and the gentle sound washed over her. "I'm sorry I forgot to let you know. You're panicking, aren't you?"

"A little," she admitted. "All of this is pretty overwhelming, and I'm not even the one who has to sign the papers."

"Well, do me a favor and relax. You've still got plenty of time. Your work will be done. I promise."

She believed him. Blade wouldn't let her down. Unlike Dan, who hadn't even bothered to find out who her new client was.

"I'll see you tomorrow, okay? You have a good evening."

After she replaced the receiver on the phone she realized that she hadn't told Blade about her new client, either.

But as she went upstairs to bed, she knew instinctively that he would have been thrilled for her, and that he would have listened to the whole story.

She fell quickly into a dreamless sleep, a smile on her face.

Chapter Six

Cassidy felt an adrenaline rush as she heard the comforting sound of the diesel engine as Blade's truck pulled into the driveway at six the next evening.

Calm down! She told herself. He's your contractor. Some image consultant you are, you almost ran out to meet him. She paced the kitchen a moment, trying to figure out a way not to look overly eager.

A few minutes later he still hadn't knocked on the door.

Curiosity getting the best of her, Cassidy opened the side door and strolled out. He was lifting something out of the back of the truck. "Not too bad," he told her in greeting. "Only eight hundred in materials."

Having no idea if that figure was high or low, Cassidy simply shrugged. Instead of answering him, she drank her fill of this man, who for one more week, was opening her eyes to life itself.

"You've got no clue what I'm talking about, do you?" His grin widened and he lifted some bags from the pickup bed. "Admit it."

"Okay," Cassidy said, raking her gaze away from his arms. Each muscle flexed perfectly as he hoisted the bags. Today he wore a T-shirt that had the sleeves ripped out. What remained of the sides, if you could call them that, clung loosely to him, and Cassidy once again swallowed. Wow.

Never would she let Sara know that Blade's chest was smooth. Cassidy had gotten quite a glimpse as he moved, and the sight had made her mouth water.

Not even thinking of Dan, with his gym-toned body, could divert her attention away from Blade's tall, tan, lean physique. He'd captured her senses completely.

He handed her a brown plastic bag. "Carry these, will you?"

"Sure," Cassidy said. As he passed the bag over, their fingers connected. The heat that ricocheted through them made Cassidy almost drop the bag of electrical supplies.

Instead she clutched the bag close to her chest as if the boxes of electric outlets could somehow protect her from the charge that was jumping between Blade and herself. Without hesitating another moment, she turned and escaped toward the house.

As he lifted another bag out of the pickup truck bed, Blade watched her go. He would grab the boards he'd bought for the porch in a minute. He smiled to himself. She'd been staring at him.

Well, the little minx could have some of her own medicine back. He'd watched her, wanted her for too long. Well, if she could look, so could he. Too bad neither of them could touch. The electricity zinging between them hinted at a spark that would be fantastic.

He'd love to feel her creamy skin underneath his hands and, even better, feel her hands on him and her gentle touches and caresses.

Heat pooled in his lower regions, and Blade groaned. He couldn't have Cassidy Clayton. Besides, once she really saw him she wouldn't want him, anyway.

Despite having a good build, his body wasn't perfect.

Far from it, actually. She'd probably hate it if she ever saw it up close.

There was the scar from the BB gun that had left a pea-size lump on his chest. That had occurred when he'd been six and messing around with some friends. Then there was the pocket knife wound in his right thigh that had left a raised gash from being stitched poorly. He'd been fourteen and accidentally stabbed himself when cutting rope.

Then, of course, there were all the scars from the rodeos. Even though he'd lived in a lower-income part of the city, he'd still found a way to escape to the county-fair rodeo circuit for a summer. He'd seen most of the Western states, stopping here and there to wait tables to earn money to continue on.

Eventually, after a serious rodeo accident, he'd returned home before his nineteenth birthday. Jake had been doing carpentry work, and one night he and Jake had made their vow and begun their business.

He sobered for a moment. It had been that serious accident that had sent him reeling and, ten years later, right into settling with Clara.

His body now composed, he hoisted the bags and entered the kitchen. When he went back out for more bags, Cassidy came out right behind him. Without a word he lifted more bags and handed them to her. A current of understanding simply passed between them, as if they'd been in sync since before time.

That thought scared him slightly. Cassidy deserved not to settle for dumb old boring Dan, but that didn't mean that Blade deserved her. He didn't deserve a woman of Cassidy's caliber. For he'd learned that he had been wrong about her. She was nothing like his first impressions when she'd sent the peanuts flying. No, he'd learned that she was better than those women of her class. She was beyond them, in a class all by herself.

He could look all he wanted, but he could never touch.

Not permanently.

Even though he'd left his upbringing behind, he wasn't like Jake. He couldn't just invite himself into someone else's world. He could be the richest man in the world, but it would never be enough.

Underneath he was still the same Blade Frederick whose parents had failed to pay the water bill, forcing him to shower at Jake's. He was still the same Blade Frederick who had gotten into fight after fight, surviving on his fists because brains weren't respected on his street. He was the man who'd found his salvation in Boy Scouts, yet still needed to lose himself on the rodeo circuit.

Underneath he was still rough and rowdy, the type who wanted to hang out at his bar and not at fancy dinners.

He shook his head, clearing his thoughts. Cassidy had returned for another set of bags, and he hadn't even brought in the ones he was holding. He handed them to her and she stared up at him.

"I'm going to carry these boards and put them on your porch," he said. The excuse, although true, sounded lame even to his ears.

She seemed to buy it. "I'll meet you inside," she said simply.

He watched her carrying the plastic bags, four in all, some looped over her forearm.

He brushed a hand over his hair and mentally gave himself a shake. Even if she didn't belong to someone else, he couldn't be with her forever. She was above him, beyond him. She might be settling for Dan, but he couldn't let her settle for him, either. She deserved more.

He lifted the boards and put them on his shoulder. Time to get back to what was safe. Their easy camaraderie and his work.

CASSIDY WATCHED as Blade carried the boards toward the front porch. His innate strength made the movement seem effortless.

The man was incredible. She had to admit it to herself—she was attracted to him. Not that she could do anything about it except stare at him.

However, having been caught earlier doing just that and not wanting to be caught staring—again—she hurried back into the kitchen and began peering through the bags.

Half the items in the bags looked fascinating, not that she had any idea of what they were.

"You know, half of these repairs are pretty simple," Blade said as he entered the kitchen. He put the last of the bags on the kitchen table.

Cassidy shrugged. "I wouldn't know," she said.

"They are simple. You could have done them yourself if you knew how," Blade said. A grin suddenly spread across his face.

"Stop laughing at me," she said, instantly knowing what caused his amused smile—her horrified and appalled look.

He shook his head and made a teasing tsking sound. "Come on, Cassie. You aren't afraid to work with your hands, are you?"

"No." She drew herself up to defend herself. "It's just not something I'm good at."

He arched a brown eyebrow at her, challenge obvious. "Have you ever tried?"

"No." She jutted her chin forward. "I've never needed to."

"Well, you do now."

"No, I don't," she shot back. "I have you."

He tilted his head to the side, conceding the point. Besides, he didn't think now was the time to tell her that in a week he wouldn't be around. No, right now he was simply enjoying sparring with her.

She had a passion, a drive, that matched only his own. He decided not to let the argument rest.

"Actually, if you tried some of these things, you might find yourself liking to do some simple home repairs. Even Martha Stewart paints walls."

Cassidy glared at him for a moment. He had her there, darn him, and she couldn't let him win. "Yes, well," she began, but the argument she wanted to shoot back failed to come. So she just stopped. "Fine," she said. She reached out her hand. "I'll paint the trim. I'm sure I can do that. After all, how hard can it be to paint?"

Instead of replying, Blade placed a paintbrush in her hand. Then he turned and rummaged through a bag, finally handing her a roll of what looked like two-inch-wide blue masking tape.

As he passed the items into her hands, his fingers reached around her wrists, supporting her hands and the contents in them.

The same heated awareness that occurred at each of Blade's touches burned through her. Struggling for outward composure she asked, "What's this for?" about the blue tape.

"That's so the paint doesn't get on the walls." His fingers lightly massaged her wrists, and Cassidy wanted to sigh with the sensuality of it all.

Instead she shot him her best dirty look. "Smart-ass," she said.

"That would be me," he replied without missing a beat. "Want a quick lesson?"

"Are you the master?"

"That I am," he said. Before his eyelids lowered, Cassidy once again felt herself drown in those deep-blue bedroom eyes.

"Do I have a choice?" she asked, her voice one husky degree above a whisper.

"You always have choices," he murmured, and that fictitious déjà vu slipped right over her.

"What if this choice is fine," she returned, using another of his own lines against him. "What if this choice is what I want?"

"Sometime you'll discover that there's even a better choice."

"Oh," she said simply, for once again she was staring at his full lips. How she longed to put her fingers over them, to trace them, to touch them!

Besides, his fingers supporting her wrists were still massaging them, sending a wicked heat pooling many places that heat shouldn't be.

At least not when one was engaged to someone else.

That thought was like ice water, and she jerked back quickly, the movement causing the tape to fall from her hands. Amazingly he caught it. "I'd best get started," she said.

"You should," he replied. With a nod of his head he conceded that the moment had passed, but his voice contained an odd, wistful tone she'd never heard before. "Come, I'll show you how to use the tape."

And so, when Dan appeared at Cassidy's house around seven-thirty that evening, he found Cassidy standing in an interior doorway wielding a paintbrush and holding a plastic cup full of paint.

"What are you doing?" He looked up at her, incredulous.

"Hey," Cassidy said. She stepped off the stepstool and lifted her face for the kiss that should have followed. Instead it didn't come.

A bit mortified, she covered her shock by placing the cup on the floor and positioning the two-inch trim brush across the top of the cup. She grimaced as she saw the massive amount of paint droplets on her white oxford cloth shirt. Oh well. For the first time in her life, she now owned a work shirt.

It had been that or take Blade up on his offer to get one of his white T-shirts out of the truck. That had seemed too intimate, and she'd found this old long-sleeved shirt in her closet.

"What are you doing?" Dan repeated. The expression on Dan's face remained priceless, although not in a good sense.

"I'm painting," Cassidy said, defending her actions. "Even Martha Stewart paints."

Dan's jaw dropped open. Then he clamped it shut before speaking. "She's not an image consultant. You are. You could give lessons to Martha."

"That's not nice," Cassidy said. "Martha is a very beautiful woman."

"So are you, but you don't dig in the dirt. You've got money, Cass. Use your fingers the way God intended them. Write a check."

This time it was Cassidy's turn to look incredulous. "Now you sound like your mother," she finally said with an indignant sputter. "What is wrong with you lately? Didn't the Schmidts donate?"

"They did." Dan took a deep breath and visibly calmed down as he warmed to his favorite topic. "I guess that's why I've been so uptight. This museum addition has a lot riding on it. Getting it done right is my moment to shine. Do you think I want to spend my life being just Senator Ed Morris's boy?"

Some of the tension left Cassidy's shoulders. As the youngest Morris child, Dan had always been the baby, and thus, not much had ever been expected of him in the way of proving himself.

He had, however, been schooled in how important it was not to fail or embarrass the family.

"I understand," Cassidy said.

"Exactly." Dan gave a vigorous nod. "This is my moment. I need you by my side helping me. You're the one who believes in me, Cass."

Cassidy wasn't really sure about that. She understood Dan. They'd been friends forever, and she knew how to massage Dan's ego. Maybe that's all she was to him. The thought flickered in the deep recesses of her consciousness, as if it had been working its way up from the subconscious. She shoved the thought aside. "I'm glad that they donated."

"Thanks," Dan said.

Cassidy smiled, although for the first time in her life she didn't mean it. She really didn't care about the Schmidts or their donation, but it would kill Dan to tell him that.

"Speaking of the Schmidts," Dan said, as if Cassidy had given him the perfect opening, "Mrs. Schmidt wanted you to know how delighted she was to meet you the other night. She also got me to thinking. How long do you plan on working before giving up your career to have children?"

At that moment Cassidy was glad she'd set the paintbrush and cup down, or else she would have dropped it. "We've talked about this, Dan. I thought we agreed we would talk about this later. Right now I don't want to give up my job, especially now with my client list growing as fast as it is. I told you I'd gotten the—"

"Yes, well..." Cassidy frowned. Dan never interrupted her, and he'd been doing it constantly of late. Just what was going on?

Could he be having doubts?

"Look, Cass, Mrs. Schmidt just reinforced what my mother's been harping on. You should be concentrating on getting onto charity boards, not building your own business. You don't need to work now, and you certainly won't after we're married."

That thought chilled her. She wanted to work. Her

business was booming, and she'd finally come into her own. She didn't want to just serve on charity boards. That had been her mother's life, and it wasn't what Cassidy wanted for herself.

Now Lillian had gotten involved. While Lillian never had quite come out and said she wanted Cassidy to stop working, Cassidy had always been afraid Lillian had wanted it that way. What Lillian wanted, Lillian usually got.

"I don't want children right away," Cassidy said. She knew she had to win this point or she'd be lost before her marriage even started. "I want to build my career. It's important to me."

Dan paced. "Well, building my career is much more important. It's what will make a name for us in this town, Cass, a name aside from that of my family. I'm not going to be a senator. I'm just a curator."

His attitude startled her. Never had she seen this side, this strong determination. "Dan, look," she began, but he again cut her off.

"No, Cass, you look. I need you to be by my side, not traveling like you sometimes do. Speaking of that, you've got that vacation coming up. Do you think it's wise to take a trip to visit old girlfriends when we've got wedding plans to make?"

"What wedding plans? Your mother's done it all," Cassidy retorted, her irritation at Dan's attitude growing. "I've been looking forward to seeing my friends for more than a month. You know it's been over a year since I've seen them!"

Dan ignored her logic. "My mother's only trying to take the stress off you," he said. "My mother knows what she's doing when it comes to planning events, and she's only trying to help you out."

"By what, running the whole show? It's my wedding. Our wedding! What Lillian wants is just to launch your brother's senate race with my reception!"

Dan's lips pursed into a slight scowl. "You ought to be thankful, Cass. It's not like your mother is around."

Cassidy's mouth opened but the words she wanted to spew forth thankfully didn't come. Her eyes narrowed. Never before had Dan been so antagonistic. He'd always been so mellow, so laid-back. Just what was going on? In addition to the perfect Lillian and her ideas, now Dan also wanted Cassidy to give up vacation time? No way. She'd been looking forward to seeing some of her best friends from high school in the brief time they all had free. "That's a low blow," she finally managed.

Dan didn't seem too upset. "I don't mean it to be a low blow. It's just the truth. My mother is only trying to help because you got all this dumped on you and it shouldn't have happened. You sure as hell shouldn't be using a paintbrush and painting your own doorway."

Disbelief filled Cassidy and she stared at Dan. He pushed his wire-rim glasses back up his nose. She planted her hands on her hips. Time to stand her ground, or watch it slip away forever. "Pray tell me

why I can't paint? This is not the Dark Ages, Dan.
Women do more than look pretty.''

''That's not what I'm saying,'' he protested.

''I don't understand you,'' Cassidy shot back.
''What has gotten into you?''

''Nothing,'' he said with a wave of his hands. ''I
just want you to take more of an interest in what I do.
It's my career that will make a name for us.''

''While I stay home and man the nursery. I don't
think so. Let's be realistic, here,'' Cassidy said, her
brain still contemplating that this somehow was a huge
fight. She and Dan never even had a little fight, much
less a big one.

''Dan, let me be honest. I don't care about your
dinosaurs or your donors any more than you care
about my clients. It's only important to me because
you are. Now that...''

He looked stricken, as if she'd physically slapped
him. ''You don't care about my dinosaurs?''

''No.'' She moved her hands off her hips. As an
image consultant she was very aware of nonverbal
body language and she didn't want that posture.

''You don't care about what I do?'' His lip quivered, and Cassidy wanted to roll her eyes with the
silliness of it all. She hadn't thought Dan was *this*
sensitive.

How to salvage it? ''Dan, honey, I'm proud of what
you do, but no. I'm not really that interested in the
nitty-gritty details.''

His appearance was that of a whipped dog. "I thought you believed in me."

Cassidy tossed her hands in the air, her frustration obvious. "I do," she said. This conversation wasn't going well, nor was it going the way she wanted it to go. "Dan, love, I'd believe in you if you were a dog catcher or a trash collector."

"You don't love my dinosaurs," he mumbled, and with that he turned and slammed out the side door.

"Damn." Frustration overwhelming her, Cassidy uttered a rare curse word and stomped her foot.

That was a mistake.

The plastic cup toppled over, sending latex paint spilling over the ceramic tile.

The subsequent curse word screeched forth from Cassidy's mouth with such volume that Blade came running, cordless drill still in his hand.

"Are you okay?" he asked.

"I'm fine," Cassidy said, and instantly he could see she wasn't. While he hadn't overheard Dan's and her conversation, he could tell by the escalation in their tones that they'd been fighting.

"I'm sure you and Dan will make up whatever rift you're having," he said, although deep down, if he was honest with himself, he hoped they wouldn't.

"I don't care about Dan," she squealed in frustration. She pointed downward. "I spilled the paint!"

His gaze fell to the floor, and he could see the river of white latex paint running across the twelve-inch ceramic squares and seeping along the grout.

"It's latex," he told her, but that just made her lower lip quiver as if tears threatened to rain down any moment.

Never had he seen such a sweeter and cuter sight. He wanted nothing more than to draw her into his arms, smooth her blond hair back away from her forehead, kiss her senseless and then tell her it was okay.

Instead he just told her it was okay.

"What do you mean it's okay?" She stared at him, a combination of skepticism and hopefulness.

Blade wanted to groan under the weight of her doe-eyed gaze. She was lovely, and right now he wanted to be her savior! He struggled to keep his tone neutral, to keep from letting his desire for her show.

"It's latex paint. Get some paper towels and a plastic garbage bag. What we can't wipe up will just peel right up later."

"It will?" Her baby-blue-eyed gaze still held his, ever hopeful.

"Yes," he said, giving her a gentle nod of his head.

"I feel so stupid," she said.

"Don't," he replied, his tone calm. "Everyone learns the tricks of the trade one way or the other."

Two hours later the remaining paint peeled right up when Cassidy used a small flat blade.

"It worked," she told him proudly.

"Good," he said simply, and Cassie stared after him as he left the room. Dan would have said "I told you so." Blade hadn't.

Why hadn't she met him first?

Probably because she didn't run in the same social circle. Probably because men like Blade Frederick didn't approach women like her.

How she wished she'd met him first.

Without Dan and her upcoming wedding, she would have been free to pursue Blade, to walk the wild side, to see what the other half did.

Maybe the grass was greener when a yard crew wasn't the one to mow it.

She contemplated those thoughts as she went upstairs to wash off. Somehow she'd gotten a little latex on the tops of her feet, and Blade had told her that washing with water and rubbing with a fingernail would peel the paint right up off the skin.

She shoved aside the shower curtain in one of the guest baths and sat on the edge of the tub. Maybe she was settling just like Sara said she was.

But Blade?

Could she really toss aside the security of Dan and all that he offered for Blade? The man couldn't afford to fix his truck.

Instead he hung out in a bar and spent his money on custom cue sticks. He definitely had his priorities wrong. He'd love her and leave her flat. And there she would be, with nothing.

And worse, she'd be alone.

No, with him the passion would burn and fizzle, just as it had with Jeff the jerk. Jeff had promised her the moon and stars, and instead given her the cold shoulder after he'd gotten down her pants.

Cassidy shook her head and turned on the faucet. She stuck her right foot under the running water.

It was not even five seconds later that she screamed.

THIS TIME IT WAS A scream and not a shriek or a screech. He dropped his drill, not caring that the jolt on the carpet was enough to send the magnetic bit flying under some distant piece of furniture.

Cassidy was upstairs screaming.

He took the stairs two at a time. He followed her screams, which had turned more into sobs, and found her in a guest bathroom.

The one he wasn't finished repairing.

He bit back laughter, desire and sympathy all at once.

Cassidy stood there, drenched. She'd managed somehow to get the water turned off.

"The shower head came on!" she sputtered, heedless of the fact that her white shirt was plastered to her chest and was now perfectly see-through. "I turned on the bathtub and the shower came on, too!"

"I'm not done in here," he said, trying to wipe the smile off his face. She looked absolutely adorable, and she was wearing lace.

"You could have warned me." She waved her hands in despair, and Blade grabbed the nearest towel he could find, a plush blue one.

"I'm soaked." A rivulet of water ran down a strand of her hair and dripped off her chin.

"I can see that," he said, and then his laughter simply took over. He couldn't help himself.

"Stop laughing at me," she sputtered.

"I can't," he said honestly as he wrapped the towel tightly around her. He drew her into his arms and with a free hand tilted up her chin. "Do you know how cute you look?"

Her lip quivered. "I look like a wet rat."

"But a beautiful one," he said.

She shook her head, sending tiny droplets of water flying. "The shower head came on. I turned on the tub and the shower head came on, too!"

"I know," he said, and then, because fate finally had spoken and he couldn't help himself any longer, he leaned down and did what he'd wanted to do from the first moment he'd set his gaze on her.

He lowered his lips to hers and kissed her.

EVEN IF CASSIDY HAD wanted to compare the kiss to any other kiss she'd ever had before, the possibility of doing so vanished the moment Blade's lips touched down upon hers.

For there was no comparison to be made. With one kiss, Blade Frederick set a new standard, wiped the slate clean and made Cassidy Clayton feel every bit of the cliché—as if she'd been kissed for the very first time.

His lips touched hers, ever so lightly, as if almost hesitating. His greenish-blue eyes had drifted shut, as if seeing wasn't needed to feel, and his lips connected further, that sticky sweet sensation sending flutters and quivers shooting through every nerve ending to each and every region of her body.

Internal heat warmed her wet body, and she sighed, opening her mouth to his, giving him an obvious invitation that she wanted him to keep going, to kiss her, to finally let her feel what she'd been missing, what she'd been wanting for what seemed like the longest time.

He obliged.

His tongue found hers, skirted the inside of her mouth, dazzled her throat and sent light dancing behind her own closed eyes.

She pressed into him, heedless of his dry clothes, and she wrapped her wet arms around his neck. His kisses deepened, sending rivers of passion down to her wet toes.

She wanted the heavenly sensation to go on forever.

But it didn't. Abruptly he drew back, set her aside, away from him.

His eyelids guarded the expression in his passion-darkened eyes as he turned slightly so she only had a view of his side.

"That shouldn't have happened," he said.

The cold seeped in then, through the towel wrapping her wet but clothed body. The chill, however, came from deep within her, and her teeth chattered.

"You need to get changed," he said. His concern was mixed with an obvious desire for escape. "You're wet, Cassidy. You could catch cold. You need dry clothes.''

"Thank you for stating the obvious,'' she snapped. Typical male. Flee before facing the truth. Run before dealing with uncomfortable responses. She'd thought Blade was somehow different.

Couldn't he feel how she felt?

"Don't,'' he began, and as he turned, she could now see the stricken look in his eyes. "You're engaged. I shouldn't have violated you like that. You belong to Dan.''

"I belong to myself,'' she said quietly, her simple understanding of his moral dilemma creating a strange, bittersweet calm within her soul. She didn't feel quite as cold. She spoke the truth. "I wanted you to kiss me.''

"But it was wrong,'' he said.

She inclined her head slightly, as if agreeing but yet not. How could something so wonderful be so wrong? She had no argument to give him, no excuse to offer. She'd figure it out later, rationalize it somehow. "So where do we go from here?''

"Nowhere,'' Blade answered. He shifted his weight from one foot to the other. "If you weren't engaged, maybe it would be different.''

He paused, as if choosing his words carefully. He glanced at her once, and then looked toward the showerhead that was still dripping. "I'm sorry about that,'' he said with a gesture toward the showerhead. He moved another step away from her.

"Hell, I'm sorry about what else happened, too. Please don't take it wrong, Cassidy. I want you. I like you a lot, but you need to figure out what you want. I can't be a part of that. I can't influence you."

As he glanced at his watch, Cassidy felt him slipping further away, distancing himself. "Look, it's late. I'll just go clean up downstairs and show myself out. You need to get changed. I don't want you catching a cold. Go get dressed. Please."

She stared at him, and then wordlessly she complied. Wrapping the towel even tighter around herself, she moved past him and out of the bathroom. Within moments she stood in her bedroom and contemplated her reflection in the mirror.

Her hair was plastered to her face, and she did look like a drowned rat. And he'd kissed her, anyway. A small sigh escaped her, and then she dropped the towel and began to change her clothes.

She'd kissed him. It had been everything she'd dreamed a kiss could be, everything a kiss should be. She stepped into a pair of silk pajama bottoms. She might as well get dressed for bed. Besides, what else could she do? Chase after him? That wasn't fair to either of them.

What she wanted she couldn't have.

She was already spoken for. She'd already committed herself, and her life, to another.

After she had changed into her pajamas, she returned downstairs. As she'd expected, he was already gone, and from the window she could hear the faint notes of diesel rumble echoing far down the street.

Chapter Seven

She and Blade had never discussed the Boy Scout presentation. Cassidy remembered that fact the next day at work, right after she and Dan made up, without a kiss and without him even seeing her.

Yes, there was something to be said for modern technology as, around lunchtime, Dan had simply sent her a brief e-mail of apology.

In an odd sort of way Cassidy felt only relief as she stared at the electronic apology message now filling her computer screen.

After last night, she really didn't want to face Dan or even see him. Worse, after Blade's earth-shattering kiss, she didn't want to experience one of Dan's tepid ones. Not for an apology. Actually, not for anything.

Cassidy's empty stomach grumbled, reminding her that the bagel she'd eaten earlier that morning had been digested hours ago. She frowned. She knew she needed to be honest with herself. The fact was that frankly, not only did she not want to kiss Dan, right now she didn't want him, either.

But she was his fiancée, and not making up with him would be bad. Wrong.

Cassidy had never been a bad girl in her entire life. An only child, she'd always done what was expected of her. She'd made straight As in high school and college, and she'd earned her bachelor's degree in only three and a half years instead of four. No, Cassidy had always done the right thing, including taking care of her parents' house sale even when it was their responsibility.

Sighing, she hit the icon marked send. The e-mail message, stating simply "apology accepted" vanished instantly.

She twirled in her chair and looked out the window of her office.

There. Her e-mail acceptance of his apology ought to make Dan happy. But would it make her happy? She contemplated for a moment Sara's cryptic words. Was she settling for Dan?

Angrily she shook her head as if the motion made her denial more real. She wasn't settling. She had expectations, a vision for her future, and Dan fit right in. He was the missing piece to her puzzle. Besides, she couldn't give up everything she'd worked so hard for, everything she wanted, for a moment of fiery passion with Blade.

Blade didn't exist in her world. He was a handyman, a jack-of-all-trades with a truck that had seen better days. So why did he make her feel so, so special?

She tapped a pencil on the desk and mulled over

that thought. Contemplating it annoyed her, and so with strengthened resolve, she sat up straight. Pre-wedding jitters, that was all it was. Every bride-to-be got them. She deserved to have them more than any other bride—after all, she was getting Lillian for a mother-in-law. That had to count for something.

She brushed some lint off her skirt. The grass was always greener on the other side of the fence, right? Right now Blade just looked better and kissed better. That was all it was. Prewedding jitters. Fear of making a mistake that she would have to live with for the rest of her life.

But she wasn't making a mistake. Dan would be there for her when he was old and gray. And when they both had their own, joint home, on the other side of Houston, as far away from Lillian as possible, then Cassidy and Dan would be able to share all those in-timacies that other couples shared. It was hard to share anything when your mother-in-law-to-be kept popping over all the time.

In fact, after Lillian's first two "surprise" visits, she and Dan had simply given up on making love. Dan had insisted a hotel was too cheesy, especially for an unmarried couple of their social stature. Anyway, he'd argued, if the press found out that Senator Morris's son was having liaisons in a hotel, even with his fi-ancée, the scandal could be too costly on his father's political career.

His logic had made sense, and after all, tradition did dictate that a couple wait. Hence, in the end, Cassidy had simply agreed and left her relationship with Dan at some heavy kissing.

Of course, that had tapered off these past two months, but that was normal, too, right?

She nodded to herself, satisfied with her decision that Dan was the man for her. Besides, after Jeff the jerk and the passionate encounters they'd shared, Cassidy liked the fact that Dan was willing to wait before just hopping into bed with her.

Jeff hadn't, and look where that had gotten Cassidy. After he'd gotten all he'd wanted from her, Jeff had simply disappeared into the great beyond of other willing females.

He'd called it playing the field.

Cassidy had called it a painful lesson—that passion burned and, once the flame was out, died. The guy just stopped answering her phone calls and returning her voice mails. He stopped calling—period.

Angrily she brushed away a tear that was forming at the corner of her right eye. She wouldn't think about Jeff and the number he'd pulled on her. She'd lost a wonderful man she'd been dating; she'd tossed him aside for Jeff. Jeff had hit the highway, and Cassidy had been left with nothing.

Except for Dan. He'd always been there.

She'd be stupid not to marry him.

That decided, she jutted her chin forward. She'd worried her way right through her lunchtime. She grabbed a granola bar from the stash in her desk. No time to go out now. Not when she had a business to run. She had back-to-back appointments all afternoon. Time to get back to work.

BLADE HATED IT when Jake leaned over the desk. Blade shifted the chair back a few inches, but that didn't help. Even though Jake stood three inches shorter, and Blade could beat him up, and had in their juvenile youth, Jake still had a presence that just didn't stop.

And right now that presence wanted answers.

"So, are you making any progress with the hot one? What's her name? Cassidy?"

Somehow, only having sensed that the question had been forthcoming, Blade managed to control his sputtering. The cola he'd been sipping, however, still threatened to make a path through his nose, but his reflexes forced that to retreat. He was in control. He would maintain that control.

He took a deep breath and tried to relax. Jake always had an eagle eye for the truth, often catching and exposing when Blade was lying.

"So, have you?"

"No," Blade said, somehow managing to keep a perfect poker face.

He hoped Jake would believe him, for there was no way he could tell Jake the truth. Sure he'd made progress with Cassidy. He'd kissed her. Passionately. She'd been heaven to his lips, and he'd wanted her. All of her.

His lust and libido had made progress, all right, in the total wrong direction. She was engaged.

"No," Blade said again, a bit more convincingly this time.

Jake's eyes narrowed skeptically. "You expect me to believe that you haven't made any progress? None at all? Come on, Blade. We need to get an inside track."

"I tried." There, Blade thought. That sounded like something Jake would buy.

"You didn't try hard enough," was Jake's retort. "We need to get in with the politicians. Can't you make a move or something?"

Blade frowned. "I told you I tried. What type of move are you talking about?"

Jake paced Blade's office a moment before coming back to hover over the desk again. "Can't you make her fancy you or something? You know, butter her up. Get to Senator Morris somehow through his new daughter-in-law."

"No."

Blade's retort was sharp, and Jake's eyes narrowed. "What's gotten into you?"

"Nothing," Blade replied. "I just don't like this scheme of yours. People shouldn't use people."

Jake picked up a paperweight and twirled it around before putting it back on Blade's desk. "We're not using her. Hell, we're fixing her house for a bargain-basement price. We're doing her a favor. She owes us one."

That logic held. Cassidy had no idea the hundreds, if not thousands, he'd saved her.

But Blade never curried favors for money, or money for favors. "It's impossible."

"Nothing is impossible, Blade, my man," Jake said. "If I believed that, we'd still be sitting back in the old neighborhood without a hope in the world. You need to give me a better argument than this."

But there was the paradox. Blade couldn't admit the truth as to why the scheme with Cassidy was impossible and would never go the way Jake wanted it to. Blade couldn't, wouldn't. Not when he wanted Cassidy Clayton. Wanted to take her to bed. While Jake had the morals of an alley cat, Blade cared. He wasn't one to ever use a woman, even if the woman agreed to it being a "mutual" decision.

Unable to form an adequate response, he settled for a weak, "I just don't like it."

As Jake tossed his hands in an exaggerated gesture of despair and frustration, Blade suddenly wished he hadn't gotten into the scheme in the first place. Besides, he hated arguing with Jake. Blade had learned long ago that no matter how sharp he was, or how good an orator himself, Jake somehow always twisted the events and situation around and came out ahead.

That's why Jake made such a dynamite salesman and contract negotiator. It was usually just better to let Jake have his way.

"Look, Blade, this isn't an ethical dilemma," Jake insisted, still determined.

"I don't care," Blade replied. He glanced at the clock and stood up. "If I don't leave now I'll be twenty minutes late meeting the Lindbergh Heights foreman. As it is, I'm going to be late by ten."

"God forbid you use a cell phone and call him," Jake said.

"I planned on doing that anyway," Blade said. He moved around the desk and headed for the door, eager to escape Jake.

"This revenue office is important, Blade," Jake called after him.

"I know," Blade replied, "but so are the jobs we have now." With that, he strode out and left Jake standing there.

"Mr. Frederick! Mr. Frederick!"

Halfway to the elevator Blade paused. He'd walked right by Myrtle, his secretary. The elderly dear looked as if she'd just run a marathon, not ten feet.

"Sorry, Myrtle. I've got a lot on my mind."

"You have messages," Myrtle said. "I didn't want to disturb you when Mr. Jake was in there, but I didn't want you not to have these."

"Thanks," Blade said. Long ago he'd given up wondering why Myrtle called him by his last name, and yet Jake was Mr. Jake. He reached for the messages.

"You have an important one from Mel Trogg."

"That's about the camping trip we're doing this weekend," Blade said. He held his hand out, but Myrtle still kept a tenacious grip on the little pink slips of paper.

"He said he and his wife can't go," she said. "You're on your own."

"What?" Blade stared. Without Mel he'd have no program for Friday night.

"Their daughter," Myrtle said, "the one who's a freshman in college, was in a car accident. They need to go to Austin to be with her. He said to tell you he was sorry."

"No problem," Blade said, although actually it was a problem. A big one. While he empathized with Mel and understood totally, because family always came first, now Blade had a group of Boy Scouts with no program save some campfire songs and marshmallows. That wouldn't earn merit badges.

He extended his hand one more time for the message slips. "Anything else? I'm off to Lindbergh Heights."

"Oh, yes," Myrtle said. She placed the messages in his hand. "Something about the chamber of commerce dinner. That's somewhere in there. I'm off to lunch."

Out to lunch was more like it, Blade thought, but he kept that thought to himself. Jake had hired Myrtle as a favor to some now-long-ago ex, and despite that strike against her, Myrtle still worked at J & B. In actuality she really was a dear.

She just went on break a lot.

Blade flipped through the slips and sighed. There

was one from the clothing store regarding the alterations for his tuxedo. He'd need that penguin suit for the chamber dinner that Jake insisted they attend. That event was Saturday night, right after he returned from the camping trip.

Even that fact, that he had to go to the darn dinner, didn't bother him like it normally would.

Another fact instead held his attention. None of the messages were from Cassidy. He didn't know if that thought should stress him or relieve him.

She hadn't fired him; then again, who knew what she thought of their kiss.

He knew what he thought about it. He still wanted her. He wanted to kiss her. He wanted to feel her mouth under his lips, slide his fingers over the white satin of her skin, remove the white lace bra she'd been wearing.

He banged his fist on the leather-wrapped steering wheel of his, not Frank's, truck. She was settling, he knew it. She wanted Dan because Dan was safe, dependable.

Couldn't she see that there was more out there?

Passion and life involved risk. She needed to risk, or she'd become bored, sedate. She'd wonder ten years down the road who she was married to, and why they never really shared anything anymore. Cassidy's passion, her zest for living, would die.

While he couldn't make her any promises, he could not stand by and watch her waste away into just another corporate wife. No, Cassidy was passion personified. Blade couldn't let that happen.

A small plan began to form and blossom in the back recesses of his mind. She'd said she'd do it last night. She told him she would help out with his Boy Scout troop. Would the kiss change anything? Would she accept his challenge?

He'd have to try.

Twenty boys depended on it—and so did one man.

"YOU WANT ME TO DO WHAT?" Cassidy stared at him in disbelief.

"Go camping. Friday. As in tomorrow night." Blade gave her a charming smile and tried not to give in to his nervous habit and shift his weight from side to side. He gave up and moved.

He'd worked on her predications for over three hours before she'd come home, and then he'd kept himself busy for another fifteen minutes before he'd dared to even approach her. Obviously, from her deliberate ignoring of him, she'd decided the best solution to last night's event was to pretend that the kiss had never happened.

Blade took a deep breath and began his pitch again. Although not as good as Jake, he could be a killer salesman when he needed to be. "You told me yesterday that you'd do a communications seminar with the boys. One of my scoutmasters and his wife canceled. They had to go to Austin for a family emergency. Their daughter was in a car accident. If you can help me, Cassidy, I could really use it. I don't know what else to do. The boys need to earn their badges."

She sighed, and from the contemplative expression on her face he could tell she was torn. He felt a bit like a heel for using one of Jake's tactics. But it was for the boys, right?

"Please, Cassidy?" He lowered his voice, letting the plea roll over her like a gentle wave. "Mel was going to do a series of activities for a merit badge. Without him, or you, the boys won't earn a badge. Without this weekend, some of them might not make their Order of the Arrow."

Cassidy crossed her arms across her chest and then dropped them to her side. "And that is?"

"A really prestigious honor," he told her. He could see her wavering, and he pressed just a bit harder on her conscience. "You won't even have to stay the night. You can just come for a few hours and then you can leave. We'll only be an hour and a half away from Houston."

"I don't know," she said. "My schedule is open, but…"

"If you could help, Cassidy, they would be so happy. Remember, these are economically disadvantaged youth. They need all the breaks they can get."

"I know," she said. "I'd have to ask Dan. I doubt he'll agree, though. He's pretty picky about what I do."

"And you listen to him?"

"I am his fiancée."

Blade didn't want to tread down that path. He bit back the cryptic reply. "You're right," he said. "You need to ask him."

"Exactly," she said. "I need to ask him."

"So when will you do that?" Blade prodded. He knew he had to push, or Cassidy would reconsider and back out long before seeing Dan and even discussing it with him.

"I'm not sure when I'll be seeing him. I mean, I thought he'd stop by tonight, but Dan's not…"

"Dan's not what?"

At that moment, despite not liking the guy, Blade was never so glad to see the man himself walk through the door.

"What am I not?" Dan asked again as he stepped fully into Cassidy's kitchen.

"Not really big on having me go out of town on short notice," Cassidy replied.

Dan arched an eyebrow and then opened the refrigerator. He took out a cola that Cassidy had purchased earlier at a convenience store. "No, I'm not. So when are you going out of town?"

"I—" Cassidy began, but Blade cut her off.

"It's my fault, Dan. I've asked your fiancée to help me out of a jam this weekend. I'm a scoutmaster for a local troop of boys and we're having an overnight campout. I want Cassidy to give a communications seminar tomorrow night to the troop. They'll earn their badges, and afterward she's free to go."

"Why Cassidy?" Dan asked between sips.

Blade held his ground. "Mel Trogg was to have given the presentation, but his daughter was in a car accident."

Dan straightened suddenly and peered over his glasses at Blade. "You know Mel Trogg?"

How to answer that? Evasively. In Dan and Cassidy's minds Blade was a handyman, not the owner of a large construction company who would know Mel Trogg personally. After all, the guy financed most of J & B's ventures. "He's a scoutmaster, too," Blade said, simply stating a basic truth. "His troop is also going on the campout."

"Really? Interesting." Dan turned to Cassidy. "Mel Trogg is owner of Bankfirst," he said. "Largest privately owned bank in Texas." Dan turned his attention back to Blade. "So he's a scoutmaster?"

"Yes," Blade said.

"I didn't know that." Dan straightened and picked a piece of lint off his sleeve. "Cassidy, Mel donated over $100,000 to the museum last year. You simply must fill in for him. It's the least you could do."

"And I'll be sure to tell him she's your fiancée," Blade added, especially now that he could already see Dan mentally counting the amount of Mel's next donation.

"Excellent," Dan agreed with a sharp nod. He took Cassidy's hands in his. "Darling, it's just for the evening, and I do have that boring opening to attend. You really would rather help out the Boy Scouts than attend the Gregorian Gallery premiere of Cleopatra's remains.''

"But I—'' Cassidy started to protest. Did no one care what she wanted? She'd love to help out with the Boy Scouts. She'd love to help a bunch of underprivileged boys. But what she didn't want was to spend any more time with Blade Frederick. The man made her nervous. He made her see things that weren't there, feel things that she knew were only an illusion.

Dan put a finger on her lips to shush her next protest, and Cassidy took a short step backward. His touch felt clammy. "Oh, Cass, you know you were so bored last year when the Mayan artifacts came to town. Everyone demands my attention and you simply stood around like a wallflower. You know when I'm working I can't spend time with you like I want.''

She hadn't been bored, and she hadn't stood around like a wallflower. She'd spent most of her time talking to Mrs. Craft, wife of a local concrete company president. Besides, hadn't Dan complained just yesterday that she wasn't by his side enough? They'd just had a fight over it. "I did not just stand—'' Cassidy began, but again instantly Dan cut her off.

"Just think, Cassidy, how grateful Mel would be. I'd love to see him up his donation this year.'' Dan dropped Cassidy's hands and turned back to Blade. "You'll have her back that evening?''

"She can leave whenever she wants after her presentation.''

Cassidy glared at Blade. He was enjoying this, the

smug jerk. He'd gotten her right where he wanted her. Worse, she wasn't really that upset about it. He gave her a slight shrug, one that Dan missed.

"Back that night. That's perfect," Dan said. "That way you and I can do lunch on Saturday, Cass. Mother has more wedding plans she wants us to discuss. I've already agreed with her choices, but I want to give you the final say." He beamed. "There. Everything's all settled."

Cassidy didn't care about Lillian or her wedding plans. Instead Cassidy continued to lock eyes with Blade. She'd kissed this man, and she wanted him. Still. And worse, he knew it.

At that moment Dan's cell phone began to shrill. "Dan Morris." Everyone remained quiet as Dan listened for a moment. "Uh-huh. On my way."

He snapped the phone closed. "I've got an emergency. We'll have to postpone dinner."

Cassidy blinked. They were supposed to have done dinner? When had they made those plans? She frowned slightly. When had she and Dan gotten so out of touch? They'd never been like this before.

He leaned forward and kissed her quickly, a tepid peck on her lips. "I'll see you Saturday around noon. Oh, and don't forget, we also have that chamber dinner later that night. Bye, love."

Cassidy turned on Blade the minute Dan had closed the door behind him. "Satisfied?"

The cheeky grin he gave her almost undid her. "Absolutely,'' he admitted honestly. ''I wanted you, and I got you.''

The words hung out there in the air for a moment.

''Oh, come on, Cassidy. You're not really that upset are you?''

The wind left her sails, and her shoulders, which she'd been holding so indignantly, relaxed into a gentle slump. ''No,'' she admitted.

''See.'' He laughed, and her face finally cracked into a smile. ''Besides, you didn't want to go to a boring premiere, did you?''

Cassidy planted her hands on her hips. ''I did not just stand there and act like a wallflower!''

Blade threw up his hands in mock self-defense. ''Did I say that you did?'' He grinned again and then sobered. ''Actually, I can't see you ever being a wallflower.''

Cassidy dropped her arms and laughed. How had Blade changed her mood? Somehow he'd made everything better, made everything seem so right. She moved over to the sink and filled up a glass with water. ''I wasn't. Dan's just so busy that he never really notices what I do.''

''Shouldn't that be telling you something?''

Her mood changing again, Cassidy whirled around so fast that water splashed out of the glass and onto the ceramic tile floor. She glared at Blade. ''We are not going to have this conversation.''

''What conversation?''

''Don't you go all innocent and naive on me. You

know exactly what I mean. The kiss. It shouldn't have happened. I'm marrying Dan. We fit. What you and I may feel is an aberration, just some prewedding jitters.''

"I'm not disagreeing with you," he said. "But I still think you're settling. You have passion, verve."

Cassidy reached for a paper towel. "Please give me a break. What do you know about me?"

"I know enough." His voice was quiet, and it cut through the kitchen like one of the knives in the custom-made butcher block holder.

"I'm sure you have work to do," she said. She whirled around and made to leave the room. Instead she gripped the granite countertop for a moment. "I'll need directions."

"Want them now?" His voice came from behind as she had her back to him.

"Just write them down. There's some paper on the desk over there. I assume it's not hard to find."

"Have you ever been to Lake Houston State Park?"

She still didn't turn around. "I know how to get there."

"I didn't say we'd be in the park. There's a Boy Scout camp about five miles away from the park. It's not hard to find."

The man was driving her insane. "Just leave the directions on the island."

"I'll do that."

She let the countertop go and began moving toward the back stairs. Her room would be safer, and she wanted to get out of her work clothes and into something more comfortable. Her pantyhose had started to itch.

"Cassidy."

Something in the tone of his voice made her pause at the bottom of the back stairs.

"Yes?"

"Are you afraid to turn around and look at me?"

Actually at this moment she was. She was torn between wanting to hit him or kiss him. All she had to do was stand in the room and she wanted him. He tempted her like chocolate cake, but she needed to remain true to her diet of bland.

No final indulgences for her, no bites of forbidden fruit, no final flings for this one-man woman.

Slowly Cassidy turned around and looked at him, sensing the mistake the moment she did so.

His male magnetism, his pure male mystique washed over her, overpowering her senses from across the fifteen feet separating them.

He wore carpenter whites, the tight white crew shirt covering and revealing every honed muscle. His hammer hung from the tool belt at his waist, the blue handle slapping his left thigh.

She dared finally to catch his gaze, finding his greenish-blue eyes mirroring nothing but pure admiration of her.

"What?" she managed weakly.

"I still think you're settling."

And with that she fled.

Chapter Eight

"I'm not settling!"

"Cassidy, honey, I'm your best friend. Trust me, you're settling."

Sara reached a hand out across the restaurant table and patted the back of Cassidy's hand. The movement did nothing to ease Cassidy's inner torment. "I mean, think about you and Dan. Does it feel right?"

"Of course it does," Cassidy said. She frowned. Didn't it? Actually, right now she really didn't know, which was why she'd met Sara for lunch. The issue had been getting grayer and grayer lately. It used to be so black-and-white.

"This man who's doing your work, Blade," Sara said, "how does he make you feel?"

Tingly all over. Cassidy kept that thought to herself. "Not like Dan. Different. Like I'm on a steep slope and I'm sliding down it."

Sara shook her head. "How often does he occupy your thoughts?"

All the time. Cassidy shook her head as if to clear

her thoughts. "Really, Sara, I needed you to reassure me, not confuse me. It's just prewedding jitters. I know that's all it is. If you were joining Lillian's family to yours you'd feel this way, too."

"We've been friends for far too long for me to watch you make a mistake. If you truly love Dan, with that end-all-be-all passion, then marry him. If not, break it off. There's someone else down the road. Don't just settle because your biological clock is ticking."

"My biological clock is not ticking," Cassidy insisted. Actually it was, but she'd managed thus far to control it. After all, she was a twenty-first-century woman in control of her own destiny. She certainly didn't believe that she had no control over her fate.

But she did have to be honest with herself. Blade affected her in ways that Dan never even touched. In fact, Blade's touch sent fire through her while Dan's couldn't even raise her temperature to lukewarm.

"Cassidy," Sara's voice called Cassidy back to the fact that they were sitting in a restaurant enjoying a late lunch. "When will you see Blade again?"

"Tonight. I'm giving a communications seminar to his Boy Scout troop."

Sara nodded as if that happened all the time. "I want you to really explore your feelings for this man."

"I can't do that. I'm engaged," Cassidy insisted. She held out her left hand. "See, I have a ring."

Sara exhaled, a deep sigh that revealed her exasperation. "Tell me about Blade."

"What about him?"

"Describe him to me."

"You saw him in the bar," Cassidy said. Suddenly she wished her best friend hadn't majored in psychology.

"So? I want you to tell me," Sara prodded.

"He's different," Cassidy said slowly. "He's kind, gentle, yet sexy as all get-out. I'm surprised some other woman hasn't snatched him up. Perhaps the fact that he's just a poor contractor has something to do with it."

"So he's sexy," Sara said with a shrug. "Lots of guys are sexy."

Cassidy looked shocked. "Of course he's sexy. You were practically drooling over him that first night. I mean, you were the one who came up with that thumb-to-the-pinkie thing."

"So have you found out yet?" Sara asked.

"Sara!" Cassidy practically sputtered on the sip of water she'd just been taking.

"Don't you Sara me, Cassidy Clayton. You're interested in this man. I know you too well. You're doing yourself a grave injustice if you settle down with Dan without exploring what you could have with Blade."

"I can't have anything with Blade. He's a contractor. He can't afford to fix his truck."

"So? I never took you for a snob, Cassidy. You've never judged people on their financial status. Only one woman does that, and that's your soon-to-be-mother-in-law unless you get on the clue train. This attitude that he's just a contractor is Lillian's influence. You need to lose that woman, and fast. The best way to do it is to dump her son.''

"I love Dan," Cassidy insisted.

"Sure you do. As a brother. He's nice. He's safe. He doesn't make you feel anything. He's boring. Honey, my marriage fell apart, but I'm still looking. Trust me, don't settle.''

"Dan loves me," Cassidy insisted, trying that tactic.

"Of course he does, but like a sister," Sara said. "Come on, Cassidy. See reason. You've complained to me that he's never around these past few months. You have got to be realistic. You're only a priority in his life because it gets his mother off his back. You're second to everything else. Are you sure he isn't cheating on you?''

"Of course he's not!''

Sara shrugged. "That's what I thought about my ex, and look where it got me.''

Cassidy pushed her plate away, the food almost entirely untouched. Somewhere along the line she'd lost her appetite. She'd wanted validation, reassurance. Not an inquisition and a lecture on why she should dump her fiancé.

"Sara, I'm not you, and Dan isn't like your ex. I'm not settling. Could we please drop this line of conversation? It's upsetting me.''

Sara shook her head, disbelief still evident. "Of

course. Just do me a favor and think about what I said, okay? And don't be afraid to let that Blade guy in. He's hot. You deserve hot, Cassidy, not tepid and lukewarm. You're too passionate for that.''

Blade had said just about the same thing, and Cassidy couldn't take anymore. ''Enough!''

''Okay,'' Sara agreed as the waitress approached. ''Let's get coffee and talk about something else. Did I tell you I ran into Debbie Dunning? You won't believe what she's up to now.''

At last, idle gossip. Cassidy leaned back in her chair. They were wrong. She knew it.

''I'M NOT SETTLING!'' Cassidy spoke the words aloud later that night, right as a flash of lightning illuminated the tan interior of her car.

Just her luck, it had to be raining. It wasn't too bad, the early spring storm more of a nuisance than anything else.

She turned the radio's volume control up a little bit louder. She actually liked the latest Toby Keith song that was currently dominating the Billboard country music chart. She'd never liked country music much before, but even in that area Blade had been an influence in her life.

She didn't need to think about Blade and the fact that he'd had such an effect on her. She turned the radio up another notch.

However, drowning her bothersome thoughts with

noise didn't help at all. The annoying thoughts that refused to go away were simply louder than the radio.

A spray from a passing car covered her windshield for a second, and Cassidy turned her windshield wipers up a notch. The swish-swish slapped away the raindrops and the residual spray.

She was almost there. So far Blade's directions had been easy to follow, and she was just about to reach FM 1485 and the New Caney exit.

"I'm not settling," she muttered again, as the dominating thought of her day once again crept back in. "Just because Blade said it, and then Sara had to say it today at lunch, that doesn't mean they're right. Peer pressure. That's all it is. And why am I talking to myself?"

She braked, realizing she was just about to drive past the exit ramp. Concentrate, she mentally told herself. You're never this out of sorts. It's just a seminar to some high school boys. You've handled worse. Get yourself together.

Yeah, but Blade was never at any of her previous seminars. Cassidy gripped the steering wheel tighter. That doesn't matter, she told herself. All you and Blade have is chemistry, and nothing comes out of chemistry. You're a professional. Just do the seminar and go home. Nothing will go wrong tonight.

Within twenty minutes she found herself finally driving though the gates of the Boy Scout camp.

Blade waved as she pulled up into the specific

campground area. She rolled the window down. "Where do I park?"

"Right next to that truck." He pointed to a harvest-gold Ford 350 dually crew cab that was parked next to a yellow school bus. "How was the drive? Did you have any problems getting here?"

"I scraped my car on that dip back there."

"Sorry about that. If there's any damage let me know," he offered.

"I'm sure it's fine." She pressed the button, sending the power window back up before she opened the car door. He held out an umbrella and covered her as she got out. Cassidy glanced up and grimaced. Was it her imagination or had the rain gotten heavier?

She didn't have time to contemplate that as she grabbed her briefcase. Get done and go home. That was her agenda tonight. She certainly didn't need to spend any more time with Blade than necessary.

She glanced around the camp, seeing a series of tents built on raised platforms. Flashlight beacons bobbed inside the tents, and another group of boys cooked on a fireplace pit set up on the edge of a lighted pavilion. Her high heels were beginning to sink into the wet ground. She hadn't thought to change into more sensible shoes. "So where do we do this?"

"Over there." Blade pointed to the pavilion they were now walking toward. "We'll eat after you're done. Are you hungry? You're welcome to stay."

She glanced at the open stockpot as they walked by. All she recognized was that it was some sort of a blend of hamburger and macaroni noodles. "I ate on the road."

She had, if the candy bar she'd bought at the gas station counted.

"Suit yourself. The offer stands. Let me get the guys. This is Scott. He'll help you get set up. He's my assistant scoutmaster. That other guy over there with his back to you is Mel's assistant Johnson."

"Hi," Scott offered.

"Hi," Cassidy replied. She watched Blade stroll off. Within five minutes he'd gathered all the boys under the pavilion. They shook the water off their rain ponchos and looked up expectantly at her.

Cassidy calmed her nerves. She'd done presentations at high schools before, and she could handle this. Within moments she found herself pleasantly surprised. While she'd expected them to be attentive, she hadn't expected a group of high school boys to be so interested and enthusiastic about her topic.

They had questions, and they weren't afraid to ask them. Cassidy found herself enjoying the presentation and subsequent discussion, perhaps even a little bit more than she did with her adult clients.

"This has been great," Blade said, walking up after she was finally finished and the boys had moved off to do other activities.

"It wasn't bad," she admitted. Actually the session had been wonderful. She'd even felt as if she'd done some good, something besides just writing a check to a charity. She made no attempt to gather up her things. "I really enjoyed it."

He smiled and it warmed her clear to her toes. "I'm glad. The boys really appreciated your giving up your time, especially filling in at the last minute for Mel like this."

"They were a good, enthusiastic group," Cassidy said. "They were great. Really. I like groups that aren't afraid to ask questions and get into discussions."

"That's my boys." Pride was evident in the tone of his voice, and Cassidy looked up at Blade. Tonight he wore a solid blue flannel shirt and jeans. The attire would never fly in her social circle, yet on Blade she couldn't picture anything else.

She needed to go, and quickly. She reached for her briefcase and stopped suddenly. She had more to say. "You know, your boys respect you a lot."

Blade shifted his weight from foot to foot. He looked off toward a tent, as if the compliment had affected him. He brought his eyes back to hers and his greenish-blue gaze held hers. "Thanks for saying that. I try to help them and I hope I succeed at least a little bit. I was once in their place."

Cassidy blinked. Once again Blade had surprised her. "I didn't know that."

"It's not something I talk about a lot." She saw something akin to pain in his eyes. How she wanted to wipe it away. But she knew she couldn't. It was not her role, to become the woman attached to this man.

"Hey, Blade. Can we eat now?"

The intense moment broken, Blade turned to look at the fresh-faced kid who had interrupted them. "Sure. You know the drill. Have Scott or Johnson start everything so everyone can eat."

"Sure thing."

"Well, you look like you need to go," Cassidy said. Panic began to fill her. Could Sara's words be right? No. Never.

Cassidy couldn't fall for Blade Frederick. She was engaged, ready to marry someone else. She couldn't spend any more time with Blade. He may be temptation and passion, but he wasn't her future. She needed to leave. Now. "I need to get going, as well," she said, amazed that her voice didn't reveal any of her inner turmoil.

"No problem," Blade said. Even in the poor light of the pavilion, Cassidy could see the lie—reluctance was reflected in his eyes.

She picked up her briefcase off a picnic table and edged toward the parking area. She had to go. She could not explore the feelings overtaking her. "I'll talk to you, what, on Monday?"

Blade shook his head. "Earlier than that. I'll be over Sunday. I've got to get the last of the predications fixed. You've scheduled the building inspector for early in the week, right?"

Cassidy clutched her briefcase as if it were her lifeline. The thought of seeing Blade this weekend and knowing she wouldn't after early next week had just filled her with dread. She'd come to depend on him. He'd been like a light in her world. Her feelings were as confused as a kaleidoscope. She tried to picture Dan and couldn't. "The inspection is scheduled for late Tuesday," Cassidy finally managed to say as she remembered the original question.

He smiled, a wistful look that said that he, too, knew the moment was somehow bittersweet. "I'll be done long before then. I told you we'd make it."

"You did," she said. And as if remembering her manners she added, "Thank you."

"It's just my job," he replied.

And then both of them simply stared at each other. What was there to say? Nothing but goodbye, because Cassidy needed to leave, to head back to her life, to leave the Boy Scouts and Blade Frederick behind.

So why didn't she move? All she had to do was just take one step. One tiny simple step, but her feet refused to work.

The moment seemed to stretch, until the resounding boom practically threw Cassidy into Blade's arms.

He gripped her forearms gently, steadying her on her feet.

"Lightning strike," he said. "Probably about a mile or two away."

"That's a sure sign I should go," she said, but the heat spreading through her body from his touch rooted her to the ground.

As if sensing her reluctance, fate intervened. At that

moment the heavens opened up and the rain descended.

Both Cassidy and Blade turned to look at the downpour, the sheet of rain so solid that standing underneath it for even a second would soak anyone's clothes straight through.

There was no way she could run to her car or that an umbrella would offer any protection at all.

"I think that's a sign you're going to have to stay," Blade told her with a hopeful smile. "Not that I'm going to mind."

Cassidy stood there and watched the rain for a moment. In downpours this heavy, Houston roads were known to flood. The water didn't drain off fast enough.

Laughter reached her ears. Underneath the pavilion roof, the boys sat eating and talking. Everyone was having a wonderful time.

She was the only one bothered by the rain. Cassidy sighed. Just for tonight maybe she'd concede that she had no control over her fate, or at least Mother Nature. She certainly didn't want to run out to her car and get drenched in the process. Driving more than an hour in soaked clothes was not appealing.

Besides, if she was honest with herself, she had nothing to go home to. Just her house, which was now even empty of paintings. The only untouched room was her bedroom, and at this moment going straight home to her lonely bed sounded dreary.

"I'll stay until the rain slows down," she said finally. She set her briefcase back on the table.

"I'm glad you're staying," Blade said. "I hate driving in Houston's storms, and I'm glad you won't be. So you'll stay for goulash?" He gestured toward the concoction simmering in the stockpot.

The moment lightening, Cassidy smiled. "Is that what that stuff is called?"

"Absolutely. It's a Boy Scout staple. You'll love it, trust me. There's even homemade peach cobbler for dessert. It's been cooking in the coals."

"I'm hungry. I guess I have no choice." Until the rain let up, her fate was sealed.

Blade gave her a wide smile, and Cassidy felt butterflies land in her stomach. "No, you don't," he said. "Not with the food or the company. Sometimes the best choice is to just stay where you are. Just think, things could be much worse."

Two hours later his prophetic words rang true. Things could get worse. From the edge of the pavilion, Cassidy stared in dismay at the rain that still pelted down. Sure it had lessened, but the campground had received two inches of rain according to the rain gauge some enterprising Boy Scout had stuck in the ground.

Worse, that dip in the road had been over a dry creek—a creek that now flowed with water. There was no way her silver Grand Prix GTP, with its low ground clearance, would make it through the rushing water. For her the road out of camp was cut off.

Cassidy winced. She should call Dan and let him know. Then again, if she did he'd tell Lillian.

No, calling Dan wasn't an option. Not when Cassidy could almost envision Lillian's words. "I told you that you shouldn't have bought that car," Lillian would say. "I told you to buy an SUV. They're much safer and you would have been able to cross the creek."

Cassidy turned as Blade approached her. "I have bad news. You're not going to get across the creek tonight," he said.

Fate had to be mocking her. "I know."

"I feel like one of those guys on a date who runs out of gas and can't get his date home on time." He ran a hand through his hair. "Although I guess you aren't my date and I'm not out of gas. Anyway, do you want me to lend you the truck? It'll get you across."

Cassidy shook her head. She had no desire to ford a rushing stream of water, even in a four-by-four that could take it without risk to her safety. "No. Besides, what if one of the boys hurt themselves? You'd be stuck. I'm just going to have to wait it out."

"Sorry."

Cassidy shrugged and gave him a resigned smile. "It's not your fault. It's not like you conjured up the rain. I've just been standing here thinking of Lillian's reaction to the situation. She told me to buy an SUV. But no, I insisted on getting a Grand Prix."

"You have a nice car."

"I like it," Cassidy said. "It fits me."

"Do you need to call anyone? Dan? Lillian?"

"No," Cassidy said. Even in the darkness of night

she could tell that clouds still blanketed the sky. "They won't worry about me unless I don't show up by noon."

She jutted her chin forward and said the following words more for her own benefit. "You know, Lillian isn't always right."

"Of course she's not," Blade agreed without missing a beat. "She caused your predication problems. That's one thing."

Cassidy rolled her eyes heavenward. She didn't want to even think about the predications anymore. The only good that had come from the situation was that she'd met Blade. "I know she caused my problems. Is it bad if I say my future mother-in-law annoys me?"

"I think we established that the night I met you," Blade said with a heartwarming smile. "You sent the peanuts flying across the bar."

"True," Cassidy acknowledged with an "oops" look. She sobered slightly. "You know, even though it's my family home, I can't wait to move. I always thought I'd be out by now, but my parents' divorce sort of stalled my plans. But not anymore. It's high time I'm in my own place."

Blade shifted his weight from his left foot to his right. "Where are you going?"

"I bought a cute little condo in Clear Lake," Cassidy said. "I guess I can always rent it out when Dan and I get our house, on the opposite side of town as far away from Lillian as possible."

Blade's gaze was shrewd. "You don't like her at all, do you?"

Cassidy sighed. "Is it that obvious?"

"You hide it well," he teased.

She took a seat on the picnic bench, and Blade sat down beside her. She brushed a wayward strand of hair out of her face. "I like her, I guess. She's not my favorite person, but I don't hate her."

Blade waited while she took a deep breath before continuing. "I guess I just don't want her running my life. She runs everyone else's, especially Dan's, but I don't want her running mine. Especially after I marry her son. She doesn't have the right."

"No, she doesn't," Blade agreed. As if for emphasis, he reached forward and covered her hand with his. "You are your own person, never forget that."

"I try to remember that," she said with a slight incline of her head. She knew she should remove her hand out from under his, but the heat between hers and his had fused them together. She rationalized that it would take too much effort. "It gets hard sometimes to remember that I'm my own person. Everyone expects so much from me. I mean, this house shouldn't have been dumped on me."

"We wouldn't have met if it hadn't," Blade said. His touch continued to burn through her. "There's your silver lining. Just remember through all this to be yourself. You'll be fine."

"Is that your philosophy?"

"Pretty much," he said. He smiled at her, and her

skin prickled. She was not supposed to want this man! "I guess it's an okay philosophy," he added. "It's gotten me this far."

"Money isn't everything," she said, for at that moment he seemed more content with his lot than she ever had with hers. "Lillian doesn't understand that. She sees that I've got a huge trust fund, and she doesn't understand why I still work. I want to work. I love working."

"Working is all I know," Blade admitted.

"Please," Cassidy protested. She gestured around. Although most of the boys had braved the downpour and retired to their tents, a few still milled around. "Look at you. These boys respect you so much. It's amazing. Instead of building my career, Lillian wants me to serve on charity boards. You, however, actually dig in and get into the trenches with these kids. You've probably done more good in one weekend than she has done in her whole lifetime."

He readjusted his hand on hers. "I don't know about that, but what I do know is that you can help out anytime you want. I have to admit, I liked having you here. You were good with the boys. Several of them told me later I should be dating you."

Really? They'd accepted her? Cassidy brushed those wondrous thoughts away as embarrassment filled her. Even though she'd been born rich, she knew how hard it was to be teased by kids. She'd had her share of teasing during her childhood. "I'm sorry about their remarks."

Blade made light of the moment, but his tone still held an underlying current of seriousness. "What can I say? They have good taste in women."

A different kind of embarrassment filled her, this time the warm and fuzzy kind that sends a woman's heart racing. "You're too kind."

"I'm serious," he said. Fire flared through her veins. "I'll admit you've intrigued me. I wish things could be different, but they're not."

Cassidy threw up her hands, breaking the contact of his skin on hers. "Not this conversation again. I'm not settling. Dan and I have known each other forever. We suit each other. You and I, well, we'd be just some passion that would flare out."

"Probably," Blade agreed. "But that doesn't mean that I don't want you."

His honesty shocked her, and she simply stared at him as he continued. "I'd be lying if I told you that I didn't want to make love to you. I've thought of nothing else since you sent the peanuts flying. You've gotten under my skin, but you're an itch I can't scratch. I can't let myself. I'll just have to wait for it to go away."

"Oh." In the darkness she simply stared at him. Never had a man been so bold or so honest about his feelings and desires for her. Jeff had seduced her with flattery. Dan hadn't seduced her at all. Blade had just told her bluntly how much he wanted her. His honesty excited her, yet at the same time it scared her. She wanted him just as much.

The question was what to do about it. Sara had told her to go for it, to explore her feelings. Could she? Could she risk the safety of Dan for the unknown with Blade Frederick?

"'Night, Blade." The last of the boys and adults headed for their tents, the rain having finally turned from sheets into just a mild downpour.

"I should show you to your tent," Blade said.

Surprise filled her. "I have a tent?"

Blade chuckled slightly at her naiveté. "Yes. You'll get the real camping experience tonight. I'll bunk in the truck so you can use the extra tent and borrow my sleeping bag."

"Really, Blade, that's too much," Cassidy protested. She folded her arms across her chest. Taking his tent and sleeping bag somehow seemed so personal.

"The creek won't dry up enough for your car to cross until probably about three in the morning. Do you want to stay up that long?"

"No," Cassidy admitted. "I'd fall asleep driving back into Houston."

"Exactly," Blade said. "So you'll stay in my tent. It's empty since Mel isn't here. For propriety's sake I'll take the truck. It's actually pretty comfortable."

Cassidy frowned. Something wasn't adding up. "You've slept in that truck before? That's not yours, is it? What happened to your red truck?"

Blade realized he'd tripped himself up a little too late. Time to cover up, quickly. "Uh, I'm getting the parking brake fixed. I borrowed that one from Jake. I slept in it once when we went hunting. Besides, have you ever slept in a sleeping bag?''

''No,'' Cassidy admitted with a laugh. Relieved she'd bought his deception about the truck, Blade quickly changed the subject again. For the next few hours while lights bobbed and then flickered out as boys fell asleep, Cassidy and Blake talked about this and that, including both his and her respective childhoods.

He'd never found an easier person to talk to, and when he told her that, Cassidy simply nodded and told him she felt the same way. Her words made his gut clench. He wanted this woman, and now that he'd found her he couldn't have her. Maybe he should get some of Jake's alley cat morals.

The thought that he should stoop to Jake's level disturbed him, and to avoid it Blade glanced at his watch. The illuminated dial told him it was getting close to midnight. He and Cassidy had spent more time talking than he'd originally planned, but now he wouldn't have had it any other way. Cassidy Clayton was one special woman, and he wished he could spend more time with her. But after Tuesday night, when her predications were removed, he'd need to let her go.

She didn't belong in his world, or he in hers.

''Come on,'' he said. ''Time for bed. Everyone else is asleep.''

''Okay,'' she mumbled, her tiredness evident.

Blade's heart went out to her. She was so special.

Didn't she realize that fact? Somehow he had to let her know. "I'm going to carry you," he told her. "Your heels will sink in the mud, and you'll ruin your shoes and get muddy feet."

His logic held, so Cassidy simply let him sweep her up into his arms. She tried to ignore the heat of his touch and the steeliness of his chest as he carried her through the darkened campground.

The inside of the tent was warm and dry, and Cassidy found herself pleasantly impressed with her accommodations. Blade's sleeping bag covered a cot, and a Coleman lantern added enough light to send the shadows dancing into the four corners of the wooden platform.

"Here you go," he said setting her gently down on the cot. She instantly missed his touch.

He gestured toward everything. "Breakfast is at eight. I'll make sure you're up, although you'll probably hear everyone moving about. The guys are usually up at least an hour before breakfast. Anyway, that's plenty of time to get you back to Houston before lunch."

"Thank you," Cassidy said. She looked up to where Blade stood in the tent. At the tent's triangular peak he had just about an inch clearance.

In the flickering lantern light she drank her fill. She'd felt muscles under that shirt, heard the heartbeat that thudded under the body of steel.

Sara's words that Blade was a sexy man didn't come close to describing him. The whole man wrapped together into a package that somehow was tender yet tough, sensitive yet sublime.

This man did something to her, for her; heck, she didn't know what preposition to use to describe how just touching him made her feel. Right now the only thing she was certain of was that she knew she wanted nothing more than to have him kiss her again.

At that moment the raw truth slapped her right in the face.

She didn't love Dan Morris. Not with the passionate love a couple needs to survive. Marrying Dan would be a marriage of convenience, like settling for the safety of standing on the edge of the pool instead of jumping in and swimming.

She couldn't marry Dan. Not when her feelings, especially those of "death do us part" and "for better or worse" weren't there.

Yes, she needed to talk to Dan. Whatever wedding plans they had needed to go permanently on hold until she sorted out all of her feelings. For some strange reason she didn't think he'd mind postponing the wedding indefinitely. Deep down she didn't think she or Dan really wanted to get married. Sure, they loved each other, but Sara was right—they only cared for each other like a brother and sister would.

Of course, Lillian would mind the wedding postponement, but right now Cassidy wasn't going to let Lillian run her life. Not anymore. Not when freedom was so close and about to leave the tent.

It was time to get what she wanted for once.

Chapter Nine

As Blade took a step toward the tent flaps, Cassidy flew to her feet. She couldn't let him go. Not like this. Not yet. She had to take Sara's advice.

She had to grab the brass ring and see where it took her. Even if the end wasn't worth it, she needed to get back in the game and risk it.

''Blade.''

He turned and waited while, for the first time in her life, Cassidy jumped into the water feetfirst without testing it. She walked right up to him, put her hand on his shoulder, then around his neck, and lowered his head until his lips were right by hers.

Blade stood perfectly still, and Cassidy, emboldened by the fact that he hadn't run or said no, simply kissed him.

The fire that she had wanted, that she had craved, ignited the moment their lips fully touched.

Yes, Cassidy thought, as she boldly kissed him, pressing her lips to his, pulling back slightly and pressing delicately again. Then, as he sighed, she parted her lips and slowly ran her tongue over his bottom lip.

He groaned, and Cassidy felt his desire press into her belly. She stood on her tiptoes, sending her tongue inside his mouth.

This was her man. She wanted him, and tonight she would have him. She kissed him her way, sliding her tongue and her lips down his neck, eliciting the groan of pleasure that indicated exactly how Blade felt.

She continued to kiss him, stepping back slightly, leading him to that single cot, covered with the soft down sleeping bag. She guided him down upon it, so that he covered her body with his, kissing him all the while.

As his lips traveled up her jawbone and to the crevice behind her ear, she sighed with the glory of it all. This time she knew the truth. This was passion, this was what had eluded her with all men before Blade.

His lips traveled down the right side of her neck and to the hollow at the base of her throat. She arched her neck, sending his lips farther. ''Blade,'' she whispered.

Upon hearing the throaty whisper of his name Blade knew he was lost. At this moment in time nothing else mattered. He had to touch her, taste her, love her. His very life, his very essence depended on it.

And he knew everyone else in camp was asleep. The rain intensified, pattering on the canvas fabric. No one would be about. He could steal the moment.

His hands reached up, stroking over the soft-gray

cashmere sweater she was wearing. As his right hand caressed her breast she whimpered, and at that sound Blade spiraled out of control. He needed her, and not just because his lower half throbbed with painful intensity.

He desired this woman like no other. She'd wanted him just for who he was. His fingers slid their way under her sweater, across the lace he lifted away.

Her nipple pebbled under his ministrations and she cried out. Instantly he brought his lips back to hers, fusing their mouths together in a passion predetermined before the world began.

As if sensing they needed time and space, and no way to back out, the rain suddenly beat harder on the canvas roof of the tent. With that increase in intensity, Blade lifted Cassidy's sweater away and brought his mouth down upon her rosy peaks.

Cassidy's head fell back as Blade's tongue laved each breast in turn. Already she was riding on some mystical crest, and her hands fisted in Blade's chestnut hair. She could see the intensity, see the drive etched into the expressions on his face as he returned his lips to hers.

With one hand the zipper to her slacks slid down and away, and within moments the last of the lace barriers disappeared.

"I have to taste you, honey," he whispered, and Cassidy knew she couldn't deny him anything, especially that wish. "My darling Cassidy, do you know how long I've wanted to taste you?"

And with that he slid his head down between her legs until he captured her heat with one spine-tingling and rapturous kiss.

She cried out with the rapture of it all as he lifted her legs, spreading them wider to kiss the inside of her thighs, as well.

Her hands continued to stroke through his hair, the soft strands sliding silkily over her fingers.

"Come apart for me, darling," he told her, and with that command Cassidy discovered that his fingers had replaced his sensual mouth. Barely a second later she was lost to the intense sensation he called from deep within her.

Wherever it was he was taking her didn't matter. She was somewhere she'd never been, somewhere she'd only go with him, somewhere she'd never be able to find again without him.

Cassidy let herself go, feeling the waves of new-found freedom, of life itself crash over her. His mouth found hers and she tasted that life, that freedom, and Cassidy shuddered with the joy of it all as he sent her spiraling over the edge.

She reached for him afterward, craving more, needing more, needing his release, but he was already pulling away and covering her with the sleeping bag.

"Blade," she said, calling him back, wanting him again, for in reality she could never have enough of this special man.

"I have nothing to protect you with, honey," he told her, and even though she reached for him, for there were other gifts she could bestow and wanted to bestow, he was already slipping away and out of her wanton grasp. "The rain's lessened. I need to check on the camp."

Somewhere a latrine door slammed, and Cassidy heard the laughter of some Boy Scouts returning to their tent. "I've got to go," Blade whispered. He leaned over her and kissed her quickly, a hard, passionate kiss that sent her spiraling again. "Good night, love."

And with that he was gone, the tent flap settling softly into place.

Cassidy stared at the still tent flap. Suddenly, without his presence, the inside of the twelve-by-ten tent seemed almost spooky. She'd never slept in a sleeping bag, much less outdoors, and she fumbled back into her clothes and pulled the down bag up to her chin with only her thoughts to comfort her.

She reached up and touched her swollen lips. He'd kissed her, touched her. She smiled to herself. The truth was out.

He wanted her. She wanted him. Determination stole over her as she snuggled into the down sleeping bag. She left the light on, and within moments fell asleep, her resolve to have him strengthened.

As HE STRODE toward his truck, Blade's resolve to do the right thing faltered. How he wanted nothing more than to go back to the tent and make love to Cassidy Clayton until the sun came up.

But that would be a mistake.

Not only would it set a bad example for the high school boys, because Blade wanted them to learn how to respect women and treat them right, but he'd also already done way too much with her. Cassidy was engaged. Blade comforted himself with the fact that he knew she was just settling for Dan and that she didn't love him. Still, he mentally berated himself, he'd just poached another man's woman, something he swore he would never do.

Heaven help him, but he wanted her.

Even as a randy teenager he hadn't wanted this much. Even his first time, all those years ago with that older woman who had picked him up at a rodeo, hadn't meant anything to him.

But just kissing Cassidy meant something. Making love to her would be special. It would mean more than he could ever know.

Hell, he was man enough to admit that whatever feelings he had for this woman scared him. He wasn't one of those weak-kneed men who couldn't say when they were beaten or that they cared.

He cared for Cassidy—unfortunately he cared way too much.

He wanted her way too much.

If only circumstances were different! If only he weren't a boy from the wrong side of town whose idea of fun on a Friday night meant camping with the Scouts.

Cassidy could never be in his world. She didn't understand it. Heck, a glance out the windows of his truck revealed that she hadn't even turned off the lantern. The battery would be dead long before morning.

He took off his boots and dropped them onto the floormat. It still amazed him that even at six foot six, he could actually curl up comfortably in the full-size back seat of his pickup truck.

Not something he liked to do often, but something he'd had to do occasionally out of necessity. This wasn't the first time he'd been trapped in one of Houston's unpredictable tropical storms. He'd spent twenty-four hours in the truck during tropical storm Alison.

He closed his eyes, but the much-needed sleep he so desperately wanted didn't come. Instead his brain processed information, planning out his Saturday. Tomorrow he'd get her home on time, then later that night he'd attend the stupid chamber of commerce dinner. On Sunday he'd get her predications fixed.

He frowned. Somehow he felt he was missing something important in the schedule, but as he couldn't put his finger on it, he decided that whatever it was, it didn't matter.

What mattered was that after this weekend he'd be free of Cassidy. He needed to be free. He had to get away before he lost his heart. She wasn't his to have, and it would drive him crazy not being able to touch her, to taste her again, to love her.

Heck, she'd accomplished a feat no other woman had. She'd pulled his chain, whipped him into shape with only a smile and some flying peanuts.

Heaven help him.
The mighty had fallen.
It had finally happened.
Blade Frederick had fallen in love.

Chapter Ten

The pounding noise resounding in her bedroom wasn't in her head. Good grief. Whatever the infernal noise was, why wouldn't it stop?

Cassidy blinked herself awake and lifted her head off the soft pillows that graced her bed. The clock next to her bed read eleven-fifteen.

The annoying noise didn't cease; if anything it got louder. Cassidy slowly got out of bed. Surely it wasn't Blade making that noise. He hadn't been out and about when she'd woken up and made her escape from the camp. Besides, he had a key.

As she pulled on her robe she mulled over that morning. She'd escaped without seeing him, and when she'd left, the clock in her car had read 6:50, and a quick glance at the low-water bridge had revealed just a bit of water flowed over it. The rest of the rushing water went under. The bridge was safe and passable.

Her Grand Prix had forded the trickle just fine, and she'd hightailed it home over the almost-deserted roads.

Cassidy drew her robe tightly around her and went to her front door.

The leaded glass didn't let her see who it was, but already Cassidy had guessed.

She opened the door, readying herself for the encounter. "Hello, Lillian."

"Finally!" Lillian admonished as she entered the room with a dramatic whoosh. She turned around immediately and started in on Cassidy. "I've been ringing the bell for hours. Didn't you hear me? Well, of course not or you would have opened it."

Lillian eyed Cassidy's bathrobe suspiciously. "Are you still in bed?"

"I just got up, yes," Cassidy said. "Is there something wrong with that? It is Saturday, my day off. I do not have to get up on my day off."

"My you're snippy lately," Lillian chided. "Must be the stress of selling this albatross. Now don't look at me like that. I only have your best interests at heart, and really, Cassidy, you haven't been yourself."

"I'm fine," Cassidy said, but Lillian ignored that statement.

"Remember that I told you I have the name of someone who can help you. You need to make an appointment for next week. You're too pretty to let yourself get run-down and you know that too many of the major life stressors in one year can bring on premature aging. I mean, moving is one, so is divorce in your family, as is a marriage and—"

"Good advice and I'll remember it," Cassidy said,

instantly throwing Lillian's words into a mental trash can. "So what brings you by, Lillian? I thought we weren't meeting until noon."

"This just couldn't wait," Lillian said. She waved her hands dramatically. "Cassidy, love, tell me it's not true. Tell me that you did not just spend last night in a Boy Scout camp. I mean, you are an image consultant! Do you know how it looks? You have a reputation to think about. The Morris family has a reputation to think about."

"What are you talking about?" And how have you heard about it already? Cassidy didn't add.

"Johnson Bacon, I mean, who would name their child Johnson? With the millions they have in oil I guess they can do what they want."

"And?" Cassidy prompted.

Lillian sighed, a sure sign of her disapproval. "Yes. Anyway, he's a volunteer with the Scout troop, and he called his wife last night to make sure that she was all right in the terrible storm and all. He also told her that this wonderful girl named Cassidy had just done a fantastic presentation to the Boy Scout troop. He also told his wife that she would have to spend the night because of the storm."

Lillian paused, and when Cassidy didn't oblige her by talking, the woman drew a breath and continued. "Well, of course Sonya just had to call me this morning and tell me everything. I mean, Cassidy, how could you? She told me you spent the night in a tent."

Cassidy shrugged, more to stretch out her shoulders

than for effect. "I did. Spend the night in a tent." Cassidy added that last part so Lillian would have no confusion as to what occurred.

"Cassidy," Lillian began.

Cassidy cut her off. "So what? If you think about it, Johnson Bacon spent the night in a tent. I mean, he's got oil millions. If it's good enough for him..." She let her voice trail off.

Lillian was not to be out-argued. "Cassidy, dear, you're a female. You are not a Boy Scout. You should not be sleeping in a tent under any circumstances. It's just not proper. If only you hadn't been the only female present on the trip."

Oh, please. Lillian wouldn't ever win support with the female voting demographic. "Well, pray tell, what was I to do, Lillian? Drive my Grand Prix over the low-water bridge and let the water sweep me and my car away?"

"That's not funny. Two people died in last night's storm. Tropical storm Larry is its name. Anyway, of course I don't want you to have done anything like driving through a creek, Cassidy. You need to be alive to marry my son. But I told you to buy an SUV."

"So you were right about that one thing," Cassidy said with a roll of her eyes. "Look, Lillian, just leave it. Dan knew where I was and exactly what I was doing. He thought it was a great idea, especially since I was filling in for Mel Trogg. You know, the owner of the chain of banks?"

"He's not in our political party," Lillian said with

a sniff of dismissal. "But I guess he does donate to Dan's museum. Speaking of the museum, you really should be more supportive of Dan. You should have been at the opening last night, not shacking up in a tent with a bunch of Boy Scouts."

"I was not shacking up, and I had a tent by myself." Cassidy threw her hands into the air. "Oh, why am I bothering with this conversation? Is Dan up? I need to talk to him."

Lillian's eyes widened at Cassidy's abrupt tone. "He's not home," she said.

"What do you mean? He's not home?"

Lillian shrugged. "He probably spent the night in his office. You know how he keeps a cot and a change of clothes there."

No, Cassidy hadn't known that. "Really?"

Lillian stared at Cassidy as if she'd grown two heads. "Really. I tell you, Cassidy, you shouldn't be working so much. This is a clear example of how you're failing your fiancé. In the future you need to support Dan more and know what is going on with him. His career is extremely important, much more than yours I might add. Anyway, he started staying at the office a few months ago, especially when he's had to work late."

Cassidy bit her tongue to keep the emerging cryptic remark from becoming voiced. "Thanks for the advice," she said instead.

"No problem," Lillian said. "I'm your second mother, dear, and you know the saying is true. Mothers do know best. And I've had such a successful marriage myself that I want you to be happy in yours.''

Cassidy simply nodded. It was easier that way, especially when Lillian was on a roll. "When you see Dan tell him I need to talk to him. It's important. Now, if you could excuse me, I need to clean up before I meet you both for lunch.''

Lillian peered over her glasses. "Oh, yes. Lunch. Don't worry about it today, dear. I have an appointment to have my mother-of-the-groom dress fitted. Besides, with time being so short and all, it was easier if I just made the decisions regarding the arrangements myself. Dan agreed with me, so I took care of everything already. You don't have to worry about a thing.''

"You're so efficient," Cassidy replied.

"I know," Lillian gushed. "I've got to go. Don't forget that you've got the chamber of commerce dinner tonight. And first thing Monday I want you to look for an SUV.''

"Sure thing." Cassidy gave a curt nod, and with that, Lillian was out the door.

Cassidy slumped into a chair the moment her worst nightmare had cleared the driveway and was definitely on her way to her own home.

Cassidy closed her eyes for a brief moment. She'd have to deal with Lillian and finding an SUV later. Those were actually the least of her problems. Right now she needed to talk to Dan and get the wedding plans, if there was to ever even be a wedding, on permanent hold.

Cassidy knew Dan wouldn't mind stopping the preparations, but he wasn't the problem. With Lillian on full throttle, Cassidy knew she was about to have a war on her hands.

"DAN, WE REALLY NEED to talk," Cassidy said when she finally caught up with him that evening at cocktail hour before the chamber of commerce dinner.

It had been two that afternoon before he'd called her from the museum. Then the conversation had been less than a minute in duration. It had only been long enough for him to tell her that he was so swamped he'd just meet her at the dinner. "I need to be sure I have all my facts straight," he'd also told her. "The chamber is about to do a huge arts campaign to encourage tourism. I want to be sure our museum gets a good plug."

Always the museum. Sara had been right about that, too. The museum, not his fiancée or the upcoming wedding, was definitely Dan's priority.

Dan leaned over and gave her a quick kiss on the cheek. "We'll talk after dinner, love. Mr. Fischer! How good to see you!"

And with that he'd moved off.

Later Cassidy took a seat at Dan's right and smiled as Dan held conversation after conversation with the people seated at their table of ten.

She had to admit there was a silver lining. Driving herself to the event meant that she could always go home whenever she wanted. It wasn't as if Dan would miss her. There were over a thousand people in the room, which meant that he had over a thousand potential donors to socialize and schmooze with.

Because, of course, the museum needed funding.

For a moment Cassidy had a vision of her future if she married Dan. Endless dinners, endless social engagements and parties, endless boredom, all just so the museum could be funded and Dan could grow his career at the expense of hers.

"Excuse me," Cassidy said with a bright smile. She needed a respite. While she couldn't leave yet without embarrassing Dan, a trip to the ladies' room, with a stop by the bar, sounded right up her alley.

The men stood as she left the table.

Cassidy shook her head, mentally clearing the dusty cobwebs that had developed during the dull dinner. She strode purposely toward the hotel foyer, not really paying attention to the people she passed. Many of them were her clients, but that didn't mean they should acknowledge her, their image consultant, in public. A catch-22, but that was the way life was.

Concentrating on just moving as quickly as possible, she didn't see the elderly woman who suddenly stepped into her path. Cassidy's heel wobbled as she moved out of the way.

A strong hand reached out from somewhere to steady her. "Hey, careful."

She would know that voice and the touch now spreading heat throughout her body, anywhere.

She looked up, seeing the blatant shock and surprise

that crossed his face at the same time it crossed hers.
"Blade?"

He masked his features quickly. "Cassidy," he acknowledged with a slight, guilty chuckle. "Fancy seeing you here."

"Exactly," Cassidy said. She stepped back away
from him, and he dropped his hand from her arm.

What was Blade doing here? Not caring if her shock
was evident, Cassidy simply stared. Not only was he
here, at an expensive dinner, but never before had she
seen him like this.

Gone were the carpenter whites and the flannels,
and in their place was a tuxedo that fit as if it had
been custom-made. Blade stood every inch his six-six
frame, and nothing about him was unimpressive. More
like just the opposite. Cassidy swallowed.

"Blade?" A different voice, this time female. The
woman laid a light touch on Blade's right forearm and
looked at Cassidy curiously. Blade slowly turned.

"Nicole," he acknowledged.

"Don't forget Mr. Trent." she said, as if gently
prodding.

"Uh, yes," he replied, and the woman named Nicole turned her gaze further on Cassidy. Cassidy felt
herself sized up and dismissed.

Hackles rose on Cassidy's spine, and she realized
she was jealous. After what had happened in the tent,
didn't she have a right to be?

"Blade," Nicole said again.

Cassidy found her backbone. No, she didn't have a

right to be jealous. After all, why shouldn't Blade Frederick have a date? When had he or she ever become an item? While they wanted each other, she had to admit that's all it was—just some powerful chemistry.

She *did* have the right to be angry. Here he was giving her the moralistic lecture when he was two-timing someone. It was as bad as Jeff the jerk saying, "I just want to be friends," after he'd already made love to her and told her how much he cared.

"It was nice seeing you," Cassidy managed, the image-consultant control she'd worked years to maintain not failing her. With that, she hightailed it toward the ladies' room.

Blade turned back to Nicole the moment Cassidy had excused herself, and just then Jake caught up to them. "Hey, who was that?" Jake asked. "I missed her."

Blade's eyes narrowed into dangerous slits. "Jake, forget it."

Jake threw up his hands as if defending himself. "Hey, sorry. What's gotten into you? Care to tell me who she is? All I saw was some blond hair. You know I like blondes, but if you saw her first then that's fine."

"You'll be glad that you didn't get a look at her," Blade said with a slow exhale. "If you did I might have to kill you. That was Cassidy Clayton and for you she is hands off."

Jake's face fell. "You're kidding."

Blade's greenish-blue eyes glittered with agitation. "Do I look like I am? Hands off."

"No," Jake admitted. He broke out suddenly into a wide grin. "I'll be. You could have a thing for this one. Better yet, I'd say you do have a thing for her, if the tension in your neck is anything to go by. Isn't it a shame I know you so well?"

"Luckily for you we're not somewhere private," Blade threatened. He didn't need Jake's teasing now. Not when his whole cover—that of being just a poor carpenter—was about to blow up in his face.

"Gentlemen," Nicole, their vice president and public relations wizard interjected, "we have Mr. Trent to speak with. Whomever the lovely lady is, business must come first right now."

"It is business," Blade mumbled. It was business of the heart. He followed Nicole, anyhow. After all, what was he to do? His cover was as good as blown. Cassidy was an image consultant. He knew she could spot custom-tailoring. Worse, how could he be at a chamber dinner that cost $500 a plate?

There would be no lying his way out of this one. He'd have to tell her the truth.

Out of the corner of his eye, he saw her reenter the ballroom. He let his gaze follow her, watching and appreciating the woman in the silvery slip dress that he'd fallen for.

Fallen in love with but couldn't have. He saw her approach Dan. He frowned. Even from his distance he saw that all Dan did was turn and give Cassidy a chaste kiss on the cheek.

If Cassidy was Blade's fiancée he'd be kissing her on the lips with a passion that promised things to come. Yes, Dan Morris definitely had problems.

It was time to let him know it.

"Blade," he heard Nicole's voice, but he ignored it. She and Jake could deal with Jim Trent and the damn revenue office. J & B wouldn't go under if they didn't get that project.

No, Jake could work on landing that job. Right now Blade had his own job to do. He needed to somehow make everything right.

CASSIDY HAD BEEN prepared for chaste kisses upon her arrival back to the table. What she wasn't prepared for was Dan's announcement that he had an emergency and needed to leave the chamber dinner, and that he was leaving right at that very moment.

"It's lucky we took two cars," he said. "You can stay and do some networking if you want. I'll catch up with you tomorrow, okay, love?"

"Sure," Cassidy said. After he'd given her another chaste kiss, she simply stared as he left the room.

What was it with the men in her life? Dan had all but become a stranger she couldn't talk to and couldn't seem to catch. And as for Blade, well, could she really even call him a man in her life?

He was just her contractor. They'd shared kisses and some heavy petting. She was a grown-up. Grown-ups knew that passion was just chemistry and it didn't mean death-do-us-part love. It was not a big deal. Just a temporary aberration. Just a little lust.

Right?

"Cassidy?"

At the sound of his voice, she jumped. Off balance once again, she tottered unsteadily on her high heels, and he reached out a hand to steady her. Immediately fire burned through her veins, all caused by just his light touch on the bare skin of her shoulder.

"Blade," she said, mentally cursing herself that her voice sounded so breathy, so wanton.

"We need to talk," he said simply.

"Talk?" Cassidy parroted.

"Talk," he repeated, his tone serious. "Can I get you away from Dan for a few minutes?"

Cassidy gave an unladylike roll of her eyes, for after all, this was Blade. She could relax around him. "Dan's gone. You can have me all you want." Manicured fingertips flew to her now-open mouth. "I didn't mean—"

Blade grinned. "I know what you meant, although I really like your proposition. How about we get out of here, then?"

"You paid a lot of money for this dinner," Cassidy said. She grimaced. How snobby that made her sound. She recovered quickly. "Besides, what about your date? Won't she mind if you take off with me?"

Blade's grin turned cheeky. "Nicole's not my girlfriend. She's vice president of J & B. I'm sure she and Jake can take care of themselves just fine.''

''Oh,'' Cassidy said as she comprehended it all. Nicole hadn't been his date. Blade wasn't a two-timing cheat. He'd come to the dinner with his business partners. That thought warmed her to no end.

''I know a great little late-night restaurant that has the best coffee and desserts,'' Blade said as he cupped Cassidy's elbow. ''How about we go there? The ice cream they served tonight certainly wasn't edible.''

''No, it wasn't,'' Cassidy replied. Blade's touch on her arm was sending tremors through her, and it took a moment for her to gather her wits and walk straight.

''I assume your car is here? We can pick it up later,'' Blade said as he handed the valet a claim check. Within moments the valet brought around a full-size BMW convertible.

Cassidy turned toward him, her eyes wide with confusion. ''Yours?''

''The company owns the red truck,'' Blade told her. ''This is my indulgence.''

''I see,'' she said, although deep down she didn't see anything. None of the puzzle pieces that she'd assigned to Blade fit anymore. Somehow he'd switched the puzzle, or maybe she'd had the wrong picture with the right box for the longest time.

She contemplated that as they rode in silence the brief journey to ZuZu's, an after-hours restaurant.

Within moments the waiter had seated them at a

corner table in one of ZuZu's many small, dimly lit rooms.

Blade ordered a strong black espresso while Cassidy simply settled for a hazelnut blend. Although she wasn't exactly hungry, the brown-sugar nut cake looked to die for and she had to have a piece. Blade chose some apple and cinnamon concoction that Cassidy couldn't pronounce if she tried.

But enjoying what was on the dessert menu wasn't why they were here.

"So, what do we need to talk about?" Cassidy said.

BLADE DIDN'T REALLY want to talk, but he knew now that nothing but honesty would do. He had to come clean with Cassidy about who he was and what he'd become.

He wasn't looking forward to this, but he was a man now. He'd given up running the day he and Jake had started J & B Construction.

"I told you about my childhood last night, right?" he asked.

"Yes," Cassidy said. "You told me about your mother and your father, their terrible marriage that still exists somehow, and about your brothers that you never see anymore."

Blade sipped his espresso. "Then I guess the next thing I need to tell you about is Jake."

"Jake? Your partner?"

Blade nodded. "Jake and I have been friends for thirty years. Since I was six, to be exact. We lived in the same neighborhood and he accidentally shot me with a BB gun. Once we got done fighting and pulled ourselves up off the ground, we ended up becoming friends for life. Both of us had this dream to make something of ourselves, and we started J & B Construction when I was eighteen. Well, to be specific, a month shy of my nineteenth birthday.''

He paused and Cassidy waited. This was another side to Blade, and she found herself admiring him. He'd come through so much in his life. ''I'd been on the rodeo circuit. You could say I'd run away, trying to escape the drudgery of my home life. Not that I was good enough to get into any type of standings. After all, I'd been raised in the city. But I waited tables and saw most of the Southwest. Then I got hurt and came home. And when I got here I had absolutely nothing to do, no work waiting for me except with my hands. I didn't want to wait tables all my life, and I didn't have a college degree.

''So Jake and I got to work. J & B started as an odd-job service and a dream that we sketched out on a cocktail napkin. We broke our backs in the figurative sense, and we somehow began to get job after job. Our growth was phenomenal. We could afford to hire college graduates, engineers and architects, and with our profit-sharing plan for our employees, the company grew even more and was named one of the best places in America to work.''

The scale of what he'd told her hadn't quite sunk

in. "So you aren't a three-person operation," Cassidy said aloud.

He gazed at her and she blushed. "I'm sorry, but I thought that, when I first met you," she said. "I guess if we're being honest I'd have to say I thought that you were a one-man operation."

He gave a short laugh. He'd suspected that and knew her confession had been embarrassing. "No," he said simply. "We're not a three-person operation. More like three thousand."

"Oh my."

He knew he'd floored her. That number she hadn't been contemplating. "Based on revenue, J & B is the tenth largest construction firm in Houston and thirty-third in the United States."

Cassidy simply stared at him as if he'd grown wings, and Blade shifted uncomfortably.

There. The truth, about who he was, was finally out. He'd told her everything. Well, not quite. He'd not told her about Jake and his outrageous scheme to get to Ed Morris through Lillian. Although he didn't want to, he'd tell her that next. She'd probably hate his guts, but he had to risk it. He couldn't live with the deception or the lies any longer.

The silence at their table seemed to stretch. "So you're rich," Cassidy finally said. She tilted her head and stared at him as if seeing him for the first time.

Blade took a sip of his espresso. "Yes," he admitted. "Very."

"Oh my God."

Busy setting his cup down, it took Blade a moment to realize that Cassidy wasn't talking about him or his newfound wealth.

Instead she was staring off into the darkness at another table, one neither of them had paid any attention to upon their arrival into the candlelit room.

Dan Morris sat at the table with a very attractive brunette. And it wasn't ZuZu's dessert that Dan's tongue was busy tasting, but rather the creamy skin of the brunette's neck.

CASSIDY GASPED AGAIN as the irony struck her like a low blow. Everything made sense now. The emergency phone calls. Dan's aloofness. His lack of time for her. His staying at the museum.

From the deep kiss he was now sharing with the woman, the ugly truth of the matter was crystal clear. Dan Morris was seeing someone else, and from the looks of it, he probably had been seeing her for quite a while.

Cassidy rose to her feet, grateful that somehow Blade was already standing, supporting her. His hand rested lightly on her arm, the touch providing emotional and physical comfort.

''Are you okay?'' he whispered.

Would she ever be okay again? Of course she would. She'd dealt with two-timing cheats before. Just like after Jeff the jerk, she'd rise from the ashes like a newborn phoenix. She'd survive. She always did, no matter how much damage her heart and ego suffered.

"I'm fine," she said, although deep down she knew she was lying.

Right now she was angry. Bitter. This was Dan. Dan Morris, her fiancé. Two months ago when she'd accepted his ring they'd promised each other that they'd always be honest with each other. He'd told her that he would never deliberately hurt her. They'd promised each other that before that would ever happen, they would set the other free.

She'd been planning on doing just that earlier in the day, but he'd been "out" all afternoon. Now, as if she'd been a fly on the wall, she knew exactly where he'd been, and who with—the brunette who was currently looking at Dan with love written in her eyes. As he played with the brunette's fingertips, Dan's eyes revealed he felt the same way about her.

He certainly had never looked at Cassidy like that. How could she not have known? All the signs had been there, yet she'd sworn to Sara that Dan wasn't a cheat. Comfortable in the relationship, she'd turned a blind eye to the truth—she and Dan had been settling for each other.

Her ankles wobbled, but Blade's strength flowed from the fingers he had on her arm. Cassidy found her stride as she headed the short distance toward the other table. She stood by it for a good second before Dan realized anyone was there. He broke off the kiss and looked up.

His surprise revealed he'd been expecting the waitress, not a glowering fiancée.

"Dan," Cassidy said simply. She reached for her diamond engagement ring and slid it off her finger. "I think you need this back."

"Cassidy." The expressions crossing Dan's face ranged from guilt to relief. "Cass, this isn't what it looks like."

"Save it," Cassidy replied. She knew exactly what she'd seen, and she didn't want to hear any excuses. For a moment she stared at the other woman. She looked so familiar, and it took Cassidy a moment to place her. "You work at the museum, don't you? In the public relations department."

The other woman had the courtesy to look away and stare at the wall.

Dan struggled to his feet, but Blade stepped forward. "Dan," he said.

Recognizing Blade's dominating presence wouldn't allow the movement, Dan sat back down.

"It's okay, Dan," Cassidy said gently. She started to touch his shoulder but then thought the better of it. Her hand dropped to her side. "We weren't right for each other, anyway. You just didn't need to tell me like this."

"My mother," he began, a stricken look crossing his face.

"Your mother can cancel the wedding plans," Cassidy said. "It'll give her something to do." She took a step back, away from the table. "I hope you two are very happy."

With that she turned to Blade.

"Take me home," she said simply.

And it wasn't until she was safe inside the leather interior of his BMW that she let herself cry.

Chapter Eleven

Snakes like Dan Morris deserved to be filled with buckshot. It had taken all of Blade's mettle, back at the restaurant, not to plow his fist through Dan's face. Dan Morris's actions had hurt Cassidy, and that was absolutely unacceptable.

"I planned on calling off the wedding today," she told Blade over sobs as he drove her back to her house. "I knew something was wrong. I mean, my feelings weren't there, either. Both you and Sara have been right. I would have been settling. But couldn't he have told me his feelings had changed long ago? Did he have to cheat on me?"

"He should have told you," Blade agreed, although he knew he was biased. He'd have been happy to dance on Dan Morris's grave if it meant Cassidy was no longer going to marry the man. "Be grateful you found out now and not after the wedding."

"I am," Cassidy said into the facial tissue Blade had stopped at a store to buy for her. "Sara kept telling me, insinuating that Dan was cheating, only marrying me because of his mother. I didn't want to believe her. It hurts the ego, you know? Was I not good enough?''

Then she'd cried some more, and for lack of knowing what else to say, Blade had simply put his hand out and covered hers for the rest of the wordless journey back to her house.

Blade pulled into her driveway. As he took the keys out of the ignition he wanted to pull her into his arms and tell her that, yes, she was good enough. Too good for someone like Dan Morris. Too good even for someone like himself. He would never deserve her, although he wanted to try. Now wasn't the time to think of his needs or his love for her. He needed to just be there for her.

So instead of holding her, he said, ''Some things aren't meant to be, Cassidy. I know you don't see it right now, but believe me, you'll feel better in the morning. Come on. Let's get you inside. I'll make some coffee. I bet you could use a cup of decaf.''

''I could use a stiff drink,'' she told him.

''Decaf,'' he repeated, knowing her statement had been more of an expression than a request for alcohol.

''Okay,'' she mumbled. She leaned on him, and a feeling of protectiveness flowed through him. He hated seeing her hurt, especially by someone as slimy as Dan Morris. Blade put his arm around Cassidy as they walked toward the door.

''Dan was only marrying me because his mother wanted it that way,'' Cassidy said as they entered the house through the kitchen door. "He asked me at the Morrises' New Year's Eve party, did I tell you that? By then he must have been seeing that woman already, but he still asked me to marry him. Lillian even picked out my engagement ring and had it ready."

"Lillian Morris needs to learn to mind her own business," Blade said, his tone unusually harsh even to his own ears. "She's not everything in this town."

"I guess she thought she was helping." Cassidy sniffed back another fresh round of tears. "Dan and I have been friends forever, and after all, I'm not getting any younger."

"She saw an opportunity and she took it," Blade said grimly. "You are not too old, and you will not end up alone. You are a beautiful woman, Cassidy. Absolutely, positively beautiful."

She turned to gaze up at him, her baby blues ever hopeful, ever needing his reassurance. How he wanted to protect her. "Really?"

He knew her ego had just been shattered. She'd just received the worst rejection anyone could ever have—to learn that they weren't enough and that the other person had found the grass greener elsewhere.

How to answer her question?

Her insecurity, her disbelief made him want to protect her, to convince her, to love her.

At the same time, though, he couldn't let himself do any of those things. Cassidy needed time to be free, to find herself, to grow into the woman who had been hidden under Dan Morris's shadow.

As much as he loved her, Blade knew he could not be a complication in her life. As of Tuesday, when all the predications would have passed reinspection, he'd be out of her life forever.

He couldn't risk any more of his own heart. He'd already lost it to her, and she didn't know it. He loved her, yet he had to let her go. He had to set her free, let her become the woman she was meant to be.

He'd accomplished his goal—proven to her she would have been settling if she'd married Dan. Unfortunately, the unplanned side effect was that he'd lost his heart in the process. How he'd hurt long after she was gone. Penance for Clara perhaps. Penance for his wild youth.

It didn't matter.

Those baby blues of hers simply held his, and his resolve faltered. He was lost, torn between his desire to do what was right for Cassidy and what was best for him.

Too bad they weren't the same thing.

He took her hands in his, immediately feeling the fire that always flowed between them. He let his gaze rove over her, taking in her blond hair, her high cheekbones, her perfect nose. He saw her creamy skin, the silvery slip dress, her perfect legs whose feet wore thin strap high heels.

It was all there in her posture, the expression on her face. She trusted him; every inch of her radiated nothing but hopeful expectation. It was his undoing.

"You're a beautiful woman, Cassidy," he said, telling her nothing but the honest truth. He sighed, and took the plunge of admitting his feelings. "I've wanted you from the moment I set eyes on you."

"Make love to me, Blade."

Her words echoed in the kitchen and they called him. How he would love nothing more. For the first time in his life Blade understood the childhood cartoons that showed a devil and an angel sitting on a character's shoulder, helping the character make a decision. "Cassidy, we, I—"

"Make love to me," she repeated. She stood before him, a vision in her silvery slip dress. His hands still held hers and upon her second request his blood had begun to boil with the passion that only she stirred in him.

"You're grieving," he told her, struggling to do the right thing. Making love to her would complicate her feelings. She was already in turmoil because of Dan. "You need a good night's sleep. You'll feel better, see things more clearly in the morning."

"Make love to me," she repeated, taking her fingers out of his gentle grip and running them over his tuxedo-covered forearms.

He groaned aloud as his body fully responded to her touch, the fire burning even through multiple layers of clothing.

"I wasn't grieving last night," she said simply, her fingers reaching up to trace his jawbone. Then her gentle touch feathered over his eyebrows. He closed his eyes, letting her magic wash over them. It was as if someone had nailed his feet to the floor. He couldn't have moved if he had wanted to. Not with her touching him the way she was.

In the midst of sensations, sensations he'd felt with no other woman but Cassidy, he heard her speak again. "I want you, too, Blade. I'm free now. No longer engaged. I'm free to ask. Make love to me."

Her words shattered his last restraint.

She was a siren. She'd asked not three but four times, and that was more than he could handle. Each time her voice became stronger, and each time his resolve to leave her alone slipped.

"Cassidy." He tried one more time, but his voice had simply whispered her name, as if knowing that his heart had already overruled his protesting mind.

With a groan of despair and desire, he caved. His head came down and he found her lips.

Heaven waited.

YES! A shiver of pure joy slid through Cassidy's body as Blade's mouth descended upon hers. Finally.

Finally there would be nothing to stop them, nothing to get in their way.

No baggage. No engagements. Nothing.

She threaded her hands into his silky chestnut-colored hair, deepening the kiss. Her tongue traced the outside of his lips before darting inside to claim the mouth that had claimed hers.

His fingertips burned a trail of passion as they flared over her bare shoulders. She clung to him, drank her fill of his mouth before he sent his own lips moving down her throat to kiss the hollow at the base.

Quivers of desire shimmied through her, and Cassidy arched her head, sending his head lower, toward the bottom of the V-neck of the dress. She needed this man. Now. Quickly. They could be slow and tender another time. If she had her way, and she knew she would, this time would be the first of many.

His fingers slid under the straps of her dress, his touch becoming magical.

"You're not wearing a bra," he said, his tone husky and teasing.

She smiled with pleasure as his forefinger traced a line just above her nipples. "No."

He groaned and bent his head farther to capture what waited beneath the dress.

"You are driving me crazy," he admitted as his mouth returned to capture hers again.

"Good," Cassidy said, for tonight she was all woman—a woman that knew what she wanted. "You've been driving me crazy, too."

She lifted her arms, and the dress slid away revealing only a tiny slivery G-string for underwear.

He groaned again, his kisses now hard and demanding. Cassidy met them with an equal fervor. Within seconds he scooped her up and carried her up the back stairs toward her bedroom.

He gently set her down on her bed. Now terribly impatient Cassidy kicked off her shoes, tossed aside the annoying decorative pillows and reached for him.

Her turn. Boldness overtook her and her fingers went to work on removing his jacket, bow tie and shirt. She kissed him all the while, feeling nothing but the hard steel of his flesh. She touched scars; she touched perfection. There was no fat on this man. He was nothing but beautiful. Muscles rippled on the broad chest and Cassidy tasted, licked and laved, drinking her fill of the body that had tempted and tormented her for the past week.

She worked her way lower, toward the straining erection she could already see waiting, waiting just for her.

Her hand slid across the fabric concealing his straining bulge, her touch light and feathery. Blade groaned and shifted under her ministrations.

"Tease," he whispered.

"You ain't seen nothing yet," Cassidy said in slang, her tone made sultry by being a woman in charge of her destiny. As he made to kiss her lips again, she shook her head, escaped from him and worked her way lower, caressing him all the while.

Suddenly she swallowed a secret, womanly smile. She knew the size of his hands, and there were some things a woman needed to keep just between her and her lover. Sara, who had been right about Dan's infidelity, would never know how right she had been about Blade, especially regarding that thumb-to-pinkie comment.

"Off," she commanded, and he helped send his tuxedo pants flying into a far corner. Now his body was nothing but naked glory like hers, and she captured in her mouth that magnificent part of him that had tormented her and given her sleepless nights for so long.

His fingers clutched her hair, massaged her back, and she delighted in what she could do to him, what gift she could bestow.

His skin tasted divine, richer and better than the finest sweets, and Cassidy knew she could linger and taste him forever.

He strained against her and suddenly he pulled her up and flipped her onto her back. His lips crashed down upon hers, and she tasted again his mouth—the delicious combination of espresso and something that was simply him. His fingers were everywhere and suddenly so was his mouth, and Cassidy found herself no longer the giver but the taker as he drove her over the edge and into the great beyond that only lovers know.

A few minutes later her fingers felt the determined shift in his steely arms, and suddenly she knew what he planned as he kissed the side of her neck again. He would pleasure her and then retreat. ''No,'' she said. ''Not if...''

''I'm clean,'' he confirmed.

She smiled. ''You better be because there's no way I'm letting you escape tonight.''

''I don't have anything with me.''

''I'm on the pill,'' she told him. No way would she let him stop making love to her. Not when she'd finally found passion, found the type that didn't burn out but instead intensified as time went on.

She'd found her soul mate, and heaven help him he wasn't getting away.

She reached her hands up, bringing his lips back to hers. She kissed him, her hands then free to roam, to caress, to cause him to groan again with the powerful passion he had for her. She could see how much he needed her, and she needed him as much if not more.

And suddenly the need was assuaged as he drove into her. His being filled her, immediately causing her to detonate. She had never been so complete, so whole. She'd think about it later, contemplate the difference between his lovemaking and previous others', but for right now all she could do was let the powerful current she rode sweep her along with it.

His strong stroke completed her, took her to heights never imagined and carried her to a place where only lovers of the heart go.

She clutched his arms as he raised her legs up, deepening the thrust, and she cried out as he took her over the edge and sent her spiraling into pleasure's delightful abyss.

"I'm with you, darling," he told her, and he was. She could feel him—the pulsating, the driving intensity—and she shattered again and again until finally he simply held her, both of them spent.

Later, as she lay curled up in his arms, the back of his fingertips lightly caressed her face.

"I never slept with Dan," she told him.

His dark-brown eyebrow arched, and she could see

he was pleasantly surprised. He continued to trace her nose as he waited for the rest of the story.

"Lillian always interrupted," she said, her eyelids drooping under the soft romantic stroking of his gentle fingers.

"Maybe she was right about something," he teased. As he planted a kiss on her nose, her eyes flew open. The need for sleep was vanquished under one feathery touch of his lips. Sleep could wait.

She reached for him, desire evident, causing a smile to spread across his face.

I love you, Cassidy thought, and then because that thought was close, on the edge of her tongue wanting to be voiced, she kissed his collarbone instead. She tasted his skin, using every one of her senses to imprint his memory deep into her soul.

What words could she share? All she had was now, this one moment with this incredibly special man.

"Insatiable," he whispered. She nodded and saw that, as he looked at her, those bedroom eyes of his held something. Could it be promise? She didn't know, and rationalized that whatever it was, it was probably only a trick of the moonlight now streaming through the window sheers.

And when he traced her nose lightly before lowering his lips again, she didn't worry about it or care, as once more they were off on another magical journey to where two hearts and souls join together to become one.

THE PERSISTENT RINGING of the doorbell and the subsequent angry pounding on a door woke Cassidy from her dreamless sleep. Not that she'd been asleep long. She turned, seeing the man she loved resting beside her.

They'd made love most of the night.

Cassidy slid out of bed without waking Blade. He needed his rest. She smiled down upon his sleeping form. She'd loved him well. She covered him with the comforter, then slipped into a silken bathrobe.

Time to go deal with Dan.

She went downstairs to the side door and tossed it open.

"I don't believe you," Lillian said as she entered the kitchen. Her high heels clattered over the ceramic tile floor. "You tramp!"

Cassidy took a step back, colliding with the countertop. Ouch. She winced. "Excuse me?"

"I saw shadows through the window last night." Lillian gestured toward the second floor, her face filled with fury. "That's not my son you have up there in your bedroom, is it?"

"Lillian."

Lillian was not to be stopped. "No, don't even bother to deny the truth. You have a strange car in your driveway, and besides, I know everything already, including how you tossed your engagement ring in my son's face at the restaurant last night."

Cassidy drew herself up, away from the cold granite countertop. Today was the start of her new life, one free of Lillian Morris and her infernal meddling. "You listen to me, Lillian. Your son was making out with some woman he works with in the middle of ZuZu's last night. He's been her lover for months. As for who happens to be upstairs, that is my business, not yours. Nothing I do will ever again be any of your business.''

"When you hurt my son, it is my business. What you did to him last night is unforgivable. He's marrying you, Cassidy, not whatever her name is. So he's sowing some wild oats before he settles down. Men do that, well, all except for my Ed. That's why they're men. You need to just deal with the indiscretion and move on. He loves you and wants to marry you, not her.''

"Lillian, Dan has been doing a whole lot more than sowing oats. I saw them with my own eyes!'' Cassidy threw her hands into the air. Why was she bothering to even defend herself? "Did you ever consider that he may love her and not me?''

"He doesn't love her.'' Lillian planted her hands on her hips and gave Cassidy The Look. "Besides, Dan knows how his father and I feel. The woman is totally inappropriate to marry into our family.''

Cassidy's jaw dropped, and she quickly shut her open mouth. Disbelief and anger filled her. Lillian had been aware of the situation from the beginning. "You know her?''

"Of course I do,'' Lillian said with a sniff of distaste. "That mousy thing from the museum. She started running after him sometime mid-November.

Why else would I push him to marry you so fast? She's a gold digger, only after the Morris family name. Despite your father's indiscretions, you at least have good breeding and family name. Although what you did just caused Ed to have a fit. Have you seen what it says in today's society page? Absolutely scandalous. What will Luke do now?''

Frankly right now Cassidy didn't care about what Dan's older brother would do. He could launch his senate campaign some other way. "Look, Lillian," she began.

"No, you look, Cassidy," Lillian said with a shake of her finger. "Your recent family scandal was bad enough to deal with, but now it's personal. The papers say you went home with some man. Someone at ZuZu's reported the whole sordid scene to Katrina Sims. You're the headline in her column today. I am mortified. Do you know how many people have already called me today? I'm the absolute mockery of Houston. And, young lady, just where is your car? Whose BMW is that, anyway?''

"Mine." As Blade strode forward into the kitchen, Cassidy gulped. The man personified sex, and from his appearance it was clear exactly what they'd been doing all night. He wore only his tuxedo pants; his chest was bare. He came over to her easily and dropped a kiss on her nose. "I heard the argument."

"This is great," Lillian said, her mortification obvious. "Absolutely appalling. You're sleeping with the handyman. No better than your father sleeping with the maid.''

''I'd watch what you say if I were you.'' The growling voice was Blade's, and Cassidy looked at him in surprise. Even Lillian seemed taken aback that Blade dared to oppose her, for she took a step backward.

''I will not put up with your insults, especially when they're directed at Cassidy,'' Blade said, his meaning perfectly clear.

Lillian regrouped. ''This is between me and my future daughter-in-law. Please refrain from inserting your very unwelcome opinion.''

Before Blade could respond, Cassidy stepped in. ''I'm not going to be your daughter-in-law.''

Lillian gasped. ''You can't mean that.''

''Yes, I can,'' Cassidy said with a nod. She planted her hands on her hips and jutted her chin forward. ''When I finally get married it will be because I'm marrying for love. Dan and I do not love each other. Sure, maybe as brother and sister, but that's it.''

''That's enough to begin,'' Lillian argued. She drew herself back up and peered through her glasses. ''Many marriages don't even have that.''

''It's not enough,'' Cassidy said with a vigorous shake of her head. She brushed her hair back. ''As for any debts you may have incurred, Lillian, as soon as this house is sold and I've moved into my condo, I'll reimburse you for every penny.''

Lillian gave a short laugh. ''I'd expect no less. Many of the deposits aren't refundable.''

Cassidy shrugged. Blade dropped his arm easily around her for a moment. "I'll start coffee," he said, painfully driving his point home to Lillian that he wasn't leaving anytime soon.

Lillian glanced over at him, her derision now at full throttle. She sneered her next words. "So you really think you can afford to take care of Cassidy?"

"Actually, yes, I think I can," Blade said. He smiled, a Rhett Butler type of smile that melted Cassidy's insides while at the same time frying Lillian's. "You see, I own J & B Construction."

"That means nothing to me," Lillian said disdainfully. She shrugged.

"Tenth largest commercial contractor in Houston and thirty-third in the nation," Blade said. Lillian still looked as if she couldn't care less.

"It means he's really rich," Cassidy added, feeling that a little spite was justified. Lillian would understand money, and if she thought that Cassidy had found a richer man, so be it.

Heck, hadn't Lillian just demanded that she marry the philandering Dan all to save Luke's senate race and the Morris family honor? As if. Cassidy would only marry for love, and only when each party was equally in love with the other.

She hadn't known she was just settling for Dan, but thankfully Blade had walked into her life, opened her eyes and saved her from that fate. She would never settle again.

Lillian opened her mouth, but now empowered,

Cassidy immediately cut her off. "Lillian, don't even think about it. I know you and your mind, don't even stoop to being petty enough to try to touch Blade with your tentacles. Go instead and salvage your relationship with your son, you know, the other one. Dan. Maybe if you'd accepted who he loves, then you wouldn't be in this mess you created in the first place. You can still have a wedding. He just won't be marrying me."

Lillian stood her ground, and for a brief moment Cassidy felt sorry for the older woman. "We'll talk later when you aren't so," she sneered the last word, "indisposed."

"We have nothing left to say to each other," Cassidy said, her tone indicating that there would be no future talks.

Lillian slammed the door on her way out.

"I did it," she told Blade in triumph as soon as she was certain Lillian was on her way home. "I stood up to her."

He smiled. Pride showed in his greenish-blue eyes. "You did."

She tossed her arms around his neck and pulled him close. "I couldn't have done it without you."

He sobered for a moment and disengaged her arms from around his neck. He set her a step back so he could look at her. His hands, however, rested lightly on her forearms so that they were still connected. "Cassidy, you could have done it without me. You must believe that. You are a beautiful, strong woman capable of anything, including standing up to Lillian Morris.''

''I am,'' she said with a happy laugh, ''but you must admit you helped.''

''You just needed to see that there was more out there. You have so much passion. You'd have been dying a slow death.''

His tone made her look at him. He was trying to tell her something. ''You seem to know a lot about that.''

He sighed. ''I guess I should tell you about Clara. She settled for me and I settled for her. Sure, we were happy, but it was the happiness of not knowing any better. In the back of my mind I knew something was missing. Something important wasn't there. I broke her heart when I let her go.''

Cassidy's blond eyebrows furrowed as she thought about that for a moment. Blade had once settled for a woman named Clara.

''It was long ago,'' he told her as if reading her unspoken thoughts. ''Clara's now blissfully married to someone else, and I couldn't be happier for her. Deep down, I just knew I wasn't the right person.''

''I know now that I'm not the right person for Dan, nor he for me. However, I don't think either Dan or I will be breaking each other's hearts. Damaging each other's egos, maybe, but not breaking hearts. I guess I convinced myself I loved him, probably because he was safe.''

''That's what I'd done, too,'' Blade admitted. He

drew her back into his arms, and she snuggled up to his broad chest. "I don't know about us," he told her. "I don't know where this relationship is going, but I don't think I can get off this path I'm on with you. I don't want to."

Relief filled her. When he'd started telling her about Clara, she hadn't known what to think. "I want to explore this—us—too."

His hand reached up to cup her chin. He lifted it, and his intense gaze bore down upon hers. "It scares me," he admitted. "I'm a man who's not afraid to say it. I'm afraid it's too soon for you after Dan. I'm afraid we'll crash and burn."

Heat simmered in her body from the touch of his hand on her chin. "We'll take it as it comes," Cassidy said, for deep in her heart she was not going to lose this man. She loved him. Now was not the time to tell him, though, not at the beginning of a relationship.

There would be time for those words later. Right now she wanted his kiss. He lowered his lips to hers.

An insistent buzzing of her phone ended the kiss before it started. "You need to check that," Blade said.

"I don't want to," Cassidy said. She reached for the annoying contraption and sighed when she saw the words "pay phone" on the caller ID display.

Right now she didn't want to deal with anything but more of Blade's magical kisses.

"Hello?"

"Hello, darling!"

Cassidy almost dropped the phone. "Mother!"

"Exactly. Don't be so surprised. I do still exist," her mother said. "Anyway, I see good news in the paper. It's about time you dumped that spineless weasel. Anyway, that's not why I called. I'm at the airport—IAH. I've got a stopover on my way to L.A. I figured this will be a perfect time to visit with you, plus I need some things I forgot. Get a pen, love. I've got a list to give you. I need everything before four. That's when my flight is out, so could you do this now? I'll treat you to lunch and we can catch up. I'd really love to see you darling."

"I'd love to see you, too," Cassidy said truthfully. Whatever weird relationship they had, she still loved her mother. She just wished her mother had better timing.

Blade set about making coffee as Cassidy wrote down the items her mother dictated. He even located some bread and made toast.

"I'll see you in what, about two hours?" Cassidy said into the phone.

"That sounds lovely dear," Cassidy's mother said, and with that she hung up.

"Sorry about that," Cassidy said as she placed the receiver in its base unit. "My mother isn't known for having great timing."

"Yeah, but that's probably a good thing in this instance," Blade said. He handed her a mug of the fresh brew.

"What? She interrupted our kiss and wants me to meet her at the airport."

He smiled and ran a finger down her nose. "True, but today I must finish your predications. If you're here in the house with me, I won't get anything done. Instead I'll be very tempted to make love all day to a beautiful woman who right now is wearing a silky robe."

"Really?" Cassidy said with a wicked smile "I can tempt you that much?"

"Really," Blade answered. "You have that power over me."

"I do?" Cassidy put down her coffee mug and began tracing circles on his chest. He groaned. "Did you know that it's a forty-five-minute drive to the airport and that's in heavy traffic," Cassidy said.

Blade shifted, and his male hardness pressed into her stomach. "Your point?"

She gave him a seductive smile and reached for him. She needed to have him as much as he needed to have her. She kissed his neck and brought his ear down to her lips. "I'm not wearing anything under my robe."

"Vixen," Blade said with a groan. He tried one last time to escape. "But you don't have your car."

"My mother's is in the garage," she said, defeating his last argument. "I'll use the Jag. Come here, Blade. Time's awasting."

He groaned, and Cassidy gave herself up to the sensations as he crashed his lips down upon hers.

More than an hour later she gathered the last of her mother's things. She and Blade had together just finished a long, hot shower. "I won't be back until about four-thirty," she said.

"I'll be done long before then," Blade said. "How about you meet me for dinner at the bar? I've got to meet Jake there, anyway, and after that we can get your car from the hotel."

"Sounds fine," Cassidy said. She melted into the long, slow kiss he gave her. It was full of promise of the night to come, and she delighted in it. "See you then."

Blade watched Cassidy leave the house, and instantly he missed her vibrant presence. Within moments he saw her wave from her mother's Jaguar. As soon as she was down the street, he retrieved his cell phone from the car. As he thought, he had four missed calls, all from the same number. He groaned and dialed.

"About time. Just where were you last night?" Jake said in greeting, having recognized Blade's cell number on the caller ID display.

"With Cassidy. Don't you even say it. I'm in love with her, and the revenue office can go to hell as far as I'm concerned."

Jake was momentarily silent. "But what about her fiancé?"

"It's off," Blade said. "The details are in today's paper. Anyway, that's not why I called. I've come up with a strategy that I think we can use to maybe salvage the revenue office job. This one doesn't involve Cassidy or that infernal Lillian Morris.''

"Well, now that Lillian is obviously out of the picture it's probably good that Mr. Trent liked us," Jake said. "When do you want to talk?"

"Meet me at the bar. Four?"

"I'll be there," Jake said. Blade heard his friend laugh. "So mighty Blade Frederick has finally fallen, has he?"

Instead of answering, Blade simply hung up on his best friend. He knew Jake well enough to know that his friend wouldn't be offended by it, especially after that last wisecrack Jake had made.

Yes, the mighty had fallen. Big-time.

But right now Blade wouldn't have it any other way. He loved Cassidy, but he had to go slow. It was too soon to tell her about his feelings. She'd just broken off her engagement. He couldn't ask her to turn right around and commit to him.

So they would take things slow. Blade frowned for a second. Last night he'd never had an opportunity to tell Cassidy about Jake's scheme regarding Lillian.

But it was over now. Tonight he'd tell Jake to forget it ever existed.

After this morning's debacle with Lillian, Blade figured Cassidy didn't need to ever find out about that.

Chapter Twelve

Cassidy's visit with her mother was shorter than she'd expected, so she arrived at the bar early. Her mother had been flying first class and had wanted to spend some quiet time in the first-class passenger lounge before her flight to LAX.

"You know flying just stresses me out," her mother had said. Which simply meant that her mother would take advantage of a few cocktails before takeoff.

Whatever. Her mother had appeared thinner but healthier than ever. Cassidy loved her mother, but she'd dealt with enough of the woman's messes with the sale of the house. It was time her mother, too, stood on her own two feet.

Cassidy shook her head as she took a seat at the bar. It was ten to four. If she knew Blade, he'd be early, so she really would only have to wait twenty minutes. It had seemed just so much more practical to come here.

"Dee," she said in greeting.

"Fancy seeing you here," Dee said. The question was unspoken but Cassidy read it in Dee's eyes.

"I'm meeting Blade here," Cassidy said.

Dee nodded. "What can I get for you?"

Cassidy tapped her fingers on the wooden bar for just a moment. She'd had one glass of wine with lunch. "Right now I think I'll just have a glass of water. I may have something else once Blade arrives. We're planning on eating dinner."

"Yeah," Dee said as she brought back the glass of water. "Blade likes eating here."

"He says it's the best strip steak in town," Cassidy said.

"Well, he does have bragging rights," Dee said as she moved off down the bar to help another customer. "He owns the place."

Cassidy's hand shook and she managed to put the glass down without spilling any of the contents. Blade owned the bar? Unable to hide her shock, Cassidy was glad Dee's back was now toward her.

She really didn't know much about Blade, did she? Her mother had said much the same thing, especially after learning that Cassidy had only known the man for less than two weeks.

"Cassidy, love," her mother had said. "Of course you shouldn't settle for Dan, but you shouldn't rush right into settling for someone else."

"He's rich," Cassidy had said. Usually her mother loved money.

"Love, your father was rich. He thought it gave him

a license to do whatever he wanted. Now after all these years I'm finally free and I'm doing what I want for a change. Now that you're free of Dan, do yourself a favor. Don't cage yourself in right away. You know I only want what's best for you.''

But what if what Cassidy really wanted was Blade? What if her soul knew it?

Then again, what did her mind really know about him? She'd learned all about his childhood and his former girlfriend Clara, but other than that, what else did she really know about the man? He hadn't told her he owned the bar. Maybe that went along with what he'd told her about women just wanting him for his money.

So the brutal question remained.

Could she trust her feelings?

She had trusted her feelings with Jeff and Dan, and look where that had gotten her. Not a good track record, that was for sure. Maybe she didn't really know what love was. Maybe what she had with Blade wasn't even really love. Maybe it was lust, too.

They'd decided to take the path and see where it led. Blade had told her that he was afraid, as well. She comforted her mind with that thought. Everything would be fine. She was stronger now, no longer a foolish girl who wanted to settle for safe.

She'd risk it, risk loving Blade.

A man brushed by behind her, so close he almost touched her back. "Hey, Dee. Blade not here yet?"

Hearing Blade's name, Cassidy straightened and turned to look down the bar.

"Not yet, Jake," Dee answered. Without waiting for him to say anything, she poured him a whiskey and cola and placed it in front of him. So this was Jake, Blade's partner. They were night and day in appearance. Jake had blond hair and stood maybe about five-ten.

"Figures," Jake said as he took a slow sip of the cocktail. "He's probably still tied up with that girl he spent the night with."

He took a seat on a bar stool. Even from her limited experience Cassidy could tell that Jake had the word *player* written all over him.

So was the girl Blade spent the night with her? If so, how had he found out about it? Curious as to what Jake was about to say next, especially if it was about her, Cassidy put some peanuts in her mouth and waited.

"Uh, Jake," Dee began, but Jake went on as if he didn't hear the warning tone in her voice. Cassidy did, and she frowned. Her fingers stilled, and she dropped the peanuts back into the plastic bowl.

Jake took another sip of his drink. "Yeah, he called me this morning from her house and told me that he's actually fallen for this one. Our Blade, falling for some upper-crust rich girl. I never expected it, even if she is a hot babe. Can you believe it? He'll finally make it into the inner circle."

"Jake," Dee warned, but Jake was warming to his topic and would have none of it.

"I'm the matchmaker you know. He met her here, and the next day she called him to fix home predications. You know J & B doesn't do home predications. Anyway, I told him to do the work if only to get close to Lillian Morris, you know, the senator's wife? Good old Lil could have gotten us in with the politicians and helped us out with that revenue office bid. Anyway, the girl was engaged to Lillian's son up until last night. Did you read about it in the paper? Her fiancé was making out with another woman and she tossed the ring in his face."

"Jake!" Dee's tone bordered on hysterical. She shot Cassidy a rueful look, and Jake slowly turned to look down the bar. Dee gritted her teeth together and made a short gesture. "That's her."

"Oh." Jake clamped his mouth shut and simply stared at Cassidy. Under his look she felt her face flare as her emotions changed from mortification to anger, from embarrassment to rage.

"Sorry," Jake finally said. He tried to make light of the moment. "Me and my big mouth. I didn't know you were meeting Blade, too. I'm Jake, Blade's partner. You must be Cassidy."

"The hot one," Cassidy said, ignoring his outstretched hand. He dropped it to his side. The peanuts she'd eaten had long ago turned to sandpaper in her mouth.

"So is it true?" she asked.

"Is what true?" Jake said. It was obvious that he was quickly trying to backpedal, trying to salvage an awkward situation.

Cassidy folded her arms and glared at Jake. "I want to know if Blade only helped me so he could get something from me."

Jake quickly masked his expression of guilt. "Maybe in the beginning," Jake said slowly, as if knowing he couldn't lie, yet he couldn't tell the whole truth. He drew a hand through his blond hair. "You'll have to ask him."

"Believe me, I will."

"Great," Jake said, relief and panic suddenly evident. "Why, here he is now. Hey, Blade, look, here's Cassidy. Didn't know you were meeting her, too. I'll leave you two alone." And with that Jake grabbed his drink and made a hasty escape to the back room.

"So you've met Jake," Blade said.

"I did," Cassidy said. She placed her hands primly in her lap and stared at him, her chin held at a defiant angle.

As soon as she made that motion Blade knew something was wrong. In fact, his gut reaction had told him something was wrong from the moment he'd walked into the bar and seen Cassidy staring at Jake.

Dee looked at him sympathetically, and instantly Blade knew what had happened. Jake had opened his mouth about something.

"So tell me, Blade—" the iciness in Cassidy's tone

chilled him ''—do you still want me to get you in with Lillian and the politicians?''

Ouch. She'd found out.

''That's not—'' he began. Then he stopped. He'd planned on telling her the truth, and it had bitten him that he hadn't gotten around to it. Mentally he kicked himself, angered that he hadn't done what he knew was the right thing to do. He was also angry that he'd thought to bury it under the rug this morning after talking with Jake. ''I've never lied to you, Cassidy.''

''You just forgot to tell me the whole truth,'' she said with a purse of her lips. ''Let me guess, is this the part where you tell me you just want to be friends, play the field some more?''

Now where had that come from? He drew a deep breath. He was going to throttle Jake. ''No,'' he said. He could feel her slipping away and he knew he had to convince her of the truth. ''I want you, Cassidy. You and only you, that's not changed.''

''Of course not.'' She slid off the bar stool and came over, invading his space. In her flats she was a foot shorter, but she still managed to glare up at him with her baby blues. ''You wanted me, wanted me to help you get into old money society.''

''It was Jake's scheme,'' Blade said, but even as the words left his mouth he knew it didn't matter. He'd participated. Guilt assaulted him. He was an equal partner to the crime.

''So, was sleeping with me part of the scheme?''

Her words froze him to the bone. He'd hurt her. He

could see it, hidden behind her controlled facade. He was a worse snake than Dan Morris.

"You know it wasn't," he said, suddenly desperate. "Look, this is too public a place to talk. Let's go back to your house and I'll tell you everything. I meant to tell you this morning, but Lillian came over and we got distracted. Then your mother called."

"It doesn't matter," Cassidy said. She moved back a step. "We've known each other what, a week or so? We've had some good times. Well it's time to move on."

Blade's heart broke. Hadn't he learned long ago that Jake's schemes often backfired? Why had he believed it would be otherwise this time? After he beat himself up for his own stupidity, he was going to kill Jake, if the spineless weasel hadn't already slipped out the bar's back fire doors.

As she retrieved her purse from the wooden bar, Blade knew he had to keep fighting. He loved this woman. He didn't deserve her, but if they had a future then he couldn't lose her.

"Cassidy, we need to talk. You don't understand. You don't have the full story. We came up with this awful plan long before I knew you."

"You knew me," she told him flatly. "You'd met me at the bar. Don't even try to rationalize away your part in this. You could have sent anyone to fix my predications. Instead you wormed your way into my life and turned it upside down. Not that I'll go back to Dan. He and I are through. As you and I are. Yes, I think we're done.''

Her voice cracked slightly. ''And if I never see you again it won't be a day too soon.''

With that she fled for the door.

''Cassidy!'' He took off after her, calling her name, but she began to run. He stopped at the bar door. He wasn't a bully. He was not going to pound on her car window and stop her from leaving.

He called her name again, but she refused to turn around. She instead got into the Jaguar and floored the V-8 engine. Her tires squealed as she pulled out of the parking lot and Blade prayed she wouldn't get a speeding ticket.

If she did he'd pay for it. He deserved to pay. A lot.

He headed back inside the bar. Dee looked sympathetic as he passed by her, heading toward the back room. Time to have a long talk with Jake.

''HE BROKE MY HEART,'' Cassidy sobbed onto Sara's shoulders. ''Thankfully I never told him how I really felt about him.''

''Shh,'' Sara said. She handed Cassidy another tissue. Cassidy had already run through half the box, and a pile sat on the floor next to Sara's sofa. ''Men are jerks,'' Sara said.

''I thought Blade was different.''

''I don't know if he is,'' Sara said. ''Only you can decide that. Did you listen to his side of the story?''

"No point," Cassidy said. She lifted her head and wiped away her running mascara. "I just left the bar and came straight here. Do you know he owns the bar, too? He's rich. He's just like Dan and Jeff. He just wanted me for something."

"It works that way sometimes," Sara said.

"I didn't want it to work that way. I thought he could have been the one. He was so special." Cassidy reached for another tissue. "It felt so different. But did I really even know him at all?"

"You'll go forward."

"Like a phoenix," Cassidy told her. "I'll get stronger."

"Of course you will," Sara said. "And I'll be right here for you like always."

"We girls have to stick together," Cassidy said. And then she cried some more. "We're all we've got."

Hours later, sobbed out, Cassidy finally returned home. The answering machine was flashing. She had five messages. She pressed Play, steeling herself for his voice. The first three were from Dan, and Cassidy found herself torn again. Blade hadn't even had the decency to call! Relief filled her as the last two were from him. "Please call me, Cassidy," he said. "I'm sorry."

Anger overtook her again. He'd used her. She was not going to call. Not now. Not ever. In fact, right now she didn't feel like talking to either of them. The work on her house was all finished. She didn't need to talk to Dan or Blade ever again.

"WHAT DO YOU MEAN the work isn't finished?" Cassidy stared at the building inspector. Looking like a thin version of Santa Claus, he certainly wasn't the bearer of good tidings and joy.

"I mean, Ms. Clayton, that you still have one electrical receptacle that is not wired properly. It's still reverse polarity. I cannot issue an occupancy permit for your buyers until you get it fixed."

"It's one outlet," Cassidy protested.

"One is all it takes," he said simply. "The rest of your predications are fine. I will reschedule and come back at 10:00 a.m. tomorrow. I'm sure you can have it fixed by then."

Could she? She only knew one person who could fix the problem. Blade. And she certainly didn't want to see him. Ever.

Not even for a stupid electrical outlet.

Twenty minutes later not one electrical contractor had said they could come by today. Her problem was too minor and too last minute. "Get a book from the hardware store, turn off the power and do it yourself," one receptionist had told her.

Frustrated, Cassidy tossed the phone down. Then she picked it up again. To put closure to her life, yesterday she'd sent J & B a check for the work. Well, she'd paid for it to be fixed; they could send someone to fix it.

"J & B Construction," a receptionist announced.

"Blade Frederick," Cassidy murmured. She stilled fingers that were winding around the telephone cord. Not all of her parents' phones were cordless.

"Mr. Frederick's office, this is Myrtle speaking. How may I help you?"

"This is Cassidy Clayton. I'd like to speak to Mr. Frederick please."

"He's not in."

Figured. Irritation filled her, and she gritted her teeth. "Find him please. It's an emergency."

The secretary wasn't buying it. "Who did you say this was again?"

"Cassidy Clayton."

"Cassidy Clayton," Myrtle repeated.

"Exactly. I'm returning Blade's call. He'll want to talk to me."

"I'm not sure I know you," Myrtle said on the other end of the line. Cassidy heard a fax machine beep.

"He knows me and I'm returning his call," Cassidy repeated, trying to keep her calm. Did he not want to talk to her now? He'd called yesterday, Monday, this time only leaving one message.

Suddenly she heard another voice. "Give me the phone, Myrtle."

"Yes, Mr. Jake."

"Jake Prescott speaking."

"Hello, Jake. This is Cassidy Clayton, and I want Blade—now."

"He's not here," Jake said.

"Myrtle has already established that," Cassidy said, her fury now reaching a crescendo. "I really need to talk to him."

"Cassidy, I can't reach him. Seriously, I've been trying for a while. Can I help you?"

She tightened the phone cord around her pinkie finger. It went white and she released it. "If you can fix my remaining predication, yes. I've got one lousy reverse polarity outlet holding up the sale of my house. The inspector will be back at ten tomorrow. It has to be done. Today."

"I'm sure someone here can do it. I'm sorry Blade failed to fix it and do all the work correctly."

She glanced at the annoying outlet. It was right there, in the living room. "Skip the PR, Jake. Right now I don't care whose fault it is. Get someone over here to fix it." She remembered her manners. "Please."

"I'll have to search around. Of course, we have electricians on staff, but I'll have to pull one of them off another job. But I'll do it because it's the right thing to do. By the way, did you know you broke Blade's heart?"

That took the wind right out of her sails, and she sat down on a chair with a thump. "What?"

"You broke Blade's heart," Jake repeated. "I don't appreciate any woman doing that to my friend."

Cassidy's gumption came back. "I don't appreciate being used."

"My idea, my fault, and I accept full responsibility. You shouldn't hold it against him. If you want to know, he chewed me out something fierce when he got ahold of me after you'd left."

"Look, this is a pointless conversation. Are you sending someone or not, and if so what time? I need to go into my office today."

"I'll have to get back to you on the time," Jake said. "But I will send someone today to make the repair."

"Thank you," Cassidy said. She heard a knock on her door. "I have someone at my door. I'll look forward to your call." She set the phone back in its cradle and went to her kitchen door.

Dan stood outside.

"Hi," he said. "I saw your car."

Cassidy waited. Sara had helped her retrieve her car. "I told the museum I'd be in late, around one. If you'll let me, I've come to apologize. Can we talk?"

She let him in.

Two hours later, after she'd shed even more tears, Cassidy finally felt totally free. Yesterday Dan had run away to Las Vegas, marrying the woman Lillian still referred to as "that gold digger."

"I hope it all works out," Cassidy told him.

He gave her a lopsided grin, his hand on the doorknob. "I think so. Mother doesn't like it much, but she'll get used to it. I'm just sorry I hurt you, Cassidy. We always said we'd be honest with each other. I meant to tell you everything, but it never seemed a good time. And I never expected Mother to push for such a fast marriage. I thought that by becoming engaged to you I could buy myself some time with Jessica. I figured when I told you why, you'd go along with it.''

"It's okay," she told him, for honestly now it was. She'd heal. She'd never loved Dan the way she had loved Blade. Dan hadn't hurt her even half as much as Blade had.

But had Blade really hurt her? Her heart protested a moment and her mind began to contemplate the question. For the most part he'd resisted her advances, until they'd both lost control. She'd gone after him in the tent. Once her engagement had been off he'd set her free. She'd asked him to make love to her. Had he really used her? She didn't know anymore. It was all too confusing. Her life just felt empty without him.

She grimaced. She needed to get into work. That at least she had. Then she'd call Jake back at J & B and give him a piece of her mind. He still hadn't called. Exactly when was he planning on sending someone anyway?

WHEN BLADE RETURNED from the job site, Jake was pacing in Blade's office.

"It worked," he said without preamble.

"What worked?" Blade said absently. Ever since Cassidy had left the bar nothing else seemed to matter.

Jake came to stand by Blade. "Ye of little faith. I told you my scheme would work."

"Oh, that," Blade said. Then he snapped to attention as he remembered exactly what scheme Jake referred to. He dropped his briefcase on his desk. "She called? Cassidy called?"

Jake grinned. "Of course she did. Just like I said she would. See, I told you she'd call, especially after her house failed reinspection. She needs one outlet repaired, and I'm sure you know which one."

Blade did know. It had been the one he'd reversed, right after he figured out that Cassidy hadn't gone straight home after leaving the bar. He'd been calling Cassidy at home, and she hadn't answered. It had been Jake's idea to fake the outlet problem. Desperate to make amends to Cassidy, Blade had been ready to try anything if it would get her to talk to him.

So he'd gone to her house, and upon finding her not home, he'd had to change horses midstream. Instead of being able to talk to her, he entered with the key she'd given him and changed the outlet. Then he'd left another apology message asking for her to call him. She hadn't called even after his message yesterday.

He loved this woman, and he couldn't let it end like this. She was his soul mate, and somehow he'd have to prove it to her. He would make her happy all the days of her life.

As soon as he got her back by his side, he'd have all the time in the world.

That meant that right now he had plans to make and a woman to woo. "Did you give her an arrival time?"

"No," Jake said. "I was waiting to talk to you. I

need to call her back. I've already kept her waiting for over two hours, since you were late getting back from Lindbergh Heights. I tried calling you several times. Did you have your cell phone off?''

No, but he'd had the radio up too loud to hear the phone. He'd been trying to drown his pain. Blade thought for a moment, reviewing all his options. He loved her. He'd been wrong. He couldn't blow this last chance. ''Call her and tell her four-thirty. Maybe even five,'' he said.

Jake shook his head. ''I was thinking later. More like six-thirty. She said she has to go into the office and this would give you time to—''

Blade squared his shoulders. For once Jake was not going to be the salesman and the planner. Not when it came to Blade's heart. ''Jake, I know you mean well, but from here I'm on my own. I'm doing this my way. Understand. You stay out.''

''Okay.'' Jake made a gesture of surrender. Blade's tone had been crystal clear.

''Mr. Jake.''

Both men turned as Myrtle came moseying into Blade's office. Blade blinked. Wasn't it time for one of her constant coffee breaks?

''Mr. Jake, really, I must tell you, that woman is annoying me again. She's called for you at least two more times. Can't your secretary answer your phone? Why does she have to bug me?''

''What woman?'' Jake asked.

''That Ms. Clayton,'' Myrtle said with a sigh of

exasperation. "She's disturbed two of my breaks. She keeps insisting that you're to call her back and wants to know why you haven't yet."

"I am going to call her back, Myrtle, and by the way, you'd better get used to that woman and learn her name. It's Cassidy."

"Mr. Jake?" Her eyes widened behind the thick glasses. Jake laughed.

"Let me let you in on a little secret. She's not my girlfriend. No sirree. Before long that lady is going to be Mrs. Blade Frederick."

Myrtle frowned. "But she keeps calling for you—"

"It's okay, Myrtle," Jake put his arm around the secretary and guided her back to her desk outside Blade's office. "Some things just don't make sense, but they just are you know?" He looked back over his shoulder. "I'll call Cassidy and set up the repair for between four-thirty and five."

"Thanks." Blade glanced at his watch after Jake and Myrtle had left. Four-thirty was not that far away. He barely had three hours, which left him not much time to spare.

He strode out of his office. Myrtle, amazingly, sat at her desk. She looked up at him, blinking.

"I'll be out of the office the rest of the day. Reschedule anything I've got and take messages. Any emergencies go to Jake."

"Yes, Mr. Frederick." Myrtle stared at him for a moment. "By the way, congratulations."

"Not yet, Myrtle," Blade said as he walked to the express elevator. "But by the end of the day I hope."

Myrtle simply looked confused and Blade shrugged. He'd explain it all later.

Right now he had work to do.

"I'M PLEASED." Diane Rothchild looked up from the dossier that Cassidy had prepared. "Excellent work, my dear."

"Thank you," Cassidy said. She wiped her clammy hands on the little terry-cloth towel she kept hidden under her desk. As always it was a totally unnoticed but necessary movement. She'd been so worried about Diane's impressions, especially after the wonderful little gossip column on the society page.

But Diane hadn't cared about that. "Absolute trash that means nothing," she'd declared. "They try to nail my husband all the time. Anything to help sell papers, I suppose."

Diane stood and Cassidy rose to shake her hand.

"I'd like you to come over to Austin in three weeks," Diane said. "You could fly in each morning and out each night. I'll have my secretary call you by Friday to set the schedule."

"Excellent," Cassidy said. She almost jumped for joy after Diane left the office. Cassidy had finally landed her biggest client yet, and this one was ongoing.

Three weeks was perfect timing, too. It was right

after her vacation, and right after she'd moved into her cute condo.

She'd finally be living away from Lillian.

So why wasn't she happy?

Because she loved Blade Frederick and the man was a liar.

Her secretary poked her head in the door. "If you don't need anything else?"

Cassidy blinked and glanced at the clock. The hands told her it was ten to five. She sat up straight, the back of her chair hitting her with a thump. Where had the time gone? She was late. Way late.

Hopefully whoever Jake had sent over to fix the outlet was still waiting in her driveway. Jake had said between four-thirty and five. Hopefully the workman hadn't left.

If she rushed she could make it home in fifteen minutes, that was if Houston traffic wasn't its normal terrible self.

With panic escalating, Cassidy broke every speed law and whipped her Grand Prix into her driveway. A truck stood there, and relief mixed with disappointment.

Oddly, somewhere deep inside of her she'd wished it had been the familiar red Ford 350. Part of her wished that it was Blade, that he'd come. For what, her mind wasn't certain, but somewhere deep inside her, her heart knew. Her heart longed for one more chance.

But the truck was a harvest-gold color, the same as

the truck in the parking lot that night at the Boy Scout camp. Jake's truck.

Cassidy sighed. One thing she'd learned yesterday after some Internet research was exactly how large and prosperous J & B Construction really was.

Of all the people she didn't want to see, she didn't want to see Jake. If he'd just kept his mouth shut.

Then what? She asked herself that question as she walked toward the truck. If Jake had kept his mouth closed then Cassidy wouldn't have discovered any of Blade's lies. She and Blade could have been happy. They could have gotten to know each other before the other shoe dropped. She would have been able to forgive him if the truth had been revealed.

She wouldn't have had her heart broken.

Well, she still would have—eventually. But not until later. She still would have had a brief moment to know what love was. She sighed. She was deluding herself. It was the same as before, except that unlike with Jeff the jerk and Dan, Cassidy had learned the lesson upfront this time.

She'd learned her heart suffered no matter what.

She raised her hand to knock on the driver side window, only to discover that the truck was empty. Odd. She attempted to peer through the back privacy glass. Nope, no one was sleeping in the back seat.

So where was Jake if he wasn't in the truck?

She exhaled slowly, trying to calm her frayed nerves. Blade must have given Jake her key. Well, at least she wouldn't be needing to see Blade in order to ask for that back.

She'd just get her key from Jake.

Cassidy walked to the kitchen door and put the key in the lock. It turned, indicating that someone was opening the door from inside.

"Hello, Jake," Cassidy said.

"Hello, Cassidy," Blade said.

Chapter Thirteen

"Blade." Somehow Cassidy managed to recover and find her voice. "What are you doing here?"

As soon as those words left her mouth she mentally kicked herself. She knew what he was doing here. She should have expected it.

She put up a hand before he had a chance to answer her question. "Wait, don't tell me. It's your job that you screwed up, so your male pride says that you had to come fix it yourself."

He nodded and shifted his weight. "Something like that."

"So is it done?"

"No."

"No?" She stared at him, indignant. He didn't look himself. Instead he seemed haggard. Dark circles had formed under his eyes, as if he hadn't been sleeping well the past two nights. Stress lines creased his forehead.

Well, tough, she thought angrily. He'd broken her heart. She wasn't feeling too sorry for him right now, especially since here he was in her house, having used her key, and the work wasn't even finished yet.

"What do you mean it's not done?" she asked again, her tone more than a little angry.

"It's not done," Blade repeated. Those greenish-blue eyes glittered slightly. "Yet." He paused. "You didn't return my calls."

"I really don't think we have anything to discuss," Cassidy said. She set her purse on the counter and planted her hands on her hips.

"There I disagree," Blade said. He didn't seem too worried about her stance. It was almost as if he knew he had the upper hand. After all, she had to have the outlet fixed.

She checked the anger threatening to bubble over, and steadied her gaze. She was a professional. She would not erupt into unladylike, and even worse, un-civilized, behavior. "What do you mean?"

"You walked out without hearing my explanation. You gave me no chance to make things right."

She exhaled, blowing a loose strand of hair away from her face. "The only thing you can make right is my predication problem. I'd appreciate if you'd fix the electrical outlet and go."

"Not until we talk," Blade said. "Hear me out, and I'll fix it and leave."

She opened her mouth to protest but stopped when she saw the expression on his face. "Please," he said.

He looked gaunt, and Cassidy's heart overruled her

protesting mind. She might as well hear him out. After all, could she hurt any worse?

"Okay," she said, not caring if her tone sounded rude. He'd hurt her. She took a seat at the kitchen table and looked at him expectantly. "Speak."

Blade inwardly groaned. He'd expected that convincing Cassidy of his love and devotion would be rough. However, he hadn't expected her to be this angry or bitter. He'd hurt her more than he'd originally thought.

Let me make it up to you, he told her with his eyes. Please be open to what I have to say. Heck, he'd metaphorically hog-tie her down if that helped, but he knew it wouldn't. This would be his toughest sales job ever. He was selling himself, and he had hurt her. He was the one deserving to be filled with buckshot.

"By the way," Cassidy said, turning her head back from where she'd been gazing out the window for a moment, "whose truck is that, anyway?"

He'd forgotten about telling her it was Jake's truck. "Mine," he admitted.

"So another lie you told me," she said flatly, as if all emotion inside her had been drained away long ago.

"Yes." He winced. "That's my truck, not Jake's."

"And the red one?"

"I borrowed a foreman's truck for when I came over here. I swapped him for the BMW."

The hurt expression on her face struck him. He really was a heel who deserved whatever she gave him. He should just fix her outlet and go.

"Why did you do all this?" She stood up suddenly. "No, don't tell me. I don't want to know. Just fix my outlet and leave. Please. Please just leave me alone."

But in the end he couldn't do that. He loved her. He may not deserve her, but he would make her happy. If she'd have him. "Cassidy."

She must have heard the pleading, the desperation in the tone of his voice, for she turned back around from her flight upstairs.

"Cassidy, I know I've lied. I was wrong. Please, hear me out and then I'll go. That I promise you. Please just listen."

Slowly she reentered the room and sat back down at the table. "All right. I'll listen."

"Thank you." He shoved his hands into his pockets and then removed them again. He hadn't been this nervous since asking out his first date. Even that now seemed so minuscule by comparison. He had one chance to make this situation right. If he didn't, he'd lose Cassidy forever.

He took a deep breath and began.

"When I first met you, that night in the bar, I misjudged you. I thought you were one of those women who comes in and slums with men's hearts."

Cassidy began to stand, the affronted look on her face telling him exactly what she was thinking. "Cassidy, please, honey. Sit down. Hear me out. Don't judge me until the end. Can you do that?"

"I don't know," she said, the look on her face doubtful. But she sat.

"Thanks." He paced some more and then planted himself for a moment by the kitchen island. "I realized quickly how wrong my first impressions of you were. But, correct me if this isn't true, you'd misjudged me, as well. You thought I was trying to pick you up."

Cassidy fidgeted for a moment before bringing her baby-blue gaze up to meet his. How he loved her eyes. They were like stars. "Yes," she admitted slowly. "I did. But does it matter? You played the role, especially after I called you the next day."

She stood up and looked out the window for a moment. He knew she was staring at his truck. "Perhaps I should have known what J & B Construction was, or at least how big it was. You were honest with me about that. You at least told me you were a president. It was on your business card."

"But in a sense I wasn't truly honest," Blade said. He gripped the countertop for a moment. "Jake told me to bring my own truck but I didn't want to. You had this notion of me, and I'd already fallen for you. When he concocted this whole scheme, I agreed because it meant seeing you. He even said he'd do the work himself. But I wouldn't stick Jake with my sister."

"You don't have a sister," Cassidy said.

"Exactly. If I had a sister I would never let her around Jake. So I took the job. I still don't care about the politicians or the revenue office job. Sure, getting the project would be a feather in our cap, but I later told Jake his plan was off. I can't ever use you like that. I don't use anyone like that.''

''That's good to know.'' She shifted slightly, and Blade could tell she was really listening. He felt his first glimmer of hope.

''And by that time you'd totally intrigued me, Cassidy, and it's rare that a woman intrigues me or gets under my skin. But you did. You still do.''

He saw the doubt on her face and pressed on, anyway. At this point there was no turning back. She had to know it all. ''The next day several things happened besides you calling me and Jake's scheme. When I came over here I discovered that I still wanted you. But you were engaged. Off-limits.''

He fumbled for the words. How to say them, without making her bolt. ''Worse, you were a woman that I couldn't stay away from. From the moment you told me your problems in the bar I wanted to help you. Then the next day I still did, but that meant that I needed to protect you, and me, from what I saw as trouble with a capital *T*. Aw, hell, Cassidy, I wanted you the very moment I set eyes on you, and that's the trouble. I don't poach another man's property. Never have, never will.''

''I'm no one's property but my own,'' Cassidy said. She twisted her hands.

''Well, yes, but you know what I mean. Jake has no problem taking whatever he can get, but I'm not like that. I might want you with a burning desire, but you'd committed your life to another. It's not my place to come into that situation and stir things up.''

She nodded, as if understanding his reasoning.

Blade took a breath and continued. ''When I came over here to work, I wanted to give you as many reasons to stay away from me as possible. If you came near me, I knew I was going to be in trouble. I was going to fall flat on my face and break all those rules I'd set down for myself. I did anyway. I kissed you.''

''That you did,'' Cassidy said. Unconsciously she reached up and touched her lips, as if remembering. Blade groaned. He didn't need that image, not now. Hopefully if he could convince her how he felt, and why he'd done what he had done, there would be time for kissing later.

A lifetime of kissing.

''I had another reason for why I pretended to be someone else. I wanted you to like me for who I was, not what I had. Women don't necessarily throw themselves at me, but there are a lot of gold diggers out there.''

Cassidy laughed hollowly.

Blade felt confused. ''What?'' he asked.

''That's what Lillian called Dan's 'girlfriend.' A gold digger. Do you know that Dan ran off and married her in Vegas yesterday? Seems she's pregnant, too.''

''Cassidy, I'm so sorry.''

Cassidy held up her hand, stopping his flow of sympathy. "I don't need or want your pity. Every day I get stronger, and the last thing I need is men lying to me. Jeff lied, Dan lied, and you lied, Blade. You can't deny that you lied, can you?"

"No," he said. He shook his head and brought his gaze up to hold hers. Cassidy looked away. "I can't say that I didn't lie. What I can say, just like I did before, is that I was wrong. Cassidy, in two short weeks you've come to mean more to me than any other woman. You've captured not only my heart but also my soul."

She blinked, and Blade instantly knew he needed to reassure her.

"I fell in love with you, darling, and that was not a good thing. It left me vulnerable, for the woman I loved was going to marry another man, and I would have to stand by and let her."

"You were in love with me?" Cassidy said. She touched the base of her throat and wobbled a little. Before Blade could reach her, she'd steadied herself.

"I'm in love with you," Blade repeated. "And right now it scares the pants off me that I could be losing you for good."

Cassidy swayed slightly, and Blade pulled her gently into his arms.

"I want us to have a future," he said simply. "Get to know each other, have kids, be married, all that. I'm so in love with you it hurts, and I lied more to protect me than to hurt you. You hold my heart and soul, and it scares me. You still do, Cassidy. I love you.''

Held against the safety of his chest Cassidy could feel and hear the rhythmic thump of Blade's heart. He loved her. Could she forgive him? Could she trust him?

As she'd learned with Dan, love wasn't a feeling sometimes as much as it was a choice. That was the paradox. And, when she'd chosen Blade, the feelings had overwhelmed her.

''I love you, too,'' she said simply, for whatever other words she wanted to say didn't matter. Not now.

''I want to marry you, Cassidy. Will you marry me?''

Cassidy looked up at him. She'd marry him tomorrow, but part of her held back. Perhaps it was her own emotional baggage, having been lied to.

''Yes and no,'' she said slowly.

He touched her cheek, sliding his finger over it, feeling her smooth skin. She hadn't said an outright no. ''What do you mean by that?''

''Yes, I will marry you, but not right away. I want us to have time to be really certain. I love you, and if this love is real then time will only strengthen that. And I don't want a big wedding. Nothing fancy. A few family and close friends. That's all.''

''No seven-thousand-dollar dress?''

''No marshmallow fluff that I'll only have to donate to charity,'' Cassidy said. She tilted up her head, and

Blade leaned down to kiss her lips. Heaven awaited, but she drew back.

"And I have a trip coming up to see one of my friends. I'll be gone a week. I've also got a new client, and I'll be making day trips to Austin." He knew she was waiting for his reaction, his possessiveness.

But he was not Dan Morris. He cared what she did, and he wanted to be with her at all times. But he also knew how career oriented she was.

"I'll miss you," he said, "but I know how important your friends and career are. Just promise you'll call me often if you're gone overnight. I love you, and I'll want to be sure you're okay."

At his words Cassidy swayed against him. He held her tight, his arms a secure haven of love. She delighted in being next to him. She didn't have to tell him she'd forgiven his lies. He already knew.

This was a man who truly understood her, and deep down she knew she'd found her soul mate. She let her lips connect with his again, feeling both the steel and the silk of his kiss.

His lips slid down her neck, skin on skin, fire on fire. Cassidy delighted in the feel of it. She'd miss him on her day trips, but, oh, how the nights would be!

He drew back slightly, the look on his face holding a question. "I've missed you," he said scooping her into his arms. "May I be presumptuous?"

Cassidy felt as if she floated all the way up the stairs to her bedroom. "Absolutely," she said somewhere along the way.

Later as he held her in the sweet aftermath of their lovemaking, he propped himself up on one elbow and leaned down over her. "Cassidy?"

The seriousness of his tone caused her eyelids to pop wide open. "Yes?"

"I have to make one more confession."

"This sounds serious," she said.

"A bit underhanded," Blade admitted. He stroked her eyebrows. When his forefinger traced down her nose and touched her lips, she caught it and kissed the edge of his fingertip.

He groaned. "I came back over here yesterday and changed the outlet so you failed your inspection."

"I know," Cassidy said. She kissed his finger in between words.

"You know?"

"Uh-huh," Cassidy said. With her free hand she began to trace shapes on his chest. A part of him began to strain. "You're too conscientious to miss one outlet. So when you told me you loved me, I figured you must have come back over and changed it. Desperate times call for desperate measures, or something like that."

"Honesty's the only policy from here on out," he said, flipping her over onto her back. He lowered his head to her neck.

"Absolutely," she told him. "And no games."

Suddenly Blade stopped kissing her. Not caring about his nakedness, he instead got out of bed. Within a moment he'd found what he was looking for in the pocket of his pants.

As he returned to kneel beside her, Cassidy delighted in watching his naked, magnificent male body move. She'd never get enough of him, and when she saw what he'd retrieved from his pocket her heart had overflowed with joy.

"Although you won't marry me right away, will you still wear an engagement ring?" He opened the small black jeweler's box. "I stopped and got this on the way over. Will you wear my engagement ring, darling?"

"My finger does feel a little bare," she admitted playfully. She held up her left hand and looked at it. "And I don't exactly remember saying an emphatic no."

"I'll wait as long as it takes, Cassidy. I love you. I know this isn't the most romantic way to ask you, but I can't wait, my love. Will you be my wife?"

"I will marry you," she said. She rose up onto her knees so that she could face him. She watched as he slid the ring onto her finger. The white gold instantly warmed as it touched her skin.

"I love you," he said.

With those words she tumbled him back to the bed, back to her body, back to make her complete. "I love you, too," she said.

"SO WHO'S THE CLIENT you need to be making day trips to Austin to see?" Blade asked.

Cassidy shifted under the weight of his arm. Dusk had settled hours ago, and they lay in the warmth of skin to skin under the fluffy down comforter of her bed.

"I guess I have a little confession to make, as well," she said with a languorous sigh. "Jake may be able to get what he wants after all."

"What does he want?"

"A way in with the politicians." She placed kisses on his chest. Already she wanted Blade again.

"How's that?" Blade groaned, and Cassidy felt him grow next to her leg.

He was all she wanted. He was all that she loved. He was her soul mate.

"My new client is Bert Rothchild."

Blade groaned as she slid herself without preamble upon him.

"The governor," he managed, as instantly both of them shattered.

"Uh-huh," Cassidy said. She began to work her hips, sending both of them spiraling.

"So I got very lucky when I met you, didn't I?" Blade said. He thrust upward, meeting her, stroke for stroke. "Is that what you're saying?"

"You did get very lucky," she said, her train of thought about the governor vanishing. Instead her focus became on Blade and his actions.

"I knew I got lucky," Blade told her as he changed the pace, "the moment you sent the peanuts flying with your purse."

"Beware of flying peanuts," she said, for as he flipped her onto her back, she lost control of whatever words she'd been trying to say.

"I love you," he said. "Just don't make me wait long, darling. I want to be able to call you my wife."

"I won't make you wait too long," she told him, her double meaning clear as he sent both of them spiraling over the edge into where dreams come true.

Epilogue

"They really use golden shovels and all that?" Cassidy said. She'd never been to a groundbreaking ceremony for a new revenue office before, but after all, her client the governor was at the ceremony.

Blade looked down at his wife. His wife. Finally. They'd had an engagement of exactly eight months before he'd been able to whisk her off for a romantic wedding on a beach at Saint Maarten.

There had only been about twenty people at the entire event, mostly family and friends. They'd been married five months now, and Blade couldn't have been happier. He'd found his soul mate in Cassidy, and she often declared him to be hers. And since they'd had their honesty policy, he knew it to be true. She'd convinced him he did deserve her. They both deserved the very special love that fate had dictated they share, and they knew how lucky they were.

"So do you have to go back to work after this?" he asked her.

As Cassidy glanced up at her husband, she saw the intense expression on Blade's face.

"I had some paperwork to do," she said.

"Can it wait?" he asked as flashbulbs popped.

She didn't answer him right away as her attention was momentarily diverted when Jake and the governor tossed the ceremonial dirt marking the official start of construction. The photo-op had gone well. Diane gave Cassidy a slight nod indicating her approval.

Cassidy turned back to look at her husband. He stood a regal figure in his custom suit. But his clothes didn't matter. She'd loved him in his carpenter whites, and each day she discovered she loved him a little more. "My work can wait," she said knowing exactly what his expression meant.

"Good," he said, placing a hand on her arm and easing her back out of the small crowd. "Jake's the showman, and he can handle whatever's next. Right now, my darling wife, I need to show you how much I love you."

She smiled, secure in the love of a lifetime. "Lead the way, my darling. Lead the way."

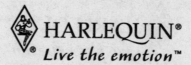

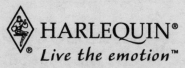

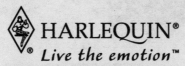

Bestselling Harlequin Presents® author

LYNNE GRAHAM

Brings you one of her famously
sexy Latin heroes in

DARK ANGEL

This longer-length story is part of
the author's exciting *Sister Brides*
miniseries! Convinced the
Linwood family framed him for
embezzlement, business tycoon
Luciano de Valenza seeks
revenge against them. His plan:
to take everything that is theirs—
including their daughter, Kerry!

*Look for DARK ANGEL
in March 2003!*

HARLEQUIN®
Makes any time special®

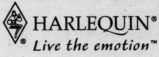

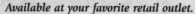
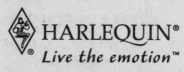